THE GOOD LISTENER

THE GOOD LISTENER

HELEN BAMBER:
A Life Against Cruelty

Neil Belton

Weidenfeld & Nicolson
LONDON

First published in Great Britian in 1998
by Weidenfeld & Nicolson

© 1998 Neil Belton

A CIP catalogue record for this book is available
from the British Library.

ISBN 0 297 81904 6

Typeset by Selwood Systems

Set in Monotype Perpetua 12.5pt

Printed in Great Britain by Butler & Tanner Ltd,
London and Frome

Weidenfeld & Nicolson
The Orion Publishing Group Ltd
Orion House
5 Upper Saint Martin's Lane
London, WC2H 9EA

CONTENTS

Brendan George Belton
1917–1978

In Memory

ACKNOWLEDGEMENTS

I have tried to re-imagine Helen Bamber's life from the 1920s to the present. The text is built on many hours of interviews with her, and with those who influenced and affected her. She allowed me to excavate her life and to reach conclusions that may not always please her. We first met six years ago at an evening organized by the Medical Foundation for the Care of Victims of Torture. She seemed to me then the archetypal Hampstead lady working for a good cause, though it was one I could barely think about. In November 1995 we met once more, on a train going to the North East of England, and she began to tell me something of her life. Within weeks, the shape of that life had lodged itself in my mind. We began a conversation that lasted two and a half years. Helen Bamber gave me her full co-operation and made no attempt to censor any aspect of the text. For this I owe her my deepest thanks.

Others made time to speak to me, patiently and unflinchingly, about events that are communicable only with difficulty. The experiences of Rudi Bamber, Roman Halter, Ben Helfgott, Adriana Borquez, Luis Muñoz, James Mubiru, and others who must remain anonymous, are inseparable from the individual life at the heart of the book.

The staff of the Medical Foundation were generous and patient with a questioner who must often have seemed unprepared for what he was hearing, nursing a project that must at times have seemed eccentric. My use of their statements, which were always informative and serious, has inevitably been selective and personal. I am grateful to Sherman Carroll, Betty Gordon, Jenny Grut, Gill Hinshelwood, Antonia Hunt, Michael Korzinski, Susan Levy, Sheila Melzak, Michael Peel, Perico Rodriguez, John Rundle, John Schlapobersky, Derek Summerfield, Gordon Wills and Erol Yesilyurt.

Dick Barbor-Might gave me very useful insights into the political culture of human rights campaigning in the 1970s and 1980s. He was candid and reflective and willing to discuss these issues with someone of a different political temperament. I also benefited from talking to Jim Welsh about this period. David and Jonathan Bamber spoke to me openly about their family, and showed me that some accounts can't be settled in a single generation. Henry Lunzer and Alison Wood kindly shared their memories of postwar Germany and the JRU with me.

Hugh O'Shaughnessy and Tony Gould prepared me for Chile with good advice. James Dunkerley will see that very little of his vast knowledge of Latin America has rubbed off, but I am grateful to him for his unfailing supply of hospitality and books and contacts. In Chile, Alex Wilde opened doors for me with great tact. Monica Gonzalez, Hernan Montealegre Klenner, Jose Zalaquett, Jorge Lopez Sotomayer, Malcom Coad and Luis Valenzuela were all, in their different ways, better guides to Chile than I deserved. In Israel, I was given much to think about by Hannah Friedmann, Daniela Yannai and Hedva Radanovitz. Patrick Cockburn was helpful and shrewd, and Rami Heilbronn a provocative interlocutor. Daphna Vardi was a counterweight, and as sympathetic in Jerusalem as she is in Oxford. In Gaza, Eyad el-Sarraj was a wonderful host and an impressive, disenchanted commentator on recent Palestinian history. His colleagues at the Gaza Community Mental Health Programme, working in such adverse conditions, were nonetheless patient, thoughtful and illuminating about the work they do.

This book would have been quite impossible to write without the support of my friends, some of them also critical readers of the work in progress. I owe Anthony Barnett a lot for his support at a turning-point many years ago, and for his continual encouragement. Fintan O'Toole and Roy Porter lifted my spirits when I wasn't quite sure what I'd written, and I'm also thankful to Orlando Figes, Veronica Hold, Stephen Howe and Daphna Vardi for their comments. Moerida Belton scoured Colindale for me. Bill Schwarz has been a great ally and a sharp-eyed reader. Misha Glenny, above all, has been an unstinting provider of goodwill, humour and criticism, especially during the difficult months of 1997. No one could ask for more from a friend. My colleagues at Granta Books, especially Frances Coady, have put up with my disappearances more gracefully than I had any right to expect of them. Rea Hederman has been a rock of support from the beginning.

Ravi Mirchandani, my first editor, treated my first drafts with immense care. He was the best and most sensitive reader I could have hoped for, and I'll be pleased if he can recognize his influence in the final text. The book was inherited by Rebecca Wilson, who has also been tremendously encouraging. She combined firmness of purpose with gentle diplomacy in steering me through what was, for her, a nightmarish publishing schedule. I probably wouldn't have written so much as an outline if it had not been for Georgina Capel. She convinced me that my half-formed idea should be developed, and it was a meeting of minds all the more enjoyable for being so unexpected. And my publisher, Anthony Cheetham, has shown faith in me for so long that I sometimes forget what a difference it has made.

PREFACE

This piece of writing considers a life shaped intimately by the violence that we've come to accept as the bad weather of our century. It is not a conventional biography.

Helen Bamber, now in her seventy-fourth year, has since the age of sixty led an organization dedicated to helping men and women who have had extreme pain inflicted on them by the state. It is called, bluntly, the Medical Foundation for the Care of Victims of Torture, a name that says more than most of us wish to hear. It is impossible even to write the word 'torture' without the feeling that communication has been threatened, that ears are closing.

Bamber's journey towards her disturbing vocation makes up the greater part of the narrative that follows. Her childhood was lived in the certainty that war and genocide were inevitable. Her family did her the risky courtesy of not treating her like a child, and not shielding her. As a young woman she witnessed the Nazi air-raids on London, and in 1944 she volunteered for service with the Jewish Relief Unit in the British Zone of occupied Germany. Back in England, she worked until 1950 with young survivors of the death camps. Between then and 1985, when she started her Foundation, she was drawn again and again to men and women who resisted the barbarism that nothing could justify to her after the defeat of Hitler. She made connections between the mistreatment of patients by unscrupulous doctors, the neglect of children in hospital and the abuse of political prisoners. Though she knew how to enjoy herself in the years of well-being after the war, her peacetime had an aspect that most of her contemporaries didn't need to see, and that she refused to ignore.

Helen Bamber discovered that she would be compelled to end her working life (and life without work is inconceivable to her) attending to images and statements that should not form part of civilized discourse. She learned intelligently from her instincts, and from the experiences of other people. I reconstruct as best I can the stages of her strange self-education. Her openness has been one of her great skills, and so this cannot be just her story. It must also speak about those who left their mark on her, and often changed her. The narrative at times has to loop away from her, and enter the lives of others, in order to try and catch what she was hearing.

If this is not a straightforward account of a life, still less can it claim to be a systematic study of political cruelty; with its focus on one passionately alert woman, it barely mentions some of the worst catastrophes for which humans have themselves to blame. There is nothing here on the Maoist policies that killed millions and institutionalized cruelty in China and Cambodia, because it did not touch on Helen Bamber's experience. This book is a footnote to the scholarship of an infamous period. It does, however, try to imagine how the extreme violence of our world affected one woman, beginning with the Holocaust, and how she did something creative about it. I have tried to give a stand against cruelty the force of a human story.

Fifty years after governments representing most of humanity declared that they rejected 'cruel, inhuman or degrading punishment', an elderly, formally unqualified woman and her colleagues, working from a row of terraced houses under a railway bridge in North London, hold up a flimsy, necessary barrier against torture. There are people like Helen Bamber in other countries, in human rights and medical organizations, who surely must be as committed and complex as she is. She may not be alone in what she does, and Bamber's may not be a representative life; but perhaps it is 'typical', in the way that good lives were once supposed to be, of the second half of a century that has degraded the language of horror. It certainly tells us something: like an exposure of black light, an image from the dark of her time and ours. The future is still heavy with violence, and the ground she stands on may be a last ditch of hope – defending the human body against torment for not being perfect, for not speaking the right language, for containing information that might be useful; sometimes simply for being in the wrong place. History has demanded a price from Helen Bamber, and this is an account of how she paid it.

1

THE LIBERTIES OF BERWICK

And it's been proved that soldiers don't go mad
Unless they lose control of ugly thoughts
That drive them out to jabber among the trees.

Siegfried Sassoon, 'Repression of War Experience'

Helen Bamber, when she was just over twenty years old, crossed into Germany in 1945 and saw the miles of rubble stretching off on either side, with thin children standing on the edge of the railway track. People threw bread to them from the train. In what was left of a town she would see 'men in long grey belted raincoats, their long, sullen, grey faces'. She said that this was what Germans were supposed to look like; but the children still looked like children. The gaunt men in their coats would notice the six-pointed star on the shoulder of her army uniform; their eyes always seemed drawn to it. She wore a metal badge on her left breast-pocket, two intersected yellow triangles set inside a blue and white hexagram with the letters JRU at the centre. Jewish Relief Unit. During the long waits in railway stations she rested her arms on the edge of the carriage window, her chest pressed to the glass, and she could sense them looking at her. She felt singled out, naked: not because she was a good-looking woman but because she was a young Jew travelling through Germany, wearing that badge.

She was driven up some days later in a noisy British Army lorry from the village of Eilshausen to what was by then called the Number One Camp, or Bergen-Belsen. The wire and gates were still there. Clinging to the grass and in the air was 'a smell of burning, of petrol fumes, burned wood and earth' and 'other smells', which were imaginary perhaps, but not impossible even then, two months after the Germans surrendered the camp. The great mounds – long barrows thrown up in the sandy soil of the heath – were still raw earth. Plants from the heath would not start to take on the graves until the following spring. Around the empty field were the most beautiful silver birch woods she had ever seen.

The newspaper photograph of the burning of the last hut was still vivid in her mind. It was a low wooden structure forty yards long with a German flag nailed up at one end and at the other a large banner printed with Hitler's face. Gun-carriers, open half-track vehicles mounted with flame throwers, lined up and sent three ragged arcs of fire at the walls of the shed. The burning petrol consumed it very fast. It was to prevent the spread of disease, the army said; but there was an element of celebration, the liberators congratulating themselves on a job well done while turning the evidence to ash.

In the late summer of 1945 there were still 20,000 survivors, the majority of them Jewish, living a mile up the road in the former Panzer training depot, austere buildings around a barracks square. The survivors' war was not over yet. And it would not be long before memory began to play tricks about what had happened here; fifty years later, British newspaper could talk about the 'gas chambers' of Belsen. There were none. It was not like Auschwitz; here extreme carelessness and racist indifference were enough, as tens of thousands of human beings died of typhus and starvation, lying in their own wastes.

Helen Bamber has always remembered the lingering smell, and it is one of those very physical memories, infiltrating all the others, that returns to her even when she forgets the precise sequence of events from half a century ago.

With old age, it seems easier to make deep connections between memories, to cut through calendar time and bring events together because they are intensified in relation to each other. The essential stands out; chronology blurs, dates fade and merge; moments far apart in time are linked by a code which it is possible to feel can at last be understood, which may be the nearest we come to feeling part of history. In 1995, the anniversary of the war's various tangled endings, Bamber needed to find a way of dealing with her sense of time closing around her, with the discovery that her life had run so long that it had become a surface on which she could trace patterns.

She felt unhappy during the official commemorations of the end of the war and the liberation of the concentration camps, that myth of 'liberation' – as though that had all along been the goal of the war. And the rhetoric of it grated, the lauding of 'survival' and 'the tenacity of the human spirit'. The tone of the expressions of official memory saddened her: 'There is always such pride in *our* generosity and bravery; the complacency of it is suffocating.'

Her own way back was to go to the far north of England, to Berwick-upon-Tweed, to be with a group she always refers to as 'the men'. She calls them that perhaps to distinguish them from the young Jewish survivors of the camps with whom she worked after her return from Germany and who are widely known as 'the boys'. She also saw them that year, men nearly her own age, dancing their vigorous dances, singing, exulting in *their* jubilee. These 'boys' are a magnificent group, orphaned and enslaved by the Nazis and ingenious beyond belief in their refusal to go under. They have done well, married, and have good lives, and there was a great, understandable desire to celebrate them. But Bamber felt that they had a bleak time of it while they struggled to live in post-war England after so much loss, and it was painful to remember what it had cost them, their defensive toughness. 'They were courageous and extraordinary, but many of them had had to bury their feelings so deep that they were unable to reach them or even know, sometimes, that they had them.'

She could not dissociate their youth from their apparently triumphant old age: 'People who went through the Holocaust survived because they were very tough in very many ways, and because of sheer chance. Many people survived at great cost. It is difficult to pretend that they did not, and I think we could do very little for them in the 1940s.' Remembering the frustration and failure of those years was like stripping a bandage from an unhealed wound. It was too close to home, in all the senses she knew of that complicated word. So she went north for several long weekends, the nearest thing she would have to a holiday that year from the Medical Foundation and its staff, its volunteers and the unending flow of new 'clients': their word for victims of torture, since all the others terms are so loaded.

The men in Northumberland are no less used to keeping their own counsel about their feelings than other men that Bamber has known, but they were never victims of a genocidal plan to change the human race, and they had families to welcome them home. They are the survivors of the machine-gun battalion of the Northumberland Fusiliers captured at the fall of Singapore in February 1942, barely off the ship after fighting their way in with their new weapons, and shooting down three Japanese planes; a glorious entrance, followed by four years of humiliation and slavery.

They were put to work on the Burma–Siam Railway, and because they came from neighbouring villages in Northumberland and were led by the same young officers who had recruited them into the Territorial Army in their school halls, these miners, farm labourers and gardeners from the big estates helped each other tenaciously, laying heavy rails and digging cuttings through hills on twelve ounces of rice a day. Work was a form of slow murder, especially higher up the line where many of them were based. They taught each other to slow down, always to dip their spoons in boiling water and sterilize them, to feed each other and protect the weak. Less than a fifth of them died; the average death rate on the railway was almost twice that. Their discipline and clannishness helped them outlast the war; their solidarity since then has helped them come through the sufferings of peace.

In this kind of endurance, place matters; and the Berwick area is one of the most distinctive places in England. The town itself is a quiet borough of grey and pink stone laid out where the River Tweed meets the North Sea, on the Scottish border midway between Edinburgh and Newcastle. Power and technology seem to have passed it by. The trains running between those serious modern cities cross the high arches of the Royal Border Bridge, which open like huge doors onto Scotland. Edward I's river fort is a tiny ruin under the railway viaduct, which is so lofty and beautiful it makes the Victorian engineers' dream of progress and peace nearly heartbreaking. Yet the flagstones of the river promenade are laid on top of the Elizabethan ramparts, now softened and rounded under grass, but still recognizably forming a barbed machine for ripping up attackers, and the walls still close around the old town.

The sandbar in the mouth of the river regularly changes shape, like a tongue probing out from the south bank of the Tweed. Boats come in through a narrow vein of water between the old McCreath fertilizer factory and the fortifications on the other side. The pier is a breakwater: 'A defence against the sea rather than a pier for shipping,' according to a terse leaflet about the harbour. The artery is closing, the port dying. In the fourteenth century it was the London of the North, a major trading post with Scandinavia. Now the sandbanks at low tide nearly fill the harbour. Everything here seems to be about enclosure rather than growth and connection; in the 1930s a travel book already called it 'the clean sequestered town'. But it feels like a good place, especially under the cold light of an autumn day.

It has narrow cobbled streets, blackened early-Victorian squares and terraces weathered by the cutting wind and rain coming off the sea. The old restaurants and hotels, behind frosted glass and plywood partitions, serve roast meat, the flesh of Northumberland cattle well done on big plates with gravy and potatoes. Many of the shops still have the feel that stores had in the 1950s; the same dry unchanging windows, like an old spirit-grocer's in a small Irish town: dummy tins of beans, empty dried-soup packets, little cardboard boxes of cubed jelly.

Like many other quiet British towns, Berwick has a long association with violence. The Barracks Museum has an exhibition devoted to 'the regiment', the King's Own Scottish Borderers (in the complicated geography of the imperial army, it recruited mainly to the north, in Scotland itself, unlike the truly local regiment of fusiliers). It is a collection of medals and uniforms, and of captured weapons – old pistols and bolt-action rifles mounted behind glass, the lethal shapes of polished metal and wood; the memory of Nazism in a few Lugers and machine guns and the inevitable dagger with *Deutschland Über Alles* chased on the blade. But of course everyone knows that the town has been touched more intimately than this by a war which to 'the men' seemed, for a long time, almost forgotten.

Bamber thinks of the place as 'untouched, almost other-worldly', and perhaps it has that disturbing quality precisely because it is a border town, where 'the North' becomes another country, its accent a mixture of Geordie and Lowland Scots. It is difficult to forget that Berwick is on the shifting threshold of sea and land, fresh and salt water, and of two nations; this is the enchantment of the town's indecision. Legally it was a neutral zone between England and Scotland until well into the nineteenth century, the 'Royal and Antient Borough' still technically at war with Russia because the government forgot to add its name to the peace treaty after the conflict over the Crimea; a near-republic, 'a peculiar jurisdiction, neither in England nor in Scotland'. Until the end of the fifteenth century it was a marcher town: taken and lost by William Wallace, Edward I of England, Robert the Bruce — a seizure and massacre every decade, on average, for two hundred years. 'Half of the body of the executed Wallace' was exposed here in 1305, and the walls felt 'the astounding effect of cannon shot, the first ever fired in England'. (The town museum primly refers to 'eighteen changes of hands' before the frontiers of the English state were finally settled.)

Now Berwick rests on a line between identities not worth killing for. Helen Bamber came to Berwick to find something in herself, as it is possible to do in border zones — there is a stillness, an absence of pressures, a sense of frontier isolation; as though the border were a real one, invisible but unforgotten. The usual rules don't seem to apply. Silence and survival and discretion have marked the place. Perhaps that is one of the reasons why it seemed so attractive to her when the world was insisting she remember.

Every month, except when the winter gets too bad, 'the men' meet in a pub in Chatton, a village thirty miles from Berwick. Those who live in Berwick — quite a few of them now — can easily reach it, and it is convenient for the men who live in the outlying villages. Bamber was driven out from Berwick on that occasion by Henry McCreath, eighty years old, in his green Barbour jerkin and sporty grey cap, handling his Rover with ease at seventy miles an hour. He's slightly deaf, an old problem, but otherwise alert and quick. He drove hard and well. He is still very much the officer. He has a hearty warm bark and a strong Northumberland accent, and made polite enquiries as to everyone's comfort. Arch Hattle, who was one of Henry's fusiliers, sat in the back. Henry drove between great plain green fields. Long columns of black cattle stood in the chill haze: fog obscured the tops of the Cheviot Hills to the north-west. The light seemed very high over the brown ridges, the trees bare, horizons endless.

The roads were empty; the farmhouses with their large wealthy sandstone buildings sat far back amid wooded gardens. This is very good land. The mines and shipyards of the Tyne were off in the south of the county, and since they are almost all gone now, the industrial revolution survives only in these large cattle farms selling beef to the cities. The talk in the car was of the men who had died – 'He took a stroke and slipped away, poor lad' – and of agricultural news – the thieves who had rustled four hundred sheep in the last few weeks, backing up trailers to the fields and taking the animals away forty at a time. Nearly impossible to round up sheep like that, Arch and Henry said, especially at night, so they must have had a really well-trained dog. They thought they knew who was behind it, and that he was greedy and stupid.

We passed a walled hundred-acre stand of trees that Arch Hattle, as a farm labourer, planted with larches, firs and oaks soon after the war: one of his first peacetime jobs. He laughed, as well he might, a man who has seen his own forest grow since coming back from the dead.

Henry wanted to show his guests the villages the men came from. He drove through Crookham, where he recruited his platoon, and pointed out the grass patch in front of the church where he drilled them, and the Victorian school hall which they used in bad weather. In Norham, where his oldest friend Archie Veitch raised his platoon, he mentioned that this is where their 'little club' of ex-prisoners of war started, in the Victoria Hotel, a pub by a grass triangle in the neat stone village.

Chatton was quiet, the same strong square houses as in all the other villages, little prefabrication anywhere in sight. Inside the pub there was a crowd of grey heads and dyed perms; many of the men wore blazers with small enamel lapel badges showing the torch circled by a laurel wreath that is the emblem of the Far Eastern Prisoners of War Association. Some wore a badge with the crest of the Northumberland Fusiliers: a round boss like a split musket ball, surmounted by a flame and showing St George slaying the dragon, inside the legend *'Quo Fata Vocant'*: wherever fate calls. The bar was full of tanned wrinkled faces; some plethoric noses; a crowd of large hearty men. They had handshakes like craftsmen or farmers; big old fingers and hard palms emerging from neat cuffs.

Henry made a quick speech, after calling for silence in a cheerfully bluff military tone. He welcomed the wives, mentioned a 'lad' who was very ill and could not be with them, and said that Mrs Helen Bamber was here because she always enjoys these gatherings and they were glad to see her.

*   *   *

They have been meeting like this for fifty years. The Chatton meeting is the continuation of a wartime democracy, the officers from the merchant families like the McCreaths and the Veitches who supplied the High Sheriffs of Berwick over the generations, and the men coalminers, farm labourers and shop managers, talking together over beer and sandwiches. The mutual respect and kindness is absolute, as the tolerance for the odd drunk or obsessive among them shows. They help each other out, with money or with sympathy when they lose their wives or fall ill, and they are extraordinarily physical with each other for men of their generation, touching each other to underline concern, hugging each other after longer absences. The fellowship of their suffering is irreplaceable.

They are vigorous, well preserved, lively and very old, but they have a hardness about them that they keep in check, and which it is easy to see could be quite difficult to live with. One of the men once told Bamber that you had to have an inner drive, a wit that kept you going; the experience of captivity made such gifts stronger. They don't pity themselves and they despise the modern business of public distress. Yet Helen Bamber – one of whose trades is 'therapy' – is an honoured guest here, a very small and rather stately old woman moving among these big men in their blazers. She greets them and their wives with pleasure and curiosity, and sits at the round tables with some of the men she has come to know, nursing her glass of whisky. They are rather gallant with her, and there's a lot of laughter, whilst some of them speak more quietly, and some with great intensity.

Three friends from Alnwick come regularly to the Chatton meeting. They went to the same school, sat at the same desk, joined the Boy Scouts and then the territorials, and were all on the railway together. They survived, and are delighted by their longevity and good fortune. One of them, like many former prisoners of the Japanese, has a physical aversion to rice. It has a dead smell, he once told Bamber; he can't stand the stuff. He was also badly beaten by a Korean guard for stealing bananas, and still can't understand, he says, how he can eat bananas yet not eat rice. When he returned to England and was still sick with malaria his mother found a bunch of bananas, exotic fruit in the rural North of England in the winter of 1945, and brought them home for him. He was revolted by the sight of the yellow fingers; yet in the end he forced himself to eat the fruit and was almost able to enjoy it. But he dug away at this ambivalence of his, which seemed to annoy him; and Bamber suggested that it was because they had been given with love, by his mother, that he was able to eat the bananas. She said something like, 'The love of your mother was greater than the hatred of your torturer.' She had not meant it as a very profound point, but after a long silence he had agreed; he said he couldn't bear to pass the hatred on to his mother, nor admit how distressed he really felt. 'You swallowed everything; that was the way it was.'

Being here has nothing to do with Helen Bamber's work with survivors of torture, and everything to do with it. It is not really work at all: she is here because she wants to be here, and it is a way of revisiting her war as well as avoiding it. She and 'the men' rather like each other's company. But they move her because they are not much older than she is, and because they are an intact society of the damaged and unheard-from, despite their success at coping with life. None of them could speak much to anyone, not even – perhaps especially not – to their families about what happened to them in Asia. Henry McCreath says of his wife, 'She thought I was a bit crackers, you know? And so I kept quiet about it.' They have, mostly, shared the past with each other: and are perhaps closer to each other than they have been to their wives.

They touch Bamber for more personal reasons too. She can understand the necessary discipline of their women, who could not share in this brotherhood; and, as Bamber has known to her own cost, could not heal their minds as well as mother them and their children; who couldn't do it all.

'I lived with a man,' she said, 'who could not speak about what had happened to him in Nazi Germany for many years, and I realize the capacity people have to survive and apparently survive well but at the price of numbing and depression. I think this is what moves me to the men. The men came back to their wives, to their homes, to that beautiful place, as no Holocaust survivor could do, but they came back as the Holocaust survivors did, with memories of brutality, of grotesque death; and nobody really wanted to hear it any more than they wanted to hear from the Holocaust survivors; and it's very difficult to deal with this in a marriage. I can guess the price the women paid. You'd have to be very selfless indeed not to want undamaged love, not to want undivided affection, not to demand of a man something that you believe is your right and which violence has made it hard for him to give; and I believe I did all that in my marriage. I could not pay the price, in the end.'

Living in the quietness of the border country has helped the men; communities here have been stable, and good land is an anchor for people who don't anyway much want to move. And although it would be untrue to suggest that they are incapable of talking about their experience without the help of outsiders, some of them have spoken to Bamber very frankly, about things that they have found it painful to discuss. It is as though her age and record, and her capacity for empathy, exempt her from embarrassment. ('She has a bit of a knack, am I right?' Henry McCreath said.) They do so with fine modesty – always insisting that I, personally, got by all right, but that Jimmy or Jackie over there *really* had a bad time. They suggest by the way they allow her in that they have kept a certain silence. Her interest is evidence that certain things were not done properly and never properly expressed after they came back.

There is also the unspoken matter of undeserved shame. Singapore was the single biggest defeat ever suffered by the British Army, and after it the empire never looked as strong again. No one would have dared say to their faces that they were not proper soldiers; still less would anybody have suggested openly that it was somehow their fault. But they felt the humiliating implication in the flatness between sentences, in the things that were not said and in the dreariness of their unexcited welcome in 1945. No families were permitted to meet them at Southampton, though the men were not told that at the time. It was decided that the less publicity attracted by this legion of the rearguard, the better; fewer emotional scenes, and fewer questions about why the big guns were pointing out to sea, why the aircraft never came, why the men were sent there in the first place. Churchill had wanted them to fight to the last man, and here they were. Few of them even got a pension from the army until a couple of years ago.

All of this matters a great deal to Henry McCreath. He seems biologically very young for an eighty-year-old, with fine silver hair and a handsome intelligent face. But his eyes, when he takes off his heavy glasses, are the oldest thing about him; the long-tolerated grief and depression in them make him suddenly look tired. His own wife died a year before the anniversary celebrations, and her passing affected him deeply.

He still has great authority with the men: 'Much-loved authority – we find that very hard to understand these days,' in Bamber's words. Watching him worrying about this group of survivors does bring alive what it meant to 'have' men, and to be loyal, to love a man across the deep English barrier of class – to return from the war knowing that you could be this man's driver, clerk, labourer, and still remain devoted to him because of what you had been through together.

Bamber noticed the first time she came to Chatton how Henry fussed over them, how he wanted to see them eating: 'It's a very basic thing, and very touching when you see it. I saw that when I was at Belsen, the need for people to feed each other; to see other people getting better. It is like a recognition of life itself. I see so much in the men that I also saw in Germany.'

This relationship between the men, which seems so paternalistic, has kept them in some condition of dignity for fifty years, and helped them to remember when no one else could help them, either to remember or forget. For Jackie Pyle, who was Henry's NCO and right-hand man, the relationship was always democratic; Henry was simply a decent human being. He was the 'mother hen' in charge of a hundred of them doing dangerous heavy work under violent guards, and that is what he still is when twenty of them are left. He intervenes, very quietly, for anyone in hard times, and he keeps the club going. Jackie feels people should remember what he calls 'the Beveridge principle' that the rich should help the poor, and says that they put it into practice on the railway. Every man got 10 cents a day from the Japanese when they worked, but nothing if they were too sick to move, so the working soldiers put 2 cents a day aside for a general fund, and so ensured the welfare of all.

He speaks about what helped them: their homogeneity, the fact that they were all from the same area; their adaptability, their skill as farmhands and miners in making tools and foraging. The most important thing was simple trust. They helped each other cut the side off what Henry calls 'a muckle great hill of rock at Wampo' to make a flat bed for the track, mainly by driving long chisels with mallets into the hard rock hour after hour, day after day. They called this 'hammer-and-tap', and the impact jarred the wrists, travelled up the arms and down the spine with every single blow. Several men died falling off the sheer cliff they were creating over the river, big stones sliding with them and crushing them in the water.

Jackie Pyle was the dynamiter. If he got it right, he could save lives by lessening the number of times emaciated men would have to climb long ladders with two-handled baskets full of splintered limestone; if he made a mistake, he would kill himself and many of his friends, since the Japanese guards didn't care to withdraw men out of range of flying rock. He would lay forty charges in crude cylinders, with cord twists for the tapers; matches were the only form of detonation he had. He would have to run fast along the line of pipes in the cleft split by the diggers and light all the charges from flaring matches, then get around the corner of the hill before the blast.

Images come back to him. Naked one-legged men diving into the river for fish: they'd had to undergo amputation of their gangrenous limbs by a surgeon using a tenon-saw while they were held down fully conscious on a bamboo bed, a reversion to medicine before anaesthesia. Men beaten with the flat of swords for dropping a tool; or forced to hold a massive stone over their heads for eight hours in hundred-degree heat. And through all of it, the endless reinvention of good humour.

He talks about the culture of 'counselling' with good-natured contempt, and says that men have become soft. Back in the war you had to have 'phlegm', you had to laugh and just get on with life. He told Helen Bamber once that the virtues of talking about pain are exaggerated, and he speaks of a fire that keeps a person going, which comes only from being struck hard. He implies that they had become steeled by their experience, but also that the spark struck from them is not easily extinguished.

Yet later he speaks of how little he could suffer fools gladly, and how he had to choose who mattered, and how the war had made him over-discriminating in his attitude to people. He had been to the edge of the cliff and looked over, so he did not want to waste any time, and got on and lived after that. But it also made him a hard overseer of himself; he could never relax. He speaks of not taking days off during his thirty-five years as a teacher, of still being at work when his colleagues had gone home, and them almost fearing and resenting him.

The source of this toughness, he suggests, is the feeling of guilt for having survived. After his denunciation of modern psychologizing it is strange to hear him say this. But he insists that many of them felt that they did not deserve to live, and that it made them determined to carry on, to prove they deserved their luck.

The turns of his quiet anger are difficult to follow – the admission of damage and pain, the simultaneous denial of the importance of talking. But it is clearer when he talks again about solidarity. There are seven deadly sins, he suggests, but the eighth is arrogance. The Japanese had this in the war: utter contempt for the integrity of another person, 'superiority run mad'. Henry and his men resisted this, in part, by showing themselves and each other that another way of life was possible: the democracy of the battalion, so that the war became the crucible of their own good commonwealth, of a solidarity they have never found again anywhere else. They insist on retaining a memory of trust and fellowship against the world they see around them, and defy us to do as well as they did. What they have to say can only be cheapened, Jackie Pyle seems to be saying, by public discussion. They know that they can be quoted and photographed, and that everyone now says their 'sacrifice' was important; but feeling it is a different matter.

The end of the war meant liberation from starvation and grotesque diseases, and the end of that life in common. Another man, a rank and file fusilier called Joe Cumming, says that 'the one thing that nobody can understand is how unimaginably painful it was to part from your friends. After disembarkation, after detraining, we just went, like that.' He makes a sweeping gesture with his hands, as though he were brushing something off. 'That was terrible. These were people who would do anything for you. And they still do: that man Henry mentioned who was very sick will be visited this evening without a doubt.'

It is as though time stopped in 1945, despite the years of hard work and responsibility that followed. They all refer again and again to the squalor of their homecoming, the insolent silent way in which it was conveyed to them that the authorities – the state, the army, the whole of official Britain – would prefer to forget about them. It still angers and humiliates them half a century later. And the single event that symbolizes this for all of them, without exception in Bamber's experience and of anyone who now speaks to the men, is the return of Jimmy Virtue.

Jimmy was from Norham, and served in the platoon led by Archie Veitch, Henry McCreath's childhood friend. Veitch may speak in the languid registers of the English upper class, a contrast to the Northumberland burr in the speech of the others, but the former captain is no less passionate than his ex-private soldier comrades about Jimmy's treatment. 'He lived out in the country about twelve miles from here. He was let off the boat in Liverpool, on the other side of the country, and was given a railway warrant. He managed to get to Newcastle at some *ungodly* hour at night, with no one to organize him or get him a billet for the night, and he eventually got himself to Berwick at four in the morning by hitch-hiking. From whence he set off to walk home. You know, we didn't expect to come home as heroes, far from it, but *we were human beings.*'

Jimmy Virtue was dead by the time they celebrated V-J Day in 1995, but he was one of the men who had spoken a lot to Bamber, and she was helping him to record his testimony in the year before he died. In one long conversation he told her of the battalion's first action in the disastrous retreat from France in 1940. They were a machine-gun unit with very few machine guns, walking along the coast in the rain, and he spoke of 'miles of beach black with men' while Stukas bombed and strafed them whenever the cloud lifted. He dived into the sand-dunes again and again to find shelter, and saw friends die. 'Sudden death was beginning to mean something to me; before, you brushed it aside but now you saw the reality of it.'

When he got back to Britain, he was given leave and saw his mother read a telegram informing her of his death. It made him feel as though he had been 'written off'; it brought back 'with a bump' that his task as a soldier was to offer himself for death. He spent the late winter of 1940 helping to clear buildings on Clydebank after Luftwaffe raids, and digging people out of the ruins; and at Easter 1941 he was sitting on top of a gasometer in Liverpool, a grey gas tank, watching incendiaries coming down out of the darkness. If one landed near him, he had to get it over the side of the tank fast. It was 'like minding a bomb the size of a house'. Bamber remembered the same incendiary bombs falling in London when she was a very young fire-watcher, the hiss and fizzle they made, and she and Jimmy compared the relative merits of buckets filled with sand or water for putting them out.

He felt he had been part of such an efficient formation; they all did. Henry talks about how his men would take machine guns home for the weekend to practise stripping them blindfold, so they could reassemble the firing block at night: he loved their sheer naive enthusiasm. So what failed to happen in Singapore affected them very badly. They had been given special Vickers machine guns with a longer range than the ordinary model, and the men were full of fight. They were sent in, they came later to believe, for political reasons, to 'leaven the lump' as Archie Veitch put it: Churchill was under pressure from the Australians to add British contingents to the largely colonial garrison of the city. Jimmy was quietly proud of their spectacular arrival. Their troopship was an unarmed French liner, and when Japanese bombers found it the ship was struck three times; so the fusiliers brought up their arsenal of thirty Bren guns and two dozen Vickers guns, removed the elevating joint pins and lashed them by their tripods to the deck rails. On each side of the ship, a hundred riflemen were lined up on the hurricane decks. When the bombers came back they flew into a curtain of bullets. Seven fusiliers were killed, but they shot down three Japanese planes. They slid the bodies into the water in the strait off Blakang Mati Island, and then made landfall.

The docks were 'a wee bit panicky' (Henry's phrase), and from then on it was the now-familiar story of the great debacle: the island's water was cut off; the Japanese attacked not from the sea but from the landward side, so that the great guns making Singapore 'impregnable' were useless; there was no air support. The troops fought well, but there was really nothing they could do. In London Churchill blustered about resistance; on the island, the generals knew they had a choice between asking their men to commit mass suicide or to surrender. Jimmy had to capitulate with the rest, 85,000 men rounded up like sheep. A few months later he was in Siam working on the railway that would eventually claim 200,000 lives. He was in a bridge-building party. 'We had barely seen a bridge, never mind built one, in our lives.'

'The rations just dwindled and dwindled but the work didn't, the work went ahead.' Jimmy contracted dysentery and chronic diarrhoea, and developed the large tropical ulcers that were caused by malnutrition and filth. An ulcer, in the dictionary definition, is a 'purulent open sore', and in Jimmy's case, as with so many other men on the railroad, his leg was eaten away to the bone. 'You could see the muscles and sinews in behind the knee, how they functioned at the back of the knee.' It was very painful. (Bill Brown, another of the men, described helping the medical officer on another stretch of the line clean out ulcers with a spoon: 'We used to sit on the bloke, sit on his arms and stuff a towel in his mouth so he couldn't scream until the doctor finished with him. The smell was disgraceful. Then carry him back into the hut.')

What saved Jimmy's life was also what nauseated and terrified him then, and gave him nightmares for years afterwards: because the doctor had no field dressings, his leg was exposed to flies all day, and his ulcer became infested with maggots. But he was lucky; the maggots were a species that prefers dead to living flesh, and so they ate the rotting tissue and cleaned out the sore; he made himself learn, he said, to see them as friends, at least with his conscious mind.

Jimmy ended the war with malaria, a duodenal ulcer and the lingering effects of all his other illnesses. The merciless labour exactions stopped a short while before the ceasefire. On April Fool's Day, 1945, they were taken down the line, wearing G-strings and vests in cold rain, squatting on heavy bridging girders that formed the base of the open wagons. They dreaded being made to carry the girders when the train stopped. But the Japanese ordered them off at Prachuab, a town on the Siamese coast. A Japanese officer let them go into the surf. 'With the cold and the diarrhoea and the colic and the cold, we were in such a mess with the sparks and the soot from the engine coming back onto us. Never mind, we got washed off in there.'

After his journey back to Norham, Jimmy Virtue went before a medical board and was judged '9 to 15 per cent disabled', and was given a small lump sum, but not any form of pension. As Bill Brown put it tersely, 'The village was good to us, the country wasn't.'

This lasting sense of insult is why a man like Henry McCreath, with his successful life and his large family, remains so attached to 'his' men. Looking back, he wonders at their own innocence: he had never been abroad before, but most of the others had never even been out of the county. (Now when one of his grandchildren breaks his leg on holiday in Thailand, it seems a normal mishap for an eighteen-year-old.) The Tyne was 'down there', with the coal and the ships, big companies and strong trade unions, but, he said, 'There's always been a feeling that we were part of the lost souls up here.'

They had come so far – across the Atlantic to Nova Scotia, then sailing in American ships to Cape Town, and over the Indian Ocean to Bombay and thence in their Free French liner to Malaya. He describes standing on the deck of the *Felix Rousselle* as they buried the dead from the fight with the Japanese bombers, watching the flames and the black smoke from the oil yards on the island as greasy soot settled on their light tropical uniforms – a young captain who had accompanied his men halfway around the world into a trap. 'One of the other officers said to me: "What do you think of this, Henry?" "Not very much," said I, "the last time we saw that was at Dunkirk and then we were sailing away from it."'

He never actually saw the city of Singapore. They were landed and hurried away to a defensive position to the north, and they were effective. Bill Gibson, one of the men who comes to Chatton, 'stitched a Zero front to rear' with his friend Barlow from their position in a Chinese cemetery.

At the surrender, Henry McCreath says, 'We were heartbroken, that's the word, to think we had come all that way and trained for years and been in France without very much to fight with and we put up a good show despite that, and in Singapore we were well equipped and we never got a chance.' One of his lads from the village of Alnwick saw a British staff car driving up the road flying the Union Jack and a white flag, past his Vickers gun emplacement. He was outraged; says that he said to his mate, right; if they come this way again I'll stop them. But an officer came round and said that it was true: they were to give up.

Henry was ordered to get some men and help build a wall of breeze-blocks around the Japanese Military Police HQ and 'it wasn't very pleasant, they were torturing these people inside and you could hear the screams.'

Like Archie Veitch, he can quote by heart from his old 'nominal roll' and has a head for exact figures (he remembers the casualty rate in his company as '19.5 per cent'), but his precise narrative falters in 1943, the year the Japanese decreed that the line must be finished at any cost so that they could bring up men and material to invade India. The beatings were now very bad, the diet awful, the Korean guards given complete licence over the men. As an officer, Henry was a target, punished for whatever his men didn't do to the satisfaction of the engineers: 'You had to grin and bear it if you were beaten. There was a guard we called Silver Bullet and he used to bring his arm up and hit you on the ear as hard as he could and if you moved the other way his other arm came up as well. In '43 I wasn't well at all, I had a very bad ear, very septic, and there was nobody to turn to really and one really got a bit down. I had yellow jaundice as well. Somebody would say to you, "Come on, pull yourself together," and you would do the same.'

He did get through, with his hearing badly affected; like the rest he was landed in England, given his railway warrant, examined to see if he was carrying any tropical diseases and sent on his way. 'When we got home we thought there might have been a bit of appreciation of what we had gone through, but that didn't turn out to be the case. People did not believe what we talked about, they did not believe it and I think it's true to say as a result of that we all shut up and very rarely talked to anybody. We formed this little club, and therefore we kept quiet.'

His wife Pat had been on her own, waiting, not knowing if he was alive or dead. They had been married the day war was declared and had two days together before he was sent overseas. Archie Veitch remembers it as the saddest wedding he ever attended. Pat had not wanted to impose on Henry's parents, had perhaps been too proud to rely on them, so she brought up on her own the child she had while he was away. His daughter was five and a total stranger to him when he came back. There were problems at first, he says, but later their life improved, though he implies that there was always a shadow of unrecoverable happiness. They went on. There were more children, and eventually even great-grandchildren.

He had great energy; he reacquired the family feed and fertilizer business which had been sold to an agribusiness combine, and made a success of it. Henry McCreath must have been an excellent buyer and negotiator with farmers, cheerful, straight and funny, and fair-dealing, a man they would look forward to seeing. That was how he spent the post-war years, and 'the club' was already meeting once a month. Such and such a lad could not be found; so and so had seen him; enquiries, letters, meetings. Pensions, disability entitlements, tactful help; and always the bad dreams.

What made it so hard for this kindly and sensitive man not to be able to articulate his feelings was the sense that 'the powers that be were not interested in us, a bit of resentment that we were forgotten; and I always think that there was a wee bit of a stigma, the fact that we had been part of the collapse of the British empire … Sometimes you could sense it, you could feel it. Maybe I was too sensitive about it but … it was so wrong, you know, because it wasn't the fault of the man on the ground, it was complacency on the part of our leaders. The Japs could have been held a wee bit longer.'

It was worse not being able to communicate within the family, and he says it made him very difficult to live with, a hard admission for such a sociable man to make. He thinks that they all, in some way, became very reserved and that something was 'bothering us, hidden inside us'. In his house he keeps a large colour photograph of the cutting at Wampo as it now is, a rickety trestle bridge along the side of a hill: he is both there and here, a complicated thing to explain to those close to him; like most of the men, he has lived in two dimensions of time. At the end of his life it is as though his business successes and reputation are indeed behind him, but the rest, what he shares with his oldest friends, is not.

Even to be able to point to this reserved place within himself was a form of release. Helen Bamber was helpful – the relief of 'speaking to somebody who understands and is prepared to listen ... I found it extremely difficult to talk, I never talked in public about it because you could see people looking at you as much as to say, "He's talking through his bloody hat," you know?

'Helen came up and met Archie and me and one or two others and then came out to two or three of our little meetings, and talked to our lads and they took to her; she has a way with them if you know what I mean and they talked a bit to her ... I thought she was rather an amazing lady, she was so quiet and peaceful in her talking, so very sincere, you felt that she encouraged you a bit to talk. She could put it into words that you could listen to, she certainly has a knack of doing that.'

Although Bamber's arrival may have been coincidental, there were some small breaches in the silence that had been allowed to grow and almost choke parts of the past. Not long before she died, Pat McCreath spoke of how she had wanted to come and meet Henry but had been ordered not to: the order was 'wives away from the dock'. She became very upset as they talked about it, with some of their old friends in the room. She had never been able to say how much she wanted to welcome him home. But Henry went across, in front of the others, and awkwardly comforted her.

* * *

Bamber's allegiance to 'the men' stems, she says, from 'a shared resistance to the sweeping away of a whole terrible experience as though it didn't really matter, as though it doesn't have *any bearing on what's going on now*. That's what upset me when I came back from Germany; it was as if somehow the sands were shifting and the imperative was to hurry on and forget the past. Today, it's tempting to imagine that cruelty can be put behind us, but if we refuse to hear about it we are allowing states to get away with it. When for asylum purposes you do documentation and take testimony from people who have been tortured, it's also about validation, you are bearing witness, you're understanding someone's story. Although "the men" seem so comfortably part of a traditional society, that society never really validated their experience.'

She recognizes, as she began to do a long time ago in the barracks at Belsen, that people who have been shattered by violence need to feel acknowledged: if the particularity of their experience is abolished, they feel traduced. We should expect what Thomas Browne calls 'the iniquity of oblivion', but the premature oblivion of silence is impossible to face with tranquillity.

More is at stake here than self-expression. Primo Levi writes of a dream in which he returns home and with huge relief tells his sister and his friends about Auschwitz; and she gets up and silently walks away. For too many people, that has been their actual experience after atrocity, what Levi calls 'the ever-repeated scene of the unlistened-to story'.

For Bamber, the idea of human rights seems inseparable from the simple belief in the sharing of experience, in conversation – in that almost archaic sense of the word as having one's being among people; and most of us achieve something like this through the medium of gossip, passing the time of day. Bamber and people like her, however, are willing to pass time that can't be traded as social small change: to speak and hear of events that remain finally incommunicable.

For some, there can never be any erasing of that moment of utter fear and anguish, when they felt themselves destroyed and could no longer believe in the possibility of return. They feel that they no longer deserve to be whole. But even if they can learn to live with it, as Henry McCreath and his men did, it is still possible to value a person like Bamber who knows what had to be done in order to go on.

It would be difficult, nonetheless, to imagine a more unlikely meeting than the encounter between these fusiliers and Helen Bamber. What do they really make of this tiny old Jewish lady in their rural pub, when they

pass around sandwiches and chips with the pints of beer? Her engagement with the worst the world can do is an expression of European
Jewish culture at its most alert, generous and painful, a culture indelibly
marked by genocide and suspicion. The ex-fusiliers' stoicism, shyness,
the very conservatism of their courtesy, their reluctance to dramatize
their suffering, their quiet decency and comfort with their place in the
world are the kind of English qualities that, in other circumstances,
might suffocate her. They represent things that she has never had; and,
difficult as their lives have been, they have returned to a place where they
are safe, something which she has had to struggle to create for herself.
But there is a serenity about this encounter in old age that is notable.

When Helen Bamber first spoke to the fusiliers in Berwick, trying to
explain what she does at the Medical Foundation, she mentioned her
time at Belsen. She talked about the camp's peculiar smell, and said that
it was somehow the smell of geraniums. Not an unpleasant smell,
necessarily, but a sort of dank, sweetish odour that she cannot forget.
She keeps geraniums on the patio of her small flat in London, and sometimes she is compelled to go out and smell them in their pots, for no
reason that she can really articulate: the need to forget; the wish to
remember. When she had finished speaking, one of the men came up to
her, took her hand and said, 'I know why you smell the geraniums.' He
could not explain either, though he is one of the men who cannot bear
the smell of rice, an aversion that is perhaps not very different from her
way of remembering Belsen.

2

THE JIGSAW

A generation that had gone to school on a horse-drawn streetcar now stood
under the open sky in a countryside in which nothing remained unchanged
but the clouds, and beneath these clouds, in a field of force of destructive
torrents and explosions, was the tiny, fragile human body.

Walter Benjamin

The story of most lives becomes guesswork when it reaches back to
childhood; what little we can remember has the power and
reliability of myth. Helen Bamber has few documents that would
authenticate her own past, and beyond the events that her memory has
shaped into fact, there is much that she is unsure about. In most families,
no-one is vain enough to assume that scraps of writing will ever illumin-
ate anything other than the ordinary, like a torch shone into an attic
where junk is kept; but in very unhappy families, Bamber is convinced,
'things are not preserved; you want them to go away.' An archive might
help her piece together a more coherent narrative, but would hardly
mitigate the tension willed her by her parents; she sometimes wonders
whether she had a childhood at all. What remains of hers are a few
letters; some black and white photographs fading to the brown colour of
old paper, the images fragile as though the light they contained were
growing too strong; and that is nearly the whole of her physical
inheritance.

Her father was Louis Balmuth; her mother was Marie Bader. Helen
Bamber knew that her father was born in America, whilst her mother
was born in Britain, and that both her parents' families came from

territories that are now part of Poland. This 'Poland' in her memory of her father was an indeterminate zone extending off into Tsarist Russia, but beyond that he gave her little in the way of place-names and dates. She remembered him talking about moving from country to country, and she was aware that he and his brothers had connections in many European states, but she could not trace these migrations: her family history was a sealed box. She wondered, for example, how her father had escaped conscription during the First World War, with its insatiable demand for male bodies: 'another odd bit of a very disjointed jigsaw.' He would speak to her about almost anything except, usually, himself. By the time locations and origins came to matter to her, it was too late: her grandparents were long dead and the world they left in the nineteenth century had been destroyed. By then, too, she seems to have been incapable of tearing off the seals and looking for herself, as though anything she found would reproach or hurt her.

Louis Balmuth did tell his daughter that his parents took him back with them to 'Poland', where they lived on his grandfather's farm. Bamber remembered imagining this journey through the eyes of her father as a child. He told her how young people were made to earn their passage on the ship, scrubbing the deck and cleaning the cabins, and that life had been bad for them in America; he spoke of dirt and hunger. The most potent 'fact' about America for her was that he could not go out on the streets in the summer because he had no shoes and the sidewalk was too hot under his bare feet. Whatever motivated the decision to return is hidden in the childhood legend. Perhaps they went back to claim a legacy from his grandparents, giving them enough capital to move and start over yet again.

It must have been a compelling reason, for her father also told her stories of persecution that he must have heard first in a tenement on the Lower East Side or in the steerage of the ship on its way to the Baltic. Somewhere he seems to have acquired a fearfulness that almost destroyed him in later life. The ease with which mobs could be turned on Jews throughout the Polish and Russian lands was one of Louis Balmuth's earliest lessons to his daughter. ' "Pogrom" was a word I learned as a small child; and my father would describe horses and violence and fear, as though he had seen them. Perhaps he really had.'

And yet the place, wherever it was and if it existed as she remembers it on his behalf, seems to have worked some kind of enchantment on the boy. It was, paradoxically, one of the few times in his life that he spoke of with affection and enthusiasm. 'It seemed to be almost his only period of happiness and freedom, of being an ordinary child – climbing trees, and throwing stones at the local count's bay horses. There was more there for him than the threat of violence; he had anecdotes about farm life, and the forests. At least this is what he remembered.' She has an image of her father banging on the window of a wooden farmhouse trying to scare away prowling bears. 'Like most children I didn't pay that much attention to what he was telling me. What is sad now is that I remember so little, and I asked so little.'

In her father's account of his childhood the nostalgic focus was on a farm, and it may be that Louis's grandparents really did own a farm. But why his parents dared to go back, and what they were doing there, had become romanticised: an East European idyll, with long shadows. These glimpses of his childhood were some of the few concessions Louis Balmuth ever made to his own daughter's infancy. Every other memory of her father's side of the family is shot through with apprehension and secrecy.

When his parents left the east for the last time, they came to Britain. Bamber could not recall the adults around her ever discussing how they entered the country, or in what circumstances, as though the urgency of their lives made them impatient with their own recent past. The rediscovery of their death certificates upset her, almost angered her; she had all but forgotten the dates of her grandparents' deaths, which made her ignorance of their lives more galling. She suspected that she was the granddaughter of illegal immigrants; and this may charge her impatience with the bright young civil servants at the British Home Office whose task it is, a century after her family came ashore at an English port, to falsify the stories told by refugees, and expel them.

The British state still leaks its secrets very slowly, and at the Public Record Office in Kew, in the deceptively light and open rooms furnished with pale wood and steel, the paper of her grandfather Jacob Balmuth's Home Office file has already worn thin and friable. An original stamp on the cover instructs the archivist not to release it until the year 2023; a liberal concession makes it possible to read Jacob's application to be naturalized as a British subject, and the police reports on him, after a mere seventy-five years.

He was born in 1856 in Debica (pronounced 'Dembitsa'), a hundred miles east of Krakow, in the Polish province of Galicia which was then part of the Austro-Hungarian Empire: Galicia had been Maria Theresa's prize in the first partition of Poland in 1772. The poorest and most backward of the Hapsburg provinces, it was inhabited by Polish landlords, Ruthenian peasants and Jewish craftsmen, labourers and merchants. The Jews were less burdened here than in Russia with civil disabilities and menaces, though it was not until after the failed revolution of 1848 that they were allowed even to own land, and they were vulnerable in times of trouble. Perhaps Louis Balmuth was passing on stories of lynchings and riots he had heard from his own father's childhood.

Jacob Balmuth married Lena Rosner from Rzeszow, a larger town twenty miles east of Debica, in 1883; the Special Branch officer, whose job it was to vet would-be British subjects in case they were security risks, reported that Jacob's 'proof of birth and marriage lines have been lost'. The policeman recorded that the 'memorialist', that is, the 'alien' applicant, 'speaks and reads excellent English'. He was a 'retired hat manufacturer', and seemed 'very respectable' to the officer, who also noted Jacob's statement that he left Galicia 'in about the year 1884–5 and was employed as a hat-manufacturer at Newark, New Jersey'. Yet the place of birth of his first son Abraham, on the latter's naturalization certificate, is given as Rzeszow, Galicia, in 1886. A year missing; but Jacob somehow became a US citizen in 1892, and claimed to have entered Britain in 1895. Louis Balmuth was born in New York on 28 August 1887, followed by his brothers Michael in 1889 and Leo in 1892, born, they would later claim, in the same city – not in Newark, on the other side of the Hudson River. Did the mysterious return journey to Eastern Europe take place in the years between acquiring the security of American nationality and the family's emigration to Britain, at a time when Louis would have been six or seven? The pieces refuse to fit neatly, and it is unlikely that Jacob would have told a policeman more than he needed to know: the process of naturalization was difficult and expensive enough.

The state could not decide what in fact he was. He described himself on his official application form in the entry under 'nationality' as 'Galician' – a touching local patriotism that none of the region's nationalisms would have recognized. An official crossed this out, and wrote in 'Austrian', at the time, presumably, of Jacob's first application in 1915. Galicia had reverted to Poland by 1920, when his application was considered again, and in that year someone corrected the entry, drawing a neat inked line through 'Austrian' and writing 'Polish'. The ambiguity seems to have troubled the civil servants, for at the time of his acceptance as a British citizen they described Jacob Balmuth's nationality as 'Doubtful', before finally settling on the term that appears on his certificate of naturalization: 'Uncertain', as though he couldn't be located anywhere on the new world map.

But of course there was never any doubt about his position and history, indeterminate though its traces may have been. Other neat copperplate annotations in blue ink make this clear. He was refused citizenship during the war, and again in July 1920. 'Lay by until pressed,' an official then wrote on the file. When his application was finally going through, an anxious note records a civil servant's awareness that he has been asked to slow down the processing of 'these cases'. Not many people could afford the time or money to become formally naturalized, as few as 2,000 a year, but the issue was less money or social status than race. Another note summarizes a letter received in response to the advertisement in the local press that all applicants had to take out, announcing their intention of becoming citizens. 'Anonymous (An Englishman) protests against the naturalization of Jews' and a civil servant adds: 'Lay By'. The letter is preserved, with its faultless handwriting and demented punctuation, on good notepaper sent from an address in Amhurst Park, the street where Balmuth lived. 'An Englishman' speaks on behalf of 'hundreds of neighbours who strongly object ... to these dirty people, we cannot breathe where they are, they neither respect us nor ourselves nor our customs ... more of them are Bolsheviks than the Government knows.' But three months later, on 6 February 1922, Jacob Balmuth finally became 'entitled to all political and other rights powers and privileges ... to which a natural born British subject is entitled'.

The sons, especially Michael Balmuth, who in 1919 became the first member of the family to take out citizenship, had meanwhile made the family prosperous. His three brothers were naturalized within three weeks of each other in August 1923. They had been in Britain for almost thirty years: if naturalization had been easier, they might have become British in time to be conscripted during the war. Louis Balmuth's

American citizenship may have saved his life. A year later, he married Marie Bader. Helen's first memories are of the 'huge' house on Amhurst Park, which belonged to Michael and where all the brothers lived with their parents.

The world shifted in the years between Jacob Balmuth's departure from the area that would nearly become a cemetery for his people, and the birth on 1 May 1925 of Helen, his first grand-child. The historical nineteenth century ended late, in the abdications and civil wars of the years between 1917 and 1922. 'Kaiser' and 'Tsar', different versions of 'Caesar', became obsolete overnight. The men who had been lent the magic of power by such words became ordinary citizens, and were discarded or murdered. The Bolshevik Revolution destroyed an old empire, and an elite of liberators made the imperial palaces their own, disciplining the people with unrestrained violence for their inadequate grasp of revolutionary necessity – terror for the sake of generations yet unborn, and terror for its own sake. To the west, the Treaty of Versailles created a mosaic of new states containing minorities and territories claimed by their neighbours, a map disputed by nationalist cartographers for the next twenty years. In Germany, the experience of defeat, the French demands for reparations, the intact strategic arrogance of the general staff and the volatility of the world market would open a road to power for Europe's most vicious utopians: small-town napoleons who had learned the jargon of science and medicine, of Darwin for anti-Semites, raging, like Hitler, against 'the terrible poisoning of the health of the national body' by Jews and democracy, and obsessed with 'blood, sin and desecration of the race'.

The frayed leather-bound volumes of naturalization papers at Kew reveal that the officials who drew them up had trouble with Polish names. Debica, on the correspondence about Jacob Balmuth, is written 'Dembica', written almost as it is pronounced, the mistake perhaps originating from the notes of an early interview; by the time it is sealed officially as his place of birth and he has taken the Oath of Allegiance it has become 'Dembria'. Jacob Bader, Helen Bamber's maternal grand-father, was born in a town that a Home Office clerk has typed out as 'Oszwieneim'. There seems to have been no such place in Galicia, or anywhere else in the Habsburg Empire. The only location that corresponds to it and might sound like it to the English ear is the town of Oszwiecim, in German Auschwitz, on the western border of Galicia with Silesia, a railway junction near the River Vistula where 5,000 Jews still lived in 1939.

*　　*　　*

North and east of Finsbury Park the ugliest terraces of small houses in London form ladders of streets. They reek of the unexotic poverty of the emigrant worker, single men frowning with anxiety outside cafés or the doors to first-floor cab offices: the terrain of the legal and illegal alien, successive waves of migration out of Europe and the old British Empire inching up through what used to be 'outcast London' – Whitechapel, Bow, Spitalfields, Shoreditch – and on through Dalston and Clapton to the drained marshes on the banks of the River Lea. Many of Bamber's 'clients' in the closing years of the century – Kurds, Turks, Iraqis, Somalis – live along this refugee trail. She has known it all her life.

Near the Walthamstow Marshes, the river has been diverted to form interlocking artificial lakes, sources of water for the population of North London. The smallest of these are two lung-shaped reservoirs, and around them lives a community of Hasidic Jews, followers of the Satmar and Lubavitch Rebbes. Between the wars the area was politically electric – religious orthodoxy was challenged by secular Zionism, parliamentary socialism by communism. The houses around the reservoirs are bigger, older and more solidly built than in the newer streets to the north; it is now an area of large families and worlds that co-exist but rarely touch. Stoke Newington Church Street, a crooked remnant of an 18th-century village, forms a hip border along the southern edge of the orthodox Jewish world – a string of fabric shops, Asian restaurants and nearly-new bookstores, of white jazz and freelancers looking for a deal. In a side road off Church Street, Daniel Defoe found a shape for two of the central myths of modernity: the man or woman abandoned and alone, forced to invent their lives; and the city struck by plague, with terror almost the only connection between its people.

Amhurst Park is a wide street that runs close to the northern tip of the lakes. The people who lived here in the 1920s had reached a social ledge higher than the other Russian Jewish immigrants – the pressers, boot-makers and carpenters of Bethnal Green working double shifts to have enough to eat. On the north side of the road there are still a few of the massive Victorian family houses that once lined it, four windows across and very deep: homes for doctors, merchants, lawyers, with big rooms and wide gardens. Blocks of council flats took their places after the war. On the south side, where Helen Bamber's grandparents lived at no. 45, there is now just one of the old houses standing, opposite the small local railway station. Many of the others, including the house she was born in, were damaged or destroyed by German bombs in 1941.

She remembers it as 'quite a splendid house. It even had a billiard room, although I never remember anyone ever playing billiards because they weren't the sort of people who would; it was an absurd symbol of the good life they could not bring themselves to enjoy. And there was a horrible rug with the head of a bear, growling silently, of which they were all incredibly proud.'

The Balmuths were a noisy, divided, bitterly inseparable family. Relations between the siblings were close and abrasive. Bamber remembers vicious disputes in Yiddish, French and English: 'They were clever and all of them were good linguists. But they quarrelled about everything, each other, their politics, and their partners. They were all curiously mad and none of them, really, understood children. All the brothers, apart from my father, died early. They never made good relationships, and most of them never married: they were very unconnected. Refugees develop in great jumps, they live disjointed lives, full of strange gaps.'

The brothers quarrelled in English when they wanted to hurt Helen Bamber's mother Marie; their women seemed to be a projection of their rivalries. Even her mother's sister, Mina, who was able to give as good as she got, was not spared, and avoided the house if she could. Bamber can recall remarks about her mother made deliberately in her father's presence. For her the extended family was a childhood battleground. 'I think that whatever ability I now have to contain anger and upheaval started with that family, because it was my only means of surviving. You were targeted for having a mother who they disliked, or for your father's inadequacies, for anything. They picked away at my father's discomfiture about his unhappy marriage. He was outwardly calm, most of the time, but sometimes he would explode, and then he frightened me.'

The most powerful figure in the household was Michael, the second youngest of the brothers. He was often away in Paris, where he kept a French mistress, a scandal to Helen's mother and an occasion for provocation by his brothers. But Michael had made a lot of money, and it was he who paid for the unused billiard room and the bear rug and the large house. He described himself as a 'merchant', and the Special Branch report on him in 1919 lists his referees: a stockbroker, a fruit merchant and the senior partner in the firm that Michael seems effectively to have controlled, John G. Raphael. The police sergeant who investigated Michael found that he had 'an excellent reputation in the City of London'. His fortune had been made in the colonial trade, rising from a clerk in the Lima Railway Company to a directorship in Mr Raphael's concern, which was 'connected with the East India export business'. To his niece he was a rude brilliant self-made thug, dressed in expensive suits and 'flaunting wads of money' – she has an image of him once 'plonking down on a table a great roll of notes to settle some argument'. Her child's-eye view of the fast-money years before the great crash is of this wide-boy uncle riding high, and the nervous aggression of his insecurity.

She was entranced by the thought of Uncle Michael's French mistress, who nobody ever seemed to have met. He would come back from France with bizarre presents: 'Once when I was ill he brought instead of toys or chocolates some rather repellent warm underwear, childish versions of elderly combinations, which I never wore, but I was puzzled by his idea of me even then. It was as though he had no sense of me as a child.'

He supported his parents – gentle shadowy characters, in Bamber's memory. She cannot remember her grandfather *doing* anything at all, but since he was seventy years old by the time she was born he must have earned his leisure in the years of hat-making. 'They were sad figures – they gave no light and no joy.' The old man exists for her now in her recollection of her own father's devotion to him, and in the Yiddish diminutive which Louis used to address him, 'Fadi' – a rare expression of affection in that family. 'My father's parents allowed all the activity and anger and violence – and there was a real current of violence – to pass right through them.'

She remembers her father's mother, Lena, as 'beautiful, fastidious, the kind of woman who always dusted a seat in any public place before taking it and made you do the same'. Bamber recalls a Persian lamb coat with a high collar, the old woman bringing a whiff of expensive scent with her and always looking good. A picture of Lena as a girl survives: she is wearing a tight leather vest and a leather belt, like a Chekhov heroine; a handsome, narrow-waisted young woman with a shy, hurt face. 'She was very small; actually no bigger than me.' (Bamber stands five feet nothing, without her heels.) 'She had produced all these children in different countries; for her it must have been a very hard life. She took refuge in cooking, incessantly, for these sulky men.'

Her mother's parents lived a mile to the east in the London Borough of Hackney, just off Mare Street, its main avenue. Jacob and Rebecca Bader made a much deeper impression on her. They also lived in a large house; here too, for a time, there was money. Helen Bamber would sit on a high stone wall around a garden where she was allowed to play, and sleep in a huge bedroom; it had high ceilings with swags of amaranth and bunches of grapes in the white plaster moulding of the cornice. Here there was affection, and a child could be as nearly herself as our illusions of the good childhood demand. She could enjoy herself, and be doted on, and she loved being there.

Family tradition believed that Jacob Bader had carried on a correspondence with Peter Kropotkin, the aristocratic Russian radical and theorist of anarchism. It isn't impossible: Kropotkin visited England many times after his escape from a Russian jail in 1876, and was a regular contributor to *Nature* (where he developed his ideas on mutual aid among animals, as an alternative to the vulgarized Darwinism of 'the survival of the fittest'), and other British journals. In 1886, he founded *Freedom*, an anarchist–communist monthly still published today out of a blind alley in Whitechapel for a tiny readership. Anarchism had a base of support among radical Jewish craftsmen in the East End in the early years of the century, enough to support a Yiddish newspaper, the *Arbeiter Fraint* (The Workers' Friend) and to carry a bitter strike by tailors to victory in 1911. But Jacob Bader's hostility to the discipline of the state and his vision of replacing it with what Kropotkin called 'the constructive work of the unknown masses' scandalized his family: it is said that when he died his wife revenged herself on politics by destroying his correspondence with the revolutionary prince.

It would be intriguing, in the light of what his granddaughter became, to know something of Jacob Bader's own ideas about power. Kropotkin died in Russia in 1921 after returning from exile, a brave but hopeless 'constructive critic' of the Bolsheviks. In one of his outspoken letters to Lenin during the civil war, after the announcement that officers of Wrangel's army were to be used as hostages, Kropotkin wrote: 'If you admit such methods, one can foresee that one day you will use torture, as was done in the Middle Ages. I hope you will not answer me that power is for political men a professional duty, and that any attack against that power must be considered a threat against which one must guard oneself at any price. This opinion is no longer held even by kings.' In that last sentence the nineteenth-century belief in the inevitable decline of barbarism impales itself on modern power. (Lenin is said to have remarked: 'I am sick of this old fogey. He understands nothing of politics.')

Helen Bamber remembers her maternal grandfather as an austere but loving person, which seems right for a follower of one of the anarchist movement's gentler sages, moving between his study and his garden, wearing a dark suit and a fob-watch across his waistcoat. She knew he had studied and that he was considered a cut above others for his learning. She never saw him at work – he always seemed to be writing or gardening. This surely disillusioned revolutionary would let her hide silver coins in his white brush of hair, which shot straight up from his forehead, in his own odd version of hide and seek.

He seemed immensely old to her, a figure from another time, and so he was, but when Helen was four he was still under sixty. For a purist and intellectual romantic, he had an unusual trade: he was a barber who by the mid-1920s owned a chain of women's hair salons. When he died his family was careful to insist on his death certificate that he was a *master* hairdresser.

His sons made little impression on his granddaughter, but she certainly remembers his daughter Mina, who become a communist, took up 'beauty culture' and later ran a hair parlour herself. This combination of style and politics was to have an effect on Helen when she grew a little older, but in her visits to Mare Street she was aware at first only of her aunt's vigorous physicality. On Sunday afternoons she would teach her niece to dance, and fill the Bader house with music and freedom; Helen's mother lived for these experiences, which were unknown amid her in-laws' quarrels.

Rebecca Bader, the grandmother, was open, sensual and hospitable. Helen Bamber thinks of her as a great earthy peasant. 'Her husband would say, "She still has snow on her boots." He seemed rather to despise her, in an affectionate sort of way.' But she knew how to amuse a serious and lonely child. She taught Helen the 'Krakowia', a stomping, booted dance from the Pale for people who knew the value of celebration, her massive body processing firmly and in stately rhythm around the floor of the large room, guiding the child through the steps with a fly swatter.

Jacob and Rebecca would go on holiday together contentedly, despite their differences, to France or Belgium, and in one surviving photograph the pair of them stand in some cathedral square outside an open-air café, the dapper little barber in his neat trilby, white shoes and light cane beside his large beaming wife, who is posing with her arms held away from her sides as though she were balancing a couple of buckets, a straw hat the size of a parasol on her head.

Rebecca would appear at the top of the stairs in the Mare Street house after Sunday lunch, which was a heavy affair, and in her best dress, the dress of a respectable wife of a prosperous tradesman, she would announce, 'Und now ve vill go to sleep.' The right to sleep when she wanted to must have seemed a great luxury once. After Jacob died suddenly in 1937, from a heart attack at the age of sixty-six, his widow never again dressed in anything but black. She died on her day for visiting and entertainment. On a Sunday afternoon in the first year after the war, she walked from Brent to Cockfosters, a distance of five miles, after a terrible row with Helen's mother and called at the house of one of her sons. She was shown into the drawing room, sat down on the sofa and did not get up again. Helen Bamber, who was in Germany by then, could not grieve for her very much. From where she then was, it must have seemed that the old woman had a good death.

*   *   *

Around 1936, while Jacob Bader was still alive, the Balmuth family fell on harder times. The world slump had ruined bigger adventurers than Uncle Michael, but by the mid-1930s the recession had disbanded productive energies everywhere in Europe; the Popular Front was in power in France and Spain; all of the East European states (except Czechoslovakia) had become dictatorships, and the Nazis were rearming Germany without hindrance. Bourgeois civilization looked doomed; communists wrote cocksure forecasts of its crisis and death; for fascists it was axiomatic that democracy would, as Hitler put it, 'drag the nation into the abyss'. The global world market of the imperialist age before 1914 had split into armed camps.

Whatever Uncle Michael traded had lost its salt, and his money no longer ran to a big house on Amhurst Park. With his unmarried brothers and his parents – his loyalty to the old couple seems to have been unwavering – he took a flat in Hendon, a few miles to the north and west. There the arguments went on, made more concentrated and frightening by the narrowing of their space. The child dreaded having to visit her uncles: 'Plates were thrown, furniture was shoved about in the most explosive way in retaliation for misunderstandings, the loss of money enraged and filled them with anxiety. I was very, very uneasy with them. They would want to hear about my other grandparents, who in turn were eager to hear about the racket they made, and I would pretend that nothing at all had happened.' She was probably made much of, and it would probably not be wide of the mark to see her as a small, pretty and self-possessed girl discovering that adults were cryptic but needed to be heard, and that she had a capacity to mediate their secrets.

Her father moved his family half a dozen blocks north to Wellington Avenue, a residential street in Stamford Hill. Here the houses were identical cramped units finished with the minimal elements of Tudor styling, the kitsch of pre-war suburban England: 'Shakespearean' half-timbers riveted onto flat terraces. Each porch had a little sloping roof of red tile, and was supported by wooden struts; each floor was separated by three fake wooden beams. A raised voice could tell a life-story to the rest of the street. Helen Bamber imagined the audience for her parents' quarrels through the uninsulated walls. Inside the house, there was no escape from who she was.

Her parents had salvaged too much from Amhurst Park: oversize 'Japanese' willow-pattern sofas, lacquered black corner-pieces, Axminster carpets with florid Second Empire designs. None of it was appropriate for such a small house, as far as Bamber can remember, and the heavy furniture added to the sense of claustrophobia. The bear rug snarled at them from the floor.

Free of the constraint as well as the hostility of his family, Louis and Marie began to abandon what was left of the common life they had imagined for themselves. 'My father was quite a remote person emotionally,' Bamber recalled. 'It had been an arranged marriage, in some way I can't now reconstruct; both of them were getting on by contemporary standards when they married; he was well into his thirties, and both families despaired of them. It was at least a *concocted* union. They were extremely ill-matched: you could not have found, if you had sought, a more ill-matched couple. Their quarrels never abated.'

Her father had a larger burden to carry than an unhappy marriage. Even before Hitler's electoral victory in January 1933, he had become convinced that fascism was a mortal threat, an absolute evil; and it is difficult to convey adequately Bamber's feeling for her father's absorption in menace. She remembers his talk of bad men from the moment she could read. It was not a premonition of danger in the sense that much contemporary opposition to Hitler is now retranslated into post-war language, a language that pays conventional heed to the genocidal consequences of National Socialism. To British Conservatives calling for rearmament, the Nazis' challenge to Britain's strategic interests was more worrying than their capacity for racial violence; and for many on the left, fascism was a class dictatorship, the 'iron heel' of their nightmares. Even for many Jews, at first, particularly those German Jews hoping to retain their citizenship and property-rights, it was better to hear the language of racial extermination that infused Hitler's speech as mere rhetoric, not a grammar of action; as the historian Golo Mann put it, they 'could not believe in the sentence that threatened them'. To accept that it meant what it said – that Jews were the human equivalent of a virus or a cancer – was to be considered an alarmist, a Jeremiah.

In Britain, as Alfred J. Sherman has noted, 'the Jewish community itself could not imagine anything like the scale of actual persecution and its consequences.' In 1933, Jewish community leaders thought that 'there might be as many as 3,000 to 4,000 refugees coming to Great Britain', and on this basis gave an explicit, formal undertaking to the Home Secretary in April of that year 'that no refugee admitted to England under their auspices would become a public charge'. (This pledge was to become a burden, later in the decade.)

Louis Balmuth, by contrast to some of his contemporaries, had a literal belief in the imminence of war and extermination. He never relaxed; he wrote incessantly, alone in his room every night. He wrote on ethics, on religion, on fascism and violence. He had, according to his daughter, a 'beautiful hand' and filled children's exercise books with neat short paragraphs, philosophical fragments, observations, comments on items he had read in the newspapers; and of course not a line of it has survived. His daughter can say now with a stern weariness that it was 'all very lofty', as though her father were some cracked suburban philosopher keeping his journal, finding the key to it all every night only to lose it during the day. What matters, of course, is how she sees him: the fact that she sees in his intransigence something mad but essential: 'He had a tremendous sense of urgency. He was utterly preoccupied about war, by the fact that nobody as he saw it was prepared to act, and he was haunted by what would happen when it came – he was very clear about what would happen if it came. And of course he was right. My father was fascinated by mathematics, and had a rather rigid geometric approach to politics and life. Fascism in power must result, he believed, in vast slaughter. It was like a theorem. He was obsessional, but visionary in the way he saw that it would spread and destroy so much. And I have to admit that I lived in some terror because of this. By the time I was nine or ten I was certain that when war came, and if the Germans came to this country, my family and I would be eliminated. Much of my childhood after 1933 was overshadowed by the fear of grey German figures in polished boots coming, as it were, up the garden path.'

By day Louis Balmuth was an accountant, working for a metal-supply firm that had connections in Germany, and which his daughter thinks enabled him to help Jews inside the Nazi state and to get money and people out. He may simply have been part of the network established by the Central British Fund. This was an organization founded by the British Board of Deputies in 1933 to help Jewish refugees from Hitler's dictatorship; and after the Nuremberg Laws removed all civil rights from Jews in the autumn of 1935, its members must have seen the writing on the wall as clearly as Balmuth would have wished. He was probably closer to the left-wing and Zionist underground railroad, for Jewish activists, Quakers, communists and other mysterious strangers came to the house, 'and there would suddenly be great anxiety and tension in the house about a particular individual. My father spent a lot of his own money, and used the telephone relentlessly, for short- and long-distance calls – and "trunk" calls were very expensive. The telephone had a hook, and separate receiver and transmitter. I was allowed to use the telephone when I was very young. And as the decade wore on, and although my mother never spoke about it and I never asked, I could see that she grew more and more resentful about the money disappearing into this work. My father was completely unaware of it even as a problem.' What an Amnesty official would say of Helen Bamber, very much later, could be applied to her idea of her father: that paid work was an inconvenience to his real work.

Her father, who like his brothers was not much troubled by ideas of childhood as a realm of innocence or play, simply shared his terrible, rational fears with his daughter. 'He told me too much, made no attempt to protect me. I don't think he knew what a child was. He never shut me out, as he shut out my mother. He would talk to me all right, though I often wished he wouldn't. And as the situation became worse in Germany, he would tell me more and more. At night, he read sections of *Mein Kampf* to me, or translate articles by Goebbels from the Nazi press; he said he was making a study of Goebbels' propaganda methods. He understood how brilliant Goebbels was, in his use of words, his drum-like repetitions of words, his ability to craft a deadly phrase, and my father wanted me to understand how language could be corrupted. And of course I was afraid of him, afraid of his anger, and I was always trying either to please my mother or to achieve what he wanted of me. And you could not do both.'

Some children are precocious, but there is something altogether more than mere precocity in the image of this man reading from *Der Angriff*, the paper controlled by Goebbels, to his solemn-faced child as she sat up in her bedroom in the cramped terraced house. She recalls reading, at her father's instigation, copies of the *Daily Mail*, which was then running a campaign against 'aliens' and in support of Oswald Mosley's local fascist party. ('Hurrah for the Blackshirts!' it shouted in January 1934; and its German correspondent Ward Price greeted Hitler as 'the saviour of Western civilization' in September 1936.) In his way, perhaps her father valued innocence so much that it had to be destroyed, made aware of danger from the earliest possible moment before it became lulled into a false sense of safety; that way led, in John Bunyan's phrase, to 'the ministration of death'.

As far as he was concerned, that is where his wife was taking their daughter. Like most of her family, Marie seems to have had the gift of living sociably and for the moment. A rather shy, handsome woman, in Bamber's memory of her, she sang and accompanied herself on the piano, and attended the theatre – always serious plays, Shaw, Ibsen, Shakespeare, O'Casey. Her daughter was going to shine; escaping the anxieties of money and politics, she would have culture. Helen was sent to elocution lessons (there is no trace of North London's glottal stops in her measured enunciation, which is that of a BBC announcer of the old school) and while there was enough money she attended a Jewish private school, a place she calls 'a hammer for little minds'. She was also taught to play the piano, and to dance, skills which her father thought absolutely frivolous. He wanted her to be a scholar; his wife wanted her to go to the Royal Academy of Dramatic Art and become an actress. 'She was building me into this precious little girl. She took great pride in my appearance, and in the way I spoke; I danced quite well, and I loved ballet, and she was imagining her kind of future for me.'

As a Jew and the daughter of an anarchist and sister of a communist, Marie could hardly have wished away the fascist threat if she had wanted to, but in her rejection of her husband she grew as cool as his temperament was hot, not showing her feelings or her affections very easily even to her only child. She drew away from Louis, and there came a moment when sleeping apart became habit. The small house then had three separate bedrooms, separate lives and meals, and a careful silence. Marie and Louis would not speak for days at a time, and would ignore each other's friends. Her Belgian cousins taught her the heavy cordon-bleu cuisine that seemed so exotic in England in the 1930s, and she would hold dinner parties in the small house, the best cutlery gleaming. 'The house would open up and people would come, and my father would disappear into his room.'

Soothing these incompatible dreamers, speaking confidently on the telephone, that symbol of adult urgency and seriousness, keeping secrets and not asking questions, was 'this apparently confident little thing dressed in patent shoes and white socks, always white socks. Quite obnoxious, don't you think?'

The stress might have weakened her, or perhaps a damp North London terrace and the burned chemicals in the smog were enough, but the child was often in no position to help anybody. She spent months in bed, suffering from what doctors diagnosed as a mild form of tuberculosis.

That doesn't seem to have been the whole clinical story; but there must have been some physical basis to it. One winter passed in weakness and fever, and she was intermittently bedridden at other times. 'I hallucinated, I had very high temperatures and I'd imagine people and objects and animals in the room.'

She did not imagine the German-speaking men who were now coming to stay. They would have been Jewish socialists, or left-wing Zionists – none of them particularly welcome in Britain. Grave men in dark suits, with the academic formality of the Central European intellectual, they had lost position, libraries, money and power. Their presence was heavy in the small house, on the stairs, outside her sickroom. They would talk to her, if they spoke English, probably seeing in her a quaint and unusual child. Bamber's memories of these guests are tied to her experience of illness and the overcoming of weakness.

One man, a pianist, had a very thick accent; he was humourless and demanding. She loathed him. When he was in the house he would play for hours on the upright piano (another fragment of culture rescued from Uncle Michael's crash), and very beautifully, the sound of German romantic music flooding the cavities of the jerry-built houses on either side. But this wasn't his contribution to her education. 'He used to come to my room and read to me during one of my periods of illness, and once he came and said, "You know, if you *want* to get better you can make yourself do that. If you wanted to, you could get out of this bed and walk around the room ten times and you could touch pieces of furniture very firmly and then get back into bed." Then he went away. And of course I did it, I walked around the room. And in a strange way this man became a turning point for me. I realize that my illnesses were very convenient, they were a way of escaping from my parents' demands; but his was such a brutal challenge. He knew exactly what I was about. I felt completely found out. And whilst I remained ill for some time, that "walking around the room" is something that I still do.

'Years later when I was in Germany I had to get up very early in the mornings, and I hated it. I was working with a man from the Jewish Brigade, who was doing clandestine work in the British Zone. He didn't say a thing at first, but he was very irritated that I couldn't wake up and he said almost exactly the same thing as that pianist: "If you want to rise at a certain time, if you want to wake up at six, you can do it." And the awful truth is that you *can* do it. It's not a lesson that I would admit to learning with great pride, because I don't think that life should impose that kind of discipline on people. But two people who were involved in dreadful situations had shown me that you can face things if you have the will to do it.'

In a decade that so widely exalted hardness and believed that nothing could resist the will if it was properly disciplined, there is a prescient subversiveness about this child learning to conquer her body's protests, but not, as it turned out, in order to storm the future. The doctrine of the sacrifice of bodies for a world without contradictions could be challenged by the determination to persevere and to resist.

*   *   *

Other visitors came to the house, to whom she was expected to feel closer. Her mother's cousins Chaim and Mendel Bader had also made themselves hard. Their work was another, and very serious, mystery. To the child of the family, who was now thirteen, they seemed to know more about life and death than anyone she knew, including her father. Bamber's mother's and father's families rarely touched each other closely, but Chaim and Mendel made time for Louis Balmuth.

They were revolutionaries, bearers of an idea: of a home for the Jewish nation, in the modern form of a state with an army and a politics and definite borders. Chaim and Mendel lived on a kibbutz in Palestine, practical socialists out there behind the sun in an 'empty' but hostile world, or so it seemed to the child in her overpopulated street. Everything about the cousins was like a folk tale: their doubling of each other, as though they were twins; their almost magical appearances on the scene; the legend that they had married a pair of Russian sisters they met on the boat to Palestine (in fact they went to Palestine separately, and four years apart: Mendel in 1920 and his brother in 1924). She recalls them as big bristling men with red hair and calloused hands. Her mother spoke guardedly about how they had been lashed by soldiers when they were boys in Galicia, how the welts could still be seen on their backs if they lifted their shirts. Helen imagined them peeling up their white stiff collared shirts, the scars standing out in relief, like ropes under the skin, but this was almost unthinkable, and certainly unsayable, either to them or to her mother.

Her father told her that they went into Germany, helping people to escape. She imagined them slipping across frontiers, moving through dark streets. Once Chaim came to stay and there was an atmosphere that could be cut with a knife. No one, for once, would speak to her. While he was there her dog, an old spaniel, lost the power of its legs and had to be put down. She took it on the bus to the local veterinary surgeon. On top of a double-decker she cradled her mangy pet, and came back after it had been put to sleep in floods of tears. 'Chaim said to me, "How can you be crying about a dog when Mendel is being held in a Nazi prison and there are all these people dying? How can you be crying about a *dog*?" This didn't make me angry, but I was desperately upset. I was told Mendel had gone in to get a woman out, a well-known activist of his party, Hashomer Hatzair, and he was caught. He was released in the end, perhaps because his brother bribed his way out.'

It is not clear how much time Mendel Bader spent on false papers in Germany itself. But he had certainly crossed dangerous frontiers, and had, according to his own later testimony, survived for a week in Nazi-occupied Prague in March 1939, meeting Jewish activists on park benches and in cemeteries. When he left to report to the Jewish Agency in London he smuggled a list of 150 names of prominent Jews in immediate danger. His plan was to get them out to Poland and from there to England or Palestine. Ordered by the Jewish Agency to return to the Czech lands, and bearing an invalid visa, he was arrested that April on the Czech–Slovak border. He escaped the Gestapo by a combination of bribery and luck. This may have been the episode that was linked in the young Helen Bamber's imagination with the death of her dog.

Secrets within secrets. She overheard Chaim saying to her father that he should let her go to Palestine, that war was coming, and that she would not be safe.' "Send her *away*." This "away" was a very big word, for a child of thirteen. It was the one thing that was never openly discussed with me. I was half-excited, half-terrified,' she says. Yet where now would she ever feel safe?

For Chaim and Mendel Bader the only imaginable refuge was the historic biblical land of Israel – the 'national home', in the language of ethnic rootedness to a particular soil. Bamber's childish impressions about her mother's cousins were, she later discovered, remarkably accurate. They were trusted agents of the Yishuv – the Jewish government-in-waiting in Palestine. In their lives they enacted the purism of the dream:

both were members of Kibbutz Mizra in the Galilee, sharing their goods with their comrades, working the earth as a symbolic political act of self-transformation.

Chaim and Menachem (as Mendel became in Palestine) were leaders of Hashomer Hatzair, the most left-wing of the Zionist parties, which believed in Arab participation in the Jewish rebirth: Israel, when it came, would be a progressive state of two nations. Menachem's duties in Europe were, eventually, more serious and painful than it was possible to imagine before the war. In the early summer of 1944 he became one of the key negotiators in the most controversial of all attempts to save Jews from the Nazis, the proposal to swap trucks and money for the lives of Hungarian Jews. The SS leadership was prepared, after Stalingrad and Kursk had revealed the imminence of its defeat in the east, to toy with what it saw as 'world Jewry' – to see if it could get Jews to pay for the privilege of sparing a tiny fraction of their people, while – incidentally – supplying equipment for the Wehrmacht. The moral and emotional dilemma of the Zionist leaders was extreme. They felt they could not refuse to negotiate, but it was quickly obvious that the British and Russian governments would never send material to the weakening Nazis. Menachem Bader stayed in Istanbul, the closest city to the German empire in which to conduct espionage and intrigue, talking to the go-betweens from Hungary and reporting to leaders of the Jewish Agency.

In Israel in the early 1950s the leaders would be accused of 'selling their souls to the devil' for having considered a deal at all; and in the end less than 1700 Jews were allowed to escape. Someone had to choose who would leave Budapest on the trains to the West. The man who made the choice was Reszo Kastner, and of course he could not help but include members of his own family and his neighbours. Adolf Eichmann would claim later simply that Kastner naturally chose 'the best biological material'. Kastner was vilified in a famous and long-running libel action that he lost, and then won on appeal. But by the time the verdict was reversed he was dead, shot by messianic nationalists who believed he should have told the unarmed Jews of Hungary to rise up and fight. The trial lit up the back rooms of Israeli power, and became a symbol of the conflict between a politics of blood sacrifice and retribution, whose spokesman was Menachem Begin, and the stern pragmatism of David Ben-Gurion. Begin's campaign against the compromisers, the collaborators, the traitors who saved people like themselves, helped him to become a real force in the country. It was the beginning of the end of the left's dominance of Israeli life. Menachem Bader had been an MP, a Director General of the Ministry of Development and a member of the executive of the Histadrut, the Israeli trade union federation. His mission to Istanbul, the most dreadful moment of his long effort to renew the nation on grounds of brotherhood and equality, ironically helped to bring about a situation that would surely have been unimaginable in his youth.

In a passionate memoir first published in 1954, during the Kastner trial, Bader insisted that his many 'sad missions' were not simply partisan operations for his tendency of Zionism, and that any act of rescue inevitably transcended the concerns of one movement. 'Living in those years in the shadow of the rampant power of the Swastika … sharpened your eye and your sense of what was to come, and if you did not go mad from knowing and seeing the truth, you could see that a terrible disaster was about to rend our nation and destroy it.' In those conditons, he wrote, when the whole House of Israeli was threatened, it was pointless for a man to 'save his own tent'. He spoke of the desperate attempts to smuggle 'money, passports, information, escape instructions', the limitless 'devotion and bravery' of the agents, and their abandonment 'with no supporters or helpers in the entire world'. He wrote of the money spent – 'a million and three hundred thousand pounds' – and of the small numbers helped by it, 'a drop in the raging sea of blood and tears'. Eichmann's offer – 'the bedevilled offer of the chief murderer Eichmann' – could not be rejected outright: 'Each one of us asked his soul how could he answer "No" … and have on his conscience the loss of this chance, even if it were very doubtful and the intentions [of the Nazis] mocking and misleading?'

One of the Supreme Court judges in the Kastner appeal, heard in 1958, tried to imagine what it was like, dealing for lives with bland fanatics like Eichmann who thought you were unfit to live, and were offering at best a reprieve for the Jews. The judge considered the alternative, the idea that it was your duty to die fighting rather than submit to death: 'This means that the Jews of the provincial ghettos in Hungary should all have fought and died as martyrs for the people's honour,' like the Warsaw ghetto fighters. 'This is one way to look at it.

The bloody history of the people of Israel tells of many such heroes. But there is another point of view, different and opposite, and this view also has roots in the pages of our history.' The judge mentioned the example of Jeremiah, who made a necessary compromise with the Babylonian enemy, and Rabbi Yohanan Ben-Zakkai, who took the sacred books out of Jerusalem during the siege by the Romans in the year 70 and 'chose to save what could be saved in a time of trouble. Despite this, no one accused them of selling their souls to the devil.'

*   *   *

Helen Bamber, when speaking about her childhood, recalls certain moments as though remembering how she taught herself what to do when she reached a new place. Death was such an event. Once when she was still very young, her mother asked her to take a gift of some kind to the Irish woman who helped her with housework twice a week and who was ill and bedridden. She lived in a very poor part of Tottenham; Helen can't now be sure what it was she was carrying, but when she got there, the front door was open and the narrow hall was full of red-faced, distressed women. She was drawn in because they wanted to share their grief, into the sharp fumes of whisky. In the front room a coffin lay on trestles, its lid propped against a wall, and under white crêpe she saw the corpse – her first – of her mother's charlady. She sensed that they wanted her to show that she knew how to act. She stayed, took her first drink of whisky, and talked.

At home the rough emotional music played on. Her father, so sensitive to hurt himself, seemed indifferent to its effect on her. He told her almost casually that her mother had had an abortion rather than give him another child. With whom could she share this? She buried the memory, and it cut deep: nearly sixty years later it was almost the last thing she could bring herself to reveal about her father.

His isolation was telling on him; his brothers did not support him in his work and he seemed to have no sustained political friendships, of the kind that would have given him the social half-life of the party member. He had become a collector of journals, newspaper cuttings and books, never throwing anything away, so that the whole house was cluttered with yellowing and dried-out paper, the carbon black of the ink coming off on hands and clothes. The house was more and more like a junk shop in which odds and ends express the mind of the owner. His wife refused now to clean up after him; the squalor was a contest between them. It was not a house to which their daughter could bring her friends.

Helen Bamber came home from school one day and after turning her key in the lock could not push the door open. Through the keyhole she saw that papers had been piled in the hallway, bales of them. 'For one moment, I thought that there had been a catastrophe and I had a hope that there would be some kind of end to all this and I remember thinking, "Are they dead? I hope to God they're dead."' Her mother came out and cleared a pathway, her rage calming, but the papers stayed there for weeks.

The child's education was taking place, clearly enough, on different levels, but formal instruction went on in Down Lanes Central School. The private school she had attended before was a Jewish establishment, so from the age of nine she found herself part of the London immigrant experience, less melting-pot than spitting frying-pan. Whilst Bamber escaped the worst forms of racism, she still had to endure the anti-semitic double-bind: Jewish children were expected to perform, and criticized if they failed to reach high standards; but if they did too well they embodied the caricature of the clever Jew. Irish Catholic girls taunted them each day outside a convent school, until she and two friends went for them with rulers, pen-nibs and fists. She reached school with a gashed face and ruined dress, and a new understanding with the London Irish. 'There's a bit that's terrified, and a bit that fights.'

When she was about thirteen, her aunt Mina became an ally and friend. Mina was a woman who, in the language of self-improvement then current, 'made the most of herself', and must have stood out like a sexy exotic among the dour puritans of the British Communist Party, for whom style was an unfailing indicator of social betrayal. She had a reputation: she had been at Cable Street in 1936, one of the thousands who prevented a march by Mosley's British Union of Fascists through Whitechapel and the London docklands; she had young men, and one of them had gone to Spain with the International Brigades.

Cable Street became a party myth: we stopped the fascists; *No pasaran!* It was recycled around the British left for the next five decades, but it is easier now than it was then to see the feebleness of Mosley's effort, a ruling-class adventurer hoping to find his way to power through the gutter. Yet in the areas where Jews lived, he created terror: there were streets that Jews did not dare to walk down; they were maimed, their shops and stalls were wrecked, and Mosley's mannered imitation of Hitler's oratory whinnied over the street-markets of Dalston and Shoreditch where he provoked riots. Wellington Avenue was a partly Jewish street and the fascist youth would sometimes rampage through it in the small hours. The Balmuths woke one night to the crash of shattering glass, and found a milk bottle among the splinters of their front window.

The glow of self-congratulation in some post-war discussions of resistance to fascism obscures certain unwelcome truths. The British press was full of innuendo and scare-stories about the refugees being allowed into Britain from Germany, and of course the numbers, though relatively insignificant – a total of about 65,000 reached the UK before the war – were overwhelming to a Jewish leadership that had taken responsibility for all of them. The very concept of asylum was rejected by professional organizations. The British Medical Association demanded limits on the entry of Jewish doctors to the UK; in a hospital in Liverpool, soon after the *Anschluss* had caused the mass flight of Austrian Jews in 1938, a senior consultant told a brilliant young Jewish physician that no Jew could be a gentleman: he should not think of applying for a consultancy at a great teaching hospital. The Colonial Office refused to allow Jews to emigrate to Africa, though in the months following Kristallnacht in November 1938 Britain's refugee policy was more generous than that of its dominions or the USA. In the summer of 1938 the Evian Conference had drawn the Western powers together in an effort to solve the refugee crisis. The chance was missed: the United States raised its annual quota of immigrants from Germany to 27,000; Australia agreed to take a grand total of 15,000. These figures must be set against the half-million Jews still trapped at the time in Austria and Germany. Norman Bentwich, a prominent figure in British Jewry's efforts on behalf of the refugees, looked back after the Holocaust on 'the cautious insensibility of the free world' in the last year of peace.

Helen Bamber had already been drawn into skirmishes with the British Union of Fascists. A group of teenage Jewish anti-fascists under the leadership of one Barry Sherwin, on whom she had a serious crush (pavements in Hackney were chalked with the obscure coupling of BS and HB), trained on the site of a dump by the River Lea. The cocktail of politics and sex: there has been nothing, she once said, to compare with Barry Sherwin's first kiss.

The blackshirts marched up Seven Sisters Road, along the edge of Finsbury Park, towards the Jewish area of Stamford Hill. A group of children climbed trees in the park and banged saucepans, jeered and yelled at the strutting squads with their heavy Union Jack banners. The police charged into the park, and the protesters had to run hard, scattering to escape the truncheon blows. Up beyond the park a cinema with high steps leading up to it offered a platform for hecklers; Helen Bamber got that far with her friends and, when a line of policemen walked through them, was thrown down the steps.

Her friendship with her aunt was a tangle of erotic and political yearnings. Mina was not beautiful, and neither family thought of her as clever, but she was a slim energetic woman with an extraordinary capacity for doing and having; a maker of parties and events, and probably, one imagines, very lovable. Every surviving photograph of her, with one exception – a coy cameo, in which she is cut out of a nimbus of sepia wearing a string of pearls, and which, according to Helen, she had made to please her mother – is a snap of sensual and roguish humanity, an action shot. In each of them she is accompanied by a different man; one of them is the classic 1930s lounge lizard, standing with his hands in the pockets of his white pressed slacks, showing off his neat blazer and the folded white handkerchief in the top pocket. In that photo, Mina is perched on the wooden wall of some seaside pier – Brighton or Bournemouth – with her arm around her lover's shoulders, but the real focus of the composition is her thighs, which emerge defiantly from her wrap-around dress.

In another photograph, printed as the front of a postcard, Mina is caught in the centre of a group, mainly men, all laughing at some holiday game: a bet won, a throw made. She is slapping her thighs, her face joyous, looking towards and past the camera, her tanned feet bare under a white skirt. The others seem energized by her uninhibited delight. Bamber feels that her life was turned by this woman, and it is easy to see why. It would be difficult to resist her uncomplex vitality.

They went out together, to Lyons Corner Houses, to Italian restaurants; and she would go with Mina to Hampstead Heath to watch her play hockey on Sunday mornings, charging with her stick, her skirt flying up, as though street politics and sport all flowed from the same energy. She took Helen to plays considered too adult for her, and confided in her about her boyfriends. Her advice about sex included the keeping of a certain room for manoeuvre: 'Always remember that the shoes come off *last*.'

She left her mark: the combination of elegance and sensual enjoyment with commitment remains for Bamber a kind of model of how to live. Mina's communism owed more, she thinks, to the fact that the party was seen to be doing something about fascism: the hook used to draw in so many decent people at the time. Bamber learned to see through the Stalinist clichés to something else, a political attitude that valued the concrete and the symbolic over the utopian: do what you can now, don't beggar the present for some millennium, and don't get lost in abstractions. She hopes Mina would have lived according to that more humane impulse.

Once Mina took her, when she was still fourteen or so, to the Unity Theatre. She remembers the Bader cousins joining them. 'The play was a rather propagandistic piece about tillers of the soil – nothing as acerbic as Brecht. But it was terribly seductive and romantic. It was in some way the Baders' ideal too, their vision of people working together in kibbutzim, sharing everything they owned. The atmosphere in the theatre was wonderful that night. It's as though all of us – Zionists, communists and others – had agreed that it might be possible to realize a life in common, despite the coming war.'

*   *   *

When Bamber was a child of seven, Hitler had come to power, smashed German democracy and begun to put his enemies in concentration camps; by the time she was ten, the demilitarized zone of the Rhineland had been reoccupied by Germany and the Nuremberg Laws were in place, stripping German Jews of their rights as citizens; in October 1938, after her thirteenth birthday, the Nazis seized the Sudetenland, the German-inhabited areas of the Czech Republic, with the complicity of Britain and France. A month later the regime staged a violent attack against Jewish homes, businesses, and synagogues, the so-called Kristallnacht. Hitler and Mussolini were able, by the end of the year, to celebrate the crushing of the last resistance to General Franco's rebellion against democratic Spain, which had pioneered a new fusion of civil war (the killing of the renegade brother and sister) with war against an entire people (bombing civilians, destroying towns). In the Soviet Union, Stalin's purge took the lives of countless new victims and the NKVD, his secret police, tortured tens of thousands of people to extract false confessions from them.

Osip Mandelstam, himself a victim of the NKVD's 'conveyor' – relentless deprivation of sleep, of food and of all sensory variation for weeks at a time – found in the night sky over Voronezh, his place of exile on the Sea of Azov, an image of the coming slaughter:

> The incorruptible sky over the trenches
> a sky of vast, wholesale deaths;
> so integral, I follow you, flee you
> and the words I mouth take flight in the darkness.

All the shambling demons of modern warfare were converging: Sherman's realization during the US Civil War that the destruction of an enemy's productive capacity, and the displacement of his people, could break his ability to fight; the pitiless use of technical superiority in colonial wars; the willingness to calculate coldly how many millions of people the state could afford to lose and still win; the effective abolition of the distinction between combatants and civilians; and finally the belief that the good of the race – defined as an ethnic group, or the whole of humanity – justified the surgical removal of the unassimilable, the unproductive or the unfit.

When war finally came it hardly surprised a fourteen-year-old already taught to fear the worst. Her experience between 1939 and 1945 was that of millions of Londoners; but for her, the onset of violence was almost a relief.

She learned to handle a gas mask and to run into the Anderson shelter as soon as the air-raid warning sounded. This piece of curved sheet-iron, placed over a hole dug in the back garden and covered with earth, looked like a dog-kennel, or a tomb. And the bombers did come, but not until the late summer of 1940, after the British Army's retreat from the Belgian coast. Mina's latest and most serious lover, a Jewish man, described for her niece the laden swim to the trawler that picked him up, and the terror of sitting among thousands on a long beach while planes machine-gunned the crowds.

Meanwhile her school was evacuated to Mildenhall in Suffolk, where Helen was boarded with a genteel and parsimonious woman who liked her, but half-starved her. She made an ally of the husband, who would make great fry-ups of potatoes, onions and tomatoes when his wife went to play tennis. She loved the freedom, and the illusion of being an ordinary English child in an ordinary English village. She became 'captain of something or other' at her school, and for once did not have to negotiate between emotional extremists.

After about ten months, however, her mother brought her back to London. The serious bombing raids began in September. Stamford Hill and Stoke Newington escaped the worst of it, but they were hit again and again, residential areas without military significance. Bombs landed a few streets away, the decisive blow of the detonations beating against the folded iron hut in which the Balmuth family sheltered. The Germans were coming up the garden, and in loud boots, murdering civilians on the way. Helen Bamber said later that she was no longer very frightened: the rituals of crawling and running, of collective sheltering, had a way of normalizing fear. Death and injury came every night; Britain had seen nothing like it for three hundred years. A man in the next-door house was blinded by a piece of shrapnel; on 13 October 1940, less than a mile south of where they lived, a direct hit on a block of council flats at Coronation Avenue brought the whole structure down on the basement in which the tenants were sheltering. One hundred and fifty-four of them died, many drowned as the water-pipes burst; twenty-six of the dead were never even identified. Closer to home she saw the wreckage on Amhurst Park, the house she was born in still standing, its windows broken, a house further down the street a pile of brick and timber. She grew familiar with 'the smell of burned wet wood'.

In the air-raid shelter at the bottom of the garden she started to teach herself shorthand, and later took a class at Miss Gottschalk's Private School in Stoke Newington. One day as she walked down through the blind curves of Church Street and past the gothic Abney Park Cemetery, with the faces of its stone angels turned away from the street, she saw that the typing-school had been wrecked by a land mine. The old machines, their long carriages returned by gravity, were hanging down off the edge of a row of desks tilting over the street.

In 1941, when she was sixteen, she volunteered for fire-watching duty, and became one of thousands around the city standing on high structures in the darkness, waiting to catch and extinguish incendiaries. Holborn was bombed one night, and she had come down from the roof of the office building in Bedford Row on which she was stationed a half-mile to the west. She was on some wooden steps that led down to the vaults of a solicitor's office, where they kept the legal documents in foolscap folders tied with pink ribbons. The stairs on which she was standing lurched, and she fell heavily into the basement. She wasn't seriously injured, but she has never since been comfortable going down stairs, her only phobia, and a real one: she will suddenly grip a banister as though her life depended on it, even on a short rise of steps.

The only time she actually dealt with an incendiary bomb was once late at night in the silent blacked-out streets off Clerkenwell; she was walking home when a stray magnesium bomb came down, hissing like a firecracker. She and her friends covered it in sand from a bucket. The worst thing that happened to her in the blackout was running from the panic of a bomb-warning into a tree, and her face was covered in blood. She says she worried far more about that, her young vanity terribly affected, than anything else that happened to her during the Blitz. It was a lucky time for her; a lucky country to be in.

Yet the war had not closed the vein of anti-semitic hatred that ran through English society. The very newspapers that had supported Mosley, and even Hitler, in the early 1930s, now detected a spy in every German–Jewish refugee and led a scurrilous campaign for their internment. In March 1940 the *Daily Mail* was sure it spoke for 'millions of relatives of the men in the fighting forces [who] are perturbed at the latitude allowed to the aliens within our gates'. Bamber heard that Jews were not 'doing their bit', and once rounded on some bigot in a bread line and told her what her aunt's lover had gone through at Dunkirk, like thousands of other Jewish soldiers. More often, she said, she stayed silent, letting it ride.

Mina remained a good friend. She lived her dream of style to the last. On the second Saturday night in March, during the late winter of 1941, and after a long break in the nightly raids, she told her envious niece that her lover was taking her to hear the black bandleader Snakehips Johnson and his men play at the Café de Paris, on the border between Piccadilly and Soho, the louche neutral zone of the city where the barriers of race and class dissolved. Helen Bamber was able to imagine going through the blackout curtains at the top of the stairs and then down into the famous basement, through the arch of mock elephant tusks; the floor would have been an archipelago of coloured silk, black wool and white cotton, shimmering in the band's light society swing. The place was modelled, it was said, on the ballroom of the *Titanic*.

The bombing started again very violently that night, without warning, and Helen could hear it from way up in Stamford Hill and see the light of fires in the centre of London. The two-week lull made the vicious thunder of the explosions more terrifying. The next day, she was alone in the house when the phone rang. 'An uncle said that Mina had not come home. He had called her boyfriend's house, and he had not shown up either. I suppose I knew then.' She and her mother learned later that day that a bomb had broken through the four floors of the building above the Café de Paris, which was supposed to be the safest public place in London, just before ten o'clock, and exploded over the orchestra. In that confined space it was awful. 'Mina and her man must have been obliterated. I was told that there was no flesh to associate with her. I seem to remember a metallic evening bag, which had a gold chain. For all I know that is what was buried. Mina had been my saviour; she had drama and humour in her bones. It felt as if doors were closing, after that.'

In photographs of the aftermath (which were never released during the war) tired men in helmets and enormous mittens lift objects carefully out of the splintered wreckage. A soldier in a leather jerkin carries an almost undamaged electric guitar over his shoulder, the back panel of a double bass held in his other glove. He is standing inches deep in blackened sheet music. The band had begun playing the uptempo 'Oh! Johnny!', and dancers crowded the floor when the bomb mangled the room.

Among the dead were officers of the Scots Guards, debutantes out on the town, and Snakehips Johnson, who was decapitated; the survivors included best-selling genre writers and slumming aristos, including Lady Betty Baldwin, daughter of the former Tory Prime Minister, whose face was mutilated by shrapnel and had to be reshaped with skin-grafts by the surgeon Sir Archibald MacIndoe. On the list of the dead were Greek, Italian and Polish names, some of them probably Jews. The high-toned diarist Charles Graves noted: 'It was full of aliens, and if any restaurant had to be hit that was the one to catch it.' The enemy within, even with the worst enemy at the gates.

Her aunt's violent death is as real to Helen Bamber as her own existence; yet if the state's reluctant disclosure of her grandparents' origins was a revelation, the disappearance of Mina from official memory created a bewildering gap in memory. No death certificate for her is listed in the records; her name does not appear on the roll of civilian dead kept in the Imperial War Museum. Perhaps she was blown to pieces, buried in the rubble and never registered; perhaps she never reached the Café de Paris that night and met a nameless death in the streets. The only sign of her death is an inscription on her father's grave in Willesden United Synagogue Cemetery: 'Mina Bader died by enemy action on 8 March 1941, mourned by her heartbroken mother, brothers and sister.' She is the missing piece of the jigsaw that Bamber feels most painfully.

Helen Bamber had learned by now how to live in a state of emergency, placating but also believing in her father, refusing his zeal as much as she was driven to preserve its rational core. She might have pulled away from all this, gone to university and become a doctor or a lawyer, and led a more conventional life. No doubt it could be said that she later found her way to situations in which pain had to be assuaged, in men like her father perhaps; that she was conspiring with events. But few of us can read our own stories so lucidly, at least while we are making them. She could not have known what was to become significant later, and buried some things so deeply that rediscovering them in her seventies still shocked her.

In Belfast in 1997 she was talking with a group of disabled ex-police officers, RUC men crippled by IRA bombs. They were in a hotel. The handle of the coffee pot was pointing towards a man, and he asked her if she wanted a cup, and she wondered how he would be able to pour it with his remaining fingers, and she suddenly remembered an instruction from years before: 'Never, ever to do something *for* them if they want to do something for themselves, like handing you a cup of tea; however awkward and terrible, you don't do it for them.' And the ex-RUC man poured every single cup for a dozen of them, 'and it was excruciating, this big pot of coffee balanced in his stump of a hand'.

At that moment, she said, a scene flashed through her mind, of herself in lipstick and high heels, dolled up as though for a dance. 'I was about seventeen. It was a posh London hotel and one talked and drank and tried to treat it as a normal party, and danced with them formally, careful not to stare. They were MacIndoe's guinea pigs, as they were known, most of them airmen who had been terribly injured, whose faces were no longer human faces. He used skin-grafts to do what he could; he was a great pioneering surgeon. I suppose they must have gathered various respectable young females together and had little parties, as part of the rehabilitation process. Before that moment in Belfast I would never have remembered it.'

This must have been her first, awkward experience of the gravely insulted human body; and also with the idea that wounds demand a kind of healing that is not merely physical; that the mutilation of a person's body demands from others an extraordinary effort of sensitivity.

Soon afterwards she would have to live with the notion that there are wounds which are not even physical, which act like 'thorns in the spirit', in the beautiful phrase of William James. These were already becoming known as 'trauma', an attempt to link the mind and the body through the Greek word for a wound. (It is ironic that at the end of the century, as the word has become almost debased through repetition, it has become more and more disembodied.) The notion of shell-shock, of the breakdown of the mind under the terrors and exhaustion of combat, had reluctantly been accepted during the First World War, and as the new war took its toll of young men's will to fight, the reliving of traumatic memories through hypnosis was tried out on front-line soldiers in order to get them back into line. But the long-term effects of life-threatening, degrading experiences was not much thought about. Many of those whose minds were breached and overwhelmed relived the experience, helplessly. And those who had seen combat would turn out to be the least resistant to outside help, to be, at least relatively, the lucky ones.

*   *   *

In the final twelve months of the war, Helen Bamber took a job as secretary to a physician in Harley Street, the beginning of a long association with that district of private merchant-doctors. She would discover, after the war, a maverick network on this street, outsiders sensitive to dangerous currents in medicine and society. She also discovered that she was skilful and competent.

Her parents, bitter and incommunicative to the last, broke up the household during that summer of victory and mass death, as Hitler sacrificed millions of lives to save the German core of his empire. Her mother took a small house miles away in Brent, a sprawl of brown terraces on the northern edge of residential London, with the great circus of Wembley Stadium on the skyline. Helen went with her. The house in Stamford Hill was sold and her father moved into a flat nearby, his papers stuffed into boxes, piled under windows and in hallways. His daughter kept going back to see him, her guilt and helpless love for the man driving her to witness his depression, every piece of news making him worse. He felt hedged in, unable to go out, chained to his own impotent prophetic truth.

In the early autumn of 1944, against the rising tide of optimism as the British and Americans fought their way out of Normandy and the Red Army pushed its tank armies towards Poland, Bamber went to a camp in Shropshire, an experiment in Jewish communal living in deepest England. Her visit reflected a commitment she had made almost impulsively earlier that year. In a canteen for service people where she worked in the evenings, she had seen an advertisement asking for volunteers to work with Jewish survivors of the concentration camps; she applied the following day. She was nineteen years old.

In 1943, when the scale of the continuing Holocaust became clear, the Jewish Relief Unit had been set up by the Jewish Committee for Relief Abroad (itself an offshoot of the Central British Fund of the Board of Deputies and the Anglo-Jewish Association). The Jewish Relief Unit was intended to be its operational arm: it would do what it could for the remnant when the time came. Two hundred or so young English Jews (and a few non-Jews) came forward.

Through this network, Helen Bamber met a Russian–Jewish woman who introduced her to an international club in London, a coffee house where the world was reconstructed night after night. She met Rudi Bamberger there at a euphoric New Year's Eve party at the end of 1944. They had gone to Trafalgar Square at midnight, and she had met a black American GI earlier in the evening. There was some question of how, or where, the night was going to end. But something about the slight, German-accented young man, who seemed so funny and diffident, made her choose him. They went back to his flat in Willesden. The place was dilapidated; cockroaches rattled in the bath. They stayed up all night talking. Nothing else happened, that night, but she knew there was no going back.

Rudi Bamberger – he shortened the name to Bamber years later, to make it sound less German – was born in 1920 into a Jewish family in Nuremberg. His father Karl owned a restaurant in the town. The end of the son's childhood coincided with the start of Hitler's rule, and Nuremberg became the perfect stage-set for the Nazis' reactionary modernism. There is no more striking image of this high-tech cult of the past than in Riefenstahl's film *Triumph of the Will*, when the SS troops march like a loud rifled machine through the cobbled streets, past the turrets and walls, during the Nazis' annual Party Day. 'Our dream of a feudal city realised,' wrote an English traveller before the First World War, quaint down to the celebrated collection of torture instruments in the basement of the Rathaus. Thomas Mann captured the spirit of Nuremberg in his description of Kaisersaschern, the hometown of his Faustus: 'there hung in the air something of the state of the human heart during the last decades of the fifteenth century, a hysteria out of the dying Middle Ages, something of a latent psychological epidemic – a strange thing to say about a sensibly practical, modern town. But it was not modern, it was old, and age is the past as the present, a past only veneered with the present; and this may sound bold, but one could imagine a Children's Crusade erupting there – a Saint Vitus dance, some utopian communistic lunatic preaching a bonfire of vanities, miracles and visions of the Cross, and roving masses of mystic enthusiasts.'

Rudi Bamberger could imagine them all too well; from the flat roof of his parents' house he could see the fireworks and searchlights sweeping the sky; and because he was blond and blue-eyed he could pass among the Nazi crowds, and once saw Hitler, Hess and Goering drive by in open-topped Mercedes cars giving stiff-arm salutes to the adoring citizens. 'The excitement of the atmosphere was incredible,' he said in 1997; 'but despite that I could not have imagined it would go so far. Living in the midst of it, one developed an emotional non-acceptance of it, and tried to detach oneself from what was going on.' It cannot have been easy. His father's restaurant was only allowed to serve Jews when the racial laws named after his native city were decreed in autumn 1935. The local party boss was Julius Streicher, the most unhinged demagogue in the entire Nazi leadership, whose tabloid *Der Stürmer* was fixated on the most pornographic anti-semitism. Rudi recalled cutting out and rearranging material from the paper in order to satirize it, with two other Jewish boys at his school; but in the breaks, they would be ordered to sing the 'Horst Wessel Lied' in the courtyard with the rest of their class.

On 9 November 1938 Rudi was woken by stormtroopers breaking down the door of the family house. The pogrom was under way; his father, everything that had made him a respected local citizen now inverted, was a prime target. Rudi slipped on his dressing gown. Because he was afraid, and hated feeling 'impotent against this massive thing', he slipped his target pistol into the pocket of the gown. The SA men grabbed him and kicked and beat him. Jews were not allowed to own guns, even .22s for shooting rabbits. If they found it he would die, and so instead of protecting himself he held onto the gun all the time their boots were hurting him. The stormtroopers attacked everyone they found in the house, but they beat his father with truncheons and fists, men with faces like boxers in drink, working-class thugs let loose for the first time since their leaders were purged by Hitler in 1934. Several of them survived the war; until he read the witness statements for their trial in the late 1940s, Rudi Bamber said he did not realize how badly they had beaten him.

They dragged his mother and sister Maja around by the hair and ripped the pictures off the walls; they trampled books; they tore the curtains and the beds. They even destroyed the heating system, a detail that struck his new lover when he told her about it in the first weeks of 1945, perhaps because it was such a profound disturbance of the most basic form of civilization, the need for shelter and warmth. 'When you hear that radiators were actually pulled out of their sockets in the wall with bare hands, it is like an attack on the right to be in a house; the whole of life is being destroyed, everything that encapsulates family life: it was an indication to me of what was to follow. The idea of somebody tearing with such physical force gives you a measure of the rage they felt.'

The SA left Rudi behind, after making him stand all night outside the front door 'under arrest'; Rudi thinks that the squad leader wanted to go home, and could not be bothered to take him in. The strategic aim that night was terror rather than murder. While the SA broke up property, the SS arrested some 26,000 middle-class Jews and took them into concentration camps for purposes of extortion. A few hundred Jews died during the riot; one of them, Rudi Bamberger's father, did not regain consciousness after the SA men left. He was an upstanding burgher of Nuremberg, thousands of its citizens had enjoyed his restaurant, but since to his killers he was, by virtue of the body he inherited, part of a global biological conspiracy, Hitler's 'world plague', 'a parasite upon the nations', nothing he had ever done could save him.

They boarded up the house and went to stay with relatives. Because of the fear and the collusive silence, Rudi didn't dare ask what had happened to his father's body; nobody asked. The body had disappeared. It had been cremated in a hurry, he discovered a long time afterwards, and his father listed as a 'suicide'. Rudi's mother worked on him to leave the country, while he had a chance. Too old for the *kindertransporten* that brought Jewish children, including his sister Maja, to Britain in the months following the pogrom, Rudi took a steamer down the Rhine from Mainz to Rotterdam; from there he sailed for England. He stayed in a Rowton House in Whitechapel, a thousand-bed hostel for homeless men, for a shilling a night, his cubicle wired over to stop the thirsty climbing in for the price of a drink.

As a condition of his entry, he became an agricultural labourer. Helen Bamber remembered his description of arriving in Derbyshire in his father's long black fur coat, looking very much the elegant young bourgeois, with a portable typewriter under his arm and a suitcase full of books following after him – an exotic alien in the hills above Lockington. It was August 1939. He boarded with an elderly, kindly farming couple who taught him how to squeeze a cow's teats down to get the milk pumping at five in the morning, and how to snag turnips in cold fields while kneeling on a sack.

He wanted, more than anything else at that time, to study; but in May 1940 he was arrested with 60,000 other Jewish 'enemy aliens'. After a few months sitting in a terraced house on the Isle of Man surrounded by barbed wire, convinced that the Germans would invade and find the Jews already trapped for them, he was sent away that July with some 2800 other male enemies of the state (of whom less than a tenth were genuine prisoners of war and supporters of the Nazi regime) to Australia. The fiction that German Jews were in a juridical and political sense *German* before all else, despite their ineluctable status as enemies of the Nazi republic, is of a piece with a general British difficulty with nationality: Britain was one of the last great multinational states, wary of national particularity. It was, as a historian of the internees wrote later, 'an Alice in Wonderland situation'.

The ship in which Rudi Bamberger was deported was the *Dunera*, and the commander in charge of the prisoners, Lt.-Col. William Scott, was later court-martialled for his treatment of them. 'The guards attacked us and stole watches, rings, money and identity papers; medical equipment and supplies were thrown overboard, together with the deportees' suit-cases,' Rudi said. The ship had on board half as many men again as it was designed to carry. They were confined to a foetid hold, with inadequate sanitation, and beaten at will by soldiers and NCOs for infractions of discipline. The food was often rancid; in rough weather the hold turned into a sewer. Rudi recalled one occasion when they ran out of water. At least one man threw himself overboard.

In Australia they were taken 450 miles north of Melbourne to Hay, a town at the edge of the desert on the Murrumbidgee River. The Australian guards were humane; their officers realized that the Nazi fifth-columnists they had been told to expect were imaginary creations of the British Home Office. 'It was a land of milk and honey; actually, of beef and lamb,' in Rudi Bamber's memory. The camp regime was not petty or severe, and for many it became an open university. The pianist Peter Stadlen, a pupil of Schoenberg and Webern, gave recitals on an upright piano donated by the Quakers, and organized a choir that performed Handel's oratorio *Israel in Egypt*, writing out the scores on lavatory paper. The brilliant ex-communist theorist of Comintern policy, Franz Borkenau, held classes on world politics. Rudi has a vivid memory of a performance of *Journey's End*, R. C. Sherriff's anti-war play.

Helen Bamber likes to think of the camp as an Athenian society, with boys sitting at the feet of sages, but Rudi was glad to escape it when he was allowed to return to Britain in late 1942. By then the government had been shamed into admitting that the deportations were unjustified. Rudi went to a government training centre and spent the rest of the war 'lying under transporters and lorries at Albion Motors in London: I did not make a striking contribution to the war effort'. For some part of the first year he lived with his cousin from Berlin, Dr Johannes Pulfer, and his wife Gertrude, a German woman whose pro-Nazi family had cut her off for marrying a Jew; but they were people of regular habits and Rudi seemed to disrupt them, so he was asked to leave. He moved to where Helen found him, in a cold cheap flat. He felt detached from the war, which now rarely came closer. Together at night they watched the searchlights from the parks illuminating V-1 missiles, and heard the explosions when they fell.

Rudi and Helen started sleeping together soon after they met. She says matter-of-factly that 'it took much longer to get down to it in those days because the fear of pregnancy was so oppressive, and it dominated relationships. During the war, especially, it was often the man that had to take "precautions", so it was always quite an interesting marker, to see if a man was competent enough to arrange these things himself.'

She loved him, but thinks now that she didn't really want marriage and all that it entailed. Instead she already had 'a *determined* need to go to Germany. Rudi really didn't want me to go; he wanted me to be there and be with him. What I hadn't realized was that there was a melancholic quality to him. I remember him when we met as vigorous and active, but there was a deep, deep sadness there that could engulf him. I had not understood that, or what the limitations of my relationship to his sadness could be, and I had not thought enough about what he had witnessed when his family was destroyed.' He must have known by then, at the end of the war, that his mother was dead; but they did not talk about her very often. He seemed to prefer it that way.

Her need to go, and to serve, seems to have been pre-political; an impulse from her family, certainly, but also an ethical impulse that didn't need articulate expression. She was influenced by the universalist ideas that flourished as the war ended, as were so many young people: racism, fascism and barbarism can be overcome; evil need not triumph; this must never happen again. Her recognition of the complexity of her need to help others, and what it would cost, came much later.

* * *

If her need had many sources, it was confirmed by certain words and images that began to appear in the British press in the third week of April 1945, in the days following the death of President Roosevelt, which at first dominated the news.

The British 2nd Army had broken into Germany in the final week of March. While their US allies drove for the Elbe, the British aimed for Hamburg in order to complete the destruction of the Nazi armies in north-western Germany. On Thursday, 12 April, near the town of Celle on the edge of Lüneburg Heath, a representative of the German 1st Paratroop Army approached the British lines. He stated that an 'epidemic of typhus' had broken out at a nearby camp and offered a truce. Brigadier Taylor-Balfour, commanding VIII Corps, agreed to a ceasefire in a 48-square-kilometre area around the camp.

The sign in front of the camp read BELSEN, KREIS CELLE, REGIERUNGSBEZIRK LÜNEBURG. The first British vehicles went through the outer gate, after driving through green forest for a few miles, on Sunday, 15 April, at '3.07 in the afternoon', according to the official record. That precise military idea of time – of tasks completed, objectives achieved, minds cleared – would disintegrate during the months to come. The SS Kommandant, a man called Josef Kramer, surrendered with fifty of his male subordinates and thirty women. He had at first the air of a put-upon manager glad to be relieved of an impossible task. At 3.30, the voice of Captain Derrick Sington, an artillery officer, amplified and metallic in the loudspeakers on the roof of the lorry he sat in, echoed over the compounds: 'You are free.'

The practical tasks were dire, but achievable; finding words for what the soldiers had found was more difficult. The Imperial War Museum preserves a letter from a Gunner Walker; dated 20 May 1945, which includes the sentence: 'This letter will read like fiction and will seem to be an exaggeration but I swear that as sure as there is a God in heaven that what I have told you is the Gospel truth.'

Brigadier Glyn Hughes, chief medical officer of the British forces in the area, said on 18 April: 'I am afraid you may think I am exaggerating, but I assure you I am not. It is the most horrible frightful place I have ever seen. Anything you have ever read, heard, or seen does not begin to prepare you for the story.'

R. W. Thompson of the *Sunday Times*, exactly one week after the British arrived, and paid to write words, also struggled with the duty to express the unspeakable. He was already aware that memory is a delicate thing: 'It is my duty to describe something beyond the imagination of mankind ... Soon now this fearful evidence will be destroyed ... The fires burn ceaselessly, destroying the obscene litter of the shameful enclosures.'

The doctors described symptoms as they had been taught to do in clean unemotional prose in clean hospitals, and even on battlefields. No training had prepared them for this. Brigadier Melvin, a senior medical officer of VIII Corps, made some hurried notes in his diary after a tour of the place: 'Death rate 17,000 in March. Thousands of corpses lying unburied. Inmates starving to death every day. Water and food finished. No light or sanitation. Hundreds dying.'

Ten thousand dead bodies were lying on the ground or in the huts when the British entered, 60,000 more were barely alive, and of the living more than 12,000 died in the following weeks. This dying took place in an area measuring one kilometre by half a kilometre. The doctors saved those they could, and the hardest thing was knowing they had to let thousands die if they were to save those who were still strong enough to survive. The soldiers made the SS guards carry bodies one by one to the graves. Twice they had to order their own men to drive excavators, handkerchiefs pressed to their faces, and shovel bodies into long pits.

Glyn Hughes, at the trial of the SS guards six months later, found words to describe what he saw, though like everyone who made the attempt, his awareness of their inadequacy can be felt in what he said: 'The compounds were absolutely one mass of human excreta ... There were various sizes of piles of corpses lying all over the camp, some outside the wire and some in between the huts. The compounds themselves had bodies lying about in them. The gutters were full and within the huts there were uncountable numbers of bodies, some even in the same bunks as the living. Near the crematorium were signs of filled in mass graves, and outside to the left of the bottom compound was an open pit half full of corpses. ... Some of the huts had bunks but not many, and they were filled absolutely to overflowing with prisoners in every state of emaciation and disease. There was not room for them to lie down at full length in each hut. In the most crowded there were anything from 600 to 1000 in accommodation which should only have taken 100. ... That was the general picture.'

Helen Bamber read the aghast press, which could not match the quiet assessment of the physicians: newspapers were trying to describe an unconformity in the human. The photographs were more accurate, (though few of the papers printed images of the worst conditions in which the inmates had died). The tabloids used them extensively in the later part of the week of 16 April and from 24 April the *Daily Express* office on Regent Street mounted an exhibition of photographs from Belsen, as well as Buchenwald and Dachau, in its lobby. (These camps had been liberated by American forces earlier in the month.) It stayed open nine hours a day, seven days a week. Visitors, including Helen Bamber, went and looked, stood in front of the mounted black and white prints among hundreds of people as they moved silently around the gallery, and then had to walk away from the images. She cannot remember if her father came down to the West End to see the photographs, a fulfilment not even he could have imagined.

There were 'stick arms in pyjama stripes', young and once-beautiful faces thinned to bony hatchet ugliness, illness leaching skin of its youthful resilience, old women's faces blurring out of the images of young girls like a double exposure. Their dark hair seemed so young: 'There were great heads of hair over living skulls,' she recalled. They crowded squatting on the floors of huts, grinning at the camera.

She remembers being struck by 'the unbelievable density' of people in the huts: women literally crammed, sitting and lying side by side along the floor. No space to turn, no beds.

The ground was covered with rags and litter, low-hanging smoke, dust, tents, piles of ragged blankets. Some of the rags were corpses.

There was a photo of a British soldier with a gun in his left hand leaning over a dying woman, who looks barely able to move, out in the open in front of a hut.

In one photograph an emaciated woman dressed in heavy wellington boots and apron and cardigan screams past two exhausted, old-looking young squaddies holding their Sten guns, fags hanging from their lips; relaxed, professional, they are squinting with distaste and doing their job. Past them, just out of shot, are some of the SS guards.

In another picture, a man lay against the barbed wire with his hand under his head protected by a piece of cloth; his slack mouth exhausted, beyond caring.

A few people sat slumped around an open fire. A dozen wasted bodies lay near them on the ground as though that were not unusual. Through a walkway between single-storey huts, a narrow alley had been cleared between the thick piles of bodies that had covered the entire intervening space.

Bamber said she was struck by the image of women in baggy striped trousers and headscarves as they carried away a body on a stretcher. They seemed to have lost all urgency about it. This was not the rush of helpers at some disaster; disaster had taken possession of them.

Burning shoes were taken from a seven-foot high wall of shoes; leather as fuel, their owners all dead.

A man in a dirty long overcoat, his shaved head reduced to stubble and bone, sat on a kind of ditch over a drain, his hands on his knees, his body thrown back, his mouth open, crying out.

The mayors of neighbouring German towns, in their long and good-quality coats and neatly rolled umbrellas, were made to look, and were photographed, a little apart from the SS men and women, at the filling in of one large grave. This is what happened down the road from their little *Städte* and *Dörfer*. The frown of official denial, of legal correctness, is noticeable on the tall old men's faces. One of them at least must have come from the beautiful sixteenth-century town of Celle, the nearest to the camp.

A shabby SS man wearing a collarless shirt, with jodhpurs tucked into knee-high boots, stood, legs apart, his feet on the earth between one stick leg and another head in a large shallow pit filled with dead bodies. Three more SS men were doubling around the perimeter under the pointed rifle of a British soldier. The man in the pit stood with his arms by his sides; he had probably carried a body into it. He stared off to the right. He looked tired, like a labourer contemplating the height of a pile of earth he still has to move before he can rest. He had a long, quite handsome weak face, a shock of untidy dark hair above unshaven cheeks. This photograph has a narrative in it that may not have been obvious in 1945, for it was a picture of Dr Fritz Klein — graduate of the medical school of Budapest University, former general practitioner among the German minority in a small town in Rumania, taker of the Hippocratic Oath (we assume) and healer of the world's sickness, which was Jewry. (As the draughtsman of Hitler's Eugenic Sterilization Law told an American correspondent in 1933, 'We go beyond neighbourly love; we extend it to future generations.') Klein had 'selected' alongside Dr

Mengele at Auschwitz in a year that saw the near-obliteration of the Jews of Hungary, and ended his medical career as camp doctor at Belsen.

These and other photographs that appeared in magazines at the time do not lose their power. By themselves they cannot tell a whole story: the British public was not then aware, for example, that the majority of the survivors were Jewish.

Such images were not then, and are not now, *like* anything else. Looking at them with someone who first saw them in 1945 is a reminder that every prison camp in the Balkans is not 'like Belsen', still less like Auschwitz.

Kramer, and the SS guards he brought with him from Auschwitz, turned an entire camp, which housed the population of a small town, into a stinking jakes. Men and women with typhus and dysentery were reduced to lying in their filth in the freezing cold, to crawling into the rafters of the huts and lying on bare boards, unable to stop their bodies evacuating, the people below them unable to move. The floors and ground were slimy; the smell became the air. A total negation of civilization on the sandy north German plain: the last spontaneous achievement of the republic of racial purity.

Belsen was never intended as a death camp. It had at first been an almost privileged enclave within the SS system, a place where Himmler stored a few thousand Jews that he thought he might be useful for bargaining: he called them 'exchange Jews', as though they were human coinage. (The 1700-odd Hungarian Jews released by the Kastner negotiations passed through Belsen in July 1944.) As defeat loomed, the original detention and insurance policy became irrelevant; the camp disintegrated into a mixture of reservation and dump. It was retitled, in a typical parody of the language of cure, an *Erholungslager*, a recuperation camp, a place for healing.

The survivors from Auschwitz and other true death camps were sent on forced marches, in thin clothing, without proper shoes or food, or were crammed into open wagons and pulled for days through the collapsing Reich, starving, thirsty and unprotected from rain and snow. At Belsen they were put into broken, cold and filthy barracks, with less than a pint of thin gruel a day to keep them alive in the freezing winter. Their guards came straight from Auschwitz, killers so insensible that they gave themselves up to the British, unable to understand that what they were presiding over would haunt the young liberators for the rest of their lives.

The German historian Eberhard Kolb gives a concise explanation of the mechanics of it. 'In the spring of 1945 20–25,000 prisoners had just as many toilets and washing rooms as 2,000 people had a year earlier, or rather even less because the camp administration had not let the water taps and other installations be repaired.' In one self-contained section, 8,000 prisoners did not have a single toilet or water tap between them.

Kolb writes: 'This was the last great National Socialist mass murder, after the end of the mass killings in the gas chambers of the extermination camps.' In the last week of its existence, an avalanche of prisoners broke over the camp. Slaves from the Lower Saxony region were driven there on foot; and the 30,000 survivors of the huge Dora factory, the underground galleries where they made the V-2 rockets, reached Belsen after 4 April. On 15 April, the camp held 60,000 people. Kolb says that a total of 35,000 died in the three and a half months before the day the British came.

What killed most of them was 'the last great typhus epidemic in history', according to Paul Kemp, the Imperial War Museum historian. The disease spread 'only because the camp administration failed to provide sanitary conditions which could have kept the camp clean … [it was] the dirtiest and most unhygienic of all German camps, which certainly says a great deal'. The lice could breed and eat and shit in the blood and breed again. There was never any attempt to disinfect and clean the beds and huts; never enough water to wash. No clean clothes had been provided since mid-December 1944. For the SS, Jews were vermin, a disease of humanity; this sickness was living proof of their inner nature. 'The condition of the prisoners was so bad that one had almost a horror of them,' said Irma Grese at her trial, the young chief of the SS women guards explaining why she did not like to strike them with her hand.

The Nazis could say, almost truthfully: Belsen was an accident. Kramer was the epitome of carefully considered indifference; perhaps this is as good a definition of his evil as we need. A mile up the road a Panzer training barracks had a bakery capable of producing 40,000 loaves a day, and stores containing tons of potatoes and dried milk, yet Kramer said he continued – it is possible to believe him – to send out trucks to Hamburg and Hanover in search of food, for he had been ordered to get all his supplies from civilian sources. The water tanks were almost empty, and a dead child floated in one of them on that April afternoon; Kramer had made no attempt to run a pipe to a stream 500 metres away. British engineers did it in a few hours.

*   *   *

The training for the Jewish Relief Unit was rudimentary: a camp with some farm work and a discussion about 'gaining the confidence of people who no longer had any trust'; this was 'group work', as Bamber calls it, of a high standard: 'They put us through some quite difficult tests, forcing us to think about how we would handle misery and degradation.' She already spoke some German, and now learned a little Yiddish; and she was taught about general nursing principles, and how to set up a search bureau. There were even classes on a form of self-protection, 'some rather crude jujitsu'.

She had a spell at the National Association of Mental Health. This was the organization responsible for the 'boarding', the reviewing of people who had been invalided out of the army on psychological grounds. The emphasis was on drugs, on getting servicemen back into action – on restoring morale. This was Bamber's first encounter with the practice of 'therapy', and it left her cold. It seemed instrumental and brutal, but of course the demands of total war are exactly that.

A psychologist came and gave an evaluation of each volunteer. He asked hard questions and dealt firmly with stupid answers. Helen looked at his assessment of her when he left his notes behind: he praised her, said she had certain gifts of insight, and had contributed well in one or two discussions about how they would deal with the survivors, but that she was 'intolerant'. (It may have been 'arrogant'.) She was upset by his analysis, but perhaps she had been too serenely didactic for her own good: 'This word "intolerant" (or "arrogant") did stick. He was probably right. The discussion was about how we were going to deal with very distressed people. He went round the circle and I was towards the end and I said that I believed that there were some people that we would not be able to affect in any way at all, people who would be almost impossible to reach. But that if there were children around, we should concentrate a lot of our efforts on working with the ones who could be reached, if we had the opportunity. But even if I was wrong about the children – there were so few left alive – I never imagined, even though I was very young, that we would go there and be able to help everybody. It was not going to be like handing out soup and sticking plasters and getting them up and about again.'

Rudi did not want her to go; and her mother was so outraged that she would not even speak to her the night before she left. Her mother's disappointed opposition was one thing; her father needed more careful handling.

His new flat was already littered with newspaper cuttings and documents. He was losing his capacity to work, to go through the motions of his job as an accountant, and as the war went on he became less careful about his appearance. He seemed utterly hopeless.

'The *winning* of the war didn't have the same meaning to him; it did mean that we had survived, and being terrified of annihilation I was of course very relieved that I could finally stop thinking about them invading our houses, as I used to imagine it; but my father was beyond that kind of feeling. I think he felt that there had been so much destruction, so much death and carnage that it could no longer be given a meaning; he was overwhelmed, as I think he expected to be.'

It wasn't madness, she thinks, but there was simply no means of expression left to him; perhaps there never had been, sitting up in his room writing to himself and preaching to his young daughter, the only convert he could make, about the coming genocide. Now he floundered through information, nothing ever cohering into a manuscript or an action. She would come to see him. making room for herself among the papers, and try to console him.

Victory, or the certainty of it after the autumn of 1944, seemed only to make things worse for him. He would never have been able to make a calculation like the military historian who suggested that compared with the cost of victory for the Germans and Japanese, 'the human cost involved in the destruction of evil was not great but small, that perhaps 57,000,000 dead was, in the balance of history, a small price to pay for ridding the world of depraved wickedness'. Perhaps: but some immensities destroy thought; some accounts will never balance.

The righteous optimism, the cheery uniform voice of propaganda, grated on him; but Helen Bamber was elated by the retreating Nazi legions, the young Allied soldiers in their uniforms, the sheer vindication of winning, and the sense that something better must now be created. Everyone she knew wanted the Labour Party to come to power in Britain, and Europe and the world would never be the same again.

She and her father met for the last occasion on which she would play the role of his child – as if she had ever been allowed to grow into it – near St James's Park. They were overlooked by the back windows of the great imperial offices on Whitehall, and walked out onto the Mall, the boulevard that connected the monarch's palace with his ministries. The park now had trenches dug in it, and sandbag huts.

When she told him that she intended to go to Germany he was not upset about the danger, or the epidemics, or the effect it would have on her. He told her she must do what she felt to be right, but he had wanted her to be a scholar: to go to university, and to be perhaps what he had never been able to achieve. It saddened him that, in some way he must have been able to predict, she was denying herself that formal discipline for ever. But he agreed with her that the camps had created something that needed to be attended to. He took it very well. And he never said, 'You are too young.'

Looking back on their conversation in the chilly spring of 1945, in the heart of that great rectangle of British power, Bamber suggests now that she went to Belsen because of a need to do something that would acknowledge the disaster, but repair it without illusion. 'It was nothing to do with feeling guilt, I think; it was about *trying to save what could be saved*. I know we can't save everybody, but I believe that we can save some. I think that was my principle then. It certainly is now. My father felt that nothing could be saved, that there was nothing left, and I felt there was, and we had to work with that. My father could never accept that some things cannot be changed; perhaps he wanted to change too much, and paid the price of impotence. He had a strange life, being tossed about from country to country, never really belonging, and was crushed by the thought of the millions dying. I don't mean to say that I don't ever despair like him, because I do. But at least my house is not filled with old papers.'

Bamber is not given to citations from religious tradition, but in this unconscious evocation of the Rabbi who preserved the sacred books, who saved what he could – and of the judge in the Kastner trial who called on him as an historical example – she strikes a chord that resonates across her wider family history.

Many people who were young in 1945 talk about the war as the most formative event in their lives, but then ordinary life started again and they embraced it, whereas her narrative is more complicated. The end of the war, despite her conventional dreams about the shape of the world that would emerge from it, was as notional an event for her as it was for her father. He had won her and lost her; the rest of her life would be the clarification of a distinction between them.

3

GRIT IN THE WHEEL

Surely this war was made to abolish Dachau, and all the places like Dachau – we must know that there can never be peace if there is cruelty like this in the world.

Martha Gellhorn, April 1945

She set off into Europe dressed as though for war, a very small young woman in junior officer's uniform with a shield of David on her arm instead of a rank. She was not carrying a weapon. More kit than body, she moved inside a pile of khaki: a rollbed, a haversack containing vests, drawers, socks, tin hat, clasp knife, plate mug, first aid kit, greatcoat and a folding bath. She could barely lift the equipment, but she had been told not to lose any of it and lugged it everywhere. She still resents the weight of the canvas bath, which she never once used.

In the grey weather the ruins of Calais stood out dark and rotten; the imprint of violence was everywhere she went. Buildings looked soft, pitted with coin-shaped holes or larger bite-marks. Less than a year before, half a million German soldiers had retreated across France, drawn back by a state that retained to the bitter end its power to concentrate the making of death; they had mined and bombed Calais before they left. Helen Bamber had a pass for a village in Lower Saxony called Eilshausen, which she could not locate in any atlas or gazetteer that she consulted before leaving England. The rough map she was given placed it near Herford, the British HQ for their Occupation Zone. She was to find her way there from a station at Bad Oeynhausen, but the trains ran on arcane schedules; military policemen scoffed at travel plans made in London and gave out new ones as though they controlled entire road and rail networks, and would then be baffled by the arrival of a locomotive hauling a chain of Belgian or Dutch wagons.

Everything was an emergency, but apparently not this young woman's desire to reach something as unrecognizable to the official mind as the Jewish Relief Unit. The first people from the unit had finally been allowed into Belsen in August. The Military Government of the British Zone was still uneasy about them, and kept aloof: no humanitarian gesture was free of dangerous implications, when examined with the eye of the foreign affairs professional.

The rhythms of travel seemed to depend on chance and privilege. She saw British soldiers, journalists and men in dark suits disappear towards the Zone; she saw trains snuffle in full of cement, machinery and food. Before long she would discover that with the right connections it was possible to secure a whole train and put it to good use, but for now she was the lowest priority of the war machine on the northern French shore. So she stayed in Calais for a week.

She remembers it as very cold, though it was still early autumn. She was billeted in a small unheated room in a Nissen hut by the railway track and swears she did not take off her uniform for a week. As an honorary officer she was allowed to use a military canteen, and during the day she would go to the town hall and sit, looking out the window at the traffic and the rubble. It rained without stopping, and the coastal fog of the Channel lay on the wet streets, the khaki vehicles grinding all day through muddy bombed-out places that looked as though they would be ugly for ever.

She felt very lonely. In the midst of all the wreckage, she went looking for cosmetics, deciding suddenly that she had to have some white nail pencils, which would give the tips of her nails a fashionably pale translucence. She does not know how she paid for them, or in what currency, but somewhere in the rationed back streets she found a set of the clay pencils she wanted. She has since had the impulse, when she is in danger of being overwhelmed, to treat herself to some small luxury. (After a grim three days in the Gaza Strip, once, it was Dead Sea mud exfoliant.) She thinks she is vain; but the preservation of a certain style seems to contribute to her capacity to persist with work, and reassures her about the possibility of living decently.

That week, despite her isolation, she also felt the last of a solidarity she has never witnessed since among the British, as though everyone was present at the funeral of someone they imagined they had all loved. It was the tribal feeling of living in a broken-down social world, which she had experienced in bomb-shelters during the air raids in 1940, an extended sympathetic conversation among total strangers. 'You spoke to one person one day, and you revealed a lot about yourself, whom you had lost in the war, and people cried a lot, and you never saw them again. It was like a continuation of the war. You had this sense of being totally alone and yet in touch with a massive community moving around you. We sat with blankets around us in cold rooms and talked. How I got on the train to go to Germany, or who told me I could travel, I could not remember to save my life. You just had to keep pushing, keep asking and almost fighting.'

Crushed against the weight of her kit, she sat for hours in a space between carriages as the train took her towards Germany. When they set off she had not slept for a whole night. Soldiers chatted her up, young men going back to their regiments; and everyone smoked: it was even more sociable than talking. Tobacco permeated the wet cotton of her shirt and heavy wool of her battledress; inhaling the smoke kept her floating on the surface of tiredness. Once they all had to stand up and move to one side of the train as it crossed a Bailey bridge that army engineers had thrown over a river. The carriage's enormous weight could be felt in every inch of its slow movement over the structure. Later they stopped and were ordered into a compound where tureens were steaming on tables, and were given bread and soup.

She tried to fall asleep and nodded off intermittently; too many halts at stations in the dark. None of the place-names meant anything to her; after the first few hours her eyes ached from looking out the window. She was aware, however, of being in Germany, of a shift in the density of the field of ruins, of broken partitions, which were the walls of buildings left standing, chimney stacks and gable ends. That was all that was left, as far as the eye could see, with women scavenging in the rubble, 'Like insects moving over the landscape.' She saw a boy carrying a basin out of a dump, women in bulky clothes as though they were wearing three coats. Sometimes she would see another train, rotten with grey men on the carriage roofs. 'A mass of people was on the move. There were children everywhere, on the rail stations and along the track, begging for food, and people threw bread and food out of the train windows to them. Everybody did it. And perhaps something went from me then. I want to be careful here, but it was about hatred: I did hate them, and I saw a lot in Germans when I was there to make me go on hating them; but seeing the children made it less easy to channel everything into one particular comfortable sort of hatred.'

She was afraid of missing her station and going on and on into the wasteland of Central Europe. Eilshausen was a name without a place; and she was a soldier separated from her unit, which no one she met had ever heard of. It was as though she could sense the nature of war, and worse than war, with her entire body: wearing her marked uniform, she identified herself as a Jew, and looked at Germans knowing that they looked back at her, without seeming to look. 'I've never been so self-conscious as I was under the eyes of defeated German men.' She kept repeating the name of the village she had to find as if her life depended on it.

She left the train at Hanover, another unexplained detour. Eilshausen was between Bad Oeynhausen and Herford. She hitched, knowing that the army whose uniform she was wearing would find her somehow. A British officer driving a PU – a Personal Utility vehicle: grey metal, canvas flaps and open sides, like a stripped jeep, with the suspension of a boneshaker – gave her a lift to the village. He was baffled by what she was supposed to be doing in Germany: it had not occurred to him that there was anything of particularly Jewish significance about what had been discovered at Belsen.

The rural areas looked like a country at peace: wide pastures, fat cattle, fields of grain and potatoes. The hamlet of Eilshausen was set among acres of old forest and rich arable land. The large house that was now the office of the Field Director (Germany) of the Jewish Relief Unit had belonged to a prominent local Nazi, and this was to be Helen's official home. But before she left London her map of the area was already centred on Belsen. That was why she had come, and it was where she wanted to be.

Her formal position was that of assistant to Captain Henry Lunzer, the Field Director of the JRU for Germany, who was still on his way from the British Army in the Far East, where he had been an adjutant in an infantry regiment. They were to set up a headquarters to co-ordinate the work of the Relief Unit throughout the British area of occupation, under the protection of UNRRA, the United Nations refugee organization. They answered to the Jewish Committee for Relief Abroad, which sent out supplies from London for distribution to the survivors. The volunteers in Germany were meant to see that this was done properly, to provide medical and nursing care if they had the skills to do so, and to help in general with 'welfare and rehabilitation'.

Almost at once she was hard at it. 'Having learned to negotiate the impossible in my own family, I had acquired a way of asking and getting, and persuading. So I could get help when I wanted it. There were very few others in Eilshausen when I arrived. Then drivers started to arrive, who had come with their vehicles all the way from England; one of them had his vehicle stolen when he went into a café in Paris and that was considered very shameful. And things were being stolen all the time. You got the impression that people were careless: careless with life, with their own lives, with people's feelings; you could see it in the way people drove, roaring down those endless German roads. The whole atmosphere was chaotic. You realized very quickly that you had to take some risks that you might not take in normal life.'

She worked the phone and tried to find out who in the Military Government could make a difference, and who in UNRRA, and what they would have to do with the supplies sent from England for the camps. After a couple of days she asked one of the drivers to take her the seventy-five miles to Belsen.

The woods were just on the turn, glowing yellow and red, and grew deeper around the edge of Lüneburg Heath. On the way they passed through Celle, a Lower Saxon market town, the former seat of a petty duke that looked unchanged since the Thirty Years War, marinaded in a deep-German, half-timbered prettiness that spoke to her of corrupt attachments to the past. The Germans had surrendered to Montgomery on 4 May at Lüneburg, fifteen miles from Celle.

They drove on through thick woodland broken by the silent emptiness of big fields. Very tall fir trees, with naked red trunks and an apex of green, alternated with silver birches standing in elegant crowds by the side of the road. Wrecked tanks and lorries pushed in among the trees were already rusting in the drizzle. 'We had to wait outside the gates for some time. I was terrified. What they now called Camp One, the concentration camp, had been flattened, but you could see the long earthen mounds and those markers which they put up over the mass graves, so many of them around that field. The inmates had been housed in the barrack blocks of the German army base about a mile away. The actual huts had been burned down – because of typhus, they said. So it was like a big clearing in the middle of these beautiful woods. You could smell burned earth, it was a strange sickly smell: dank, sweetish. Like the smell you get when you take a geranium and crush it in your hand. It was completely, utterly silent. Everyone who was there said this, but I remember that there were no birds, none.

'In the new camp there were still people who were very ill. The day I arrived a woman had drunk Lysol and forced Lysol down the throat of her baby which had been born as a result of rape by a Ukrainian guard. She killed her child and herself. That was the day I arrived in Belsen.'

Looking out now across the site of the camp on a chilly autumn day, like the day Helen Bamber first came, it is impossible to imagine the squalor. There is no smell. Each mound is cut like a low stepped tumulus, a raised oblong of earth held in a very low stone frame. Each has a larger stone plaque with the number carved on it in relief: all round numbers, 800, 2000, 1000. The field is now softened by grass, lichens and the tough smoky heather that covers uncultivated ground all over the heath with a stain of purple. The heather has a grip on the burial mounds; when it withers it leaves a mat of dry hairy grey twigs. The site is closed in on the west by an obelisk and a curved wall; a separate Jewish memorial stone, low and square, stands some way in front of it. Turning away from these plain stone shapes there is little to see except sky and trees. The forest is coming back: birch trees, white and slender, have grown up where the huts used to be. In the absence of the huts, of any single structure that can bear an idea of how it was, it could be a prehistoric site: an outline on the ground, of interest to archaeologists, with sepulchral mounds that were emptied long ago. It is easier to imagine the nothingness felt by Hannah Levy-Hass, a Jew from Belgrade who arrived here in late summer 1944, and who wrote in her diary on 18 October that year, after seeing the corpse of a very young girl laid out on a bench: 'A small, bare window looked out on to the grey barbed-wire fence, behind which stood more rows of bleak, grey huts. And beyond this – nothing, a cold, dark, foggy void, the rain-drenched line of the northern horizon, desolate, leaden.'

Further back in the woods, however, a rectangle of bricks has been uncovered. It is the foundation of one of the huts. Each brick is now numbered, like a shard of evidence. The area suggested by this enclosure housed hundreds of starving people. Not far off is a dirty, concrete basin dug into the loam; it was overgrown for years. This was one of the water cisterns that Josef Kramer allowed to run dry in April 1945. These accidentally preserved shapes, lacking the aesthetic finish of a monument, are a definition of mass hunger and thirst.

In the first year after the war, the recent past had none of the tidiness of a memorial site. Helen Bamber walked around the graves, and looked at the marks on the grass where the huts had been. She was driven up the road to Camp Two, the former Panzer school where Rommel trained elements of the Afrika Korps, and saw the two- or three-storey blocks that had become home for the former inmates of the Nazi camp. 'It was grim; a prison camp in all but name. They had stone buildings rather than wood huts, and they seemed incredibly bleak.' It was laid out like any cavalry barracks, solid structures around large empty spaces, except that the parade ground had been renamed Freedom Square.

That night she slept on the floor of a barrack room in a sleeping bag. A rat 'as big as a small dog' ran over her in the night. She had already forgotten to be bothered, this fastidious young woman, at not taking her clothes off for days at a time. She remembers it as 'frighteningly cold' on the bare boards, though it was not yet winter.

She met volunteers of the unit, and Mrs Rose Henriques, famous as a social worker in the East End of London, who was the JRU leader based in Celle. She also met former inmates of the camp. She smiled, spoke to them about the wave of support for them in England, and tried to absorb what they said about their needs, and she noticed the toughness and determination of the ones who spoke to her. The rooms she saw reminded her of the overcrowding in small air-raid shelters: seven or eight people in bare concrete cubes filled with beds and clothes.

It is pleasing to think of the end of the war and of liberation; comforting to imagine the survivors being fed after the gates opened and, when they were well enough, riding to freedom on a democratic truck. But the Jews of Belsen travelled a bare mile, to the old Panzer grounds, and there they stayed for another three years. They had been redefined: they were now Displaced Persons, or DPs; and the British preferred to call the camp Höhne, rather than Belsen. But naming is much more than a verbal act, and the Jewish survivors were unhappy with the new language. The DPs could not leave the camp on their own terms; or rather they were free to go, but only to the last places on earth they wished to see.

The British were both the inheritors of Belsen as a Jewish centre – the ethnic Poles, Russians and others were being sent home, leaving around 12,000 Jews – and of a strategic problem. As guardians of the people whose lives they had helped to save, they could not easily force them back to their countries of origin. Those who had gone home to Poland discovered that the Nazi persecution of Slavs had not encouraged solidarity with Jews, and made their way back to Belsen. Some were murdered before they could do so. The British, as colonial protectors of Palestine since 1919, were balancing their own interests between Arab and Jewish nationalism. They could not grasp the real nature of the disaster that had befallen the Jews, and were deeply suspicious of their emergent nationalism. For the moment, then, the Zone was ruled by the legal fiction that Polish Jews were still really Poles, that Jews who had lived in Hungary were in fact Hungarians. Norbert Wollheim, a German Jewish survivor who became one of the Belsen DP leaders, was told by 'a high UNRRA functionary' in June that German Jews 'did not represent a recognised category'. If Jews in a particular town wanted help, they should apply 'to the German mayor of the town'.

This insistence on a juridical shadow-play, against the enormous backdrop of a world order turning on its hinges, charged the air of the Zone with the hectic and the unreal; it was full of verbal violence, of connivance at formalities that everyone knew to be empty, of tolerated evasions and repressed anger. Time was suspended; the displaced persons might be said to have been in limbo, were that Christian concept of hell's margin appropriate for people who had come back from places of absolute darkness.

To Helen Bamber it would come to seem that she was always running very fast, and getting nowhere; and suddenly the world would change and what had been unthinkable became normal, and she would find herself in a different place. It was like this achieving anything for the DPs; and higher powers could change the rules of the game. In the summer of 1945 the Germans seemed irredeemably tainted by the existence of Belsen and Auschwitz; a year later former Nazi functionaries were taking office once more, and a complicated silence began to weave itself around the past.

Beneath the politics and cynicism, the pain and terror of the survivors was often invisible. Yet in Helen Bamber's memory it is the energy of that pain that is indestructible.

*   *   *

The precocious hustler was a very junior relief worker – one of the youngest in the relief unit. She says she had no administrative capacity. Henry Lunzer, her boss, and a former salesman for Gestetner in Palestine, had volunteered because his two sisters were already in Germany with the JRU and he thought he should be there. Judith Lunzer was the matron of the hospital at Belsen. Henry was a short, fiercely mobile and impatient man: 'full of that military organization and drive,' Helen Bamber remembered, 'kindly, a bit autocratic, but very effective. He may have been a law unto himself, but he was a law. I liked him very much.'

He thinks she was a fine administrator. 'The first thing I had, so to speak, was Helen – who was, in inverted commas, a secretary, but it was she who ran the administration of the headquarters. She had to be the one at the other end of the phone, the other end of the letters. And what she did was admirable, really excellent.'

Lunzer's job was to tie the strands of the work together, to travel throughout the British Zone, to find out where he needed to place people and to establish communications between pockets of survivors and those who could supply them with clothing and food. Helping trace their living relatives was one of his most important tasks. He was a doer, who had travelled around Palestine selling printing machines before the war, and the army had taught him how to organize resources. The unit improvised with what it could get, passing on supplies from Britain to the DP 'Central Committee' at Belsen and other camps. It did good work, in difficult conditions. But Lunzer had walked into a situation that demanded political subtleties which he, as a blunt, straight-shooting person, could not have appreciated. Their job was the relief of Jews; but many of his comrades would have liked to include in that the organization of transports to Palestine, which was illegal. Everything they did had to be accounted for, documented and receipted to a committee of community leaders in London, distinguished people, connected people; but those on the ground did not always feel that punctilio was achievable.

And anything that smacked of improvisation, of illegality or corner-cutting – and especially anything that might antagonize the British army of occupation – horrified the committee in London, for understandable reasons: they saw their whole relief effort threatened with closure.

Joanne Reilly, a fine historian of post-war Belsen, has caught the dilemma of the JRU and its Field Director very well. 'In theory, the neutral position of the JCRA Executive [the parent body of the JRU] on the political issue was necessary. In practice, it was completely unworkable. British relief workers inevitably did choose to get involved not only in Zionist politics but also in aiding the illegal immigration programmes. ... The grave mistake of the Executive was in not coming to terms with the situation in Germany as it was rather than how they would have liked it to be.'

Henry Lunzer said later that his job should have been to let the people organize themselves, but that there was a constant tension between his superiors and the DP leaders because the donors wanted to control the distribution of food and medicine and clothing. He believes that his committee in London had a view of themselves as a charity, and expected gratitude, and that this irritated the DPs, who wanted to take their destiny into their own hands, and distribute goods in their own way. 'So why have a fight? Yes, the distributors would take a little bit extra for themselves: that was inevitable. It was part of the culture of Eastern Europe from which they came. Why fight it? As long as the main bulk of the stuff went to those who needed it.' His superiors could not even bring themselves to recognize the elected committee of the Jewish DPs, since it was not ratified by the British military authorities. Lunzer was also aware of the poverty of his unit's resources compared to those of the 'Joint' (the American Jewish Joint Distribution Committee), which often subsidized the British effort. His task cannot have been made easier by the knowledge that the Joint, reflecting its government's pro-Zionist policy, was only too happy to encourage immigration to Palestine.

The JRU was, then, part militant charity, part self-censoring political movement, and part army platoon. Helen Bamber remembers vividly the atmosphere of the mornings at Celle when Mrs Rose Henriques would assemble her team for exercises and put them through routines while she played bouncy tunes on an upright piano. Bamber dreaded the callisthenics. She and Henry seem to have shared an affectionate mockery for Rose Henriques. 'A marvellous person,' according to Lunzer, 'but a typical Edwardian do-gooder.' He thinks that she, almost unconsciously, always wanted the donor to be given recognition, and that this blinded her to the feelings of the survivors and their resistance to seeing themselves as objects of charity. Rabbi Isaac Levy, who was Senior Jewish Chaplain of the British Liberation Army, writing about her many years later, felt that 'her one weakness was her inability or unwillingness to appreciate the role which Palestine played in the sentiments of the inmates.' 'Wonderful; the backbone of the *moral* Jewish East End,' Helen Bamber says wryly.

For her part she typed letters and made herself indispensable and persuasive. If supplies did not turn up, she tried to be calm while signalling urgency, enquiring at Military Government HQ, or talking to UNRRA. If a military bureaucrat was becoming irritated with the demands of people he found ungrateful and irrational, because he could not imagine what they had experienced, she would soothe him, and promise to talk to Captain Lunzer. 'Henry demanded a lot of discipline, and expected things to be done. But he could not hold his patience in *negotiating* for things that seemed so simple and reasonable – he would *demand* that they be done. Perhaps he used me to cajole and facilitate – I was to some extent his diplomatic alter ego.'

She drafted reports from the information she was given for the vigilant gentlemen in London. It may be that she did not write enough of them. The sending of information was a sore point. Those who required it were eminent, older men (and women, including Rose Henriques), like Norman Bentwich, historian and lawyer, former Attorney-General of Mandate Palestine, and Leonard Cohen, a successful barrister; men used to elegant minutes, regular reports – the British administrative way. Passionately committed to the welfare of the survivors, and responsible for the very existence of a British relief effort, they came from a different culture to the people they had sent out to Germany, let alone the survivors themselves.

Henry Lunzer would come back from his troubleshooting journeys around the British and American sectors – Hamburg, Bremen, Düsseldorf, Lübeck, Berlin and countless tiny villages in between. He would bustle in dictating memos, spend the Sabbath in peace, and have to leave again late on Saturday or early Sunday morning. He would take his assistant with him, still dictating, scribbling away in her Blitz shorthand. He had a big ex-Wehrmacht Mercedes which, Helen Bamber remembers, 'had one of those sunroofs that slid back, so that you could be driven in it standing up': a Nuremberg-rally limo gunning the roads of Germany in the service of Jews. It had a partition, so that Lunzer could speak without being heard by his driver, and they would bounce in and out of shellholes as he read his notes and talked on and on. Three or four hours later he would let her out where he knew she could get a ride; sometimes they had a PU following them. He would speed off, and she would come back in the jeep.

She had an office in the former Nazi's big house looking out onto the woods, the oaks and birches flanking the big meadows, the dark congestion of fir and pine. Eilshausen was so small that Bamber could walk out of the back door and lose herself for an hour. It was the kind of forest, she said, that made you want to listen to Schubert yet wonder how he could have arisen from such a people. The tranquillity and peace were astonishing. In among the trees the silence was profound, the ground springy with needles, but she felt that there was always something lurking behind her. In the street she often felt suffocated, surrounded by the villagers' inscrutable resentment, at best their self-pity and ignorance. And they were well fed, living off their produce, forming a striking physical contrast to the thin Jews on their rationed diet.

Alison Wood, the unit's welfare officer, also remembered the landscape in terms of the music that was now permanently shadowed for her: 'One had to face different sorts of confusion; for instance the land around Eilshausen was irresistibly beautiful, and that it should be so was disorienting. It should have been ugly, grey, dirty, and it wasn't. And the children were so beautiful.' She spoke of 'that long road up to the Lüneburg Heath, and those woods, and the Hanoverian hills in the spring – so romantically German, the land of Brahms and folk-song, and with people in it who had been so unspeakably dreadful'.

Frau Schoenberg and her daughter were the housekeepers for the JRU. They had fled from the East to escape the Russians. Bamber, who finds it hard to be vindictive, tried to reach them; but it was like speaking to the mildly autistic. 'There were twenty-five of us, mainly Jews, in the houses we had by then taken over – the Nazi's house and the ones next to it. She and her daughter had a billet in the village, which was very hostile to us. She had been a nurse in a hospital in the East, she said, and had tried to get away but she and her daughter had been raped in front of each other. They were always in tears, and I felt for them. But she also showed me most lovingly a photo of her dead son, a handsome blond boy in full German Army uniform, posed on top of a beautiful statue in Paris, very much the triumphant victor. This was his moment of glory, and you felt it was his mother's too. And of course I understood her loss; but I asked her, "Don't you feel for the French people too?" But she had no sense that he should never have been there at all. Her lovely boy.'

Bamber and her friends protected Frau Schoenberg and her daughter, walking them home to their house when they were abused for working for the Jews. Once there was an ugly picket of men from the village, shouting at the headquarters house and at the women inside it, these Jews occupying their country. A man from the Jewish Brigade had given her advice on how to deal with confrontations when no soldiers were around. He told her that one person should go out alone and face them. So she did, wearing her uniform, and stood silently in front of this bunch of big rustic men, who were probably drunk. They broke up and drifted away sullenly.

Henry, she thinks, loathed Germans in a way that was hard to overestimate, but he was scrupulously correct in his dealings with them; meticulous even about the crockery and furniture in the house. If they broke an ashtray they tried to replace it.

The wearing of that symbol on the arm was still a defiant act. Edit Blau was the most fluent German speaker in the unit. She was a left-wing German Jew who had survived one of the last death marches, pushing her mother into a ditch, rolling in after her. Once Helen was working in her room and out of the corner of her eye she saw Edit walking down the village street. 'There was a woman standing on the corner and suddenly I heard a loud smack, and Edit had hit this woman hard across the face. She had made some anti-semitic remark assuming Edit was English and could not understand her.'

Bamber's official duties were in Eilshausen, but she spent as much time as she could in Belsen itself. Her work took her there, but it was also a magnet for her: a city-state full of politics and anger, run by people who had come back from the dead; a self-governing Jewish enclave that no

German could enter. Lunzer knew that she was 'not totally fulfilled' as his assistant, but he left her to her own devices and 'she did things admirably.' So whenever the drivers had supplies to deliver, and she had done her work, she would ask to be taken up to the camp. It was better than sitting in the backwoods surrounded by German farmers. It is striking that although Henry Lunzer and Alison Wood paid tribute to Helen Bamber's humanity and efficiency as a colleague, she herself cannot easily remember what she was doing at Eilshausen, and was dependent on their assurances that she was useful: those office days have become empty, lost in the fog that is most bureaucratic time.

She remembers Belsen more vividly, with certain scenes cut out in relief. In late 1945 there were still 'awful sights, amputees, gangrene, festering sores. People still looked terribly emaciated, to my eyes, haggard; you still could not escape that view of Belsen. Sometimes when you were searching through things you were reminded of the enormity of it: once we were in one of the huts and came across a vast pile of shoes, sorted according to sizes, including children's shoes, all neatly lined up; you were never safe from that kind of confrontation.' The prisoners had been forced, when Belsen was a 'recuperation' camp, to do nasty and mindless jobs; and one of them was unpicking the stitching of worn-out shoes so that the leather could be recycled. The shoes that she found could have been that raw material, and could as easily have been the shoes of the dead. Slavery made little distinction between labour power and the stuff it worked on: both were there to be expended as ruthlessly as possible.

The barracks felt like cold-storage units as the year turned, full of bodies trying to keep warm. At least that first winter was mild. A year later, in December 1946, Judith Lunzer, Henry's sister, wrote this description of life in the barracks at the start of the coldest European winter for nearly a century: 'The problem of accommodation is very acute. Many patients are being discharged from hospital in a weak condition and instead of having ... extra care, return to their bare rooms, often overcrowded and lacking the most elementary essentials. Winter has come to Belsen ... the lack of warm clothing, the shoes that let in the ice and snow, the icy rooms, the coughing children, the pleading, desperate mothers. ... The coal allocation has been cut by 50%, which left enough to heat the hospital for four hours in the morning and one hour in the afternoon. There is just enough heat to prevent the pipes from freezing, but not enough to keep patients and workers from shivering with the cold. … [Two days later] This morning two pipes burst in the hospital – wards were flooded with water, and the room containing the welfare supplies inundated, so that a lot of articles, including cigarettes, were spoiled. The winter has only just begun – may God help us get through it.'

When Helen Bamber first arrived, the people in the camp had barely recovered their humanity in the eyes of their rescuers, who had to be forgiven for not realizing that the survivors were never conscious of losing it.

The young Yugoslav survivor Hanna Levy-Hass captured in her diary for the last week of the concentration camp's existence a sense that some deaths are truly inhuman, and her determination not to give in passively: 'Better to put an end to it all, like a human being. Are we supposed to let ourselves decay and perish, physically and psychologically, slowly but inexorably sinking into the void of total exhaustion, smelling of suppuration and contamination, dying bit by bit like beasts? … What dishonour, what unspeakable disgrace. … It is man's duty to die like a man and avoid a fate that is worse than any death – a death that is no death.'

The liberators' pity had sometimes tipped over into disgust and revulsion, their anger at the perpetrators degrading the victims. Brigadier H. L. Glyn Hughes, the chief medical officer of the 2nd Army, wrote later: 'It was the most moving and heart-rending sight to see those poor creatures, to hear their weak animal cries, many only just able to realise that there might still exist a ray of hope for them.' The man who announced to them that they were 'free', Captain Derrick Sington, found himself thinking of some degenerate zoo: 'On the left … stood row upon row of green wooden huts, and we came into a smell of ordure – like the smell of a monkey house. A sad blue smoke floated like a ground mist between the low buildings. I had tried to visualise the interior of a concentration camp, but had not imagined it like this. Nor had I imagined the strange simian throng, who crowded to the barbed wire fences surrounding the compounds with their shaven heads and their obscene penitentiary suits, which were so dehumanising.'

At least Sington and Glyn Hughes were soldiers who had seen violent death. The effect on others was worse. In early May, before the war was over – Belsen was behind the fighting front for three weeks after it was handed over to the British – ninety-six medical students from a London teaching hospital were sent into the camp as an emergency health service.

Before he died one of them, Andrew Matthews, a twenty-year-old from an English country town, unprepared for anything, set down in a scrapbook what he saw when he entered one of the huts: 'The hut door hung open and the entrance was covered with a curtain of hessian. I pulled this back and stared in horror at the scene before me. There was a writhing mass of humanity. No one seemed able to rise to their feet, yet I was scared as bony hands clawed at my trousers. I was pouring sweat and nauseated by the smell. ... The half-dead were lying on the dead to cushion their bones from the floor, which was a morass of faeces, urine, vomit and rotting flesh. ... The shaft of sunlight from the door fell on the ravaged face of a woman who might have been thirty or seventy. Her hollow eyes were pleading for help and as I knelt beside her, she placed her hand on her abdomen to show where it was hurting. It was covered with a sheet of dirty paper, which was adherent not to her skin but to her bowel ... The paper was now her abdominal wall as skin and muscle sloughed away, probably as the result of a simple burn. I was helpless and inadequate, I could not communicate, I had no dressings, not even an opiate to put her out of her misery. Dead bodies roused little emotion, it was the living dead that haunted me, human animals half-naked and dying, bereft of all hope and common dignity. I could not visualise them in the context of normal living yet they were still alive and breathing the same foul air as myself.'

Helen Bamber worked with Andrew Matthews as his assistant for two years, in the late 1970s. Their children became friends; their families spent holidays together; Bamber was close to him when his first daughter died, aged eight. Neither was aware that the other had been in Belsen in 1945; it was simply never mentioned. In 1995 Dr Matthews read about her work with torture victims in a newspaper, and the article spoke of her time at Belsen. He was dying by then, but they talked for three hours on the telephone. He may already have begun compiling the relentless collage – his memories of Belsen, press-cuttings about Auschwitz, Vietnam, Pol Pot's Kampuchea, stories about the use of systematic torture by governments – that his surviving daughter gave to Helen Bamber after his death. He wrote a preface to the album, his private meditation on twentieth-century horrors, describing his own father, 'a kind and gentle man', and his devotion to the Christian Bible. 'In the month of May 1945 I faced the stark reality of life for the first time. I emerged unscathed but my beliefs did not. There is no God either in spirit or substance, only a Devil and that Devil is mankind.'

*   *   *

As she reached her seventies Bamber found it no easier to understand what she had witnessed in Germany before she came of legal age. If the discovery of chance connections across her life allowed her to fill in gaps, it never offered anything like the tidy resolution of a narrative. Her time in Germany could never be closed off in that way. In 1994 she met a Belsen survivor at a conference in Dublin; they talked later at her hotel. He had been five years old when the war ended. He remembered a room in the hospital at Belsen. His mother had typhus; she was hot, moaning, convulsing, yet tormented by cold. Bamber described what happened according to the now elderly man, her voice almost incantatory:

'There was a window which was very high and [his mother] asked him to close this window because she was so desperately cold, and he couldn't reach it because it was so high, and she said go and call the nurse, go and call the nurse. He didn't want to do that, he wanted to stay with her, but in the end he went and the nurse came back with him and she went into the room first and came out and pushed the child away, saying you can't go in now, and he never saw his mother again. She had died in that moment he left her. This was the casual brutality of post-war situations; maybe it was one of our nurses who just pushed the child away, didn't allow him to mourn his mother. But that is how it was; and it brought back to me my own sense of guilt about situations where we had not been as careful as we might have been.

'This encounter did not bring any joy at meeting a survivor, but a lot of feelings about one's unthinking behaviour, and about witnessing and condoning such behaviour. There was so little time for mourning; yes, there was ritual, you had to be sensitive to that; and you had to be busy and efficient, but you can do that while detaching your own humanity from it. There is something about being the rescuer in situations like that, something terribly seductive, but when the chips are down and you've got a sensitive piece of work to do, you don't do it.'

People were indeed dying, no longer thousands a month, as in May; no longer even twenty a day, the rate at the end of June; but death was always present. She remembers an empty room in one of the blocks in which a woman had died that afternoon. It was already dark. The room was cold, stripped bare, there was grime on the floorboards and windows, and a naked bulb lit the woman's body lying on the floor, covered with a sheet. Her eyes were closed; a lighted candle stood near her head. Helen was asked, very seriously, to stay with the body. They had to go, perhaps to arrange the funeral, perhaps to mourn someone closer to them, and in Orthodox ritual a dead body cannot be left alone. She sat there for most of the night as the watcher for this dead stranger. 'They came back in the early hours of the morning. I had elected to do it, because of their need for me to do it. I don't remember being afraid, just the feeling of cold and death; as though it was part of someone else's ritual, yet I could understand its importance.

'My feeling about death, there, was almost of relief; there were times when I wanted people to die. We cling onto people nowadays; now I try so hard to stop people committing suicide. I'm not sure we had that feeling there. There was so much death; so much talk of death. I think that when memories came back, and the whole horror was open in a way that it was not when they were freezing and starving – I think that people didn't fight sometimes to live, when it all became clear.'

Beyond the practical business of distributing food and clothing, Helen Bamber was discovering a capacity and need to be open to people's experience of disaster. Perhaps this was her legacy from her parents, and she was beginning to serve out a lifetime sentence of needing too much to care. But listening to these survivors talk, as she now began to do, in the long monotonous evenings in the barracks, was not simply an expression of her own emotional harm. Her childhood had given her something good, after all. It made her available to a larger hurt – to the darkness left in the minds of those who had suffered cruelty. If she had not been prepared to take that unnecessary step during the first winter at Belsen, a step no one expected her to take, whatever need she had might have dissipated; exacting a lower price from her than the choice she actually made, perhaps, but also wasting her fear, idealism and anger.

She would be sitting in one of those chilly rooms, on a rough blanket on a bed, and the person she was talking to would suddenly begin to tell her what they had seen, or try to tell her what it was like. Often they were women. They would hold her with their eyes, and she said that she had to make a decision very early on: she could be brisk and sympathetic and matronly and evade the force of what she was hearing by pretending it could be resolved into a practical problem; or she could respond in a different way.

'Above all else,' she said, 'there was the need to tell you *everything,* over and over and over again. And this was the most significant thing for me, realizing that you had to take it all. They would need to hold onto you, and many of them still had very thin arms, especially the ones who had come from or gone back to the East and then dragged themselves to Belsen, hands almost like claws, and they would hold you, and it was important that you held them, and often you had to rock, there was a rocking, bowing movement, as you sat on the floor – there was very little to sit on – and you would hold onto them and they would tell you their story. Sometimes it was in Yiddish, and although I had learned some, it was as though you didn't really need a language. It took me a long time to realize that you couldn't really do anything but that you just had to hang onto them and that you had to listen and to *receive* this, as if it belonged partly to you, and in that act of taking and showing that you were available you were playing some useful role. There wasn't much crying at that time, it was much later that they began really to grieve; some people had got far beyond that and they might never again have been able to weep; it wasn't so much grief as a pouring out of some ghastly vomit like a kind of horror, it just came out in all directions.

'I remember some of the women were so angry about the death of their loved ones, and the fact that you could not do anything about that and they would be angry about things they still wanted, pounding the floor, sobbing, pulling their hair, banging their heads against the bed or the wall; a lot of real anger, and it could be frightening. And then sometimes it would be right to touch somebody, when you find that moment to take somebody, to hold them or to attempt to hold them. Sometimes it worked and you would sit with a person and, you would rock, literally rock with them in a kind of terrible grief and weeping. It was a weeping in which there were fewer tears than I see in the work now; the weeping seemed to come from their throats, from much lower down, a kind of sobbing. A terrible noise.

'I know other people who were there also talked to the survivors and tried to reach them; some did not. But I found it necessary to go in, to face it and allow myself to be targeted and not be contaminated, and simply to listen.'

Alison Wood, eighty-four years old and losing her sight, unable any longer to read and sitting in her dark study at the top of a mansion block near Hyde Park, could still see Helen Bamber as she was at twenty. The first observation Alison Wood made, before a question had been asked of her, was that 'Helen started listening to people a long time ago; she always had a tremendous listening quality'. The only non-Jew in the unit, Alison Wood said that not a day passed now without her being carried back to that time, and to what she had seen. She spoke of a 'vivacious, funny, pretty young woman; but with a huge degree of mature charm on top of that. All of it had depth. Like any very pretty woman, she could use that to get things done, but always with this very strong serious vein in it. And she was always finding personal things to contribute, as well as what she was officially there to do. Some of us had to detach ourselves from what was happening; some could never tolerate the closeness of some of the work with these extremely distressed people. But Helen was not afraid of feelings – it was a natural gift she had, and she found out how to use it. She could also handle the anger and fear of other young workers, and would somehow be the person that people gravitated towards; and this was in such contrast to her gaiety, her ability to fool in the hay at a picnic in the Hanoverian hills, like any other girl of twenty. I think she must have discovered an awareness in herself of her own needs, and her need to do that kind of work – to *be* that kind of person.'

Despite this testimony, Helen Bamber insisted that in her need to be receptive she was ordinary. Many of the women who worked at Belsen were sensitive to the devastation they felt around them. Eva Kahn-Minden, who worked in the Glyn Hughes Hospital (the Wehrmacht institution renamed for the senior doctor among the liberators), was given a locket by a woman for listening to her when she 'unburdened [herself] for the first time about the worst period of [her] life'. Senta Hirtz, who was in the second team that entered the Zone in July 1945, wrote that 'Our first move was to make contact ... to try to bring peace into a tormented mind', and she wrote of 'hungry people ... not only hungry for physical food but also hungry for love, hungry for life'. It was as though these women each discovered a hidden form of speech, unrecognized by army or state, or even by the relief committees. When Henry Lunzer, who was so devoted to the relief work, was asked about the possibility of talking to the survivors he said that he never had the time: 'That sort of thing I would have left to the members of the team.' His priority was to get food and clothing and medicine into the hands of the survivors. But Helen Bamber was crossing into a territory from which she would never be able to retreat – and never wish to leave.

What she heard was the unbearable counter-factual history, endlessly redrafted, of the survivor: people brooding on hypothetical conditions that they knew could never be fulfilled, even if time were reversible. ' "If only; if only I hadn't … if only he'd stayed with me, *I could have saved him*." It was almost as though they were blaming the person who was forcibly separated from them. There was a German Jewish woman, very beautiful, her hair had grown out – people did begin to become whole in appearance again uncannily quickly. She hadn't been married very long and she absolutely adored her husband. Her love and her desire for him were so incredibly strong that she couldn't get over the fact that he had been taken from her and had died. She felt she was the strong one, and if only he had stayed with her, she could have kept him alive. This was very common. It wasn't so much what happened to them, it was what they had not been able to prevent that they couldn't bear. As though they had a choice and as though the person who died had a choice.'

They expressed guilt over not sharing something that they had found, or fighting over a piece of food: 'The shame of that was quite over-whelming for a lot of people. As they got physically stronger the memory of some of the humiliation and degradation became very difficult.'

Moments of selfless bravery were described and shaped, held up as examples. Later, not in Belsen but at a place called Kaunitz, where some Hungarian and Polish Jews had been stranded, Bamber was told a story that seemed to have been passed on through Auschwitz and Belsen, about naked men and women being marched through a camp, perhaps after a 'selection'. As they passed each other guarded by SS men and women with dogs, a prisoner recognized her husband and made some gesture which her guards did not see, but he responded and was seen and as his group moved ahead the SS set the dogs on him. But the belief of those who witnessed his death was that he did not make a sound in order not to let her hear and to save her. 'There may have been heroic myth in this story, passed from mouth to mouth,' she says, 'at least a longing for heroism, but they did not cling to many myths – not like refugees I have worked with who have strong political beliefs or dogmas. The survivors of the camps had been singled out not because of what they believed in, but because of what they were; and so there was heroism, but it could never be a Sunday afternoon war-film kind of heroism. That was not an option for them.'

The young relief worker, like many others in that first winter after the war, tried her best to comprehend the scale of genocide. Whole countries were empty of Jews. This single act of racial murder has become such a familiar symbol of evil that it is difficult to think ourselves back to the moment when the very concept of its scale was being pieced together by individual minds. In those early months the infinite number of small acts of cruelty Bamber heard about seems to have marked her deeply. So many of the women told stories of violence in excess of the demands even of the exterminist machine.

Several of the women talked about Belsen itself. In particular, they described the women guards, led by Irma Grese. At the age of nineteen – the same age as Helen Bamber when she joined the JRU – this farm worker who had grown up near the women's concentration camp at Ravensbruck in Brandenburg, volunteered for the SS. She became an overseer at Auschwitz. By May 1944, before her twenty-first birthday, she was a despot over 30,000 women prisoners in Compound C at Birkenau, the labour camp that was part of the Auschwitz complex. They were mainly Hungarian Jews. Most of them died that summer and autumn: worked, starved, gassed. In early 1945, she came to Belsen with her Kommandant, Josef Kramer. She was known for her beatings, her habit of ordering prisoners to cross the wire and then having them shot, for the seeming incongruity of her blonde youthfulness and extreme violence.

At her trial she was asked to describe her whip. She did so with a kind of caressing pride, explaining that it had been made for her 'in the weaving factory in the camp': 'It was made out of cellophane … cellophane paper plaited like a pigtail. It was translucent like white glass.

organisations and congresses undertook in all seriousness and with a genuine optimism to ensure that all the horrors of the previous two decades should never recur.'

Hanna Levy-Hass had seen that new world amid the stink of Belsen: 'After a while everything will become clear and find its true form. The nightmare will pass and give way to emotions that are honest and pure. ... That time *will* come, *must* come, whoever is there to receive it. This is what matters.'

* * *

In the person of men like the SS doctor Fritz Klein, the Nazis turned medicine, the art of cure, into a science of murder. At his trial, Klein was involved in an exchange with the prosecutor which captures the blank nullity of his indifference, of technique devoid of moral content. He had been asked by his defence lawyer about his role in selections at Auschwitz:

> What happened to those people who were selected as unfit for work?
> – The doctor had to make a selection but had no influence on what was going to happen. I have heard that part of them were sent to the gas chambers.
> Was your work completed when you had divided the transports into fit for work and unfit?
> – Yes.

Klein had so tightly fused racialized politics and medicine in his daily practice that he could say to a Jew, a fellow-doctor and prisoner in Auschwitz, Dr Ella Lingens-Reiner: 'Of course I am a doctor and I want to preserve life. And out of respect for human life I would remove a gangrenous appendix from a diseased body. And the Jew is the gangrenous appendix in the body of mankind.'

This was 'killing as a therapeutic imperative', in Robert Jay Lifton's phrase. Even at Belsen, which was not designed as an extermination camp, the vile medical antics went on. An orderly called Karl Rothe murdered 200 people by injecting them with phenol, a procedure developed at Auschwitz by the SS doctors as their way of controlling typhus. The hospital itself became a site of murder.

Against this background the Glyn Hughes Hospital was a place of symbolic as well as practical importance. It contained at least 700 beds. Whole families would accompany the sick person and stay in the ward with them, urging them to recover, talking, praying, entertaining. Hospitals were no longer trusted places, and there was an instinctive insistence on moral support, on not leaving people alone to think themselves worse. For Bamber it was a revelation, a subversion of the normal authoritarian doctor–patient relationship and the ideal ultra-clean environment. 'Huge numbers of people would gather around a bed, and the nurses, who had been trained in the classic British way, found this terribly difficult. In 1945 doctors and nurses were supreme, they looked after the patients and it was not appropriate in their eyes to have masses of relatives cluttering up the wards. It was unhygienic, to them, but I began to see how desperately important it is if people are dying or distressed or seriously ill to have their relatives around them. Especially, of course, if the patients are children. Their relatives had to become part of the care. It was a necessity, but the nurses learned on their feet, and saw that there was no way they were going to keep people out, they were going to be there, they were going to be noisy, they were going to be interfering, they were going to be demanding, and the doctors didn't have any alternative but to allow this.'

Bamber was still drawing lessons from what she saw at Belsen when in the early 1960s she took part in a movement to allow mothers to stay with their children in hospital. What had become common sense in Belsen was later treated as revolutionary – the idea that medicine can have more than one correct form, and the idea that hospitals can be sociable as well as clean. Medicine perverted would remain for her an absolute contradiction; but it would take, as she discovered later, more than the Nüremberg trial of Nazi doctors (which began in December 1946) to break the insulation of medicine from human values.

* * *

The creation of a new world order is hard on those forced to carry the old inside them. The strategic imperatives of the geopolitical balance, its topographies of defence lines, blast radii and buffer zones were expressed in a language that found the concept of human rights almost meaningless. The whole of Eastern Europe had become Stalin's defensive wall, a field for slowing down any future invader of Russia. The US and its allies needed now to reconstruct Germany for the Cold War, using whatever human material came to hand – including less than recon-structed former servants of Hitler.

The British Military Government wished to end the story of Belsen, 'rounding off neatly the narrative of the war', as the historian Tony Kushner describes the official attitude to the liberation. It wanted to tidy up this enclave of 12,000-odd belligerent Jews – to define who they were, and where they were going – but not to send them to Palestine. Instead it found itself holding a protean thing which defied easy manipulation and could not be made to break cleanly with the past.

The numbers in the camp at Belsen fluctuated. People were repatriated to, or slipped out to return to, Poland in the early months, and found the anti-semitism of the Polish backwoods intact, particularly where peasants had taken over the houses of Jewish families. These would-be Polish Jews were turned back to the Allied Zones, where they were classed as 'non-repatriable'. Joanne Reilly notes that 250 a day were arriving in Berlin by December 1945. The British were not happy to see them return: in the careful prose of Norman Bentwich, 'at first they were held, under a strict interpretation of the rules, not to be entitled to the rations of the civil authority. They had to be fed by what the regular members of the camp and the Relief Unit could supply.' In other words, the army would not feed them. The British authorities set the ration strength of the camp at the level of 2 July 1946, and refused to register any new DPs. But Belsen, with its Search Bureau run by former camp inmates, its thousands of witnesses to what might have happened to vanished parents or children, and its living political community, still drew people from all over the Zone.

For the Relief Unit volunteers, caught in the human intersection between the shifting plates of global conflict, it was not easy to be pragmatic. Some of the people who came to them for help had covered four hundred miles across three zones of occupation – Russian, American and British. Some had walked all the way from Poland. The Kielce pogrom of July 1946, in which forty-one Jews were murdered, was the old East European horror – accusations of ritual murder, hysterical mobs, and a government (this time communist) refusing to lift a finger.

Helen Bamber was called out to see one man who had found his way to Eilshausen that summer. 'He had walked for so long that his feet were in the most *appalling* state, it was as though his feet were no longer like human feet, they were lumps of meat and the shoe was somehow part of the flesh of each foot. I tried to clean his feet and help him as far as I could. And I remember the look on his face: I've never forgotten it; the expression was one of pity. For me. Not scornful pity, he was actually sorry for me having to do this.'

At least on one occasion, faced with the official desire to draw a line under history, she began to founder. 'Once I think I really wanted obliteration, I wanted the heavens to open up and take us all. A group from Poland had turned up where they shouldn't have been; and somebody had asked us to mediate. These people had come in starving, their feet rotting, and there were about fifty of them. Henry asked me to go. The people were being held in some cold and grim huts, and I had to try and bargain and bully for food. And the British officer in charge said to me, "As far as I am concerned, these people don't exist. They haven't got the proper documents, they have no business to be wandering about here." As though to say the way I'm going to deal with it is to pretend they're not here. I stared at him, and it was then I thought I can't go on. But eventually I struggled on and he agreed to give them some food, but he *stormed* with anger, and he suddenly shouted at me, "My God, these people must have done something terrible to deserve this." But we got the food, and then the Joint, the US Jewish relief organization, gave us some more. You had to plead and to improvise, you knew that. But at that moment I was nearly overwhelmed.'

Authority had to make itself immune to the pathos of people searching for what was gone. Bamber recalls the Zone as a landscape of ruins, of people travelling on the tops of trains, on foot, walking from one country to another, a fluid and chaotic reality, an ominous atmosphere. The former inmates were so used to avoiding officials and rules as a way of evading death that they would set off on devious routes, ending up anywhere but the place they set out for, and this when permits were needed to leave the camp, to go to a town, to cross the Zone. From the viewpoint of the British military, it was like watching a series of random walks, people taking their direction from some internal roulette-wheel instead of a reliable compass.

In June 1946, attempts to confine the DPs to the camp under curfew became increasingly irksome. They asserted their right to walk outside the wire. Henry Lunzer's report to the JCRA (Jewish Committee for Relief Abroad) captures the strange atmosphere of orderly behaviour and lurking violence that his assistant remembers. When the crowd moved, Lunzer noted, there was some shooting in the air, and 'the Public Security Officer, Belsen, took a hose and proceeded to direct a fortunately weak stream of water at the crowd'. Germans gathered on a bank outside the main gate jeered at the DPs, who then 'surged forward, stormed the gates, opened them and passed through. They amazingly and immediately reformed into an orderly procession and marched quietly up the main road surrounding the camp. Prior to this the Public Security Officer had his pistol removed by the crowd and efforts are being made to trace and return it.' The crowd then broke the gates at the other end of the camp and, 'having proved that nothing could keep them behind barbed wire dispersed to their homes'.

*   *   *

No event caught the inseparability of the desire to rebuild civilization and the need for retribution better than the trial of the Belsen camp guards which opened in September 1945. The two impulses could not be set straight. *The Trial of Josef Kramer and Forty-Four Others* was the first Western attempt to make Nazis answerable for acts which were defined, in an older and barely appropriate language, as 'war crimes'. In the dock were the meanest grades of killer. The tribunal was, perhaps, more typical of the problem of how to judge mass murder than the later Nuremberg trials. No Prussian Junkers or icily repentant architects were in the courtroom at Lüneburg. None of the defendants had ever made policy about anything; they had followed orders to the last, even though the machine they served had broken down. By the end they were administrators of plague: guilty of 'brutal apathy', in the words of historian Paul Kemp. But they were not passive agents. Small people given the unlimited licence of racial superiority and the power of death over prisoners, they were volunteers for eugenic purification. Josef Kramer had been a concentration camp guard from the very beginning of the system in 1933: it was his career. He had worked at Dachau, Mauthausen, and Natzweiler; and in the summer of 1944, he took

charge of the gassing complex at Birkenau to put around 200,000
Hungarian Jews to death – the last industrialized massacre of the Final
Solution. His staff was made up of people like Irma Grese, the ex-
dairymaid; Herta Ehlert, a former bakery assistant who worked at
Ravensbruck and then at Auschwitz; and Karl Francioh, in charge of the
kitchen at Belsen, who shot prisoners as they stooped to pick up potato
peelings outside his window.

Yet the trial conformed scrupulously to British legal norms. It had to;
and the transcripts therefore make weird reading. Law confronted its
utter negation, and allowed it its best defence. First, the prosecution
outlined its case; the rescuers described what they saw; and a few of the
ex-prisoners were allowed to give evidence.

The defence arguments were made by clever dutiful men, British
barristers in uniform: they 'put it to the court' that standards of cruelty
and ill-treatment were relative; that it was wrong to impose our
standards on others; that the Wehrmacht did not dig latrines in the field,
so how could we expect them to do so in the difficult conditions of late
1944 with so many prisoners on their hands; that German standards of
privacy were different from our own, and who were we to judge? It
would not be right to expect too much 'in these matters': 'Nobody was
going to deny that there were beatings at Belsen; but ... to a certain
extent, the language of a concentration camp is blows.' The legal mind
that learns so well to argue both sides of any case here reached a
disturbing ethical frontier.

The SS men's counsel applied to have their clients tried separately;
disputed the linkage of Auschwitz and Belsen (Kramer and the others
were charged with murder and neglect at both camps, in order to show
that what happened at Belsen was not the result of circumstances outside
their control). They argued that 'the charge does not disclose an offence'.
They seemed, at least on the evidence of the printed record, sometimes
to speak as though they were at the Cambridge Union, though there may
have been no other way for them to get through it than by treating the
trial as a performance.

The defence hinted that Jews had brought their sufferings at Belsen on
themselves. The lawyer for Kramer, Major Winwood, felt able to argue
that 'the type of internee who came to these concentration camps was
low, and had very little idea of doing what they were told, so that the

control of these internees was a great problem'. This partly explained, he suggested, the sanitary atrocity that was Belsen: 'Amongst them there were people who naturally performed their natural functions where they felt inclined.' Irma Grese, questioned by her counsel, Major Cranfield, eagerly agreed with this line of thought: 'Later on when I had twenty or thirty thousand they behaved like animals, when food was a bit more scarce. ... it was just as if the prisoners thought that any place was good enough for a latrine.'

The lawyers 'put the case' forcibly that Kramer and the others were constrained by a totalitarian system in which the Führer's word was the only law. Kramer was a pawn while 'waves of circumstance beat around him'. Himmler was the real culprit, who unfortunately could not be in the courtroom since he was buried nearby on Lüneburg Heath, following his suicide in May.

It was the necessary, patient absurdity of doing justice. Colonel Smith, leader of the defence team, declared in his closing speech that British justice would gain 'one of those great decisions which from time to time have adorned our legal history' were the court to 'uphold the law as it governs at the time of the act'. It would 'go down in history as an act of courageous upholding of the dignity of the law which has been so severely shaken by the events of these terrible years'.

The court decided not to accept the honour proffered to it. Kramer, along with Dr Klein, Irma Grese and eight others, was found guilty and hanged on 12 December 1945.

Helen Bamber remembers the execution day as one of hard frost and silence. The local people did not stir. She did not hear any German refer to the trial or the executions, ever: 'That blank denial of responsibility. It was as if it wasn't happening: nothing to do with us, after all.'

The denial was not always silent. At Lunzer's request she saw an American woman from the Joint, who had just arrived in Germany and was visiting the British Zone. They met in a canteen run by the British army in Celle. The old town has dozens of timber-framed houses with oriel windows and high gables from the sixteenth and seventeenth centuries, their plaster surfaces painted in bright reds, greens, and pale yellows between the black edges of wooden supporting beams. On the first-floor lintel-timber each house has an inscription from the Bible picked out in gold lettering, a pious motto of self-congratulation, often linking trade and religion: '*Wer Got Vertrauet, der hat Wohl gebauet.*' Who Trusts in God, Has Built Well. Outside a scale-maker's shop, pious moderation in all things was (and still is) recommended: '*Die Zeit, ob gut ob schlecht, sorg, das der Balken waagerecht.*' Whether times are good or bad, he who keeps the right balance will flourish.

Outside the window the two young women had a lorry and driver waiting to take them into Belsen afterwards. Helen was talking about the camp and the survivors, and the waitress said to her, in German, 'I don't know what all this talk is about Belsen camp. We knew nothing about a camp.' Helen lost her temper and rose to hit the woman, and was pulled back by the American. 'That was what you could put your hand out and feel: "We've got our problems, we're starving, our homes are bombed, we've had a terrible war, what is all this stuff about the Jews?"'

*   *   *

Even the diplomatic Norman Bentwich, vice-chair of the Jewish Committee for Relief Abroad, described the atmosphere of the DP camps as 'often stormy and fantastic'. Helen Bamber was tested by the demands of confused, bereft people who took out their anger and grief on those nearest to them: 'Nobody was liked; nobody was good enough; nobody could do enough. You started at an enormous disadvantage. We were often the target of anger, and it was tempting not to listen to what they were saying as a result.' The Jewish Relief Unit's ambivalence – its impulse to solidarity undermined by its need to maintain correct relations with the British state – did not help its young volunteers.

Many of the survivors still lived in an anguish of uncertainty. The Belsen Search Bureau tried to compile lists of the living and their families. Bamber remembers that 'they would write the names of their relatives on these small pieces of what I think of as cigarette paper, this very thin paper, and they would always have them in their hands, giving them to you, pleading for you to make connections.'

The displaced persons had become what the anonymous writer of an appeal for the JCRA called 'grey ghosts at the doorway of the world'. Living in suspended time, the Jews at Belsen were told that they were no different from any other victims of the Nazis, and British attitudes hardened. Isaac Levy, the army Rabbi, was told by the Director of Civil

Affairs for the Military Government that 'emphasis should be placed on a Jew's political nationality rather than on his race or religious persuasion. ... Jews in the DP camps are treated in the same way as DPs of other nationalities. German Jews found in concentration camps are treated in the same way as other inmates. ... After their return home these Jews are treated as other Germans.'

The leadership of the Jewish Agency in Palestine knew that its moment had come. In the camps, many East European Jews who had ignored the Zionist call to emigrate before the war now demanded the right to go to Palestine. Already in August 1945 the Welfare Department of the British Army's Jewish Brigade – made up largely of Palestinian Jews – had written a passionate memorandum on emigration: 'Those who were persecuted because they were Jews have the right to live as Jews. The continued evasion of the recognition of the Jews' distinct national identity is in stark contradiction to their tragic reality. ... The White Paper of 1939 [which strictly limited Jewish immigration to the Mandate] ... must be repealed and the gates of Palestine opened wide to the hundreds of thousands whose only hope for a rebuilt dignified existence lies in that direction.'

This was the profoundly modern version of the ancient dream: the reinvention of a 'national home' out of the wreckage of European genocide. In the diary he kept at Belsen the Dutch Jew Abel Herzberg gave unsurpassable expression to the idea of history as national revelation. On the feast of 'rejoicing in the law', Simchat Torah, in October 1944, the Eastern European Jews danced in their huts. 'Tunefully and passionately and with an indomitable rhythm they sang prayers for the reconstruction of Jerusalem. Once again ... religion and nationalism are inseparably interwoven. The idea bound to politics, the principle of eternity to the opportunity of the moment.'

Helen Bamber, as a sympathetic witness, saw the new state becoming real in the demonstrations, the newspapers, the posters and placards, and the agitation of the DP leaders. The news from Palestine was of struggle and gathering tension; the Arabs rejected partition, and war seemed inevitable. But Bamber could see that support for the state was also enabled by the exclusion of other possibilities for emigration. President Truman had no wish to ask the US Senate for an increase in admission quotas for Jews, as Bamber was well aware. 'At first there was a wave of compassion and sympathy and outrage – British soldiers were outraged and Germans were dragged to look at it and so on – but over time, this changed. There was nowhere for them to go. None of them wanted to go back to their countries of origin, especially after the end of 1945. Early on I had the sense that the majority of them wanted to go to America or to Britain; these were the countries that held out the hope of a democratic culture, a mixture of nationalities, the possibility of work. But they couldn't. The American quota system was rigid; in Britain you had to be sponsored by a relative, and that meant they had to afford to keep you and house you. It was a stalemate.'

The new nation was to be a new country in every respect, cleansed of the old vulnerabilities of the Diaspora. From the barrack squares of Belsen, with Lüneburg Heath stretching away to the north, a place of sur-render and death, the Arabs of Palestine were invisible. The immemorial was entering history, and it would create new injustices, but that seemed unthinkable to the survivors in the urgent desire for reparation.

No one embodied the demand for freedom from 'the curse of national anonymity' more fiercely than Josef 'Yossel' Rosensaft, the Polish Jew who became the undisputed leader of the Belsen DPs. The British, how-ever, did not recognize his committee as legitimate representative of the DPs until 1947. He had 'an intense energy and imperious will for self-determination', wrote Bentwich. 'He was no bigger than me,' Bamber recalled, 'very dynamic, pushy and feisty.' His voice was memorable: slightly high-pitched, carrying, charged with emotion, especially if he was angry, 'which was not infrequent'. His group called itself the Central Committee of Liberated Jews and was unyielding in its refusal to accept anything less than recognition of the DPs as Jews, and of their cohesion, and their right to emigrate. Rosensaft and the other leaders 'were not easy people', in her recollection, but he had charisma and pugnacity; 'a real *macher*'. Bamber says he was a mesmerizing speaker. Photographs show him drawn up on his platform, back straight, hands resting on his jacket pockets, head arched as though projecting his voice out among the flags and banners rising around him with their slogans: 'We will outlive you, Bevin!' 'Blood on Your Hands!' Bentwich summed up Rosensaft's attitude: 'Every Jew worthy of the name should be sitting on his packed trunk ready to leave at any moment.'

By February 1946, the British had conceded permits for emigration to a limited number of people. The rest stayed where they were. And all the time, in a steady secret outflow, illegal parties left for journeys over the Alps to the ships waiting in Italian ports.

* * *

The DPs created the life of a town in Belsen while they were forced to remain there. They had schools, workshops and religious centres. Many of them were artisans and small merchants, and their workshops were ingenious: from bomb casings, tank armour, or tin scavenged from the fields as raw material, they made tools and ornaments; a locksmith trained apprentices; they had tailors, corset-makers and cobblers. A technician made artificial teeth. A newspaper, *Undzer Shtime* (Our Voice), was published in Yiddish. The first book published in the liberated camp was a list of the survivors with the Hebrew title *Sheerit Ha'pleitah*, The Surviving Few.

Belsen also had a theatre, which could be a ritual in the dark. Bamber recalls a revue in Yiddish satirizing the military government, a Sholem Aleichem play, a *shtetl* farce. The atmosphere was uproarious, with the audience talking and intervening during the play. But then, she remembers, they would perform a scene of a family at table and the whole audience would become totally still and silent. 'The family portrayed would be obviously an orthodox family; and then the Nazis would come in. And they would drag or kill the mother; and the power of the scene turned around the abuse of the mother, and the break-up of the family. The depiction of the Nazis was realistic and violent. The sense of the disaster about to happen could be felt in that hall. Nothing explicit about the aftermath was shown, as I remember it. I have never seen anything so effective, despite the crudity of the stage and the performance. It was raw and so close to the experience of the audience. There was never any applause. Each time it was like a purging.'

* * *

During her time in Germany she did not take any leave. Rudi Bamberger wrote to her, and she tried to tell him about the world she had found, but it was too far from ordinary experience and too near his own to make communication easy. He may have had enough of terror: he had seen his father murdered; his mother and grandmother had, he now knew, died at Majdanek; and despite that he had been made a prisoner, a deportee and an enemy alien. He had turned his back on Germany. It could be said that he simply wanted to live, and forget about human cruelty as much as possible. He was beyond engagement with her need to pay attention precisely to this, but she loved Rudi enough to wish that she had his comradeship as well as his support.

Two young German Jews, both drivers and fixers for the unit, both wild and damaged, were close to her. She wanted Rudi to write to them in German, to become a normal influence on them in the charged atmosphere of the Zone. One of the boys claimed to be out at night look-ing for Germans to kill. Helen tried to get him to see that this kind of justice was self-cancelling. She said that you could not really tell with this boy where truth and fantasy diverged. He promised, at least, to stop for her sake. But Rudi could not bring himself to write to him or his friend. Helen began to feel that her life in Germany would never be translated back into a language that those she loved could understand. She spoke of this later as 'a disjointing', as though it was a hidden fracture.

She met Israel Klein while she was feeling so detached from her previous life. He was an officer of the Jewish Brigade, based in Belgium but operating inside the Zone, although the military viewed the activities of the Brigade with profound suspicion, seeing its members as recruiters for the Haganah and agents of illegal emigration.

One of the unit's jobs was to help locate Jewish DPs and bring them into the network of supply and organization. Through Klein, she heard about a group of young women at a village called Kaunitz. They had been slave labourers making grenades and machine parts. With food, their bodies had begun to discover the energy and fertility that many of them had never experienced. They were suddenly awash with sexuality, although still deprived and often hungry. They were also surrounded by young soldiers.

Klein drove Helen Bamber to Kaunitz in a PU. The camp was a series of requisitioned houses; she recalls a big muddy yard. Electricity was minimal. The toilets were out of her nightmares – her fastidious dis-comfort with them is still obvious. 'It was a dreadful place.' (Other observers, it has to be said, thought it was relatively decent: Rabbi Isaac Levy described the camp as 'the best in the whole British Zone'.)

Helen remembers many of the women as beautiful, once their hair grew and their periods came back after malnutrition stopped. 'Their beauty made it so difficult: when people emerged from the chrysalis of ugliness they presented at first, it brought home the loss more acutely. Ugliness is easier to deal with – it separates you, it is a protection, but these young women had both life and unutterable loss.'

When Israel Klein took her to Kaunitz she was impressed that a man should be so concerned about the vulnerability of young women; it was unusual enough to touch her. She spoke to them about menstruation and sex, and how it was not a good idea to be impulsive. She talked about guarding themselves, or at least making choices, 'because there was a wildness in them that was not going to be helped by going to bed with every British soldier. We were trying to give them some sort of pride.' These women were a few years younger than she was herself, and she felt like their aunt.

Klein was, she says, 'a lovely man'. She felt very protected by him, which was (and is) uncommon for her in her relations with men. 'He had a combination of audacity and courage and a depth of humanity which was compelling.' They didn't have a sexual relationship, but they were very close and they might easily have become lovers.

She began to visit Kaunitz as often as she could. Her work there did not correspond to any official definition of her job. Henry Lunzer, asked about Kaunitz half a century later, could not recall the camp's existence, but he did not seem to mind where his assistant was as long as the work was done and his communications were kept clear. Inevitably, she found herself talking to the women about what they had experienced. Klein also knew, she said later, that their value there was as much about listening and talking as in the giving of practical help. 'Other people could probably have done a better job than I did. I didn't have any real skill, but I did spend a lot of time with them, and I became very much part of them. I think I may have been better with them than I was with anyone at Belsen: they were a much younger, more cohesive group and it was easier to establish a relationship with them.'

The high holidays were moments of celebration, but also of anger and grief. Others who worked with survivors noticed the tension before a festival. The nurse Eva Kahn-Minden, who worked at Belsen, was reminded later, when she was looking after young survivors of the camps at a TB hospital in England, of the compulsion to remember lost relations: 'If I think back on that terrible tension in Bergen-Belsen every year at the festival times I get afraid. It always was as though the worst of their past and the best-of-their-joy-at-being-here met, and no-one was quite his normal self. It was quite explosive.'

Helen Bamber went with Israel Klein to the first Passover after liberation at Kaunitz. Getting the right eggs and meat and suitable flour for matzos – the traditional unleavened bread – was extremely difficult, but they appeared somehow, probably from the black market. The irony of the Exodus story, of the Passover with its memories of flight and escape, hung over that derelict field in Germany: 'and when I see the blood, I will pass over you, and the plague shall not be upon you to destroy you, when I smite the land of Egypt' (Exodus 12:13).

She found it impossible to think of a protecting God; but she was moved, she said, by the young women's determination to celebrate. 'The meal was laid out on big tables in the open, and we came late, and I can remember how pleased they were that we had come. I had to be at the end of the table, and because it had already started and the tables were in a narrow alley between huts they had to lift me over the tables, right over them like the dormouse at the tea party, and they thought this was the funniest thing they had ever seen. There was surprising laughter among these women; we would dance and sing with them, and enjoy food. I loved being with them.'

For a short time she and Klein became an unlicensed team, doing whatever they felt was necessary. She knew that he was up to his neck in clandestine emigration to Israel. She did not ask him too much, just as Henry Lunzer had to hold himself aloof from actions seen as hostile to the British state. Even after half a century, Bamber is reticent about admitting any link between the JRU and illegal emigration. But according to Alison Wood, Helen would smooth the way for Jewish Brigade soldiers trying to get into Belsen, using her charm on, and devising plausible explanations for the British officers, and arranging beds and transport for the Brigade when they needed it. Occasionally, she could not help being more directly involved. 'We heard about a young woman who was dying of TB in a German hospital. We went in a truck, and when we got there were confronted by a very hostile German doctor. All the other patients in the hospital were German. He didn't want us to see this woman, and we took an instant dislike to him. We did get to her, of course. I think she was the thinnest person I had ever seen. She was *obviously* dying, and her arms were like little sticks, the skin quite mauve. She said that she wanted to go to Belgium, where her brother was, and to die there. A week later Israel said he wanted to go back to the hospital to see her, to see if she was still there. I said OK, we'll go. We took some food and blankets. It was quite late in the evening; he said come on, let's not bother with the doctor, and we ran up the stairs. She must have guessed what was going to happen because she put up her arms as we went in and Klein picked her up and we went out with him carrying her and put her in the truck, and he drove her to Belgium.'

Bursts of irrational violence still took her by surprise. On May Day night in 1946, a warm summer night in a village hall, she cannot remember where, a concert was held. It was her birthday: she was twenty-one years old. A quartet played Beethoven. It must have been strange, afterwards, coming out with the exacting form of the music still in her head, knowing that the Eurasian plain stretching off in the dark was in ruins. On this particular night, their British driver had disappeared. A lorry with a German driver was available, and they set off on a bad road. Suddenly he seemed to go berserk, and drove the truck off the road, bumping wildly over the hard furrows of a ploughed field. She was thrown out of her seat, her head banging on the floorboards as he jerked the wheel. Her three male companions grabbed the driver, one holding him in an armlock while another pulled at the wheel. It was never clear whether the driver was maddened by hatred, or simply crazy.

She spent weeks in hospital with concussion and other injuries. While she was lying there Klein was ordered back to Palestine. He tried to see her, she heard later, but he was not allowed to come. She believes that he died in Israel, fighting in the war of independence, but it is as though the relationship that formed and crackled in that highly charged atmosphere could not have survived outside it. She let it go.

*　　*　　*

The Jewish Committee for Relief Abroad was suspicious of the nervous intensity that the work in Germany demanded, and critical of Henry Lunzer and his staff for identifying too closely with the survivors. The people he had to answer to were, in his view, 'typical Victorian do-gooders. They were convinced that the only way was to go on sending clothes and food. This was not the main problem. They had no idea, really, what was going on.' Helen Bamber agreed: 'They thought that if you provided lorries and supplies everything would be all right. They could not understand the enormity of the situation, the lines we had to cross, the eruptions and clashes between relief workers and DPs, between them and the military and among themselves.'

Lunzer's relationship with the committee in London seems to have been worsened by his perceived failure to provide regular reports (and perhaps his assistant's frequent absences in Belsen and Kaunitz did not help). His principals wanted an orderly, legal operation; to know what was being spent, and who was receiving supplies: they wanted information. Captain A.C. Jacobs, the committee's secretary, wrote to Lunzer on 28 March 1946: 'I find that so many of the things which we ask you to do are ignored and questions unanswered.' On 17 August, Leonard Cohen told him, in a letter of bruising candour: 'I do not always see eye to eye with you, but I have told you this before and I will tell you again quite bluntly and without reserve that until the Committee has someone better to put in your place you are entitled to and so far as I am concerned will receive the Committee's confidence and support.'

Other letters between committee members speak of zeal, anxiety and strain, of tension between Lunzer and Rose Henriques, of his exclusion from important meetings; a stand-off between the energetic fixer and the cautious trustee, and a tragic waste of good people's time. Henry Lunzer, over half a century later, is generous in his estimate of his critics: he says simply that they were very well meaning; that they raised a lot of money; and that without them the British Jewish relief effort would not have existed.

But in 1946 the lack of clarity between him and his superiors could have only one outcome. Meanwhile, he and his team, including his assistant, continued to make things happen. He heard about a fully equipped Red Cross train lying idle somewhere in Holland. 'I got it,' he recalled laconically.

Bamber had to do something useful with this train. Many of the children in Belsen and elsewhere in the Zone had tuberculosis. The Glyn Hughes Hospital had no specialist facilities, but a sanatorium in Davos, across the border in Switzerland, had doctors, equipment and fine air, and the Joint made sure it was available. All that Bamber had to do was to get a few dozen sick children out of Belsen, across the British and American Zones and into the neutral state. She had to have certificates proving that the children were ill; that they had permission to leave Belsen; permits from the military authorities to cross the British Zone; permits for the US Zone; and of course, written promises that the children would not be a burden on the Swiss state. She also had to contend with the suspicion that the train was a ruse, to get the youngsters out of Europe. Few of the children wanted to have their chests X-rayed, because they felt that if they were known to have tuberculosis they would never be able to emigrate; but the nurses were infinitely patient. It was an auspicious event: a re-enacting of an operation that had been made obscene; a railway journey to cure instead of murder.

Two or three children were in Düsseldorf, and the military authorities there were refusing to give them the necessary papers. They needed permission from Berlin. Attempts to solve the problem were met with obfuscation and masterly inactivity: the phones were down; the major was out.

Helen was driven to Düsseldorf and lobbied the man who had the authority to sign the papers. She tried persuasion; she tried anger. She kept coming back. He was, she said, 'like a fine piece of timber, good looking, bland, completely indifferent'. When it grew dark, she went looking for a place to stay.

She found members of the Jewish *gemeinde*, the local community organization, living in a damaged house, about eight mainly middle-aged or elderly men and women, a significant fraction of the surviving Jews of Düsseldorf. She could not get through the front door, which was still blocked by rubble, so she had to climb up a long ladder through a second-storey window and all greetings were conducted at the top of the swaying ladder, shaking hands, smiling, perched above the wreckage of the Westphalian capital. She was giddy with vertigo.

That night she slept in her uniform on the landing. At breakfast the next day her hostess entered the room where they were gathered. She held a tin aloft, keeping a napkin over it, and then whipped it off and they smelled the warm yeasty smell of freshly cooked bread. She had found some white flour and baked white bread, which was such a rare event that it was a celebration. The English girl was honoured.

Bamber went back and spent all day at the military government office arguing, begging, pleading; nothing worked. 'The man was a bastard, he really was a bastard, and he was not going to budge an inch. The train was arranged and all I needed was permission from Berlin to let these people go for treatment. I even tried flirting with him. But I happened to overhear that one of their officers wanted to go to Berlin for some very important meeting, and he had no transport. I believe that I got the permission I needed by giving this guy a lift to Berlin. My driver Heinz was very streetwise. I told him, "Drive like hell." We went at an outrageous pace and the chap in the back was bounced about like a cork.'

The X-rays of darkened lungs were packed carefully, and the children filled the train, dressed in sheepskin coats and gloves supplied from the Joint's wealthy wardrobe. The adults stood along the platform at Hanover station while the children crowded the windows for the photographs. Helen Bamber is dwarfed by the height of the coaches, smiling like a small plump cat.

Modern bureaucracies, especially the great state organizations, run on a logic of efficiency and internal rationality; that is why in the wrong hands they are capable of anything. The Holocaust was administered like this. In the post-war world certain people, troubled nuisances, took it on themselves to obstruct the operation of these great machines that would now and then like to get away with murder. By the time she left Germany, Bamber was becoming grit in the wheel; she was learning to slow it down.

* * *

There was, for her, a moment of exhausted anger, of astonishment that things had gone so far, and she knew that she had to leave.

A man hung around the fringes of the unit at Eilshausen. He had papers allowing him to live in the British Zone but he seemed to go back and forth between Western Germany and the East without challenge. Bamber assumed he was a smuggler. When she got a message from her Bader cousins in Palestine asking for her help in locating another relative who, they thought, might be dying of cancer in Poland, she turned to this black-market operator for help, though there was a frantic damaged quality to his cheerful bonhomie. After his return — he had found no trace of her distant relation — he came to find her. She was working in her office, and was alone in the house. It became obvious that he thought she owed him more than thanks. When she resisted he put his hands around her throat. She was up against her desk, the man's fingers cutting her breath, when Alison Wood and Henry Lunzer arrived in the hallway.

But the man stayed in the room and when Henry came in a few moments later she said nothing. She still cannot understand why; some combination of guilt and fear. Soon afterwards the man left the house and she carried on as though nothing had happened.

Norman Bentwich and Leonard Cohen came on a tour of inspection of the unit, then returned to Eilshausen and told Henry Lunzer to pack his bags. He said later, 'They threw me out. To this day I don't understand the real reason that they got rid of me.' He had been meaning, he said, to ask an old friend of his who was connected to the committee, as though it had happened last month and not over half a century ago. The correspondence held in the Wiener Library in London rehearses the break painfully. At this distance it seems like a clash of styles that got out of hand, and was also, as Joanne Reilly argues, a consequence of unclear political guidance for the workers in the field, who were expected to look both ways at once. Perhaps a further clue to what happened is contained in a book by Norman Bentwich published ten years later. Of Simon Bloomberg, Lunzer's replacement as Director, he says that he had 'the important qualification from his colonial experience that he knew the official mind and could talk on agreed terms with the military and civil authorities ... the British body had to improvise, and put into directing positions those who had many virtues, infinite devotion, and the common touch, but just lacked that official touch.'

Two months after Henry Lunzer left Germany in late November 1946, and before his successor arrived, Helen Bamber also left for home. It was the worst winter of the twentieth century, with rumours of starving wolves driven into the woods around Berlin, of cannibalism, of trains arriving from Poland full of frozen corpses in unheated carriages. The cold bit through deep layers of clothing; at Belsen there never seemed to be enough wood or coal to keep the barracks warm. The darkness and cold were depressing; nothing seemed to move without great effort, and the situation of the displaced persons to move not at all.* Bamber said once that she felt younger at the age of seventy than she did then, on her way back to England.

*The British authorities finally began to issue certificates for Palestine to the Jews of Belsen in March 1947 – between 400 and 500 a month were promised. Most of the displaced persons had left Germany by the time Israel declared its independence in May 1948.

Although she was a better diplomat than Henry Lunzer, she too would always lack 'that official touch'. She felt utterly empty; incapable of seeing beyond her reunion with Rudi Bamberger, or of relating what she had done to the rest of her life. 'I hadn't done it for Rudi; it couldn't mean the same to him. And I don't think I went to Germany because I felt I was doing the bidding of my father: I did it for myself. And I did it because the truth is that the only way I can survive is to find a way of not being overwhelmed, and to do something while I can, work with some instead of despairing about them all. And that's all really that I've ever been able to do.'

4

THE DISCIPLINE OF LOVE

It seemed to him that peace held a strange and unfamiliar aspect and that war had been the more obvious and natural condition. Throughout the entire journey ... he had grown accustomed to the idea of the sovereignty of certain death in Europe. All of a sudden, at a frontier, ordinary life began.

Joseph Roth, *The Silent Prophet*

The journey back was miserable: the slow train through Germany, the crude new buildings amid the wreckage. Calais still looked like a war-zone. The ship pitched in a freezing wind which kept Bamber off the deck as it crossed the Channel. Refugees unused to sea travel were sick around the hard wooden benches and in all the toilets.

She would like to have left the winter behind her, but the weather, indifferent to human needs, was as cold in Britain as it had been on Lüneburg Heath. The London traffic moved at walking pace in the snow and ice; the Thames was sluggish and close to freezing, in the harshest winter that any but the oldest people could remember. She was exhausted, yet in the kind of self-punishing ritual that depression requires, she had asked that no one come to meet her at Waterloo. She carried her giant kitbag onto a bus going north of the river. It was not a good start.

She noticed things about her uninvaded country that had become strange to her: the massive Victorian cityscape, its integrity damaged but hardly diminished by the bombs; the number of cars; and things that were missing, like women pushing handcarts loaded with bricks, and children begging. The soldiers lacked the tense careful look of men from an occupying power, and the people walked upright; the cold made them grin.

From Charing Cross Road she took a taxi to her mother's house in Brent, out by the North Circular Road. Her mother had never forgiven her for going to Germany: she must have been able to guess the kind of future that such a choice threatened. No ambitious mother wants her only child to grow up saving humanity. The ballet classes had been wasted; her husband seemed to have won. She still hoped her daughter might at least marry well, but Rudi Bamberger, whom Helen had taken home before the war ended, would not do at all: this witty *luftmensch* was not her idea of a good match, a Hampstead house, solid furniture and seats at the Royal Opera. She let him know it, too. When the young couple returned late at night she would shout abuse at them from the top of the stairs. Marie Balmuth had been cheated by life, and her daughter's was the worst betrayal of all. 'She was an enormous romantic, and from then on there was a resentment between us that could never be repaired. She was hysterical when I went to stay with Rudi at a country pub after I returned. I tore down her illusions ruthlessly and almost revelled in it, as children do. I felt guilty about her for a long, long time.'

To escape her mother Helen went to the flat Rudi had found in Sumatra Road, a street of double-fronted Edwardian houses converted into cheap accommodations on the seedy edge of Hampstead.

The grip of companionship and erotic release was enough at first to overcome her feeling of defeat, and even her distance from him. He cared as deeply for her as for his own lost family; his politeness was impeccable, and because she could not yet talk about what she had seen and heard, for a time what he gave was beautifully enough. She needed, she said, to be with someone who knew what had happened, and he could give her the almost wordless comfort of not having to be told too much. The barriers could only be felt when she did want to talk: that 'disjointing' she had begun to feel in Germany was slowly working beneath the tight skin of their understanding.

He wanted, she said, nothing that could be taken from him, other than her. The past was there, where nothing could be done about it; the future was unthinkable, and could only be faced by running into it burdened as lightly as possible. He had found work as 'manager' of an anarchist co-operative making lampshades: all those bomb-damaged sitting rooms would need redecoration. The job seemed unlikely to weigh him down for long.

The flat in Sumatra Road was a roof over their heads: it was only home as a place to be away from. They tried not to have too many possessions that were not held ironically. The house reeked of damp and of rotten brick. Water streamed down the grey cement cladding on the outer walls; green-black fungus ate the wallpaper inside. The flat consisted of two rooms and an alcove that was both kitchen and bathroom. A table-top over the bath became the dining area and to take a bath they had to light a geyser, which exploded with a roar to squeeze out a trickle of hot water. The house was on the bend of a railway line, and shook when the trains ran. 'We had mice; we both rather liked them. They used to come up over the bath and sit on the table top.' The toilet was down the hall, shared with an Austrian–Jewish couple who fought and screamed behind the plaster wall. Upstairs a woman, another refugee, played the piano, loudly, pressing deep badly tuned chords down into their small bedroom.

Rudi had bought the furniture from the landlord when he rented the flat, including a black mock-Chinese corner-piece, studded with dragons, lyre birds and little mirrored drawers. They kept *objets* in it that Helen's mother had given her and which they would pawn regularly, along with Rudi's tennis racket. They were very poor: she wore Rudi's gymnasium sports shirt to keep warm in bed. The house was extremely cold that winter, so every night they lit a coal fire in the grate and sat close to it keeping the world at bay in the unheated corners of the room.

Helen Bamber's father was adrift. 'The scale of the mass death, not only the liquidation of the Jews and the gypsies and the resisters, but the whole mass destruction of the war preoccupied him.' He still went on reading, and going to the library, but he had become almost reclusive, leaving the house to go to his undemanding job as accountant for a metal-supply firm and talking to almost no one, alone with his figures and his philosophical and theological books. 'When I tried to talk about Belsen and Germany and the survivors he was interested, in a way, but the most important thing for him was the impossibility of repairing the gap in creation. He had no sense of renewal or hope.' He felt he had been proved right without a grain of comfort, and she thinks he never found a way of living in the same world as the Holocaust until the very end of his life.

He had also become more Orthodox, looking for a spiritual meaning for God's turning away. To Rudi he seemed 'a very Orthodox Jew'. Like his ex-wife – their divorce had been formalized while Helen was in Germany – Louis Balmuth was shocked at the way his daughter was living with her partner. He called for marriage, and for a religious ceremony. They were willing enough to get married, since Rudi was still an 'enemy alien' and had no right to be in Britain. By a twist in the law, Rudi would gain the right to live in the country by marrying her; she would become stateless by marrying him, though it was understood that she could then reapply successfully for her nationality.

While she was thinking about remaking herself as a British subject, a stiff and well-tailored man 'from the Home Office' came to call on Helen at Sumatra Road. He affected not to notice the damp, the vibration as a train shuddered past, the grimy windows. He said he was sure that 'this citizenship matter' would go smoothly, but wondered if she remembered anything about illegal emigration to Palestine, in which His Majesty's Government was very interested. She dedicated her courteously expressed but total amnesia to Israel Klein; and then the government man went on to question her about Rudi. What did he believe in? Where had they met? He asked about the club from which Rudi had taken her home, and about the politics, but he contrived never to use the word that floated just above the conversation, the symbol of the world splitting asunder, leaving little space for innocent political commitment. He must, nonetheless, have decided that Rudi was not a security threat, because he became a citizen of the United Kingdom.

As for getting married in a synagogue, she was a tranquil atheist, but Rudi Bamberger was actively hostile to all religious establishments and fought bitterly against such a compromise – something he now regrets. But in March 1947, after the civil ceremony in Hampstead Town Hall they did, for the sake of peace, agree to be wed by a Rabbi of the old man's choice.

After the worst of the thaw and the flooding was over, they bought a motorbike with the £60 Louis Balmuth had given them as a wedding present and the JRU allowance she had saved in Germany. It was an XWD (ex-War Department) Indian, a North American trophy, powered by a 1000-cc V-Twin engine. A silver head wearing a streaming war-bonnet perched on the front mudguard. Square hessian army saddlebags hung over the back wheel: Ex *War Department*; and it still looked like a battle-courier's machine. It lacked suspension, apart from a coil spring, and it shook, but the driver sat on a saddle like a projecting tongue, and could do 90 miles an hour. This was their dream of escape and freedom.

As the weather improved they began to imagine what it would be like to ride fast down long straight French roads. Money was tight, but money still didn't matter much. In the early summer, they would come home in the warm afternoons, drive over to Hampstead Heath and swim through the reeds in a quiet pond. Nothing else seemed of any account, for a while, except each other's sun-tanned bodies and the feeling of comfortable happiness. Every night they covered the machine, the only substantial thing they owned, with a heavy sheet cut from a barrage balloon.

They took the bike on the ferry to Calais and drove towards Switzerland. Wherever they stopped on their way through Central France, Rudi's accent triggered hostility from the peasantry. But she loved it when they finally went up a pass towards Switzerland, the mountains lifting up such an amazing bulk of rock and ice around them. The difficulty was in the loop that any fantasy of life on the road builds into itself, pulling them home.

At first, it was Rudi who had friends. While she was away he had grown close to a loose group of writers and artists, most of them pacifists or anarchists. Some had been members before the war of the Peace Pledge Union, which one historian has called 'the largest absolute pacifist organization in history'. They had spent the war, Helen Bamber said with a certain ironic distaste, 'climbing up ladders with Stephen Spender types in Hampstead putting out fires'. They were alienated from the Labour government by its ardent support of the USA as the Cold War began, but few of them were tempted by the Soviet front campaigns for peace, despite their sympathy for the destroyers of Hitler's biggest armies. Within a year, the communist coups snuffed out Eastern Europe's democratic interlude. It was a time when 'Third Roads' between communism and capitalism were being laid down by radical Christians and socialists looking for their own niche in the ecology of the Cold War; within a few years, eccentric democrats who had not chosen sides would be isolated on narrow ground.

The lampshade co-operative was housed under a damp railway arch behind King's Cross station. 'It was run on the most ultra-democratic lines. The lampshades were *appalling*,' Helen Bamber recalls. They were like bad imitations of Liberty's pillaging of the William Morris pattern book. Rudi's job was to supervise the outworkers, and make sure that production actually occurred – a tricky problem, with a half-anarchist workforce. So the firm went bankrupt soon after his marriage, and the floral-print lampshades gathered dust.

Friendships survived the crash. Stuart Smith and his wife Ella entered Helen Bamber's life. He was a writer; she worked as a secretary at the LSE. They lived at 141 Gray's Inn Road and they and their friends some-how became known, at least to Rudi and Helen, as the 141 Group, with vague connections to real cultural predators of the late 1940s like George Barker, and the gay artists Colquhoun and McBride. Helen Bamber was unconcerned that she was on the outer edge of the circle. 'They were witty, kind and knowing: they gave me a refuge. And it was Rudi's perfect context – the level of debate and vibrancy and cynicism was wonderful. And they had the added attraction for me of loving him.' She was, at least on the surface, thoroughly enjoying the Bloomsbury pubs, the oily mock-continental dinners with bad wine in Soho restaur-ants and the hazy discussions that followed.

It was gossipy London talk, politics and literature and even higher things. Some sense of the milieu may be had from Stuart Smith's novel, *Derrick Preest*, published in 1941. It was an English *Bildungsroman*, its eponymous central character emerging from a world of minor public schools, stilted male encounters ('Hullo, here's old Hugh'), cocktails and dances to gramophone records. It has the necessary brave cad (who becomes a fighter pilot in the Battle of Britain) driving a borrowed Alvis up the Barnet Bypass with a faithless gel called Cherry Ling. The hero walks between cardboard figures of materialism and commercialism. Stephane Grappelli and his Hot Four cheapen mass taste; Preest listens to Beethoven and talks about 'true values'. Discussions of the meaning of life – mildly social Christianity, romantic rebellion, relationships without jealousy, and feelings of guilt – swirl in a pale soup. This was the atmosphere of pre-war British pacifism, with its search for personal regeneration and spiritual renewal. The novel closes with a brief encounter in an air-raid shelter between the hero and a working-class girl called Rose. She falls in love with him, the cellar takes a direct hit; she is wounded but can walk home, where he watches her die. He emerges onto the 'hard concrete pavement' and crosses onto the high street, waiting for the traffic lights to change colour. 'Soon he was lost in the crowd.'

Bamber, at the time, was a little in awe of her husband's friends. They were intellectuals; she was not, and in this respect she somehow remained very young. She would always lack a certain confidence, tending to revere a little the bearers of the fashionable idea while keeping her distance from it.

Stuart Smith was a committed pacifist. Looking back on the war, in an essay written in 1965, he claimed that 'the wrong done in using force is not less but greater than any good that can be defended by force; that the evils which result from not using force – that this country and others might or would be subjected to domination by Fascist powers – would be less than those which would result from the use of force necessary ... to prevent that subjection.' On the Nazi genocide, which was, he honestly acknowledged, the real test of his beliefs, he suggested that a protest by the world's 'moral leaders ... together with a readiness to take in Jews from Germany, would, without the use of war, have arrested the process of extermination far short of the figure it in fact reached'. Had there been a German invasion, of course, submission under protest would only have deferred the moment of truth; and Smith offered no remedy for the millions of Polish and Russian Jews who were invisible to the world's leaders, and most of its intellectuals.

Helen Bamber accepted her friends' pacifism as a sincere protest against militarism, but could not be unaware that the Peace Pledge Union had supported the Munich agreement in September 1938 – which sacrificed Czechoslovakia to Germany – and even Hitler's demands against Poland a year later, on the grounds that war was the absolute evil, and that all the great powers had to accommodate each other's demands in order to avoid it.

The 141 people were tolerant and sceptical, and yet there was a cocoon around them, something of that 'power-protected' moralism that can only flourish where life is basically sweet. Stuart Smith wrote in the mid-1960s of his decision to become a conscientious objector: 'England has the most gentle society I know of, and the most just. Violence to its own members lies further back in English history than in that of almost any other country I can think of, and one of the many results of this is that conscientious objectors in this country are, in the first place, recognised, and, in the second place, well treated. [This] obviously contributed to making a choice of pacifism easy.'

'They knew about *cricket*' is Bamber's way of summing up the deep security of their Englishness. She felt like an outsider, yet she loved them for being everything she could not be: tranquil, settled, secure in a safe place. When she struck out on her own path she would, and perhaps not so unconsciously, be arguing with some of her oldest friends' assumptions.

Bamber found herself observing England with the eye of a visitor: a place where innocence is not difficult, which prides itself on not needing to know too much about the worst, because such things do not happen in a culture of law that has been stable for centuries. Such a culture has some of the qualities of a fairy-tale: the invaders never come, and everyone receives justice, as an observant Italian critic noted about the greatest English novels of childhood. Retribution is visited on the wicked at the quarter-sessions, not in ambush or on the battlefield. In 1947 it took an effort of imagination, even in a country that had lost 400,000 of its people, to appreciate the wreck of Central and Southern Europe after it had paid the price of Hitler's defeat: at least 15 million dead, numberless maimed, entire regions destroyed. Still less was it possible in England to grasp as anything other than a large number the near-extinction of Europe's Jews, despite what the soldiers had witnessed at Belsen. So it seemed to a young woman trying to find her way back in, after an absence on the other side of the world.

If the choice is between laughing or crying – and she sometimes felt that these were the only alternatives available – it is probably best to choose the former, in order to live normally in a democratic society. Her husband had adapted, his gift for irony sharpening with lessons in indirection. It may also have been his way of protecting himself from his own past: a style of speech that made it difficult to probe too deeply. It helped him to enjoy the present, which was where he wanted to be. But for his wife, living in the present was more demanding.

*   *   *

Helen Bamber was in crisis, and had been for most of the winter and early summer, despite the hedonistic spell Rudi cast on her. She began to have panic attacks, to fear violent people, and to have suicidal feelings; and there were, she said, 'very black, very black days. I can remember when I went with Rudi to Virginia Water, that beauty spot in Surrey. Lovely places affected me very badly. I had the most appalling panic, looking out over the lake, a wave of grief and a feeling that there was going to be a disaster. All that I'd seen of violence and the sense of violence around me in Germany engulfed me when I got back. I regressed for a time. It was also upsetting to read about powerful Nazis – judges, industrialists, policemen – being reinstated. The atmosphere seemed to change very rapidly.'

She took refuge in the dark, watching anything on the screen to dull her sense of threat; sitting for hours on her own in the Golders Green Ionic, her neighbourhood fleapit. Some British films of the period were paranoid night pieces like Lean's *Great Expectations*, opening on the terrified boy in the graveyard, or Reed's *Odd Man Out*, with James Mason as the dying IRA man hunted through Belfast in the winter; she said later that she saw them over and over again, and recalled *The Rake's Progress* as though its Hogarthian story of an upper-class bounder hitting the lower depths held some key to her mood. It may have been its innocence that attracted her, the assumption that its hero, played by Rex Harrison, could redeem himself by dying in war. When *The Red Shoes*, that great expressionist melodrama of the ballet, came out early the following year it seemed to mock in its tale of swooning obsession and triumph her own mother's dreams for her.

She felt lost, and whilst it must have been hard to see the Cold War putting a stop to denazification, there may have been a less rational explanation for her withdrawal. She may have missed the self-importance of being with the damaged, the bit of God that sticks to every rescuer. There is a pleasure in working with people in extreme situations, and a feeling of omnipotence that is close to despair: the carer wants to do more and more, and feels more and more helpless as a consequence. Helen Bamber is not immune to this temptation; no one is, who is drawn to this kind of work. Those who work with survivors are wary of identifying with the victim, of inflating their own capacities and of the depression that comes when that illusion is pricked. Bamber has become very critical of her own need to do what she does, but at the age of twenty-two she could not begin to understand what she was going through.

There was more to it, in any case, than her own self-importance. Like her father, she felt that the Holocaust was a discontinuity, and that life could not simply go on, even though she knew it must. 'Even with sensitive and decent people, I felt the sweeping away of a whole terrible experience as though it didn't really matter: the attitude was, *it doesn't have any bearing on what's going on now.* I felt this when I described something very particular that I had seen, while they wanted to talk widely, intelligently, unhampered by detail. It had no significance for them.'

Her new friends did not find it easy to hear about where she had been. She found this even with Rudi. It was not that he did not care to know, far from it; his sensitivity and kindness were unshakeable, his pride in her genuine. But he could not connect actively with her memory of what she had seen; only much later could she understand that he was afraid to turn back, having escaped.

People complained about rationing and she would grow irritated; and she found that she had a problem with raw meat. 'Rudi had a way of using food extremely well. I used to have to go to the butcher in West Hampstead, playing the housewife; the getting of the meat with ration coupons was a serious business. You had your piece of newspaper and you stood in a queue, and there was all this flesh facing you, the different cuts, a carcass or two hanging up. I found I could not look at it, all those red chunks lying on the white porcelain top. I still find the sight of raw meat very difficult, though I am not a real vegetarian: it is a gut aversion. I wanted to please – to come home with something appropriate. Instead I would grab whatever they put in front of me and leave the shop. I could never tell Rudi that I had this difficulty. I forced myself to eat meat. What people tell each other and what they don't is very interesting.'

She also found it difficult to acknowledge Rudi's melancholy. The man she fell in love with was intelligent, sensitive and active. 'He was very integrated; he never compromised in situations where I might have given in, wanting to be nice, to be liked; he stuck very closely to what he believed.' He held her upright when he realized how hopeless she felt. Yet soon after she went to live with him, he went down his own pit for almost two weeks, and she could not reach him at all, and felt very much excluded from him, which was harder to cope with than she could have imagined. 'He was and is a very profound man. But I think I know what the women in Berwick experienced in their marriages: you can have a very good marriage, but always with some remote space between you, in which one of you is inaccessible. And we couldn't talk much about what he had lost.'

She came to accept that he would have these episodes. Yet despite her rejection of her mother's dream of respectability, she found herself wanting a home. Rudi's ability to tune out the squalor of their rooms began to seem an endless deferment of the future. He seemed happiest travelling on the big motorbike, and for that he needed a companion and friend; arrival was a different matter. Stability meant children, which she desired and he did not. For her, 'A family meant something that I'd never actually had – it sounds absurd to say it, but a kind of Sunday-lunch scenario of togetherness in a big kitchen, an ideal family, my romance. Of course I never ever achieved it, in the way I imagined it.'

The Bambers remained in the noisy primitive flat for four years, and lived out a compromise. Having a child, for someone who did not want to be tied to something lovable that he could lose all over again, was an unbearable thought. Rudi had had to restart from zero; now he had Helen, and it was all he wanted, or so she thought.

Superficially, she was better able to cope. She was determined to organize herself no matter how useless she felt. When the lampshade collective went under, they lived on her money. The pawnshops still saw a lot of them, the tennis racquet going in and out of hock along with the watches and jewellery; and she went looking for paid work.

With hindsight, which is all she has, she found a clue to Rudi's attraction to the radical pacifists and to why the two of them slowly began to grow apart almost as soon as they had come together. On Kristallnacht he had held onto his pistol while he was beaten and his father was murdered. 'I remember him saying to me that he would never, ever carry a gun again. And I think that he was saying something about himself, and his life, and about the difference between us. He would use his intellect for thinking about issues, but that was all: he would not commit himself to anything; he needed that distance.' She repeated herself, emphasizing each word separately: '*He would not carry a gun again.*'

*   *   *

The Jewish Refugee Committee had rooms in Bloomsbury House. She had to force herself to work, and it was a logical place for her to come; here she did not have to explain herself. She was given a job in the

Emigration Department, trying to help Jewish survivors join their relations in the United States. The US still had a quota system that favoured 'Nordic' immigrants and her job was to persuade officials whose faces she would never see that they should make an exception for a woman, say, who wanted to live with her last surviving sister.

Bloomsbury House contained many committees in small crowded rooms. She lost herself in the work, a lifelong habit, coming in early and leaving late each evening, and had very little contact with anyone outside her section.

A man appeared at the door of her office one night as she was preparing to leave. He introduced himself as Oscar Friedmann, from the Committee for the Care of Children from Concentration Camps. He had heard that she was good with people, he told her abruptly, and wanted her to come and work for him. His wiry greying hair was brushed back off a high forehead; his face was sharp, smooth-skinned, ascetic, almost immobile on one side, as though frozen in irritation. He looked confident and used to being obeyed. His bow tie and immaculate shirt were those of a dandyish scholar. She said that he intimidated her, though at first she was not sure if she was more intimidated by him or by what he wanted her to do.

In August 1945 the British government began to admit the first of a group of child survivors of the camps. It had been persuaded that a thousand children could be absorbed by the United Kingdom, then the third most powerful country in the world, though not all ministers were convinced. The Home Secretary, Chuter Ede, worried that they would form 'a permanent addition to the foreign population competing in the employment market with British subjects', while the Foreign Secretary, Ernest Bevin, hoped to confine them to farm labour in order to prevent them from finding 'openings in commerce'.

In the event, not even a thousand could be found. Seven hundred and thirty-two young people were eventually gathered together and flown from Czechoslovakia to Britain. They had to be under the age of sixteen, and though several were older than that they looked small enough to pass for children. The Jewish community, through the CBF, had to take complete financial responsibility for them.

Mostly boys and young men, they had emerged from slave labour at camps like Auschwitz, Stutthof, and Dora-Nordhausen. Before that they had been pent up in ghettos like Łodz where the Nazis forced them to work until they were transported to die. Many of them had witnessed the death of close relatives, or been separated from them in a way that they knew guaranteed death. They had worked in factories where murder was a routine form of labour discipline; they had stood for 'selection'.

Oscar Friedmann was now in charge of their general welfare. The former head of a progressive borstal, he had come to Britain with a *kindertransport* in 1939, and retrained as a Freudian analyst. That tense face which Helen Bamber noticed was at least partly the result of nerves cut by a rifle butt in Sachsenhausen in 1933, where he was interned after the Nazis came to power.

Friedmann asked Helen Bamber to become one of his case-workers, helping him monitor the state of mind and living conditions of the children as they adjusted to life in Britain. She would be a sort of counsellor to them. Most of them, by this time, had been in Britain for well over a year, but she understood that many of them were still finding it difficult to adjust. She would have to show Friedmann that she knew how to be around survivors without patronizing them. It was not going to be easy, he told her with a harsh frankness that she would come to know as his normal style; but she would have a weekly supervision, and he would train her.

She could see that he would be a martinet: 'You know when you are meeting somebody with whom you are not going to be able to play games.' Yet she agreed to join him. She could have gone back to work for a doctor in Harley Street, or applied to a university. This seems to have been the moment when it became difficult to imagine an ordinary life for her. Even when she was not concerned with refugees and the aftermath of terror, much of the paid work she would do in the coming decades would become a marking of time, a distraction from where her mind really was.

Yet her work with Friedmann would remain, for her, the most demanding she ever did. She said, and it is obviously true, that there is a part of her that is the fixer, who enjoys 'ducking and diving', getting things done at the last minute by persuasion and guile. 'It is a challenge to me to work in a more reflective way – the contradiction between wanting to campaign, to make changes and at the same time knowing that there is a deeper level in the person which can't be touched by campaigning. I sensed that with Oscar I would have to adapt in ways that could not be fixed; I would not be able to use the techniques of avoidance and persuasion that I had learned with my family.'

She began to meet the 'children', some of them not much younger than her, in their flats and workplaces along the refugee trail on which she had grown up – Hackney, Stoke Newington, Stamford Hill and further out in the newer suburban terraces. She learned to be able to take what was coming to her, and remembers, as well as their barely credible vitality, their burning anger, their inability to pretend or soften.

It was as though all the love, even the capacity for feeling, had been crushed out of them: she cannot, no matter how well they have done since then, erase the image of their unimpressible faces. She remembers it without dismay; she was an inadequate surrogate parent to young men who had lived what she had only feared. 'They faced annihilation day after day, for years, and this doesn't happen without a blunting of emotional life, a "psychic numbing" in which the emotions become remote, so that fear and love disappear in a kind of blur, and the person merely functions. Yet they also had in them the most intense grief and love, but that is reconstructed over time, and this was still very early. They *knew* what was happening to their relatives when they disappeared; yet some of them were so young they hardly knew who they were themselves, they had shut off parts of their memory and could not even recall what their homes looked like. Nobody in this world gets the best, but something enables us to reach some normality with the parenting that we get. These children didn't have that, or had had good parents and then lost them. They achieved so much, in their different ways, but it took time; and with them you prayed for more time.'

She said that she found them 'terrifying'. 'They had very hard armour, highly defended, efficient and compact bodies. They did not honour you in any conventional way. I remember their stony little faces, giving nothing back, their sceptical eyes – a complete lack of trust, as though to say, what are you going to do for me, how can I negotiate with this person for what I want? I never saw them cry, even when they spoke of dead parents, sisters, friends. They had a way of looking past you, watchful and alert.' Once she described them as 'unbending', as though they held themselves unnaturally rigid and upright, their backs tensed against threat.

Eva Kahn-Minden, the former Belsen nurse who worked with some ailing young refugees at a TB sanatorium in Essex, wrote in her memoir of a recurrent Yiddish phrase they used when they felt they were not being given their due: '*Es kimmt mir.*' It is owing to me. And Bamber also faced this steely challenge, the implication that they had gone through enough, and that their new world should cut them some slack. She was, inevitably, a conduit for them, a provider of things they needed.

Those who had particular strengths and gifts, Bamber believes, were the most resentful – especially towards those who couldn't recognize them for what they were. The first group of three hundred, after re-cuperation at Windermere in the Lake District, where they lived in the wooden barracks of a wartime hostel, were sent to London and other cities, placed in digs or in hostels and put to work. The assumption seems to have been that they should lose their dependent status as quickly as possible; that the resources were not available to educate them more fully; and that labour would do them good.

The policy was understandable, and it was true that Friedmann and his colleagues had few resources, but Helen Bamber claims that the CBF found psychological concerns self-indulgent, and that there was always a certain tension over money. The young people didn't appreciate the dilemma, and she would sometimes find herself being treated like a probation officer.

The communal response, as Martin Gilbert shows in his affectionate and magisterial book about 'the boys', was impressive – it embraced volunteers, teachers, rabbis, philanthropists and athletes. The state was miserly, at best, and 'the committee' had to subsidize rents and medical and educational bills. One of the most useful things it did, as Gilbert notes, was to found the Primrose Club, where the survivors could meet luckier people of their own age; it had a canteen, a table tennis room, a library, and a space for dancing. But all of these efforts could not persuade some of the young refugees, in Bamber's experience, that they were treated as fully human. They wanted what parents would have given them.

Everything she did with the children was examined and often challenged by Oscar Friedmann. She is convinced that she learned more from him than she ever has from anyone. Bamber remains loyal to him, and says he could be kind and extremely funny, but she could not be unaware of his bleakness. 'He did not generate warmth.' Before the war he had been responsible for delinquents and orphans. What she did not know, until she knew him better, was that Oscar Friedmann had himself been brought up in an institution after losing his parents. First an orphan, then a reformatory head: not an obvious choice for a job as sensitive as the one he was now doing. Culturally, too, he seemed very 'German' against the earthier manners of the 'Polish' boys.

Sheila Melzak, a child therapist (and herself the daughter of a Belsen survivor) who now works with Bamber, and who has talked to her about her experiences in the late 1940s, suggests that Friedmann's limitations were those of the European child psychotherapy of his day, with its emphasis on setting boundaries, and on the need for a sternly loving figure of authority. His interpretations of his young colleague's behaviour could be hurtful. Bamber's motives were questioned, her weaknesses exposed. 'It was the most uncomfortable period of my life – much worse than working in Germany. Over there you could be very, very busy if you wanted to escape into activity, and I couldn't escape here. I had to justify everything. Compromises that I had made previously were ruthlessly exposed. Oscar let nothing pass for the peace of the world.' She remembered more than once crying all the way home, and lying awake in her dreary flat thinking, 'Is this my life?'

His greatest weakness, in her memory of him, was his inability 'to work with the light as well as the shade, to realize that part of what we must do is to enjoy ourselves, to have the courage not to be brought down by catastrophe but to move forward into life, and – strange as it sounds – to have fun with those you are helping'.

They did have group discussions with the boys, which Friedmann would lead, but he would remain aloof, silent. They would always begin with protests about clothes, or spending money, or about some having more than others, which meant a great deal to them. And sometimes, though almost always alone, they would, Bamber says, hint at where they had been: dreams of killing, of eating the dead, of guilt; their memories of people who had died very badly.

Most of these children were given very little of the attention that would now be thought appropriate for such grief, though Bamber tried her best when she visited them. 'I had to learn to talk about the fear of annihilation, which was still very strong, and the nightly fear of somebody coming to kill them. They had had to stand in selections every morning to be chosen, literally for life or for death. It was necessary to talk about facing that morning roll-call and the fact that one didn't care if other people were taken, so long as one survived. It was very important to normalize those nightmares, to make them into a relatively good thing, in that they represented something terrible that needed to be expelled.

What she was doing was largely instinctive; she never felt that anyone – helper or survivor – had permission to talk about the past. The rule was a bracing emphasis on not dwelling on things, on getting on with it. She says that, very tentatively, she would encourage a young survivor to draw or paint, and try to honour what the images revealed; or she would ask about the food their parents cooked for them, how they buttoned their coats, how they played with them. She was, in a language that was not then familiar to her, reconnecting them to good memories, trying to move past the image of grotesque death. And in her capacity to take their anger, she was showing a capacity to absorb without responding in kind, creating, however intermittently, an environment in which such feelings were safe. Sheila Melzak said that 'she could do it probably *because* she was not trained in the orthodoxy of the time. She did not stop herself listening.'

It could feel like walking under water. A Czech boy under Helen Bamber's care was in a tuberculosis clinic in outer London. She had a good relationship with him, she believed; they had talked about the past, and had drawn pictures of his home and his parents to help him mourn them. She thought she knew who he was: that she had got it right. Every week, she took a long bus-ride out to the sanatorium. She had, with his permission, told the doctors and the nurses about his recent past so they could understand why he was such a 'strange' young man.

One Thursday she arrived to find that he had walked out in the middle of crucial treatment. At such moments, Friedmann's inability to soften reality could feel like gloves coming off. He was scornfully crushing: 'How *could* you have missed it?' 'I kept asking myself, *what* had I missed? What collusion had there been between us, my not seeing the fear that was going suddenly to make him panic? I should have been able to sense that underneath his compliance this young man was going to take flight. I didn't partly because I didn't want to: I didn't want to challenge my idea of our relationship.'

Friedmann made her feel that she missed many important things. She had entered into an agreement with a landlord to rent a room to one of the boys. The boy skipped, and the man wanted to be paid. 'I could not believe a Jewish man could be so hard, demanding every single penny he was owed.' Oscar was icily cold to her about that negotiation 'in which I was not perhaps completely punctilious', Bamber admitted. 'I may have assumed his goodwill.' She could not tell Friedmann that she found the landlord's sexual innuendo and aggressive demands for money frightening. When the man threatened to take her, personally, to court for the week's unpaid rent for his room with its linoleum floor, gas ring and bathroom out in the hall, Friedmann told her, well, you'll have to appear in court. Friedmann asked her, well, did you or did you not get his agreement in writing? He never quite let her off the hook, even after the committee agreed a settlement.

She was an attractive young woman, who smiled beautifully, if photographs can be trusted, with a body that men found attractive. A woman at that time could not easily complain of unwanted advances, so she kept silent. 'If you have the fixer in you and you want something, you're tempted to try to use charm to get better conditions.' One of the employers, who manufactured handbags, was blatant, and she hated being in his office with its smell of animal hides. He would flirt sleazily with her, stringing it out as long as he could before talking about the young survivor in his shop. She took to dressing old, looking as plain as possible. Friedmann expected people to be strong: that was how you came through, as he had done.

Friedmann had high expectations of her, and so his criticism bit harder. He told her that she had skills she should not waste, and wanted her to undertake a proper training in analysis, but she sensed that if she did her marriage would end. Becoming a psychoanalyst was expensive, which made it easier to rationalize her decision; nor could she bear the thought of losing Rudi. She thinks that Oscar Friedmann in his lucid hurtful way felt that the marriage was doomed, but it was the kind of judgement that a person can spend years resisting, as though holding apart the jaws of a trap.

Rudi was not happy about the demands and disciplines of work. She was the one who seemed to grow connections wherever she set down, which would become one of her great fixer's gifts. She used some forgotten network to get him a job in a firm selling the new ballpoint pens. The lack of money oppressed her; she had had enough of the pawnshop.

She had come to accept that Rudi was uneasy in workplaces where his accent would be noticed. He had become still more sensitive to comments about his Jewishness, and admitted later that he was 'hypersensitive to anti-semitic atmospheres' outside his trusted circle of English friends.

In the autumn of 1947 a package was delivered to him from the Nürnberg Kriminal Polizei. It contained the testimony of an ex-employee of his father's describing Rudi's condition on the morning after Kristallnacht. Rudi had forgotten for nine years how badly he was beaten, but here it was in detail – the bruising, the cuts, the swollen face. The package also included six sets of mugshots of former SA men, and a letter asking Rudi to identify them. They had come to trial, accused of 'destruction of property'. He was unable to confirm that they were his father's killers. The names – Doppelhammer, Weber, Krauss, Strehle – and the faces – long, heavy, balding heads – were truly meaningless to him. 'I wanted to forget about it all; I wanted it all behind me,' he said almost exactly fifty years later. There could be no question, ever, of him returning to Germany, even for justice.

Couples lean on each other, unless a relationship has become entirely parasitic, and theirs was far from that. She was becoming so good at helping others, and was powerless to help him – the rescuer incapable of saving those closest to her, the listener not wanting to know too much. She is still capable of nearly anguished incoherence about the paradox of her relationship with this man, whom in her way she still loves and who has remained loyal to her throughout a lifetime. 'Knowing what I know now', she said, 'about people who have suffered as much as he had, and what they need, I can understand why we failed; and I wanted a normal relationship even so, wanted passion, fun, spontaneity – there was something in me quite crushed by what we were. I realized too late that that was my fault as much as his.'

* * *

Work was the official way out for the children, duty and therapy combined. Oscar Friedmann was 'brutally realistic' about this, Bamber thinks. 'He said to them, "this is how it is; this is how you can survive here." He was hard, and many of them resented him, but he had to be, because he had so few resources.'

But the slogan 'Put it behind you' was not easily combined with certain forms of work. Any hint that labour was more important than dignity was a provocation. They had been slaves in a system that lacked even the economic rationality of the worst colonial sugar plantation, where bodies were valuable commodities; these boys had been utterly expendable. They were sensitive to contempt or unreasonable complaint. 'They had been nothing,' Bamber recalls, 'so when an employer made them feel like that, as happens in small rough workshops, they would explode.'

Bamber had to walk a line between diplomacy with small businessmen – diamond-polishers, leather workers, rag-trade merchants – and defence of the boys. She finds it difficult to remember many employers who had the heart to understand what their apprentices had been through. Still, she tried to explain to her charges that they were not singled out for exploitation more than most people at the time, when the labour legislation of the post-war period had not made much impact on small factories. 'The fights with landlords and employers were about never being *controlled* again. Most apprentices take some confidence in their family backgrounds into their work – how could these boys relate to anyone except extremely?'

Inside the Jewish community there was a depth of sympathy on which they could draw; a tacit understanding of their achievement in being alive; and there were many pre-war refugees who had lost their own families and did not need to be asked to cherish the newcomers. When they had to move outside this environment, they could find themselves treading very thin air. Bamber was once interviewed by a panel of headmasters who had to decide whether a boy would be allowed to study at William Ellis, a North London grammar school. He was a bright scholar, one of those whose education was encouraged, but he was hardly conversant with the British syllabus. She had to ask them to make allowances for the boy's deficiency in certain subjects. One of them leaned towards her and asked with perfect, querulous innocence, 'Didn't they give them any *books* to read in those camps?'

* * *

Her backward look must be darkened because she has for so long, and for the last quarter of a century almost continuously, been preoccupied by the most atrocious things that human beings can do to each other. She may know too much about the psychic damage that torture can inflict, about the apparent permanence of hurt. She was also young, and was herself vulnerable, when she was exposed to these young people in the late 1940s. The overwhelming weight of their own testimony, as recorded by Martin Gilbert, is on the side of their vindication, on the achievement of stable family lives and an enduring solidarity among themselves. The Nazis did not defeat them. Bamber acknowledges this, and must admit that people can 'get over' the most extreme violence (though that common parlance hides infinite layers of ambiguity). To live an active life, to transcend suffering, is humanly preferable to standing transfixed by the graveside; and 'the boys' did move on, even if, as Gilbert records, many of them kept coming back night after night to the place of death. Yet Bamber's testimony of what it was like to work with them does catch, in its awareness of the effects of human chaos on individual lives, an anguish that can't be recuperated as a 'triumph over adversity'. As Lawrence Langer has written, in his stubborn, inconsolable reflections on oral testimonies of the Holocaust, 'the pretence that from the wreckage of mass murder we can salvage a tribute to the victory of the human spirit is a version of Holocaust reality more necessary than true.'

The tough physical energy of these young men is so memorable to Bamber because cruelty is, above all, an experience of the human body. 'The Germans used your body against you, made your survival dependent on your body, concentrated everything on it. These boys had a powerful desire to live in the body they had rescued. Their rehabilitation was partly about reclaiming "the good body", as it is with torture victims, relearning a way of respecting the body and the self with it.'

To live in such a body – one that had been starved, beaten, marked for death – must have been to experience a sharply heightened awareness of the physical self, and to resent any disparagement of it: a shoddy suit was an insult to one who had worn a filthy camp uniform; denial of education was denial of a future but also a condemnation to working at the body's expense – the distinction between mental and manual labour much more, for these youths, than a matter of career frustration.

Roman Halter knows what it was like to feel this way. He was one of the young men visited by Helen Bamber in her impossible role as carer, case-worker and good mother in 1947 and 1948. He disturbed her greatly, and she disturbed him in ways that she did not suspect.

His life has been creative: he has been a successful architect, who turned to painting; and he then began to work in stained glass and cast-iron forms. He has even made royal coats of arms, like the one on the doors of the Queen Elizabeth Conference Centre in Westminster — his seal on the state that reluctantly gave him asylum. His stained glass is in Waltham Abbey and other buildings around London.

In the Hall of Names, the quiet archive at Yad Vashem in Jerusalem where three million victims' names are recorded — the shelves of tall books full of the traces of absent bodies — Roman Halter's extremely narrow window filters a subtle light from high up along the entire length of the room. It contains small jagged shards of opaque grey or green, some almost blackened, as though stressed by heat, and set in calmes of black iron that mimic script. The glass is sparing with light. The mystery of any great library is its elusive promise of infinite knowledge, a memorial to a past continuing into a future; here the record is of destruction, of the human and the written, memory as absolute loss.

The main gates at Yad Vashem were also made to Halter's design. They are easily neglected when they are held wide open during visiting hours. The gates hang from an enormous stone frame, which has geometrical markings incised into it. They are curtains of torn metal, teeth, daggers, hooks of iron emerging out of a violent stencil: a carefully considered, ferocious expression of grief.

As he enters his seventies Halter is demanding, with other former camp inmates, compensation from the German state for the time they spent as slave labourers. None of them has ever received a penny or an individual apology. 'Even SS men get a pension; we don't,' he said drily at our first meeting.

He would have no truck with the language of inspirational celebration. He spoke of how they had all been so utterly determined to work, have families, how success became the measure of their survival; how most of them did not speak about what they had seen, for there was no way they knew how. He said that they kept going, but now that their children had grown up and moved out there was nothing to stop it coming back, in dreams, anger, depression. He said all this with an extreme lack of self-pity, with controlled revulsion from the absurdity of grief.

Once a year, he related with a kind of wintry scorn, they put on tuxedos and come together and eat and dance and people say, look at them, how wonderful they are, what great survivors they are, how successful they have been, but then they go home and no one sees what they become, 'like Peter Ustinov in his dressing room with the grease-paint on' staring at the dead glass. 'We're like little old clowns,' he said, as though to cut with acid the sweet illusion of the onlooker. For him and his friends, he implied, there was no victory to cheer about: time stopped for them in 1945; the years between 1939 and 1945 are more vivid to many of them now, in old age, than what happened last month.

For a Holocaust commemoration in the first year of the new millennium, he is helping to organize an exhibition of drawings made in the camps, which, he said, must include proper documentation, in order to prevent what happened at the last such event he curated. He mimed the gusto of an art connoisseur savouring the work: 'How marvellous, how like Toulouse-Lautrec, how deft, as good as Degas or Picasso, remarkable really, and all done with matchsticks.' He seemed to imply that in the clichés of conventional aesthetics, art becomes a disembodied escape from history. He held up a reproduction of a drawing. A few quick charcoal strokes, it depicted the morning *appel* at Auschwitz, an SS man leaning into the mass of striped figures, a dead body in front of the ranks of prisoners, the cocked hips of an SS man as another SS reports numbers to him. It is a desolate work. Halter's point seemed to be that it is not possible, morally, to 'appreciate' art made under such conditions.

At a Jewish old people's home north of Muswell Hill, a few days after we first spoke, he was dressed in an elegant collarless shirt that did not conceal his massive shoulders; his linen pants were held up with canvas braces. He has a wide strong face, a powerful beaked nose, grey hair brushed down on either side of his high cranium; a fierce controlled intensity about him, the quiet cold intelligence of the eyes impossible to ignore. He spoke evenly, in a voice still accented with Polish and Yiddish cadences, but it was a voice charged with courteous derision for the triviality of most ordinary business. His lucid calm realism was expressed politely, a slight smile playing around his mouth.

In an open area for meeting and prayer at the home, he moved around in front of a huge stained-glass window, a wall of strong primary colours, a heavy density of light made weightier by the thick black iron of the irregular calmes. He was hanging a censer in front of it from a swag of thin silver chains. He unfolded the chains from tissue paper on the surface of a lectern and cut them with pliers after measuring the drop. His hands were big; he used the small tool easily and quickly: the last touch to a thing that he had built, a piece that refracts the light as it enters a space and transforms those who use it.

He had begun by saying that truth meant a lot to him as a child. It was difficult for him to lie to get into Britain, to say that he was born on 7 July 1929 and not 7 July 1927, but they said you had to be sixteen or under to get in and so he became sixteen. He remembered the MPs who stood up and said that these young people will take jobs that British workers could be doing.

He respected Helen Bamber's 'social conscience', her seriousness, and he said she was a good person, but also that you had to realize what it was like, the total deprivation of physical warmth and the overwhelming experience of desire. The Germans had nullified his body and exacerbated its demands. I loved it, he said, as though feeling the yearning still, when she leaned towards me; she was only a couple of years older than me, listening so sympathetically to me, but I was so aware of her body, her face. And of course he leaned towards her earnestly, even though she was so serious. He wanted her in bed. He thought she would be shocked if she knew, she was so principled, so 'idealistic', but that is the way it was.

To bring home the force of discovered need he told a story about an incident at Theresienstadt, the former camp which became the gathering place for survivors who wanted to come to Britain in 1945. He and a friend found some Ovaltine and ate it out of the tin, chewing the dry malt-flavoured milk powder: it tasted so good. His friend also knew where the SS had thrown away tins of meat, and they found a tin of hash that was not too old, and with this and the remains of the Ovaltine they visited a young prostitute. He described his experience with her, with mesmerizing frankness, as though wishing to convey the physical state he was then in – what it felt like to be safe at last, his body discovering that it had a sex.

He talked about his first months in England. He said he hated Friedmann. He said, with special emphasis: 'He always wore a bow tie.' He despised this affectation, the constriction of it, with a visible physical revulsion, looking so cool himself in his heavy cotton shirt and braces.

Once, four of them were going to the cinema in Troutbeck Bridge, the nearest town to their hostel in Windermere. It was a hot late-summer day in Cumbria: anyone who has been there remembers the massive rock hillsides, the heather, the water. Three of them wore shirts; Halter was wearing a white vest. They met Friedmann on the road, his wiry short hair brushed back, his tweed jacket, his bow tie knotted. It is easy to imagine his aggressive stiffness, his martinet posture as the young men came up.

Friedmann asked where they were going, then leaned towards Roman Halter, polite and unsmiling. 'Why are you not wearing a shirt?' Halter said it was because he had not thought about it, for the last four years he had thin, worn-out rags to put on his back, and anyway he *liked* wearing this. 'No. That is not why. I ask again, why are you not wearing a shirt?' 'Because it is hot.' 'You know that is not why, why are you not wearing a shirt?' It went on, Halter said, this relentless interrogation, the same insistent crushing question, the other three boys standing to one side. Friedmann, now pale with anger, asked again, 'Why are you not wearing a shirt?' and Halter, faced with this unbending man acting like a warden, looked up at him and said, 'Because I don't want to look like *you*.'

*   *   *

There was a theory, even among people of the utmost goodwill, Roman Halter believed, that because prison corrupts, and the camps had been a kind of prison, then these little men must be somehow depraved, ruined; he felt that the attitude was, at least initially, that they should not be allowed too near normal people. He implied that they had suffered from the idea that slavery can be treated with the balm of honest toil. Despite the efforts of the notables who ran the committee and the goodwill of the voluntary network it generated, Halter sensed a feeling that he and his friends were lost souls.

Having spent his adolescence as a slave labourer, first in the Łodz Ghetto and later in the worst of the concentration camps, he was sent to work from early morning until evening in a small factory making crowns for diamond drills. The furnaces were hot, the machine noise deafening, the work monotonous. It might be tempting to treat these men as paragons of self-help, toughly loved kids pulling themselves up by their shoelaces, but the dry anger that the memory evokes in this unbelievably capable, intelligent man should be a corrective to any such reading of their experience.

Collecting what little money he had, he went to Foyle's, then the world's biggest bookshop. He still spoke English badly, but he asked an assistant how he should go deeper into his new language. The assistant spoke German, and he told him there were two kinds of books in English literature: the very formal, elegant and transparent style of writing, which the book-seller associated with the eighteenth century, and on the other hand the Shakespearean style, a rich and magnificently human language. There was no use starting at this peak, though, so he recommended, from the language's thinner branches, J. B. Priestley's *The Pleasure of Reading*, which he said would be useful as a guide, and some deceptively easy-to-read books, from which Halter chose *Alice in Wonderland*.

He said he took his books home to the hostel and went on strike. He refused to go to work one morning and stayed in bed, reading Lewis Carroll. The set of his face must have been daunting to anyone asking him to move; and it is strange to think of him concentrating carefully on the nursery geometry of Carroll's story, power imagined as a card-game, the rituals of polite language made strange, the emergence of justice even out of shrill nonsensical absurdity. Every newcomer has to invent an England for themselves, but Halter's must have been touched by a hopeless, mocking irony: Alice banishing power with the cry, 'You're nothing but a pack of cards!'; the Lion and Unicorn, heraldic thugs from the royal coat of arms, patronizing that 'fabulous monster', the human child.

He learned more about Englishness when he had won his point with Friedmann, and become an apprentice to a company called Mechanical Development Engineering in Slough, a company that would be famous for making the Dome of Discovery at the Festival of Britain in 1951, that great celebration of post-war modernism and optimism.

His new boss was a Mr Archibald, a former RAF squadron leader with a calculated taste for the absurd, who liked Roman Halter and gave him lessons in English and maths. One of his deadpan exercises, early on, was to ask his new apprentice to analyse grammatically sentences, such as, 'Is you is, or is you ain't my baby?' Archibald wore leather patches on the elbows of his tweed jacket, and when Halter asked him why, he said that it was to save wearing out the cloth when he got home late and his wife made him eat his dinner from a bowl on the floor, propped on his elbows with the dog.

Something worked; the boy's talent was drawn out. Roman Halter learned mechanical drawing, how machines were made and improved, copying meticulous technical drawings and seeing how flat plans unfolded into three-dimensional form.

At first all he was doing was retracing the drawings, learning about tradition, a copyist in a long line of careful transcribers, and understanding how changes in a plan could ruin a machine and lose money and lives, or else become an improvement, an innovation. He was careful to tell me later when he was explaining his stained-glass window at the old people's home that no two versions of the Torah were the same, that every copyist introduced some error, no matter how subtle. In Slough he seems to have found his own version of time-bound, disciplined creativity after a childhood from which the idea of any time relevant to a future had been cauterized.

When he finished his apprenticeship he was skilled enough to qualify for a course at the Architectural Association in Bedford Square, winning a scholarship, the Abercrombie Prize.

Whatever he did, he had to do on his own. One of his aunts lived in Lausanne. Before his father died he told him: when you survive – he always said *when* you survive – you must remember your aunt. He approached the Red Cross in Prague before being flown to England and they showed him how to send a card to her. The reply said: God be thanked. We are thrilled that you are alive. He wrote to say that he would like to go to live with them.

There was no very positive response, but in 1948 he was finally able to travel to Lausanne. They cooked him a lunch the like of which he'd never eaten in his life: clear soup with tiny veal chops floating in it, veal ribs, and then the main courses. He stood up before the meal was over and made a little speech about how he would love to be united with his family, and live in Switzerland. It was greeted in silence. A cousin took him aside. Now is not the time, he suggested, later, we'll talk.... That evening this cousin did talk to him, man to man: let's be realistic, you would not be happy here, it's for the best if you complete your training in Britain and then we'll see....

They gave him a parting gift. An elegant box; in it lay a Swiss watch. His relatives wanted him to wait, and perhaps this would help him measure time between visits, like a good burgher; he felt that Friedmann wanted him to fill it with mindless labour. Time was what he did not seem to have. As he crossed the Channel he said that he opened the box again, held the watch up by the strap and at the ship's rail let it fall into the water.

*   *   *

It is necessary to dwell on Roman Halter in this account of Helen Bamber's life, because as a young man he represented a quality of suffering that her practical activity could not reach. Recognizing, as she had to, the vacuity of normal sympathy and of the rhetoric of consolation, she felt impotent to help him or any of them, though she said she worked fifteen hours a day. When pressed why it was the figure of Roman Halter who stood at the centre of this feeling, she implied that his fierce pride and intelligence was apparent even then, but also said that she knew from him 'that nothing could replace his dead mother and father; that nobody could ever "make up" for that loss'. Bamber said, 'You could never touch him: he held on as fiercely to the pain as to his independence.'

What he recounted of his Holocaust experience in that space in the rest-home lit by his own richly coloured glass was almost certainly not the testimony he could or would have offered to even as sympathetic a listener as Helen Bamber in the 1940s. Yet that experience, and she knew enough from Belsen to imagine more than he intimated, supported her knowledge of his invulnerable sadness; or at least it does so in retrospect, as she tries to understand why this work with 'the boys' was, as she said, the hardest she ever did. Each of them, in their seventies, tries to give coherence to a past that is resistant to any shaping hand.

Between the summer of 1941 and the spring of 1945 Roman Halter had been a slave machinist. In the Łodz ghetto, to which he had been deported in 1941 from the village of Chodecz, he survived by working in a metal factory and had gone on doing that after he and his sick mother were wheeled away on a cart in the spring of 1942. Roman Halter escaped from that cart at his mother's insistence and ran back to the ghetto where the still-'productive' Jews were left. He never saw her again. (Between January and May that year, over 50,000 Jews from Łodz were sent to Chelmno and killed, including most members of Halter's family.) He accepted a bargain. A foreman offered to take him as his adopted son and give him work as long as he turned over the extra portion of food that would come to him as a member of the family. The foreman, who was on the ghetto council, was entitled to additional rations for his family, and in this way they would, for a while, have more to eat. Inhuman trade-offs among the victims were built into the system. Halter ate barely enough to stay alive, but he did eat.

The metal factory was not enough to save the last of Jewish Łodz and in September 1944 along with the thirsty, starving remnant Halter was sent to Auschwitz-Birkenau in a locked cattle truck. Because he had been a metal worker, he was assigned to the SS's munitions programme. He spent a short time in Auschwitz in the former gypsy blocks. From there the SS transferred him and five hundred other usable metal workers to Stutthof.

The system that combined mass production and mass murder had outlying branches few of us can recite the names of in the mechanical way that we invoke Belsen or Auschwitz. Stutthof, twenty miles east of Danzig on the Baltic coast, was one of the largest, a pure example of a camp designed to exterminate through labour.

They were roused at five each morning. When Halter was there, through a year and a half and most of the two winters of 1943 and 1944, they had thin shirts and jackets to keep out the icy Baltic wind. For warmth, when they were not working in the factory and they were left out in the open, they would form themselves into an 'oven', a scrum.

Halter made bullets for the German Army and the Waffen SS. Every day he formed hundreds of conical lead pieces, the killing missile part of bullets. He had to conduct a coil of wire made of malleable zinc and lead into a die, and after each new moulded slug was formed he cut it off, before trimming and hardening it in oil and water. He had to be very quick and dextrous, in order to survive. The SS did not tolerate mistakes, the machines were crude, the die prone to fracture. The price of cackhandedness was a finished bullet.

The Russians were close by the late autumn of 1944 and in November the machines were packed up and sent to the Reich. When they loaded the mills and lathes they had to walk past the SS, and Speer's man from the armaments ministry who was choosing prisoners they could use in Germany. They were told to stay silent, on pain of death. Halter said he was convinced he would not look strong enough to be chosen, so he said to the Speer man, 'I have dextrous fingers for small parts.' An SS guard lifted his rifle butt, but the ministry bureaucrat stopped him and told Halter to join the transport. (As Speer himself was to write of such choices, in a characteristic roundabout evasion: 'I cannot claim that humane considerations stood above the interests of a wartime economy.')

'Survival is a summation of the totality of your personality,' Halter said, and he suggested that it is not the result of a thinking process. (One of his paintings has at its centre a stone face with clear steely eyes, the faces of the starving surrounding it like angels around a Renaissance saint. Halter remarked of it that you often see the character of the survivor in the eyes.) When he was at Stutthof he made decisions, as far as he could. He offered to clean the barracks. It was the common set-up: the SS at one end, the slave prisoners crammed into the middle and the civilian overseer at the other end. This man had what Roman called a fat Brunnhilde type living with him who traded sex for food with the Hungarian SS men while her partner was at work. She would eat sardines out of a tin and discard it, and because he had the run of the barracks as a cleaner he would take the empty tin and drain the fishy oil from it. There was a look of loathing on his face as he described this and mimed the action of drinking the dregs of oil.

He has a copy of the transfer order from Stutthof. Five hundred 'Männlichen' and 'Weiblichen' are to be sent to 21 Scharndauerstrasse, Dresden. In an order dated 23 November 1944, 216 young men and 284 women are specified, and the names are typed neatly, with no sloppy errors or crossings out, on page after page. This was after the Germans had been driven out of Russia, and most of Poland, Hungary, France, Italy, Greece and Yugoslavia, and still the bureaucracy kept working, the heel stamping on an ever smaller human mass.

55. Halter, Roman   7.7.27   Pol.   84 194

Number in the transfer list; name; date of birth; where he was from; prisoner number. This was all they cared to know about him.

In Dresden he went on making bullets in a cellar as the British planes bombed what was left of the city. He was also the messenger boy, the *Läufer* carrying drawings from the German office to the machine area, and the German overseer gave him a little more food. The slaves were forced to sleep on the second floor during air raids – the important bullet-machines were kept in the safer basement. They were 'hands', in Adam Smith's term for labourers, but for the Germans literally so: 'I have dextrous hands.'

When a bomb hit another part of the factory they were forced to remove the dead bodies, an incident recounted in Martin Gilbert's book. Halter told Gilbert that 'those who did this work came back smelling of rotten corpses, and we were all invaded by this stench, which at night became suffocating in the spaces where we slept.'

He retold the story of what happened to him after the war ended, how he escaped a death march and was sheltered along with two other young Jewish Stutthof survivors by a German couple, Kurt and Hertha Fuchs, on their farm near Dresden. The journey he then made was an epic loop around Central Europe.

On 5 May 5 he set out for Chodecz to see if his brothers or his sister were still alive. He found an old bicycle and made his way across the ruined plains, barely escaping murder by a Russian soldier on the way. In Chodecz, like so many other Jews in Poland that summer, he felt mortally threatened by the villagers who had taken his family's house, and by the police. The entire pre-war Jewish population of the place – around 800 men, women and children – had ceased to exist, apart from Roman Halter and three other people. So he left. It took him nearly two months to get back to Dresden. The local Nazis had murdered the husband of Frau Fuchs and one of the Jewish boys sheltered by her after Halter's departure. So on the tops of trains, on foot, hitching on army lorries, he travelled on to Prague. He had heard that Theresienstadt was the place to be if you were young enough and wanted to get out to the West. He was already eighteen. It was then that he subtracted two years from his age, to compensate for the crushing acceleration of his life.

*　　*　　*

The people who helped them in England should have done what a parent would feel was best, he said – given them love, care, and education. What they needed was 'to know how to stand in relation to a sane world', and the ones who had some power should have raised funds and done something for their advancement, instead of dinning it into them that they must not expect any favours. It is not enough now, he insisted, to emphasize success, survival and transcendence. He did not want to denigrate the people who had done good work, and many had compassion, he believes; but there was a failure of imagination and courage. Even the Spastic Society, he said, had hired an enterprising fund-raiser from ICI after the war and raised millions of pounds.

Helen Bamber had seen the DP camps, and he said that was perhaps why she had more insight, or else she had some inner sensitivity. Halter gave her credit for her awareness of what they were going through, and for her suspicion of the employers. Friedmann, on the other hand, had preconceived ideas, and petty snobberies. He thought he knew the correct way to behave; he had an exaggerated respect for those with certain accomplishments, such as the playing of bridge.

As for 'therapy', there was none. Bamber and people like her tried to draw them out, but some of the carers urged them to forget about the past and seemed to Halter rather proud of themselves for doing so. The boys had their own shorthand for what had been done to them, and did not need to explain anything to each other; the outsiders were too crass or insensitive. Their 'morale' was good, they were not sitting round tearing their hair out, so people thought they must be fine. We strung them along, said Halter, with his effortless dignified scorn.

Film became therapy; they imitated the verbal riffs of the late 1940s cowboy movies in the hostels, killing the bad guys. He remembers Gary Cooper, stern, anxious and unsmiling: 'Drop it!' And sex was therapy; holding and caressing the warm body of a woman: 'Even if you were not in love, it was wonderful.' He needed sex. Sport was also an escape. He swam powerfully and systematically – he had started in Lake Windermere in the late summer of 1945 – and was good enough to compete in the Maccabiah Games in Israel in 1950.

*   *   *

It was Roman Halter's friend Ben Helfgott, however, who seemed to be the vehicle of a pure athletic energy trying to overcome cruelty and, in his case, the very existence of human misunderstanding. He was so good that he became a champion weightlifter, representing Britain in his class at the Olympics. He has at the age of nearly seventy the arms and shoulders of a thirty-year-old martyr to the gym and, concentrated into a body that can't be more than five feet two inches tall, the effect is startling. He bursts at you, sincerity and urgency focused by a straight gaze. He embodies another view of the young people's experience in Britain – an acknowledgement that the past cannot be forgotten, but also a passionate belief in transcendence.

He grew up in Piotrkow, a town of some 50,000 people south-west of Warsaw, of whom nearly a third were Jews. It became a ghetto in its own right immediately after the German invasion in September 1939. Helfgott's father, whom he reveres with a tangible sense of loss, was a flour merchant and, in his son's memory, a personable entrepreneur who kept his family alive for much longer than was reasonably possible: 'a man of indomitable spirit'. He secured for his son, aged twelve, a job in a glass factory, which would save his life, and even there the boy revealed an extraordinary physical agility; he was capable of lifting a sack weighing 100 kilos and carrying it up a ramp. At first he was treated badly by a *meister*, a foreman, who seemed to be a standard Polish anti-semite. His father had him moved away from this man's section, but also challenged the man when he met him later in the course of some business at the foreman's allotment when the man needed the use of a horse and cart. Ben's father shamed him, without humiliating him, and still let him use the cart; and he must have done this with great insight and skill. When the Germans were combing the town for young, ill, elderly or female Jews in October 1942 this same *meister* saved the blond young boy, claiming he was a Pole. 'My father did not believe in teaching people lessons by giving them like for like; he simply showed them decency. This is a story that has been instrumental for me in many ways. It has given me greater strength. People may behave badly but that does not mean that they are really bad. It is all a question of how you respond, how you treat others.'

Later, his mother and youngest sister were rounded up and shot by an *einsatzkommando*; and soon afterwards two of his uncles were murdered. By late 1944, Ben Helfgott and his father were among the small number of Jews still left in Piotrkow. Then, with the Red Army closing on the area, they were sent to Buchenwald. Ben Helfgott was separated from his father. He never saw him again: his father was shot trying to escape from a transport by German home guards in the last days of the war. He speaks of this in a voice that is difficult to describe. Full of tentative stops and starts, it is not a voice charged with sorrow past and overcome; his father's death cannot be accepted as an act of fate. 'But in the end he didn't save himself. Luck went against him, at the last minute.... My father and a number of others decided to run away. They were caught, by older Germans, who were in their fifties and sixties, who had been called by Hitler to defend their fatherland. They shot them all.

'Had he not run away, he would have ended up in Theresienstadt. It was one of those cases ... he had so many lucky escapes, and there was the end. ... It is something that preys on my mind a lot. As I get older more and more, I think of the futility. Having done so much. He was such a resourceful man, if he had come to the West he would have done ... been an unbelievable entrepreneur, very resourceful, very imaginative, and he had a great largesse about him. It was only a matter of months, six months when he was separated from me and my sister, six months, not even six months. We were well and everything was fine, and then suddenly there it was....'

Ben Helfgott survived the final months doing hard physical labour in a factory making *Panzerfausten*, Hitler's last-ditch weapon against Russian tanks. He came to Britain in August 1945; that year he also met Roman Halter, with whom he later shared a flat.

He is more yearningly generous than Roman Halter in his view of their first years in Britain, and more optimistic than Helen Bamber (whom he barely knew, in the 1940s). For him Oscar Friedmann was 'a *very* complex man', who was basically 'kind and considerate; he would always listen'. But Ben really only understood his apparent harshness towards them when he learned about Friedmann's background after his death. 'He had to be a hard man. He himself was brought up in an orphanage. He lost his father when he was ten years old.' (The enormity of this loss for Ben Helfgott, and the depth of his empathy, is very apparent.) 'He was a self-made man. Everything he did, he did himself. So he felt that if he could do it, never mind what happened to us, he felt we could do the same. ... I think he did a great deal for us. Because we were in a very vulnerable situation. It was quite easy to make life comfortable for us, to say, oh let them have a bit more, but this wouldn't do us any good. He said, you have had your rehabilitation; go to work;

learn a trade; and *make* something of yourself. He *pushed* us into it.'

Helfgott cannot quite forgive Friedmann for one thing. 'He thought of us as orphans. I personally resented this, as did some of my friends, for us to be called orphans. Because I was very lucky to be with my family till I was twelve years old. I knew what it meant, family life, and I was grown up enough not to feel an orphan. I always had this terrible sensitivity towards those who were brought up in an orphanage ... and now suddenly the idea that *I* was an orphan was something I found difficult to accept. I did *not* consider myself an orphan: it was *forced* upon me. But people did think of us as orphans, and he, because he was an orphan, expected us to study in the evenings, if we wanted to study.'

He is not convinced that more sustained attention to their psychic loss would have been appropriate, for most of them. 'It would have helped with some, it would have disturbed others. If we had not been pushed out, and told you're on your own, you've got to make your life up ... but we were not on our own: we had each other. *That* was the thing.'

Ben Helfgott is a communicator, in the most utopian sense of the word. He says that he himself never had any trouble talking about his experiences, and that the majority of his friends were like that, though 'there came a time when they stopped talking about it, when they got married, when they had businesses, they had no time'.

But for him, everything associated with strength under control is the best expression of the human. 'I was always very outgoing, very optimistic, and it was in sport that I could practise and live this inter-national life.' He speaks of a glorious time at the 1956 Olympics, at the height of the Cold War, when his grasp of European languages and his sheer willingness to see the best in people allowed him to mediate between Russians, Czechs, Germans and Americans. 'I was in my element. I loved bringing people together. I could see the goodness that existed among us; everything else was intrigue and exploitation, but when we were together we had so much in common.'

He was a natural. When he came to Britain he would astonish his fellow-refugees by flying over the horse at the gym, walking on his hands, effortlessly climbing the rope and looking down on the others struggling at the bottom. Without a trace of boastfulness he says, 'I had tremendous strength, great agility, and I was never afraid to do anything.' There is a photograph of him with some of the others on the beach at the

Isle of Wight in the late 1940s: Roman Halter, already powerfully developed, with a swimmer's body, forms the left base of a pyramid of three boys; but Ben, a tiny young man, is the apex, standing with one foot on each of the other boys' shoulders, looking pugnaciously at the camera and squinting against the sunlight. His shoulders are unbelievably massive; his short legs are like stone.

His healthy normality must partly have been achieved by the unremitting self-imposed discipline of sport. Peaceable physical effort for him is human, not superhuman, and for him the democracy of athletes is exemplary. The struggle between contestants in sport is, he suggests, also a struggle against violence and oppression, and as a strong man he is aware of the temptation of force. Weightlifting for him was almost a moral choice: 'I could have done better in wrestling, but I didn't like to hurt anybody. Invariably, when one has an encounter with another person, even if one does not intend to hurt, one hurts. I didn't like this, I never liked to hurt anybody. Only when I was attacked, I would automatically respond. I would never run away. If somebody challenged me I would *put* them down and I would hold them down and ask them: Enough? Finish? And if not I would hold them down until they would stop.' Thus this survivor of genocide embodies his belief in reason and goodwill, and an almost compassionate feeling for an aggressor's weakness.

Ben Helfgott and Roman Halter seem to point to different versions of their shared past. But Halter could not conceal his still-baffled admiration of Helfgott, the first time he lifted weights. It was at the men's pond in Hampstead, a haunt of narcissists, and Ben was in his trunks laughing boisterously at some big weightlifter huffing and puffing as he lifted the barbell. (Ben never could keep his mouth shut, said Roman.) 'OK, *you* try it,' said the bruiser. The quick little boy who had come out of Buchenwald, with hilarious self-confidence, went over and clean-lifted the big yoke of iron into the summer air.

*   *   *

Roman Halter said that 'sequential formulas' in describing the lives of Holocaust survivors can be useful, but that they need to be examined very carefully. The formula is too often the same: Poland as an idyll of family life, then the invasion, the Holocaust, unspeakable suffering, and the sunlit uplands of sanity and family after the war. He thought there was too much nostalgia for communal life in Poland before the war. Poland was full of racism, unemployment and repression; their childhood was hard.

He is sick of clichés: 'let us cut out the word "terrible".' There are ways of telling it that are authentic, he believes, like Primo Levi's work. But it is not easy: you have to sift with 'finer and finer sieves, one inch, three-quarters of an inch, half an inch', until you get some grains of truth that are timeless, authentic from beginning to end.

His stained-glass windows employ a cast filigree system rather than the traditional lead calmes to hold the glass. It makes the shapes of the glass panels more varied, more elaborate; and the calmes look heavy, part of the composition and not mere frames for the glass. In the window of the old people's home the religious symbols seem massive, unsentimental and defiant, patterned like big notes across a sheet of music in dark blues, reds, purples, and greens. It is not a joyous choral effect, yet it is anything but ponderous. The images are simple: a seven-branched candlestick, a plate of challah bread, a cup of wine, a Torah, a shofar – and a very small, broken Star of David.

None of his pieces invokes Holocaust images, except very indirectly, 'in order not to insult the past'. Hence the subtle hint of the Star of David, formed by pieces of yellow glass, with a minute triangle of red inserted into the star. It is a tiny element of the window: the sifting of which he spoke, but in another medium, a painstaking search for the right register; light refracted with care.

This meditated craft is far from the urgent, frustrated demands of his mind and body in the years after the war. No theory can account for the kind of integrated decency which, despite everything that should have ruined it, finds expression in a person like Halter. The very fact of his creativity is an enigma. The source of the creative, the Romantics thought and our culture still believes, lies in a relaxed receptiveness, a giving and receiving relationship with the world – Wordsworth's 'discipline of love'. We cannot mesh that delightful theory with what happens when the world offers a young person nothing but madness, horror and death. Something survives, but it is not a source of consolation, a victory of the soul. The gulf between us and him remains open.

At the end of our conversation Roman Halter began to speak of Henry

Moore, whom he knew and liked. Moore was very arthritic in later years, and one day Halter was at Hoglands, the artist's estate in Hertfordshire, on a day when one of his collaborators was putting the finishing touches to a model for a piece, prior to the making of the large-scale mould. Moore heard that the model was nearly ready and invited Halter to inspect it with him.

They drove down to one of the studios away from the main house. Moore looked at the model and praised what his co-worker had made of the idea, but said it was still not quite right, it should be more like a woman bending over, and he described the bold soft lines of a woman's spine, the flare of the hips and pelvis. He turned to Halter and told him how at the age of nine he had massaged his mother's tired back, and how his hands had never forgotten the feel and shape of that large female body. Moore stood in his studio, a very old man, lifting his hands and moulding the imagined curves of a giant woman's back. Roman Halter recreated Moore's gesture respectfully, his own hands lifted and curved, remembering a form shaped in the air.

*　　*　　*

Helen Bamber said once, when speaking about her parents, that 'the power of an only child in a divided household can be devastating. If you've sensed that power in yourself it is a permanent temptation. You can use it either way.' She had put that power to good use, and become accustomed to living as though emergency was normal. The Balmuths and the Baders had, by their unwillingness to retire quietly in the face of threat, marked out a path for her. She was as alert as her father had been to the coming of disaster, convinced that good fortune could not last; but she had rebelled into constructiveness, and it was not proving easy.

The young camp survivors grew up; some got better jobs after their hard-earned education, married, had children and lost their need for help from anyone except each other. They 'did well', a phrase Bamber loads with suspicious concern. But her own sense of failure and guilt was great, as it had been when she returned from Germany. She felt that nobody had done very much for them, and that she certainly had not, though in practical ways she and others had made a difference. She seems to have oscillated between feelings of impotence and creative action, needing the first to enable the second.

They seem to have left her with a belief that all survivors can be competent and successful, and yet remain untouchable; with a realism in which the most real thing is that which has been lost. What they had lost – their families, their entire childhood world – was not amenable to repair. 'In the early 1950s their experience seemed in danger of oblivion. So much was unfinished and unsaid, in the rush to get their feet onto the ladder. I would come out from the underground into some lovely London square and feel like a complete alien because of what I had heard from one of the boys; what must they have felt like?' When she thinks of them, the image that sometimes comes into her mind is of 'a mother and child crossing a road, intent on getting to the other side, but not communicating, not touching, walking in complete silence'.

5

A STORM FROM PARADISE

The dreams sanguine humanitarians raised almost to ecstasy about the year fifty of the last century by the moving sight of the Crystal Palace ... have vanished as quickly as they had arisen. The golden hopes of peace have in a single night turned to dead leaves in every drawer of every benevolent theorist's writing table. A swift disenchantment overtook the incredible infatuation which could put its trust in the peaceful nature of industrial and commercial competition.

Joseph Conrad, 'Autocracy and War'

To introduce into the philosophy of war itself a principle of moderation would be an absurdity.

Carl von Clausewitz, quoted by Roger Trinquier in *Modern Warfare*

In 1950, at the age of twenty-five, Helen Bamber stopped working for Oscar Friedmann. She can't remember exactly when, because for most of her life one job flowed into another, and often she was holding down two at the same time. Oscar remained in his severe way a friend, so she helped him with his work and talked to him about the survivors with whom they were still in touch. She would never quite let go of any of the brilliant, needy and angry men who were to employ her in the coming years, and who taught her more than they knew while she appeased them and helped them to function. In a sense, she stayed in one place, while always moving on; an endless conversation with the same kind of man, hearing the bad news in different voices. Their problem, usually, was that they took what they heard personally; and so did she.

In her account of herself she can seem haunted and obsessive, but this is at best partly true. She was, as many have testified, an attractive and warm person, with unusual human gifts, and if she was restless, full of unsatisfied longings to do something, to do more, she also yearned for a nice house with a big kitchen, a steady income, and children: her fantasy of the normal happy family gathered for its weekend supper. Despite her bleak sense of the world she loved good food, music, well-crafted objects: she wanted to possess ordinary contentment. It must have been hard for Rudi, every attempt to anticipate or satisfy a beloved partner tangling the knot still further; but for the moment their warm familiarity still held everything else in place.

She genuinely enjoyed the pleasures that became more abundant as wartime rationing ended. Winston Churchill returned to power, his Conservative government accepting the new consensus of welfare and full employment. He did not get her vote: as young semi-bohemians she and Rudi were sympathetic to Labour and to campaigns against war and colonialism. They had their nights in Soho, their plays and books – the poetry of George Barker and Dylan Thomas, the novels of William Cooper and Jean-Paul Sartre – with the back half of the *New Statesman* as a cultural guide. On summer evenings it was good to walk with friends from Sumatra Road through streets that grew more richly shaded the higher they climbed towards Hampstead, where an art-movie house in a side street showed foreign films. And they could escape even more easily now to the Alps. This was the beginning of the golden age of capitalism in the West, when to be young, healthy and employable was to live in a kind of paradise. Technology and the market worked, as never before; but progress, for all its chemical and electronic mastery, could not unravel the dense weave of politics. Europe and the USA lapsed into a tense and hedonistic peace; the rest of the world became the violent exception to their rule.

In May 1948, questions of legality and British acquiescence had become moot, as far as Jewish aspirations to nationhood were concerned. The state of Israel was declared after a bloody struggle following Britain's withdrawal from its former Mandate territory; the neighbouring Arab states combined to destroy Israel and were rebuffed. Hundreds of thousands of Palestinian Arabs fled across the new borders, terrorized or confused; a discreet policy of expulsion was aided by vain and bombastic promises of Palestinian restoration by the Arab powers, which have echoed down the years ever since. The Palestinians would remain a permanent challenge to the Israeli state, and the conflict became the most intractable of those in which two peoples have no doubt they belong to the same territory. Europe had solved the problem of its 'displaced persons', the Jews torn out of their places of exile in turn displacing the settled population of the once-historic Jewish homeland. Helen Bamber had seen people slip away from Belsen, heading for Palestine because they had nowhere else to go, except to the very regions where their families had been murdered; and although she came from a family that was Zionist by conviction, and was elated when the Jewish state came into existence, her attitude to it remained pragmatic: there had been no other choice, given the Holocaust and the attitude of the Western powers to Jewish immigration. This would, in later years, set her at odds with an Israeli government persuaded that ineluctable national destiny justified harsh measures against the enemy within.

Mere nations faded to indistinct shapes on the map of the new war between global ideologies, which seemed to threaten the very continuity of civilized existence. Throughout the summer of 1950 US and British troops under MacArthur fought the North Korean forces which had invaded the South. In late September, President Truman decided to reunite Korea under a regime friendly to the West. The North was now invaded in turn, and the President ordered his generals to drive on to the Yalu River, Korea's border with China. Mao Tse Tung responded by unleashing the armies which had just brought him to absolute power in Beijing. The UN army was routed in the north. Truman told a journalist that the use of nuclear bombs was 'under active consideration'. It was one of his Kansas City tough-guy gaffes, but Clement Attlee, the British Labour Prime Minister, was so frightened that he flew to Washington to talk Truman out of it. The age of nuclear paranoia had begun; two years later each side had their hydrogen bombs, and Helen Bamber remembers talking with Rudi about bringing children into such a world, and looking at people in the streets who did not seem at all worried and thinking, 'They're all right, we're going to be all right.'

She and Rudi left the damp refugee house, at last, and moved to a flat off Primrose Hill, above Regent's Park, with its high-windowed

Georgian terraces and formal gardens. London Zoo is in the park at the bottom of the hill: when the traffic on the roads through the park was quiet, at night, the cries of the larger animals, the elephants and the wolves in their open-air enclosures, were audible out on the hill. It was a decent place, and although they had no spare money they could live comfortably. On Sundays when they were not hammering country roads on the big bike they would join the strollers in the park, the most genteel of London's open spaces, which has a way of cradling its visitors in a calm, Edwardian light. It was almost possible for Helen Bamber to imagine that peace was real – 'that the war had not happened yet'.

She saw her father as often as she could, and after his retirement they would go to concerts at the new Festival Hall, among the harsh decks of raw concrete on the South Bank, but being with him was always like touching sadness. After an evening of classical music and his abject talk she would come home exhausted. Louis Balmuth retired in 1952, and lived alone. He had made enough to live on from his job with the metal suppliers, but he had almost no friends, and his daughter realized now that he never had any. He filled his time with reading – books on the death camps, accounts by survivors, and studies of the Nazis, including the man he still saw as their genius, Josef Goebbels. Hitler had been a mere demagogue, Balmuth was convinced; but Goebbels perverted his intelligence, and that was more mysterious.

The existence of the state of Israel never offered Louis Balmuth the grain of consolation that it gave to so many Jews of his generation: for him, there could be no repair. Although he saw the attempted Nazi genocide as unique, and not part of an eternal cycle of calamities that had befallen the Jewish people, Helen felt that his sense of it was perhaps better expressed by the Orthodox term *hurban*, 'disaster', rather than 'Holocaust', or *shoah*, with its implication of sacrifice and renewal.

Rudi Bamber, meanwhile, was not exactly fulfilled selling ballpoint pens. He had tried to study medicine when he came back from Australia, but he could not settle to it; something had gone. The past could not be altered, though at least he could change his name, losing the unbearable German suffix. He was prone to depression, 'very hard and very exclud-ing depressions' in his wife's memory of them. Her mother did not help their situation by deriding Rudi's failure, and melting into illness at the first sign of crisis, in constant need of placation, a permanent handicap on the marriage. She did have heart disease, but could 'produce' a dramatic cardiac episode for effect, according to her daughter. But even without her, Rudi's depression was severe enough for Helen to be concerned, both for him and for the impact that children might have on him, for she was still determined to have a family. Children stood for her insistence that there was a future, despite her dread and foreboding of it.

She was drawn to medicine, and since she lacked the money or the confidence to study the subject, she thought she would work for doctors until a real vocation took shape. She must have had enough belief in herself to know that she could choose employers who would give something back to her. The south side of Regent's Park opens into the curve of Regent Street, and the West End of London; but also onto the medical quarter that occupied whole blocks from Paddington in the west to St Pancras in the east: the consulting rooms of Harley Street; the large complex of the Middlesex Hospital; the Royal National Orthopaedic Hospital on Great Portland Street; the National Temperance Hospital; the Elizabeth Garrett Anderson Hospital for Women; hospitals for sick children, tropical diseases, afflictions of the ear, nose and throat. The human body was studied with extraordinary intensity along this mile and a half of road. This was where Helen Bamber would make a living, and slowly put her own world together.

Her first job was at a hospital much further to the east, on the river below Tower Bridge at Wapping, the headland that forms the Pool of London. She knew it well – her aunt Mina had often taken her around Whitechapel and the docks when she was a child, in part to show off to her where they had stopped Mosley's Fascists from marching down Cable Street. The area had been heavily bombed during the war.

The hospital was called St George's in the East after the parish around the Hawksmoor church of that name. Only the walls and spire of the great church were standing, blackened by smoke, a severe Palladian ruin between the housing projects and the docks. Iain Sinclair, in his poem *Lud Heat*, speaks of its 'massive, almost slave-built strength'; and hundreds of dockers and their families had died around it in the Blitz: there were still 'bald hills of rubble' in the streets all the way down the river when Bamber went there to work.

The headland at Wapping had canals, locks and wharves cut into it; at either end of the small peninsula, swing bridges allowed ships into the basins surrounded by warehouses. Although Wapping never recovered after the war, London was still one of the world's great ports in 1951. The street names listed the raw material of wealth: Tobacco Dock, Spice Court, Fig Street, Rum Close; there was even a Commodity Quay.

St George's was an old two-hundred-bed general hospital, run down and slated for closure; it had to deal with the accidents suffered by men lifting and turning dead weights, hands crushed between a load and the quay, bodies with too much beer and tobacco in them, and with women injured by having too many babies. The locals called it 'the infirmary'; part of it had once been a workhouse. It stood a few hundred feet from the riverside wharves. In Wapping Helen Bamber felt 'cut off from the world by the bridges and dam-gates': she discovered waterside stairs, reached by narrow alleys between warehouses, from which she could look across the Thames to Bermondsey. The funnels of ships passed between the buildings when the bridges were raised.

She had lived among the working class of North-East London for most of her life, but this was different, the separate world of unskilled English organized labour (though many dockers had names like Murphy and Quaid and were devout Catholics), a world lived to the rhythm of hard casual work, loading and unloading ships. Every morning men hoping for a start still gathered at the dock gates. The union had that rigid strength that characterized so many doomed institutions of the British labour movement; and Bamber had to learn about the pub, the dogs and the football. West Ham or Millwall were the teams, but not Tottenham Hotspur – known on the river as 'The Yids', Bamber discovered, because it had Jewish players.

She found the people innocent, in a way that surprised her. Marooned on their headland, fatalistic, the river bringing them heavy labour and now and then a little plunder, they seemed mesmerized by the port's long history. Work drained away, ships grew too big for the locks and canals, yet the dockers believed that 'nothing really bad could ever happen to them'.

Defoe, in his mythic journal of the Plague of London, saw the temptation to imagine Wapping as a refuge, as people watched the epidemic raging at the other end of the city: 'This made the people of Redriff and Wapping, Ratcliff and Lime-House so secure, and flatter themselves so much with the Plague's going off, without reaching them, that they took no Care ... and several from other Places really took sanctuary in that Part of the Town, as a Place of Safety, and as a Place which they thought God would pass over and not visit as the rest was visited.' God did not pass, then or later. Helen Bamber was witnessing the end of a community: in fifteen years the port would be dead. But coming here was then, for her, like an escape: 'It was my rehabilitation.' She felt as safe here as she ever could.

Bamber came highly recommended, by the CBF and by Friedmann. She was competent, self-possessed and discreet – a very young-looking woman who could calm people down, run things and talk back.

She took dictation from the doctors and took administrative work off their hands. Management was almost amateur: a handful of people could run a hospital like St George's in the 1950s. John Rundle, who was a young registrar there, and who is ending his working life as a clinician at the Medical Foundation, says that he saw then how good she was at paying attention to people, at making them feel understood. 'She was very impressive, much more than a secretary, very trustworthy and calm.' She was also, he said, 'good with language, in the widest sense'.

What she remembers is laughing a lot, and having the time of her life. The hospital was badly maintained; wild cats lived under the boards of the pavilions, and an old porter would leave food and sing to them when they emerged. She and Rundle were friends. They drank in the local pubs, and got to know some dockers' families. A man called George Marling, so badly crippled by rheumatoid arthritis that he could not turn his neck, his hands like claws, was given a job helping in the office. It encouraged him to begin to move his body again. His family brought her gifts that never seemed to have cleared customs.

To keep the work interesting, Rundle and Bamber organized lunch-time meetings for neighbourhood general practitioners where they talked about the health problems they were seeing, and asked the local doctors' advice. Bamber discovered that memories of the war were as raw as the bomb sites: Dr Hannah Billig, who had a practice on Cable Street, had stayed during the Blitz, treating the injured and listening to thousands of terrified bereaved relatives. Bamber thought her fierce and ingenious. But the dockers had no memorial. Their families still felt anger over this neglect: even merchant seamen had their monuments, but the men who kept the ships turning around under bombardment were forgotten. Many of those who died were unidentifiable – burned, shattered, blown into the river. (At the very end of the twentieth century an attempt is being made to turn the last piece of derelict land fronting the river at Wapping into a memorial for the civilian dead. A property developer has a better idea: it is an ideal site for apartments with river views, each costing a quarter of a million pounds.)

Bamber was made acting almoner – the hospital's social worker – after the holder of the post died in childbirth. She visited the patients' families in their council flats. One day on a ward she was introduced to a doctor she had not seen before, a very short, markedly energetic man with a strong Liverpool accent. He had a slight limp, dragging his leg after him with agile impatience, as though it was a distraction. She was aware of his scrutiny of her; but on his rounds – he was acting as locum for a consultant – she saw him focus with deep concentration on each patient. He seemed to revere the human body in the act of diagnosis, whilst the younger doctors spoke with unusual respect about his skill at explaining symptoms.

This was her first encounter with Maurice Pappworth, one of the most unsettling figures in post-war British medicine. He was a goad to its elite: the *Lancet* even when praising him tagged him with adjectives like 'vitriolic', 'bitter', 'haughty' and 'excessive'. All his life he stood outside the establishment, breaking windows. His obituarist in the *British Medical Journal* noted admiringly that he was 'regarded as a pestilential nuisance ... for most of his career'. In 1936 he had passed the examination of the Royal College of Physicians, which had a 90 per cent failure rate, and would normally have become a Fellow of the College and been awarded a consultancy, but he was told by a leading physician in 1939, when he applied for a consultant's job, that 'no Jew could ever be a gentleman.' Exclusion from the company of such gentlemen might have been a relief – but the denial of a merited professional honour was intolerable. John Rundle, who also met Pappworth for the first time at St George's, said, 'You could get away with murder in those days,' if you were a medical grandee, and as Pappworth would later show, this was sometimes literally true.

But meanwhile the wound festered, and because it was so visible and sore, the kind of men who had inflicted it went on snubbing him. Since Pappworth could not get a consultancy in a large hospital, he went into private practice in Harley Street. The Royal College of Physicians, housed nearby in one of those beautiful terraces on Regent's Park, became his measure of clubby complacency. It returned the antagonism, until his exclusion became a scandal. When he was finally elected to a Fellowship in 1993, a year before he died and fifty-seven years after gaining his Membership, he was given a standing ovation.

John Rundle remembers Pappworth as a small man, with light brown hair, 'nondescript-looking', but with a compelling personality, and said that he had never met another doctor as good. 'He had an *excellent* attitude as a physician. He was a real humanist, and at that time there was great austerity among senior physicians in their approach to people.' Rundle wanted to pass the draconian Royal College of Physicians exam, and Pappworth taught young doctors how to do it. (He would eventually train over a thousand members of the college, and found it satisfying that his pass rate was so much higher than that of the great teaching hospitals from which he was barred.) 'Twenty of us would attend his tutorials, crowded into a room in Harley Street. This was in about 1953. He taught us how to think about medicine; he made good doctors of us, he made us efficient and caring at what we thought we had already been trained to do. He was a rare animal. The gifted ones are ignorant of the fact that they are so gifted; and he was like that, despite the famous chip on his shoulder.'

Pappworth was immediately attracted to Helen Bamber, and made that clear; but unfulfilled desire was a manageable part of their relationship. Despite or because of this ambivalent charge in the friendship, he found her a sympathetic interlocutor, one who lived with a membrane as thin as his separating her from the world. Bamber said that Pappworth always had 'a sense of impending danger'. It was not easy for him to forget that he was a Jew; and covert anti-semitism was still rife in the medical profession. A radiologist in another hospital said to no one in particular, in her hearing, that there were already quite enough Jews floating about the place.

Bamber would come to his rooms, to help him deal with letters and teaching notes; but often just to talk for hours. 'He was not lonely, so much as cursed with aloneness, and that haunted me.' Helen chose Pappworth, as least as much as she was chosen by him; his influence on her went deep.

His abiding concern was with the potential of medicine for cruelty. He would talk to her about unnecessary surgeries, the overuse of drugs, the distress caused by acts that passed for research. The lust to know too much appalled him – the very impulse that was transforming the world around him with speed, lightness and information. He represented to her 'the Jewish predicament about helplessness and power, about how you use power, and how it can become a deadly danger, and is always something to be watched'. For him medicine was a real form of power, and he was convinced that some paths to knowledge were an abuse of an almost sacred vocation.

Pappworth had something of the Orthodox suspicion of research for its own sake, and he never fully resolved the problem of how new techniques (to which he was not opposed) could be perfected by testing on human beings. The essential purpose of medicine for him was, simply, diagnosis and healing. His own skill was won from meticulous study of the body. In his *Primer of Medicine*, based on his lectures to young doctors like Rundle, he would later write: 'Beware the crime of diagnostic greed. Overwhelming evidence is not essential for a correct diagnosis.' The proper question was, he wrote, 'To paraphrase a famous Hebrew saying, "Wherefore is this disease different from all other diseases?"'

The Nazi doctors who selected, who administered injections, who ran the euthanasia programmes, represented for him the ultimate betrayal. The perversion of medicine was a sin like no other because it was against the body of humanity. Bamber said: 'He found it literally inconceivable, beyond his imagination, how physicians could have done these things; he had himself struggled so hard to achieve what he knew about care.'

In the late 1940s, after the Nazi doctors' trials, Maurice Pappworth began to compile details of unethical experiments from reports published in the medical journals. By the time he met Helen Bamber they formed an archive.

In the early 1950s research had become almost the only means by which ambitious physicians could be promoted. Doctors in the nineteenth century cut up the dead to learn about the living; now it was tempting to use the living bodies of people who either did not know what was happening to them, or were not in a position to argue, and to play safe by repeating difficult experimental procedures on them: humans as laboratory animals. New-born babies in the public wards of hospitals, the mentally ill and prisoners asked to 'volunteer' were most vulnerable.

Thousands of experiments – many painful, certainly uncomfortable, and some of them lethal – were carried out without the subjects' consent (or that of the parents of young children). These doctors were a minority, even among researchers; but Helen Bamber said she began to understand why the dockers' wives told her it was safer to be treated in even a decrepit local hospital, and to stay out of 'them teaching hospitals – you never know what they'll do to you'. Florence Nightingale called early nineteenth-century hospitals 'gateways to death'; Pappworth gave the folk wisdom of the poor a content of real horror.

He often quoted, in Bamber's recollection, a sentence he attributed to Moses Maimonides, the great Jewish philosopher and physician: 'May I never see in the patient anything but a fellow creature in pain.' (It is actually from 'The Physician's Prayer' by the Berlin doctor Markus Herz, the first Jewish court physician in Prussian history, who wrote it at the end of the eighteenth century.) References in English and American medical literature to patients as 'the material' carried overtones, to his ear, of Nazi terminology. He began to write sharply critical, almost derisive letters to the medical press about experimental results and the standard of teaching in British hospitals, and alienated himself still further from the establishment.

Nothing upset him more than experiments on the very young and the very old, especially on those who were dying. He told Bamber of a case from California in which a group of over seventy-three patients with terminal cancer had long hollow needles inserted deeply into their livers, through which tubes were passed. Fourteen of these dying people had the needles in place for nineteen days. Blood samples were taken and a contrast medium was injected so that X-rays could be taken of the circulation of the blood in their livers. Of the seventy-three subjects only two had an illness related to the tests.

The doctors reported that there had been no real complications in the test group: some of them had arteries, bladders or bowels punctured by careless insertions; a few suffered haemorrhages.

Pappworth's collection of experiments grew and grew, in the course of Bamber's association with him; and she recalls that he often wondered what he should do with it. An open challenge to the integrity of other doctors for doing what was considered to be normal research seemed unthinkable. It would put him beyond the pale.

She believes that Pappworth hated the position into which he was digging himself. 'Some people get angry and enjoy it, but he was deeply *hurt* by the abuse of medical practice. He took it personally.' For her, his anger was an education in the ways by which care can be turned into something else — a form of cure that banks on the greater good of those yet unborn, who will be grateful to us for what we do. The connection between this and other kinds of violence cannot have been obvious to her at the time, but power focused on the human body would later drive almost everything else from her attention.

When Bamber was talking about Pappworth she recalled an occasion in Germany, which she could barely locate in time, and certainly not on any map. She found herself with a colleague early in 1946, at what she called a 'castle', somewhere in the east of the British Zone. She remembered gaunt, shuffling men, who seemed to be mentally ill, and she was told that they had been castrated by X-ray during the war. 'Gods in white coats,' as one of their nurses later called them, doctors who knew what they were doing, may have mutilated those patients. It may have been one of the asylums in which the Nazis starved or gassed the less than perfect: defective children, idiots, depressed farmers' wives — what they called *Lebensunwertes leben*: life unworthy of life.

*   *   *

St George's in the East closed in 1956. Helen Bamber went to work at the Middlesex Hospital: it still occupies an entire city block north of Oxford Street. Now she could walk to work across Regent's Park. It was a good job, helping a radiographer and the sister-in-charge run a large X-ray department. She worked for Pappworth in the evenings, transcribing his quirky brilliant lectures to his tutorial group. He was thinking of publishing them, and her job was to help turn them into coherent prose.

At the Middlesex, she met Herbert Seddon, a spiky, partially deaf, brilliant orthopaedic surgeon and Professor at London University, said according to hospital legend to know more about bones and peripheral nerves than anyone else in the world. If Pappworth was the great diviner of what ailed a body, Seddon, for her, came to represent medicine at its most creative. He was a specialist in reconstructive work, lengthening shin bones for children born with asymmetrical legs, or working on limbs crippled by polio; and he had invented modest pieces of apparatus that made a difference, such as a light splint for polio victims who often had to wear heavy leg braces. Like Pappworth, he was impressed by this serious young woman, though in his case the interest was platonic. Later he would become a good friend.

At home she and Rudi circled in silence around her determination to have children and Rudi's fear of bringing them into a world that could take them away from him. She would be thirty-three in 1958, and wanted to have a child by then. This was late for motherhood, at that time. She also wanted contradictory things, and could be difficult and anxious. They had, she now believes, married too early; she was changing, estimating herself a little more and feeling stifled by the history they shared. Yet like many couples on the brink, she and her husband clung together and turned inward. The large chaos of states had brought them close; a smaller act of violence may have kept them together for a while longer.

Rudi was still close to his cousin Dr Johannes Pulfer, despite being evicted by him during the war. He and his wife Gertrude lived in the same two-up two-down house in Colindale, on the edge of a wartime airfield. It is the kind of suburb in which a city forgets itself as a historic centre and becomes dormitory streets. It seemed safe beyond words.

Gertrude was nostalgic for a Germany that had ceased to exist in 1933, so she reproduced as well as she could a decent Berlin home in this perimeter suburb of a city she disliked. She ran the practice efficiently for Hannes. Helen and Rudi would often go out there on Tuesday evenings for *Tafelspitz and Kartoffelsalat*, a wistful middle-class German dinner. They often found themselves keeping Gertrude company: Hannes's real life was downstairs in his surgery, and perhaps he was escaping from a melancholic partner. He had a dog called Pasha, 'a revolting Pekinese', which snarled and bit ankles, and the more it snapped the funnier he thought it was. It kept him company between patients.

Early one evening at the end of March 1957 Rudi and Helen were in the first-floor sitting room with Gertrude Pulfer when the dog began yelping, a hysterical terrified sound unlike anything they had heard before. 'Then there was a noise of furniture being shoved about, his heavy doctor's table with all its instruments and its brass lamps being thrown over, and above all that cacophony I heard this strange animalish sound coming from a human being, and a pounding on the floor. I can't tell you how I knew, it was a question of seconds, but I think we all knew.

We rushed downstairs, Rudi first, then me, Gertrude behind me, these narrow stairs, in this house which she had decorated with these very German tapestries, cushions and dried flowers, and when we got to the door of the consulting room a man rushed at us with a knife, all bloodstained, with spittle on his mouth, and I just caught sight behind him of Hannes lying on the floor, covered with blood.'

Rudi backed out of the surgery, Helen pushed Gertrude and together they ran to the front door, and out into the street; the man ran after them and they scattered, but he caught Helen. 'He'd got me with his arm around my neck and he held the knife to my throat: that feeling of steel on the skin, that someone is about to butcher you. ... I felt indescribable weakness and quite absurdly thought of the word "artery" but I think he was as confused as I was, he only had hold of me for a moment. He let me go and I stumbled and he ran in the opposite direction.' Rudi shouted into a nearby house to call the police, and she held onto Gertrude to stop her going inside again. 'She was a large woman, and I had to fight with her, I was screaming that Hannes was dead, I'm sure he's dead, because in our panic we didn't know where the man was and I wanted her to understand there was nothing she could do. I was afraid he had gone back into the house. Then the police came.'

The whole ground floor of the house seemed to be covered in blood. A hand placed on a dark-painted wall by the consulting room would detect the stickiness of a patch they had missed when they were cleaning, although Helen and Rudi had scrubbed for hours.

They found the man's knife in a hedge across the road: 'a ten-inch stiletto,' said the local *Hendon and Finchley Times*, eager to note a rare murder in the area, but the man was gone. At night a detective slept on a camp bed in the surgery, leaving the door open. According to the medical notes found next to the doctor's body the murderer was Elias Georgiou, a Greek Cypriot with a history of psychotic delusions. The patients, the friends, the locum doctors who came to help, all felt the curious safety of being under siege. They drank and fed each other and told terrible jokes, but then there would be a call and someone would announce that the fugitive had been sighted in a patch of woodland somewhere in the dense housing sprawl, or along the Silk Stream that ran under the road near the house and on through industrial estates and playing fields. The suburbs seemed to be full of empty hiding places.

The manhunt was given an edge of hysteria because of Georgiou's nationality. Guerrillas under General Grivas were then fighting to expel the British from Cyprus and to unite the island with Greece. Pulfer's murder was not remotely connected with this small war, but a crazed Greek knifeman at large in the capital was too sensational an image for the press to ignore.

The police caught him, and he went on trial. Helen Bamber had to identify him. 'When he was brought into court, he looked very different, it was the same man but all that ferocity and energy was gone; he was depleted. He stumbled and had to be helped to stand, and he was completely bewildered – he could barely understand what was going on.'

At that moment she claims she felt closer to him than to the barrister questioning her. 'It was as though he and Rudi and I had shared in some terrible drama, and I felt antagonistic towards them and not to him.' There was now another life at stake: death was still the penalty for murder, and not even the distraught widow could bear to think of hanging the man as a solution to his destruction of her life. They were prepared to lobby for his reprieve, if it came to that, but Georgiou was obviously insane. The only explanation he could offer sounded like a sad violent defence against his own homosexuality: 'The doctor told me to marry one of our boys and this is very wrong and against our religion. I pulled one of my knives out of my pocket and threw it on his desk and said, "If you want me to do that you must kill me with my own knife." He stood up and I picked up the knife and cut his throat.' He was ordered to be detained 'during the Queen's pleasure'.

Gertrude remained friends with Rudi and Helen, but over the years she lost interest in seeing them. There was no question of her returning to Germany: she had married a Jew, and could never forgive her country for what it had done to Johannes Pulfer and to her. She lived on for another thirty years in her neat well-kept house, out beyond the new motorway, which opened soon after her husband's murder and cut her off from London.

The events of that night had other effects. Helen Bamber could not, for several years, pass a dark room even in her own house without anxiety; once, at the hospital, she had a panic attack when a black-bearded man, a Cypriot, was brought in for an X-ray. The killing also made it impossible to put off having a child any longer, and she was pregnant by the following winter.

David Bamber was born at the Middlesex in November 1958. It was a difficult birth. 'For the first twenty-four hours they didn't want me to hold or see him because they thought he might have been damaged. I remember the shock of seeing his head coming to a point, like a pixie's; I think I contemplated suicide then for the first and only time in my life; I felt that if David really had been damaged I wasn't sure I wanted to go on.'

She did not enjoy the experience of being inside the hospital machine, and hated the sight of screaming young children abandoned on other wards. Doctors and nurses had power and were not always aware of how they were using it. 'There was what now seems an extraordinary lack of care about how children felt, and a lack of understanding of mothers forced to abandon them, as though they were somehow a nuisance.' She recalled almost nostalgically the chaos of the Glyn Hughes Hospital at Belsen, with the families gathered around the beds of the precious children.

*   *   *

The pent-up tensions of a century of colonialism were released into the already charged atmosphere of the Cold War. In 1958, Britain was still the disputed overlord of much of West Africa, the Caribbean, Singapore, Hong Kong and parts of Arabia; France had already lost one rearguard action in Vietnam, and was waging another in Algeria against the nationalist Front Liberation National.

The British were resigned to decolonization; the world role of the City of London as a financial centre was more important than mere territorial possession. The French empire had come late, and was bound up with the lost prestige of a defeated country. Pride was complicated by an insistence on the ultimate equality of all subjects of the empire under the banner of the Rights of Man – an event postponed until the subject peoples were developed enough to enjoy it. This was 'the civilizing mission', an illusion that led France into barbarism in North Africa, one of the states that originated codes of human dignity and constitutional rights indulging in a tremendous outburst of baffled violence. Anti-colonial purges and killings were answered by disproportionate counter-savagery from the army in the field. French soldiers, encouraged to treat their enemies as beings without culture or humanity, would, like their American successors in Vietnam, later have difficulty in recognizing themselves.

'Don't read this; it will only upset you,' Rudi Bamber had said to his wife on a Sunday morning early in March 1958. That day's *Observer* carried an account of the arrest and torture of Henri Alleg, French Algerian, Jew, communist, and supporter of the FLN, by his compatriots of the 10th Paratroop Division. His testimony, under the title *La Question*, was published by Jerome Lindon, Samuel Beckett's editor. Available for barely two weeks, sixty-five thousand copies of the book were sold before it was seized by the police. The English edition was about to appear, and the *Observer* gave it the front page, quoting from the preface by Jean-Paul Sartre: a typically overheated polemic, but an effective denunciation for all that of the army's behaviour in Algiers.

Helen Bamber had met French ex-partisans in the British Zone in 1946, and had heard descriptions of Gestapo torture. She could barely credit the truth of Alleg's statements. Sartre caught that sense of incredulity in his preface to Alleg's evidence: 'one thing seemed impossible in any circumstances: that one day men should be made to scream by those acting in our name.'

It had been at least possible after 1945 to imagine that the human body must become politically sacrosanct. In war it could be burned or fragmented; nuclear weapons might destroy whole populations; but it seemed, for a while, incompatible with basic self-respect to torture bodies prior to death. For someone with Bamber's fear of being singled out for cruelty, this may have been wishful thinking. How could anyone be so innocent? Yet forty-eight countries at the United Nations had signed the Universal Declaration of Human Rights in 1948, which stated in its fifth article that 'no one shall be subjected to torture or to cruel, inhuman or degrading treatment or punishment'. The naive seemed for a moment to have inherited the earth.

Especially from the beginning of 1957, when General Massu took over the city in a successful attempt to destroy the FLN, reports of electrocution, half-hangings, drownings and beatings began to leak out of Algiers. Torture had, of course, never left the world, though nineteenth-century Europe believed that it had eradicated the practice and that it would soon be only of antiquarian interest wherever civilization planted its flags. Despotic states have always used it, especially on those suspected of treason. In police stations all over the world the use of the third degree on criminal suspects was the norm, even in England and the USA, and especially in the South. A white policeman in a room with a descendant of slaves was guided by lynch law rather than the Bill of Rights, and lived in a culture that endlessly denied their common humanity; and 'Judge Lynch' demanded 'slow torturous burnings' to mark his dominance well into the fifth decade of the century.

In Algeria, however, a severe application of cruelty was organized by a democratic state, and on a large scale. If it was designed – the verb is exact – to retrieve information, it was also intended to demoralize a political movement. In this it set the standard for modern political torture: violence used on the nerves and muscles of individual men and women because the larger body politic is too difficult to understand. For someone with Helen Bamber's experience, Algeria saw the return of beautiful cynical men in leopard-pattern jump-suits and forage-caps; the glamour of the killing machine – of Nietzsche's genial warriors, so considerate at home, 'not much better than uncaged beasts of prey in the world outside where the strange, the foreign begin'.

Bamber said she felt something give. 'I could no longer hide behind the bad Germans who had done it all, the idea that it could never happen again. Perhaps there is something more realistic in the assumption of human evil than in the hope that declarations can change impulses and hatreds. But something had come back in Algeria, and it was horrible.' That was the word that stuck in Henri Alleg's memory:

> The torture went on until dawn, or very nearly. Through the partition, I could hear shouts and cries, muffled by the gag, and curses and blows. I soon knew that it was in no way an exceptional night, but the routine of the building. The cries of suffering were part of the familiar noises of the 'Centre de Tri' [clearing centre]. None of the paras paid any attention to it, but I don't believe that there was a single prisoner who did not, like myself, cry from hatred and humiliation on hearing the screams of the tortured for the first time.
>
> ... A little later the door opened again. This time it was two paras. An electric torch shone on my face. I waited for the blows, but they never touched me. I was trying in vain to see who they were, but I only heard a

young voice say: 'Horrible, isn't it?' and the other one answered: 'Yes, it's terrible.' And they went away.

*   *   *

It is more interesting to consider why someone like Helen Bamber does what she does than it is to probe the 'heart of darkness', the mind of the sadistic killer which, with its attendant clichés of redemptive violence, so fascinates our culture. Torturers are essentially banal. Like the Nazi doctors and nurses who killed children and the mentally ill, evoked with unforgettable contempt by Michael Burleigh in *Death and Deliverance*, most torturers jump to their task out of bureaucratic ambition and the cowardice that overwhelms the ordinarily weak in strong institutions, especially armies. Stupidity and bigotry may help them, and so in varying degrees does the human appetite for inflicting cruelty. A study of Greek torturers after the military junta was deposed in 1974 found that many of them were neglected children who found in state-sanctioned cruelty a way of taking revenge on the powerless or the clever and rebellious. Their normal enemies were certified. But this is probably too charitable, and really explains nothing: childhood trauma may enable, but it does not cause, the use of torture by an institution as powerful as the state.

In pre-modern times, when torture was an integral part of the judicial search for truth, the torturer-executioner belonged to a separate caste. Richard Evans, in his great book on capital punishment in Germany, describes how the executioner had his own cup at the inn, his special seat in church, and invariably married the daughter of another hangman; between executions he lived by emptying the town cesspits, or killing stray dogs; and he was often the local knacker, rendering dead horses into useful parts. Twentieth-century narratives of torture, by contrast, hold a mirror up to their readers: in it we see decorated army officers, students, clerks, political idealists, and even medical doctors.

In the literature of torture, one report on the familiarity of the perpetrator overshadows all others, and it is the record of a terrifying hoax. Stanley Milgram, a psychologist at Yale, asked volunteers to administer electric shocks to a subject separated from the experimenters by a glass screen. The current was not switched on, but the volunteers did not know that, as they went on increasing the voltage under the calm supervision of the experimenter, listening to the screams of the subject.

The fact that destroyed any lingering notion of the born torturer was the ease with which a group bond between experimenter and volunteer could be forged, 'from which', Milgram wrote, 'the victim is excluded ... the victim is truly an outsider, who stands alone, physically and psychologically.'

Helen Bamber, with her colleagues at the Medical Foundation, insists that our moral duty is to describe and refuse torture, not to understand, relativize or forgive it. Yet there remains one important sense in which an effort must be made to understand the torturer.

Torture marks its victim physically and psychologically. Ritual torture was used in certain tribal societies – among the Plains Indians, for example – literally to mark the passage of young men into adult society, and into a kind of primitive equality. The anthropologist Pierre Clastres argues that this 'writing on the body' was a way of making law unforgettable: it was homeopathic cruelty, designed to prevent young men from wanting too much power, and so preventing much greater cruelty. Torture is always about power, and every action of the torturer is a 'translation of pain into power' as Elaine Scarry put it in her classic meditation on torture in *The Body in Pain*; above all, it is about the symbolic power of the state at its most extreme. Squads of men in war have always had the opportunity to abuse prisoners, if they so wished and if their commanders let them; but that is different from the modern organization of torture, in which prisoners are carefully logged in, 'processed', and their answers recorded and cross-checked. This is torture as a bureaucratic industry. It is necessary to confront this torturer, the one who expresses the mind of the state, or is allowed to think that he does. But he rarely emerges from his office; and the state denies that he exists.

In French Algeria, secrecy and denial broke down, but only because the French state was so divided: it was fighting an unwinnable war, in which no formula could be devised that would preserve French rule and the privileges of the settlers, yet allow the Algerian majority to elect their own representatives. In French eyes, the 'Arabs' (many of them Berbers) were sullenly enigmatic. Camus' 'stranger' shoots an Arab who is featureless and nameless, yet who seems to fuse with the harsh sunlight to form an intensely physical, oppressive threat.

This same blindness infected the army in Algeria, which imagined itself as the defender of France's historic destiny, and of Algeria from its native people. Officers in the elite units of the paras and the Foreign Legion saw the conflict in pure and ruthless military terms; the roots of Algerian nationalism were invisible to them. They dreamed a clash between terrorism and order, criminality and justice; while the FLN justified their own pitiless methods (mutilation, terrorist bombing, the massacre of wavering villagers) by the French Army's much greater violence, its arsenal of planes and tanks.

The problem could be seen in organizational terms: all that was necessary was to undo the structure of the group directing resistance to colonial rule. Interrogation of suspects would reveal the make-up of the FLN. 'Special methods' would be needed to make them talk, but gradually the empty squares in the *organigramme* on the blackboard at headquarters would be filled in and victory would follow. Who then would complain about the measures taken?

Roger Trinquier, one of the paratroop officers who strutted the Algerian stage 'like demigods', as Alistair Horne remembered them, published a book in 1961 with the bland title *Modern Warfare*. It was nothing less than 'a Cartesian rationale for the use of torture in revolutionary war', in the words of its later American editor.

Trinquier was a schoolteacher who volunteered for the army in the early 1930s. A captain under Vichy, he had always hated de Gaulle, like many of his comrades in Algeria, but it is too easy to see him as a fascist; and indeed some para officers had fought in the Resistance. They were courageous soldiers, not sadistic brutes. In the late 1940s Trinquier was a counter-insurgency operator in Vietnam, using many of the techniques (special forces behind enemy lines, strategic hamlets) that the Americans would try, with no more success, in the course of their awful decade in the country. During the battle of Algiers, Trinquier's units cross-hatched the city with a grid, surveying and collecting information from each square and picking up civilians who did not fit neatly into it. Anything between a third and a half of Arab males in the city were interrogated; and of these an uncountable number were tortured.

Trinquier worked on the assumption that 'modern warfare' is a battle against subversion: 'Warfare is now an interlocking system of actions — political, economic, psychological, military — *that aims at the overthrow of the established authority in a country and its replacement by another regime.*'

He believed that a lever could move a mountain: 'We know that it is not at all necessary to have the sympathy of a majority of the people in order to rule them. The right organisation can turn the trick.' (His claim that 'a band of gangsters' could take over metropolitan France using the methods of the FLN is of a piece with his belief in the people's weakness: 'This is the simple mechanism, now well known, which can at any instant be unleashed against us.') Given his purely technical view of governance, the aim was to take the lever away from the FLN, for 'in *modern warfare* we are not up against just a few armed bands spread across a given territory, but rather against an *armed clandestine organisation* whose essential role is to impose its will upon the population. Victory will be obtained only through the complete destruction of that organisation.'

What enables the enemy to win is terrorism. The terrorist, whose motivation is never discussed, is a shadowy conspirator carrying on 'warfare without uniform' and attacking 'far from the field of battle, only unarmed civilians who are incapable of defending themselves and who are normally protected under the rules of warfare'. He is not 'an ordinary criminal', Trinquier insists, and he writes that 'during a period of history when the bombing of open cities is permitted, and when two Japanese cities were razed to end the war in the Pacific, one cannot with good cause reproach him. The terrorist has become a soldier, like the aviator or the infantryman.'

But – and here is the rub – the aviator and the infantryman accept the risks of their work. The terrorist does not. He must be made to realize that, when he is captured, he cannot expect the privileges of the normal combatant. He must talk; and what his adversary is seeking is 'precise information about [the terrorist's] organisation'. Trinquier's account of what happens next is euphemistic, but frank: 'No lawyer is present for such an interrogation. If the prisoner gives the information requested, the examination is quickly terminated; if not, specialists must force his secret from him. Then, as a soldier, he must face the suffering, and perhaps the death, he has heretofore managed to avoid. The terrorist must accept this as a condition inherent in his trade and in the methods of warfare that, with full knowledge, his superiors and he himself have chosen.'

In a passage that foreshadows events in Chile and Argentina and many other countries, he writes that it is essential to declare war at the first symptom of subversive operations, and from that point 'any party that has supported or continues to support the enemy shall be considered a party of the enemy. The nation attacked must fall in behind the government and its army.'

Trinquier has a kind of twisted honesty. He does not waste time, for example, on the hypothesis of the 'unexploded bomb', which is exhumed and revived whenever torture needs a justification. (What would *you* do if you knew a terrorist had planted a bomb in a hospital, or a school, and you could save lives by making him tell you where it was?) But for him, as for his many successors, subversion is an infectious disease of the body politic, curable if it is caught in time. No persuasion or appeal will have any effect on 'a populace infected by clandestine organisms that penetrate like a cancer into its midst. ... It is only when we have delivered it from this evil that it will freely listen, think and express itself. A just peace will then be quite possible.' Military experts must be as impersonal as medical specialists; torture is, properly understood, a kind of rehabilitation; and as with cancer, progress has given specialists the tools they need: 'science can easily place at the army's disposition the means for obtaining what is sought.'

Even this most lucid of torturers quails from describing the reality of what actually happens in the room. In Algeria, science was embodied in an army signals magneto with a few electrodes dangling from it. Henri Alleg described the first time he saw such a machine. He was at the time roped to 'a black plank, sweating with humidity, polluted and sticky with vomit'.

> Ja— [a para sergeant], smiling all the time, dangled the clasps at the end of the electrodes before my eyes. These were little shining steel clips, elongated and toothed, what telephone engineers call 'crocodile' clips. He attached one of them to the lobe of my right ear and the other to a finger on the same side.
>
> Suddenly, I leapt in my bonds and shouted with all my might. Cha—[a lieutenant] had just sent a first electric charge through my body. A flash of lightning exploded next to my ear and I felt my heart racing in my breast. I struggled, screaming, and stiffened myself until the straps cut into my flesh. All the while the shocks controlled by Cha—, magneto in hand, followed each other without cease.

Then I felt as if a savage beast had torn the flesh from my body. Still smiling above me, Ja— had attached the pincer to my penis. The shocks going through me were so strong that the straps holding me to the board came loose. They stopped to tie them again and we continued.

After a while the lieutenant took the place of Ja—. He had removed the naked wire from one of the pincers and fastened it down along the entire width of my chest. The whole of my body was shaking with nervous shocks, getting ever stronger in intensity, and the session went on interminably. They had thrown cold water over me in order to increase the intensity of the current, and between every two spasms I trembled with cold. All around me sitting on packing cases, Cha— and his friends emptied bottles of beer.

At a later 'session', the same officer put the bare wire into Alleg's mouth, whose jaws were 'soldered to the electrode by the current'. 'My eyes,' he recalled, 'under their spasmed lids, were crossed with images of fire, and geometric luminous patterns flashed in front of them. I thought I could feel them being torn from their sockets by the shocks, as if pushed out from within.'

De Gaulle's concessions to the FLN, after he came to power in 1958 in a peaceful coup, and before his withdrawal from Algeria in 1961, were hardly motivated by revulsion from the situation that Alleg described. But they had the effect of stopping the war, and outraged soldiers like Trinquier. De Gaulle, the far-sighted old cavalry strategist, was applying political, not military or medical, and therefore more humane, criteria to a struggle that had cost a million lives, the vast majority of them Algerian. He knew that the FLN was – however authoritarian – the voice of Muslim Algeria. The colonels were technicians of violence, substituting torture for an understanding of a community's desire to reimagine itself – its members' willingness to die for an idea of the nation. Benedict Anderson has written of 'the venomous argots of dying colonialisms' (gooks, *ratons*, slants) that they have the effect of 'reducing the adversary to his biological physiognomy'. In this condition, the suspect in the room has no nationality: their identity denied, he or she cannot be taken seriously as a civil person, or even as a human being.

There is no more poignant commentary on the degradation of military thought and democratic values in Algeria than Henri Alleg's story of an episode from his time in the half-finished house that had become a torture centre, the door-frames empty, steel reinforcing bars sticking out of the walls, an unsafe house where everything needed for 'modern warfare' could be improvised using simple materials.

> One night on the floor above me, they tortured a man: he was a Moslem, quite old, to judge by the sound of his voice. Between the terrible cries which the torture forced out of him, he said, exhausted: 'Vive la France! Vive la France!' ... But the others continued to torture him and their laughter rang through the whole building.

* * *

As the 1960s began, Helen Bamber had, like many women in the twentieth century, seen the effects of war and genocide, witnessed the violent death of a friend, and given birth to a child.

Like many others, she also feared that basic human decency might be under threat; and that there were dignities and rights which the rival ideologies could not even see: the right of free expression, full of awkwardness for the state; and the right of the human body to be free from unnecessary pain. By the end of the 1950s she was struggling to reconcile her desire for a stable middle-class existence, and for emotional satisfaction, with her gut feeling that there should be some response to the tolerance of atrocity. 'I don't think that you could have my background, have the kind of father I did, have worked with survivors, and not wish to stake out some position of resistance. Anyone who had been at Belsen after the war must have been preoccupied with the responsibility of the bystanders. I did not want to be a bystander.'

Her own emotional reaction against cruelty was given powerful intellectual and moral backing as the decade ended. Pierre-Henri Simon's *Contre la Torture* had already appeared in 1957. Simon had been an inmate of German prison camps and linked what was happening in France and Algeria to the legacy of fascism. He spoke for many who had knowledge of the work of the Nazis in seeing torture as a return to barbarism: 'The nineteenth century was far from pure; in its civil wars, in its social struggles ... it was covered with blood. ... Nevertheless, the century had at least a kind of modesty which our own no longer possesses: even when its tribunals condemned the innocent ... they preserved at least enough of the humanist and Christian [sic] spirit implied in the Declaration of the Rights of Man and in the penal code which it inspired to spare those it indicted from torture.'

In June 1959, the proprietor of Editions de Minuit, Jerome Lindon, who had already defied his government by publishing Alleg's testimony, issued another challenge to French colonial policy. *La Gangrène* described the torture of five Algerians by police in the centre of Paris in December 1958, at the Special Branch building on the Rue des Saussaies. The print-run of the booklet was seized, yet Lindon was not charged with any offence. (He would be tried two years later for encouraging soldiers to disobey immoral orders). Many writers – the Catholic François Mauriac, the Gaullist André Malraux – protested on his behalf to de Gaulle; they went over to what Trinquier called 'the party of the enemy'.

Meanwhile, in Britain, the violent end of imperial rule in Kenya came under scrutiny. What was known as the Cowan Plan insisted that all detainees should do hard labour, a symbolic way of stating that Kenyan nationalism was merely criminal. As political prisoners, the detainees refused. At Hola Camp in March 1959 eighty-five of them were marched out and told to start digging ditches. All refused the order, and all of them were thrashed with heavy sticks. Ten men died.

John Calder, the English publisher of Samuel Beckett, brought out an edition of Lindon's book in September. In his edition he included a report of the Hola murders, and the story of Captain Ernest Bonar Law, an officer risen from the ranks who had objected to the systematic beating of prisoners at the Nairobi jail where he was employed. He was dismissed, denied further work, imprisoned and deported to Britain as a pauper. He had spent his entire adult life as a regular soldier in the British Army.

Calder asked Peter Benenson to introduce the book. Benenson was a lawyer and a founder of Justice, a group that campaigned for observation of the United Nations Declaration of Human Rights. Passionately, if a little incoherently, he ran through the classic arguments against torture – that it degrades the perpetrators, that it is unreliable, that it is a threat to democracy, that it provokes more violence than it stops. His preface links torture in Kenya and Algeria with similar cruelties taking place in the Soviet Union under Stalin, and insists that 'power exercised without responsibility' will have evil outcomes even under a democratic system

— especially one in which manipulation of the media has replaced political debate.

This was an important moment in the emergence of a new political sensibility, demanding a minimal space for the voice and the body, and it began with a visceral reaction against torture. Helen Bamber's instinct was highly personal, but it was typical. Arthur Miller, in his auto-biography, speaks of his own need to find 'a depoliticized human ground on which to stand and defend everybody at the same time'.

The geometry of even the best constitution can break down; the point was to make the state walk as it talks. A humanism stripped of any but the most cautious hope, a willingness to go on working for justice without illusions: 'I am up against a cliff wall yet I have to go forward,' Samuel Beckett is supposed to have said once, and his work seems to express what was at stake in its concentration on the body and voice, its concern with what is irreducibly fragile and physical in humanity, its sense of disaster. It is difficult (though not impossible) to imagine anyone who has taken the force of *Endgame* or *Malone Dies*, with their pitying comic fixation on the damaged body as the darkness closes around it, living at ease in a world that permits torture. Beckett's editor Jerome Lindon, who published the statements of the tortured so courageously and urgently, was risking his life: the OAS, the terror group of the Algerian settlers, bombed his Paris home in December 1960, on the day of his appearance in court for 'incitement to military disobedience'. Beckett, the former Resistance worker whose friends were murdered by the Nazis, helped as much as he could, though constrained by his status as a 'foreign resident' in France. He persuaded friends to hide copies of *La Question* when the book was confiscated by the state and encouraged writers to sign a declaration in defence of Lindon.

This was not a politics: it was a drawing of boundaries for any political action. If it now sounds like the common sense of liberalism, in the early 1960s it was tempting to believe in ideas that endorsed violence without limits. Nihilism could masquerade as the toughest realism. And if the refusal of torture seems a small thing, it is worth remembering how little space the ideologies of the time gave to any consideration of political cruelty. For many younger socialists, Mao's China was the promised land. It is doubtful if the words 'torture' or 'cruelty' were ever uttered in the lava-flow of verbiage about the Cultural Revolution. Sartre, who was so influential on a generation of Western Marxists, was fascinated by the dialectic of violence. His commentary attempted to give testimonies like those of Alleg a hysterical, totalizing quality. 'Europe is at death's door,' he cried in the preface to Fanon's *The Wretched of the Earth*; and one of his sentences is a classic expression of the way in which even the wildest revolutionary gestures would be defended in the years to come: 'No gentleness can efface the marks of violence; only violence itself can destroy them.' Uninhibited killing force was no stranger in the dreams of philosophers further to the right and closer to real power. The mandarins of the US State Department were convinced believers in the iron laws of progress. Walt Rostow, the great academic theorist of modernization, was an implacable advocate of ruthless measures in Vietnam, the professor choosing bombing targets over Tuesday lunches with LBJ at the White House.

Helen Bamber, an ordinary woman with a family and a difficult marriage, was groping towards something that she could decently believe in, and act on. Her old friend Stuart Smith helped her to define herself. His position remained that of absolute Christian pacifism. In an essay written after Amnesty International was established, and after torture had become a public moral issue, he argued that if war can be justified, then 'the torture of someone in order to make him give information or to make him yield', by comparison a minor matter, must be logically acceptable; but if we believe that torture is always wrong, we must accept that war is equally immoral under all circumstances. 'If a decent man,' he wrote, 'under no pressure, and in no instance, would resort to the use of a thumbscrew, how can that same man, under what-ever pressure, and in whatever circumstance, resort to war?'

Bamber found this hard to swallow. 'If we tolerate war against even a Hitler, then there is no human barrier to torture: it is like a theorem, which cannot imagine how awful life has been outside England in this century. And it meant that unless you campaign against war as a whole, you have no right to condemn torture.' Stuart Smith also wrote that it is 'better to submit than to commit murder'. This was a placid – and safe – form of resistance. He had a tranquil inability to recognize that such a posture would have condemned whole human groups (including the one that included Helen Bamber and her family) to certain death.

She could not live at this kind of moral distance from reality. But the re-emergence of torture sharpened her impatience with any ideology that distracts attention from the atrocity to the system – that pulls our eyes away from the individual violated body in the name of all the oppressed. 'I was beginning vaguely to realize that you have to be aware of both, of what causes the release of this incredible capacity for brutality – and this is about privilege and power, certainly – but always, also, the individual who is suffering. If you only care about the latter you may become some Mother Teresa figure, but if you only care about the social causes you are doing Stalinist sociology.'

Yet for the moment, despite everything, she was a mother approaching middle age, who loved her son. The murder of Hannes overshadowed the birth and, she now believes, her early years with David. It would heighten her sense of the threat latent in the world, and make her want to protect him by preparing him for that. She also wanted to earn a little money, and to have another child. She really tried, she believes, to hold back as long as she could the worst images that the newspapers and Maurice Pappworth were placing in front of her, and to let the world take care of itself.

After David's birth she went on taking down Pappworth's lectures to would-be members of the college he despised. She typed them up and edited them for his approval. He was incredibly patient with her, explaining clinical issues in fascinating detail. She loved being around this small, pugnacious, 'very Jewish' rebel: 'There was nothing refined about him, except his mind.'

A Primer of Medicine ('Being an introduction to clinical neurology, alimentary, respiratory and cardiovascular diseases') was published in 1960. A note on the title page records the author's 'profound gratitude and thanks to Mrs. Helen Bamber who typed the manuscript from dictation'. It is a strange primer, more a salty oral performance than a textbook; quirky, choleric and eccentric, it is full of quotations from Michelangelo, from rabbinical sages and *Pirkei Aboth* ('not learning but doing is the principal thing') and general dismissals of pretentious non-sense: 'I have attempted to follow a great teacher, Rabbi Nachmanides, who in the 13th century, wrote "Notwithstanding my desire and delight to be the disciple of the earlier authorities, to maintain their views and to assert them, I do not consider myself a donkey carrying books."'

He rails against specialization ('The narrow specialist usually lacks a broad view of medicine, is incapable of seeing the patient as a whole, is often abysmally ignorant outside his own narrow field'), and defends, against 'fashionable' theories, the importance of practical clinical medicine, as opposed to research work: 'Touch, hearing, and above all, sight are the foundation stones of physical examination.'

The second chapter is called 'History Taking'. It was heard and then written down by the woman who had become close to him; and in those long discussions in which she spoke to him about Germany after the war, and they talked about how the perversion of medicine can be encouraged in ordinary hospitals, there seems to have been some enduring transmission of influence, even of a technique.

Too many students, Pappworth said, grow up never to appreciate 'the true value of good history taking and never bother to practise and thereby acquire this difficult yet rewarding art'. The history is the individual's unique testimony. Pappworth advises his readers that to get a good history 'it is essential to be on good terms with the patient'. The doctor must be 'friendly, kind and sympathetic, not arrogant and blown out with the air of feigned superiority or ultra-sophistication'. He goes on:

> It is only by adopting a friendly attitude that he will obtain the confidence of many patients and complete confidence is essential for good histories. Humility and a love of people are two necessary ingredients of the good physician.
>
> Another essential quality to possess is that of being a good listener, allowing the patient to talk freely and in simple language and yet skilfully guiding him away from irrelevancies and towards a logical continuity of his story.

In this simple description of what a doctor should do, Helen Bamber would eventually discover a kind of programme, an attempt to fuse good medicine, the defence of human rights and of memory. The healer must find out, but not like an inquisitor. Help can begin with the act of listening, for nothing else leads to an understanding of the speaker's true situation. Careful attention to the voice and the body can honour the memory of pain, and begin the process that turns memory and description into a refusal of the destructive power of that pain.

*   *   *

She was doing part-time work at the Middlesex in mid-November 1960. Professor Herbert Seddon had a new patient. Sir Winston Spencer Churchill, aged eighty-five, had just been admitted to the private wing of the hospital after breaking a small bone in his back, slipping, like any old man, while leaning down to kiss his wife goodnight in her bedroom.

The next day Bamber was in the private wing of the hospital. She saw Churchill, clamped to his giant cigar in his wheeled chair, being pushed along by a nurse, flanked by the grave little professor in his white coat and by a big detective. The smell of Havana tobacco filled the corridor. Churchill looked like a grey baby – his eyes had 'the sweetness of the very young'. She felt moved to be near him, remembering those sonorous phrases of the good war when there was a clear enemy and the barbarians were all out there on the other side. Those certainties were dying with the old man in the wheelchair: 'In that moment I was conscious of a time coming to an end, and of a certain language. I think I also began to feel myself running out of time.'

6

TAKING HISTORIES

I am not your main concern.
Give me a passing thought.
I know that there is horrible discomfort
in having me on board.

The archer with the stinking wounded foot, in Sophocles' *Philoctetes*

Churchill lived on into the new decade, playing old Gilbert and
Sullivan records in the afternoons as his mind failed. Helen
Bamber's father, an ordinary man hurt by a world he could never
influence, died before Churchill, though Louis Balmuth was alert to the
end. He had been born under the father of the last Tsar; the month
before he died, the Tsars' bureaucratic heirs divided Berlin with a wall.
The global contest seemed to become permanent, like an old war of
religion; but as far as he was concerned he had seen the worst. At the
end it was not her father's age that astonished his daughter, but his
happiness. He was no longer the person she had spent her life dreading.

He had married, in his early seventies, a woman much younger than
himself, in an 'arrangement' that suited them both. Helen Bamber could
not credit how well it worked, how they could laugh at each other's
obsessions with warming the teacups or hoarding newspapers. He teased
and giggled, she remembers, behaviour altogether unheard of from him.
Suddenly, he was a contented old man, with not much time left. He let
go the character who had spent his life trying and failing to express
something about the disaster, though for him it could never be overcome; and for a few years he discovered what it was like to play. Helen

said she could imagine him then, as she had never really been able to do before, in his first childhood on the farm in Galicia, listening at night to the bears outside the house.

He died at the Middlesex Hospital, where she was working again after the birth of David. He was brought in by ambulance after suffering a mild stroke. His daughter spent as much time with him as she could. His condition did not look serious at first, but his arteries were hopeless. He kidded and rallied his very young doctor; Helen booked his X-rays and laughed along with him, wondering at what she had missed. A few days later a second stroke killed him.

She was already pregnant again when her father died. She stayed at home for the birth; an Irish midwife came to help her. Jonathan arrived in June 1962, amid sociable chaos, with ladders and boxes on the floor of their new house. They had just moved in, a family expanding and moving on as families are supposed to do. It was a warm summer night; she could believe for a time that her life was starting all over again, and remembers a good-humoured birth. Mrs Kearney had unpacked a big mirror and set it up so that Helen could see herself, and afterwards the midwife performed a swaying dance, holding the mirror away from her big body, turning the room and mother and child around in the glass.

Helen now had what she had always wanted: two children, who enchanted her, and soon even the nice house with the big kitchen. They had not stayed long in the house where Jonathan was born. The new and, they wanted to believe, final home was a roomy Victorian place in Muswell Hill purchased with a small legacy from her father and Rudi's compensation from the German government, which he had at last reluctantly accepted. She would always have to work; but at least their standard of living was rising. Rudi, meanwhile, had at Helen's suggestion approached the Jewish Welfare Board for work. To his surprise, he soon found himself running old people's homes, and discovered that his light touch made the work enjoyable: he liked the problems of his clients, and it was better for him working around people who would not question his accent or make him feel uncomfortable when they discovered that he was a Jew.

She might have enjoyed it while the going was good, and part of her did, but her father's death instead marked the beginning of the end of ordinary family life for her. At an age when many women trim their relations with the world to concentrate on their young children, she began – after an interval of calm – to engage with it more than ever before.

Her father always made her feel that she knew too much, and yet that she was powerless. She remembered as a child sitting on the edge of a playground watching the other children running and laughing, and feeling crushed by the responsibility of knowing that her mother's cousin was in danger in Germany. Play was a betrayal. (One of her later collaborators said that he thought of her childhood 'as a whole life built around keeping secrets'.) For her father, the enemy was, in a way, invincible. The defeat of fascism repaired nothing: the damage and any conceivable reparation were incommensurable. Helen felt that there was, almost until the end, something reproachful about him, and she could never quite discharge herself of the guilt he induced. His death released her, so that she could spend the rest of her life acknowledging that the situation is indeed hopeless but that it is necessary to do something about it.

Despite her restlessness, she said she loved being a mother. She was absorbed in her children, and the deep vicarious satisfaction of their needs. She was very angry once when the sister of Rudi's brother-in-law, an enthusiastic Norwegian liberal, began almost to lecture her, as activists will, about the Sharpeville murders and the imprisonment of Nelson Mandela while Helen was breast-feeding Jonathan in her pink-flowered bedroom. She told the woman she did not want to hear about it, not at that moment. At least for a time, images of violence had to be kept at bay, outside the world formed by her and her babies.

Amnesty International was launched with an article by Peter Benenson in the *Observer* on 28 May 1961. The article dramatized the situation of 'prisoners of conscience', people incarcerated for their beliefs by communist and pro-Western regimes. Benenson suggested that free expression itself was the best way to liberate prisoners of governments that feared ideas: 'The most rapid way of bringing relief to prisoners of conscience is publicity…'

Bamber joined a campaign that staked out ground on which the survival of raw elements of democracy might be hoped for, if not guaranteed, despite Cold War realpolitik and the imperious nationalism of the new states in Africa and the Middle East. She could see its importance at once, but she admitted that in the warm high of early motherhood she was unable to care very much about Dr Agostinho Neto, the Angolan poet and doctor flogged and jailed by the Portuguese, or Cardinal Mindszenty, trapped in the US Embassy in Budapest, or the six other prisoners chosen by Benenson as test cases.

Some voices could not be shut out so easily. She was working part-time for Maurice Pappworth in 1962 when he wrote an essay for the journal *Twentieth Century*. He did not pull his punches, either in the title – 'Human Guinea Pigs: a Warning' – or in the combative voice he adopted: 'Many physicians have become scientists rather than healers,' he wrote; and he accused them of 'rarely having any interest in patients purely as patients'.

He described the infliction of pain on confused and weakened people, often to confirm some banal result. It seemed obvious, for example, that if patients with liver disease were given large doses of ammonium chloride they would suffer anything from 'mild delirium to acute mania with frightening hallucinations', but a professor at a London teaching hospital decided she needed to see the effects for herself and administered the substance to sixty-six alcoholics dying of cirrhosis. At the same time, each patient had a catheter inserted into his or her heart, and another into the kidney, to measure their responses. Old Irish dossers, probably, in that part of London: who would care?

Pappworth had a way of making medicine strange – of highlighting its violence, its ability to interfere with the body – in order to question it. He asked doctors to look at their skilful puncturings and incisions and to realize that if they were devoid of therapeutic purpose they were cruel. Similar actions in warfare are described as stabbing and cutting; and divorced from either war or medicine, they are torture.

He was attacked as a medical Luddite, but Pappworth was not campaigning against new techniques as such, despite his suspicion of the rage for innovation. It was their application to those who had no use for them, and did not know what was being done to them, that galled him. Catheterization, for example, the insertion of a long thin tube into the heart chambers through a vein in the arm or leg, allowed pressure readings and blood samples to be obtained direct from the heart; doctors could use it to learn about cardiac functioning. The pioneer of the technique, Werner Forsmann, had tried it out nine times on himself in the late 1920s. In the 1960s, it was still a tricky procedure, easy to botch: the tube could jam in the vein, it could end up in the wrong place inside the heart, and 'arterial spasm' often occurred when it was introduced through a vein in the arm. The authors of a 1978 textbook wrote that 'even in skilled hands, cardiac catheterization carries a risk which is acceptable only when it is related to the clinical state of the patient under investigation.'

Few of the experimenters Pappworth wrote about were so cautious, or as heroic as Forsmann. Pappworth described 'the worst experiment on children' that he had read about. Seventeen children with rheumatic fever, ten of them with heart complications, had catheters passed into their hearts, 'and with the catheter still in position, these sick frightened children were made to pedal on a bicycle'. He asked if anyone had explained to the parents of these children 'what was to be meted out to them'.

Pappworth wanted to restrain the instincts of pure, irresponsible research among those who deal with the bodies of human beings. The attitude he shrank from was put brutally by a Dr Szent-Gyorgi at a congress in Boston in 1961: 'The desire to alleviate suffering is of small value in research — such a person should be advised to work for a charity.' Pappworth remarked: 'Let us not forget that even doctors can become degraded. Over 300 of them have been named as having taken part in the dastardly cruel experiments on the inmates of German concentration camps.'

This short essay reaffirmed the traditional principle that it is immoral to experiment on patients not suffering from the disease being investi-gated, and without their consent. Claude Bernard, one of the great originators of modern experimental medicine, had written in 1865 that 'the principle of medical and surgical morality consists in never performing on man an experiment which might be harmful to him to any extent, even though the result might be highly advantageous to science, that is, to the health of others.' Despite this impeccable lineage the essay was, in Bamber's recollection, 'fantastically provocative; he was seen as unspeakable. They tried to ignore him, but it was impossible to do so.' Even though he did not name any of the doctors who carried out the experiments, 'the article was greeted with rage and massive denial. Even liberal doctors would shudder when I mentioned Maurice's name and raise their eyes to heaven. The measured public response was not matched in private, I can tell you. He became for many leading doctors a pariah. But it made its mark.'

A cautious editorial in the *British Medical Journal* admitted that general exhortations 'seem to have had little restraining effect on those who cannot always understand the difference between guinea-pigs and human beings, especially when they are collected together in penitentiaries, reformatories and institutions for the mentally defective'. The editor pinned his hopes on a new code being written by the World Medical Association Ethical Committee; but Pappworth was not convinced that self-regulation would work: he was sceptical of a code based on the willingness of gentlemen to control themselves.

Bamber believes that Pappworth was determined to fight on, no matter how unpleasant it became. He had nothing to lose, since his private practice and his membership course for the Royal College of Physicians were untouchable by anyone with real power in British medicine. He also felt that public opinion was moving his way: press coverage of his essay had been almost sensational, but it favoured him. He went on collecting examples from the medical journals, and by the mid-1960s his archive had grown to around 500 cases. Bamber thought that he couldn't stop; he didn't know how.

In the USA, Pappworth found an ally in Dr Henry K. Beecher, a descendant of Harriet Beecher Stowe, who in 1959 had written a thoughtful essay on 'Experimentation in Man' in the *Journal of the American Medical Association*, sharply distinguishing the roles of 'physician' and 'investigator'. His starting point, like Pappworth's, was the 'gross actions' of the Nazi doctors; and he had in his papers copies of German research reports, which he may have evaluated for the US Army at the end of the war. He wrote that 'any classification of human experimentation as "for the good of society" is to be viewed with distaste, even alarm ... such high-flown expressions ... have been used within recent memory as cover for outrageous acts.'

Beecher's speciality was the alleviation of pain. Among other things, he showed that the act of caring, of being seen to do something, can itself relieve pain – even if the physician has done nothing physically significant to the body. This is the 'placebo effect': the mysterious easing of real, often acute pain by the administration of sugar or salt instead of morphine. The patient believes that good is being done, and this can be enough: the embodied mind acting on the complex pathways of pain. In their magnificent book, *The Challenge of Pain*, Ronald Melzack and Patrick Wall write that this effect is 'the common ingredient of all the healing arts ... so powerful that modern-day pharmacologists have to demonstrate that their drugs are better than the placebo'.

Beecher, perhaps not surprisingly, given his central concern with easing the body's torment, revolted against the creation of avoidable distress. Like Pappworth, he did not shirk conflict; but in every other respect, he was his opposite: a WASP, a Professor of Anaesthesiology at the Harvard Medical School, very much an establishment man. Yet when he did eventually break cover to describe, and in terms far more moderate than Pappworth was capable of using, some actual violations of experimental ethics, his status would not protect him from obloquy.

* * *

Helen Bamber, with her affinity for interesting doctors, had already met Herman Hardenberg, a psychoanalyst and associate of D. W. Winnicott. She worked for Hardenberg on Saturday mornings, starting in 1962, earning useful extra money. Hardenberg and Winnicott had earlier spoken out against the fashion for 'pre-frontal leucotomy' – better known as lobotomy, the removal of healthy brain tissue to pacify the mentally ill, an exceptionally violent 'cure' which, as the journalist Brian Inglis pointed out, relieved patients 'not only of their tensions, but their personalities'. Winnicott described it as 'the worst honest error in recent medical practice'. He wrote that when doctors talked about the 'good mental changes' supposedly brought about by lobotomy, the word 'good' was never defined; and spoke of the dreadful fear of all patients entering mental hospitals, that they would have their brains cut, or be given ECT, or insulin shock therapy. 'Nothing better than leucotomy divides psychiatry as a blind therapy, from psychiatry as a complex but interesting concern for the human being who finds life difficult, and whose problems we can feel to be represented in ourselves.'

Hardenberg backed Winnicott's claim: he found 'a very great fear of leucotomy which was deeply hidden, and my patients were unable to speak of it until confidence had been established between us'. When a doctor wrote sneeringly of his and Winnicott's 'flaunting' of 'an alleged special relationship' with their patients, Hardenberg asked, 'What else is a doctor supposed to have with those in need?'

Bamber was beginning now to work at the intersection of human rights and medicine. In the late summer of 1963 she assisted Hardenberg with a brief, tantalizing paper – delivered as a lecture to the British Psychoanalytical Society – called 'Torture and the Subconscious'. In it, Hardenberg wrote of 'wanting to understand' an outburst of 'cruelty and torture' typified by Hitler and the SS, and by events in Algeria and Kenya. The nineteenth century was naive: 'knowledge and religious belief' do not produce 'peaceful living'. What we must admit is the 'universal and persistent character of cruelty'; but 'resistance to cruelty' is equally constant, and enigmatic – 'the problem of why people are kind'. He discussed the aggressive drives of the infant, the urge to destroy and dismember, and the way it changes, in most cases, into an awareness of the mother as a whole person instead of a collection of body parts to be eaten or attacked. Guilt dawns; and with it a capacity to feel pity and concern. This is the normal human being, more or less. But aggressive urges remain and can become unharnessed in particular circumstances. Hardenberg allowed the lecture to trail off with a disclaimer of his own ability to understand those circumstances, pleading ignorance of 'sociological and historical knowledge'.

Bamber said that she tried to persuade him to discuss the reasons why states torture. What the Nazis had done, and what the French did in Algeria (and the FLN's response to the French), were less upsurges of psychic rage than conscious strategies. The 'normal', benign development of the individual explains why most of us do not wish to torture other human beings. The problem for her, and for us, is how ordinary people can stay silent when the minority of disturbed individuals, their instincts untempered by love and concern, are given a licence to feed their urges. 'The problem of the bystander, the feeling of helplessness in the face of cruelty preoccupied me for obvious reasons; but I was also beginning to wonder what reparation can be made when people have been abused. Perhaps I am reading back too much from what I do now, and of course I did nothing about it for years, instead displacing it with endless campaigning, but that little paper of Herman's was an irritant for me.'

She still disowned any pretension to being an intellectual. Hardenberg once said to her: 'You're a midwife.' He meant, she thinks, that she could draw people out, and bear with their confusion. This quality of sympathetic provocation is her gift. It certainly helped her to absorb something important from these unusual healers with whom she was working.

What she was feeling was in the air; bad dreams about medicine and torture disturbed sensitive minds in the early 1960s. One of their most enduring and moving traces is Chris Marker's short film *La Jetée*. Told in black-and-white still pictures, like the fragments of a lost movie, it is the story of a man in a post-nuclear world, held prisoner in a 'camp' ruled by 'scientists'. He has a recurrent nightmare of a man being shot down on an airport viewing jetty. The scientists want to capture such dreams. The narrator of the film tells us: 'The prisoners were submitted to experiments of great concern, apparently, to those who conducted them; the outcome was disappointment for some, death for others, and for others madness.' The man is shown lying blindfolded on a hammock, his body arching, biting the cane frame of the hammock. What the scientists are doing is 'stripping out the present' so he can be sent out into time past and time future to discover the resources they lack, so that they can restore their power, and recover the world they have destroyed. 'The man does not die, nor does he go mad. He suffers.' And as the 'treatment' takes hold, 'images begin to ooze like confessions.' He visits the past, and falls in love; in the future, he discovers what his tormentors want. He then escapes back to the past. But the man is disposable 'material'. He must die; at the end, he witnesses his own death, shot as he runs to meet his lover on an airport balcony.

*   *   *

In 1964 Helen took her son Jonathan to hospital. He had a trigger thumb, a very minor deformity. The pre-med was botched, and a surgeon was arrogantly dismissive of the mother's anxiety and the child's fear. Her presence was upsetting the child, he said, as Jonathan was brought screaming into the operating theatre. The doctor saw in her baby only a technical fault. She was told she could not visit him in the recovery ward: hospital rules forbade it. The children got used to it, they said, cried at first, but then became quiet and co-operative. It was normal. After the operation Helen walked into the recovery ward, and insisted on staying with him until he came around so she would be the first person he saw. She was made to feel difficult, an over-anxious mother.

Soon after Jonathan was born she had watched an eight-year-old film called *A Two Year Old Goes to Hospital* made by the psychoanalyst James Robertson. It is a record of time passing in a children's ward. The two-year-old girl, Laura, is a happy blonde infant in a sunlit garden, her father smiling at her; then she enters a dark, tiled admission office, bare of everything except two hard chairs and a desk, as her mother speaks to a nurse. Laura appears behind the bars of a hospital cot, staring out, crying when a nurse speaks to her, hanging onto her favourite old blanket. The camera sees it all like a surveillance system (Robertson was standing in the ward filming, at the same hours every day). She veers between silent apathy and bitter grief. Her mother's visits are short, and strained: she is afraid to take her baby on her lap in case it is against the rules. On the fifth day Laura barely acknowledges her mother, and ignores her departure; and by the eighth and final day she is 'shaken by sobs'. Robertson notices that on the way out of the hospital, 'she is seen walking apart from her mother.' For days afterwards, Robertson claimed, the child soiled herself and was angry, and months later she was still reproachful.

It is meant to be seen as a short film of a personality nearly dis-integrating; propaganda for a psychoanalytic point of view that stressed the dangers of separation – almost any separation – between mother and child. Yet it spoke to the experience of women. Helen Bamber had seen crying children like these in the Middlesex, and seen enough of medical arrogance. Pappworth agreed with her that there must be a better way of caring for children in hospital; he was no Freudian, but it is clear from his writing that the use of already-distressed infants as experimental subjects affected him badly.

The connection back to the 1940s that she made when she was having her first child now became more active. 'I was very aware of what separation had meant to the children from the camps – that was the worst thing, the loss on top of the cruelty. This came back so strongly when I saw children's wards in big hospitals, children screaming and crying and rocking backwards and forwards in their cots. And I became more confident in remembering that in Belsen we seemed to get by rather well with whole families in the wards helping with the feeding and with the dressings, and I couldn't see why we had to have this sterile uniformity with people lying neatly in orderly rows of straight sheets. It

was convenient for the nurses and for the doctors: a form of institutionalized convenience and power.'

Robertson's film was based on the work of John Bowlby, who saw the
human infant's attachment to its mother in terms of animal behaviour –
the baby clinging to its protector, as danger circles the herd: the young
ape needing its mother. Winnicott's writing had always seemed more
subtle and attractive to Bamber, she said later, in particular his emphasis
on 'play', the creative attitude to the world in which culture begins and
which the mother can help to create by being, herself, a safe environment for the child. For Winnicott, even the capacity to be alone without
fear or anxiety 'is based on the experience of being alone in the presence
of someone, and ... without a sufficiency of this experience the capacity
to be alone cannot develop'. The bewilderment of separation can lead to
a breakdown of the child's illusory but vital sense of effortless well-
being. She had seen what the effects of extreme violence and separation,
beyond all domestic imagining, had done to the boys from the camps.
'What I took from Winnicott was simple: if you can avoid traumatizing
children, avoid it. It is the first betrayal.'

Hospitals were reluctant to learn from mothers. Visiting hours were
highly restricted; mothers sleeping near their children almost unheard of
(though one pioneering hospital in Newcastle had been allowing women
to do so since before the war). Never mind that a government committee, guided by Robertson, had agreed that mothers should become
part of the care of children; few hospitals – as Helen Bamber was about
to find out – would volunteer to reinvent themselves.

Hospitals were houses where the sick were made well; but they were
also schools where medicine was taught, and where patients became
cases. Their great pride since the mid-nineteenth century was the achievement of asepsis – an ultra-cleanliness administered by professionals.
Letting mothers in went against the grain: it meant a sharing of power, a
break in the wall that separated the hospital from an infectious world. And
having protective women around would, for a certain kind of ambitious
doctor, restrict his or her access to research 'material'.

Bamber heard from her Irish midwife about a nurse called Valerie
Elder who had, with a group of women in the South London Borough of
Battersea, set up an organization called Mother Care for Children in
Hospital. She went to meet them and within a few months had found

something new in herself. 'I began speaking for the first time with authority, or so it felt to me; having spent so long feeling impotent, I discovered a way of challenging power. These women helped me to see that it could be examined quite practically and confronted. It was a tiny corner of power, but it did not seem tiny if you were a mother with a sick child. And something about a small child staring out through the bars of a cot in a large hospital ward symbolizes helplessness as nothing else can.'

They set out to convince hospital boards that they would benefit from allowing women to help their children's recovery. The heads of nursing and medical schools were lobbied, and the women visited hospitals to discover for themselves how they treated sick children. 'You had to talk about the practical advantages of having a mother there, so that we didn't seem to take away anything of the power of the doctor or nurse; and that whereas a withdrawn child can seem a very easy one to look after in a hospital, it's also a damaged child. We had a lot of committed support from the inside, from paediatricians and nurses – but it was a weary, uphill struggle for all that.' Only one hospital in twelve allowed women to stay overnight, and Bamber recalls 'mothers standing in the grounds outside children's wards in freezing weather looking in at their children'. One hospital that she visited claimed that it allowed 'unrestricted' visiting: any half-hour during daylight hours.

It was a pre-feminist campaign in which women were mothers before all else, and they were derided by a government minister, according to one of the campaign leaders, Peg Belson, as 'middle-class women in pretty hats with time on their hands'. But they had a steely polite militancy, very careful and articulate, and it isn't a small thing to change the way a state treats its sick children. In May 1963 the campaign became the National Association for the Welfare of Children in Hospital. Belson, its historian, could write with pride thirty years later that due to their efforts, children were no longer 'passed over like a parcel... visited infrequently or not at all and collected days or even weeks later'.

Bamber became the driving force of a group based in North-West London, and carried out a survey of the many hospitals in her area, giving talks in the suburbs to organizations like the Women's Co-Operative Guild, the East Finchley Young Wives' Group, the Barnet Women's Institute. She had the bit between her teeth.

Persuading mothers to have the strength to demand their rights was one of the most important things she could do. Rosita Green, who was a member of the group, recalls that when her son needed a serious operation Helen Bamber encouraged her to confront the surgeon and tell him that she would not leave her child. She was told they had nowhere for her to sleep; she offered to sleep in a chair. Within hours they had given her a large room to herself. She was the first woman ever to make such a demand, and this at the Royal Free Hospital in Hampstead, stronghold of the demanding middle class.

Bamber's fierce gentility was effective, according to Rosita Green, and she was a good speaker. She would describe the clean large wards of the modern hospital, with kids marooned on tight beds, and then offer an alternative vision of a children's ward as an untidy place, full of women talking to and holding their kids, calming their panic, with toys all over the floor. Bowlby liked the atmosphere of hospitals in the less-developed world; Bamber's unspoken model was the hospital at Belsen.

Green thinks of Helen Bamber then as quite a matronly figure, exquisitely polite, with not much humour about her and rather driven, looking older for her years than she did when Green met her again three decades later. She also remembers the tirelessness that would become a familiar element in people's impressions of Bamber the activist. If there was an obscure group on the outer edge of the city, who were prepared to listen to the argument, she would turn up at a school hall on a winter night, well-prepared and competent. What her new companions could not have known was the strength of her desperation. Her evangelism was real; she wanted to be born again.

The fear that children would be damaged enough to become violent, affectless and cruel was a common theme of the early 1960s – the problem of the 'delinquent'. (Burgess's *A Clockwork Orange*, published in 1962, is in part a reworking of this obsession.) For Bamber the images of violent children touched her deepest ambivalence about post-war society. 'We had normal – not Nazi – French boys doing unspeakable things to Algerians. What made them capable of it? I can't pretend that this sort of consideration drove my work for children in hospital, but I know that many of us did not want to be part of a society intent on fostering the destructive side of children's characters. Now, of course, I have to wonder what kind of childhood the perpetrators have had – what makes so much cruelty available to the state.'

These uppity mothers forced doctors and parents to look again at the inner workings of institutions that were taken for granted. They were made to see and hear what had been silent or invisible. Peg Belson tells the story of a paediatrician who was won over by their arguments and by watching the film of Laura in hospital. Although his office was at the end of a large children's ward, he told her later that he had never heard the children crying – heard it as meaning anything – until after he had seen Robertson's film.

*   *   *

Helen Bamber's activism was also a preface to the end of her marriage. Rudi supported her, looking after their sons when she was out, helping to organize public meetings, and taking a strong interest in the work. But Rudi's support made no difference; she was moving into a different place, widening the existing distance. 'There was something in me that needed to have the reflection from others that I was not getting from him. The more confident I became the more he seemed to withdraw.'

The hospital campaign did not occupy that much of her time, though Bowlby would surely have disapproved of her efforts to put his ideas into practice. She remembers her early relationships with her children as totally absorbing, particularly with David. The murder of Hannes Pulfer before her son's conception seems to have intensified her connection with him. She breast-fed each of her sons for over a year. When they were infants she took them to the zoo, to the parks, on picnics in Highgate Woods; all of those memories, for her, are about London summers and good times.

Rudi Bamber says now that he recognizes that he and Helen were already leading separate lives. He would leave early for work and come back late, and she always had part-time work, so that not a great deal of time was left for each other. He acknowledges with generosity and candour that she needed something different: 'There wasn't enough in a normal middle-class existence for her – looking after children, a house, seeing friends; she wanted something else, much more committed than that.'

Piecing together what they say, anyone can imagine what it must have been like. Long companionship is the most addictive drug. Every day seems like a renewal of affection and solidarity, until the moment the familiar joke or the habit is torn out of context and its banality quivers in plain sight. The ways in which disdain begins are never very different, yet they matter more than anything to those exposed to the worst form of ridicule, their own, as they learn to read the truth in the face of someone they have trusted.

Helen felt that Rudi related better to the children, about whom he had been so sceptical, than to her. 'It was as if there were a competition between him and me to mother the children. I didn't feel his passion or need; I was simply part of the pattern. The better he became with the two boys the more our relationship seemed to dwindle. There is a myth that having children brings people together: it doesn't.' Or it need not; in their case, it did not help.

Once in the mid-1960s they went on holiday to Lewes, in Sussex. She left him with the boys and went shopping in the old town. He had told her where they were going to be, and she decided to surprise them, excited by what she had bought for the children. The look on her husband's face as she walked up cut her: she had interrupted his absorption in his sons. Jealousy, guilt, vanity: the invariable toxic ingredients always work. He could not give her what she wanted because it was not his to give: only she could satisfy herself.

After that holiday she contracted viral polyneuritis, an inflammation of the peripheral nerves. She could not sleep for the pain; at times couldn't fasten the children's buttons or tie their shoelaces. Herman Hardenberg found her a neurologist who told her that all she could do was rest, so she stayed indoors for months and scratched at her need, deepening the split.

She later realized that she had never fully accepted something so central to their relationship that it seemed to require no comment. Rudi Bamber was, to use the inadequate language we possess, a survivor. He was still suffering; his secrets were not often communicable. The silence in which he lived would only be broken much later, in old age, and she could not help him do it.

When she recovered from her illness they took in lodgers to lower their costs. When the Turkish naval captain arrived he seemed a faultless guest. He was preparing for his country's diplomatic service, and had been assigned a course at the University of London. He had the cultured scepticism of the Istanbul upper class, speaking three languages, at ease with the modern West, but conscious of the great bulk of Islamic

Anatolia to which his urban world was tied. He was a humane man, yet ironic about violence, like any member of an elite that depends on an army for its survival. He and Helen Bamber fell in love. He told her what she least expected – that she was exceptional, that she was desirable – 'a lot of things that I needed to hear'. The passion shook her, and for a while she seems to have lived in a slow burst of reawakened sexuality.

He made her feel wanted, and safe, which was even more important. She had never had that from her parents, and she and Rudi had grown together knowing an infinite amount about each other's fears and anxieties; the illusion that the world a partner created was a safe place had never been available to them for long, and for her it would never be truly achievable.

Rudi Bamber behaved with immense dignity, according to Helen, and moved out to a nearby flat once they had decided that the marriage was over. The captain had already gone back to Turkey by then. The affair had been a catalyst, but her separation from Rudi was the tearing of a valued, closely knit thing, sure though she was that it constricted her. She felt more guilt than relief. Nothing could ever replace it. She was never as close again to anybody; never again lived with a man; and Rudi continued to move her. There was so much that they had been unable to speak about – his parents' deaths, the effect on her of what she had witnessed in Germany, her insatiable need to act – and it was only many years later that the gaps began to be filled in. 'I still grieve about what happened, because we struggled so much and fought so hard, we had the children, and it was when Rudi was settled at last, and life was better, that we separated. I respect him very much, and there is a great affection in our relationship; he's a person of great integrity – the one person who I know would never betray me, ever.'

The penalties of her failure were heavy, and not just for her. From now on, she had to hold down two, and sometimes three, part-time jobs. She would have other lovers, but she would essentially be on her own. The boys were at different schools, where she took them each morning; she took in students, and cooked and cared for them. She lost friends, who blamed her for the breakdown of the marriage.

She was, she remembers, almost fiercely close to her eldest son. He hated his school, at first, and refused to eat the midday food it provided, so Helen pushed Jonathan in a pram to the school gates each lunchtime and took them out to eat. She could never drive and got used to the long spells of waiting for buses with the poor, the old and the very young.

After a long disintegration into helplessness and random fits of memory as Parkinson's disease wiped out everything she had been, Marie Balmuth died of heart failure in 1969. It had been a tense, joyless and guilt-ridden relationship ever since the end of the war. Helen Bamber now had no one standing between her and death.

Her experience of her mother had been so oppressive that she was determined to lighten her own weight on her children. They enjoyed, as a result, extraordinary independence. She wanted them to feel confident in the city. Between the three of them, they seem to have accepted that the fussing of protective mothers and the helplessness of children were for other people. Jonathan recalls astonishing a school friend at the age of eleven by telling him how he had gone to meet his mother at work, travelling on the underground and walking half a mile across Central London. Though David would come to wish that he had a different kind of childhood, he and his brother were clever at school and no one's fools. They appeared to thrive on premature adulthood. Jonathan announced at the age of eight that he didn't like his primary school because he was not being made to learn enough, and asked his mother to find him a better one.

Student lodgers came from Sudan, Tunisia, Malaya, with their elaborate courtesies, their hot food, teaching the boys to dance and suck eggs (literally, in the case of a student from Laos) and to imagine a wider world. Or so she sees it. She remembers laughter, and an almost carnival atmosphere, despite the drudgery of her work. She revelled in what she was able to do. But her children were counting the cost, in the quiet inexorable way that parents cannot see.

* * *

She worked for Herman Hardenberg at weekends until he died in 1967; and for Herbert Seddon during the week at the Royal National Orthopaedic Hospital. She went there to fill in for someone on leave, and Seddon asked her to stay and work for him. He was now very grand – Sir Herbert Seddon, CMG, DM, FRCS – but remained, in her memory of him, an unpretentious man. He would approach each operation with great care; his reconstructive work had a kind of aesthetic deliberation, as though he wished to make a body more whole, more beautiful, and his surgery involved ingenious formal solutions. In a letter to her from a Christian village on Mount Lebanon in 1969, Seddon wrote with quiet satisfaction about a boy whose leg he had operated on at the Royal National Orthopaedic Hospital, and asked Bamber to dig out the name of an Iranian who Seddon thought might respond to similar treatment.

He was a person whose temper and energy are euphemized as they grow older with terms like 'irascible'; as his deafness got worse, he told her she must be his ears, and she helped screen out fools. But he was a compassionate man. Bamber said that 'he could not cut a patient and wash his hands and play a round of golf with a light heart.' She recalled him once sitting on the steps of the hospital in Great Portland Street with his head in his hands as though he were praying. She sat beside him and he told her he was about to go in to tell a patient that his leg would have to be amputated up to the thigh.

Maurice Pappworth, meanwhile, wanted to show that he had not been silenced by disdain. His *Twentieth Century* essay hadn't done much, in his view, to change the conduct of investigators, but in 1963 he was interviewed on television and made a powerful impression on the publisher Victor Gollancz, who commissioned a book from him.

Pappworth tried, with Helen Bamber's assistance, despite the fact that she was no longer formally working for him, to shape his material into coherent form. Yet the only coherence it had was in its relentless repetition of unpleasant and violent, because unnecessary, experiments. Hundreds of cases, each one repellent; it was a furious list, a book of evidence in a case against anti-humanist medicine. He had no sense of form, and all she could do was to persuade him to drop some of the more obviously repetitive examples.

As it went on accumulating, she found the material 'frightening and disturbing' to work on. Sitting in his rooms in Harley Street, with descriptions of liver biopsies, cardiac catheterizations, lumbar aorto-graphies and wild drug tests spread over desks and on the floor, the book was no longer an editorial problem; it began to feel like a conspiracy. In his earlier essay Pappworth had not named the doctors who had, as he saw it, broken their oath, but now he would have to give details: who they were, and where they worked. They included some of the most eminent medical professors in Britain.

In the spring of 1964, Pappworth delivered a manuscript to his publisher. Livia Gollancz, the owner's daughter, returned it with a note saying that it was an interesting document, but not a book. Pappworth must have wondered whether he would ever be allowed to let the bad air out. Helen Bamber, who had no confidence in herself as a writer, suggested that they ask her friend Stuart Smith to edit the book. She knew he would be discreet and sympathetic, and had no connection to the medical world. Pappworth was now very anxious about libel suits, and suspected that Gollancz had been frightened off by the legal implications of the book. The normal author's warranty, guaranteeing that there is nothing libellous in a book, was an obstacle to openness.

Smith, who was then a freelance editor and writer, said later that he was glad of the work, and liked the small, cheerfully aggressive man whom he met at Pappworth's house in Hampstead. He had heard about his legendary diagnostic skills. He was impressed by how personally the author took the cruelties he was describing, though Smith is insistent that ' "chip on his shoulder" seems far from the right phrase to describe Pappworth'. He saw that the rejected manuscript was disorganized, and that Pappworth seemed to expect the material to speak for itself.

Smith persuaded his author to organize the material into categories – experiments on the dying, on prisoners, on children, on the old – and to stick to these, and to try to inject a more personal voice into his presentation of them. Although Pappworth reversed much of this work, the published text reflects the editor's organization of the material. Helen Bamber remembered feeling relieved that it had become choppily readable, but that it was still 'like dealing with a parcel of explosives'. The phone used to ring when word of the book got around, and 'some doctor he had never heard of would lecture him about the folly of what he was doing, or denounce him for treachery.'

Most of the publishers who now saw it seemed to agree about the dangers of the manuscript. Many of them, including Jonathan Cape, turned it down because, they said, their libel insurers would not cover them. At last, Norman Franklin at Routledge – then the leading social science publisher in the UK – agreed to sponsor the book, asking Pappworth to name every single co-worker and minor researcher on every paper he cited, spreading the risk of libel suits. With unusual publishing courage, he offered Pappworth a 'weak' warranty clause that made him wholly responsible only if he libelled someone intentionally.

Because of the delay, Henry Beecher had anticipated his English co-thinker. In 1966, Beecher published a short paper with the innocent title 'Ethics and Clinical Research' in the *New England Journal of Medicine*. (The more prestigious *Journal of the American Medical Association* had turned it down flat.) David Rothman, in his book on the transformation of medical ethics in the USA, compares the impact of the essay on American culture to Rachel Carson's *Silent Spring* and to *Uncle Tom's Cabin* (the work of Beecher's ancestor). It listed twenty-two unethical experiments, naming none of the investigators. Beecher had already been denounced as 'an irresponsible exaggerator' by fellow Harvard professors, when he raised these questions at a meeting the year before. Now he was 'vulgarly abused ... and accused of sensationalism, exaggeration and dishonesty' – so he seems to have told Pappworth, who must have been steeling himself for his own ordeal.

Human Guinea Pigs was finally published in 1967. It described 205 experiments, 78 of them carried out in the public wards of British public hospitals, all in the National Health Service; whilst most of the rest took place in US hospitals, prisons and mental institutions. All the experimenters were named.

The book is surely one of the most disturbing ever published on such a technical subject. Pappworth's tone is soberly indignant, impassioned and frequently disbelieving – his voice cannot find the normal impersonality of the medical paper. He calls for the treatment by doctors of the whole human being, contrasting 'the physician–friend' who recognizes 'the mutual obligation of two equals' with the researcher who 'selects subjects'. His most damning charge is that some doctors 'have never developed the art of taking patients' histories properly'.

Pappworth looks at medicine as something so serious that every enactment of its power has to be justified; he isolates its capacity for violence, and it is this alienation effect that makes the book so shocking. Reading about cruelty is a numbing business – most forms of state-directed torture or murder, for example, are identical and predictable. Like Helen Bamber's father, Pappworth was repelled by *intelligent* cruelty, and once medical experiments are seen as unnecessary they seem ingeniously vicious. It was as if a tormented engraver had been allowed into operating theatres to see what is normally hidden, and then to print up the images: I saw this, and this; they did this.

In Philadelphia, to test catheterization techniques, nine children each had a needle inserted into their femoral arteries (the normal route) and another into their jugular veins (a more dangerous procedure), while they were forced to inhale a special gas mixture through tightly fitting gas masks. Two three-year-olds 'required some restraint', according to the researchers; and 'all the children's legs were held in place by binding to a board'. The purpose was to establish 'the normal values for cerebral blood flow in children'. Pappworth writes: 'It is difficult for a lay person to visualise what all this involves. The patient's face is covered with the complicated breathing apparatus, whilst tubes connect his heart and also the main arteries and vein of his outstretched limbs to recording instruments, so that his position often resembles crucifixion and the apparatus is reminiscent of that worn by an astronaut.'

And so it goes on, for page after page. He includes the experiment on dying liver patients which he had first described to Helen Bamber in St George's in the 1950s; he details so many that it is impossible to read the book for very long.

He writes of a 'maniacal impulse' to produce research papers, and this 'terrible temptation' always led him back to Nuremberg, and the Nazi experiments on helpless prisoners. When he began writing the book, the World Medical Association had called for a ban on using prisoners as subjects. Until then they had been used widely in the USA, especially in drug trials. Pappworth was convinced the ban would be evaded: in 1963, after the scandal of the birth defects caused by Thalidomide, the chief medical officer of Distillers, the drug's manufacturer, had called for the use of 'criminals' to test drug toxicity. Pappworth knew how the status of criminal can be applied to the innocent: 'The Nazi doctors regarded the entire population at Auschwitz as "criminal".'

The difficult truth was that the Nuremberg Code – an ethical statement drawn up after the trial of the Nazi doctors in 1946–7 – was considered by many physicians to be irrelevant to the way they practised medicine. Whatever is seen as completely evil can be ignored: it has no continuity with other evils, and the culture which helped to shape it is undisturbed. The Nazis had corrupted science with 'politics'; experimenters in the West believed they were doing pure science. A little deceit, and even force, seemed to be justified if the end was good medicine. Pappworth could not live with that self-deluding historical blindness.

The hard point of the book was his attempt to end the cherished freedom of doctors to choose when and how to experiment on human beings. In the US and Britain, experimentation was effectively outside the law. Patients could sue doctors for assault, but this was almost unknown. Pappworth argued that researchers should make proposals to a research committee, based in each large hospital and including non-medical members, which would decide whether a given experiment was scientifically and ethically justified.

This was heresy. The response to the book was savage, even for a fighter like Pappworth – and Bamber seriously doubts whether he carried any but the lightest emotional armour. When she went to see him at his home in Hampstead, he seemed more isolated than ever. The venom of the professional gossip was rarely committed to print, but some did slip through. A Dr Charles Fletcher in the *BMJ* sneered at Pappworth's clinical ethics, and asked: 'Let us have no more of this petty nonsense, and let men of knowledge and probity ensure that the difficult ethical problems of clinical research are handled helpfully and sensibly.'

The *BMJ* and *Lancet* were more measured, but reiterated the dogma of self-regulation. They mocked Pappworth's style, the *Lancet* speaking of his 'vitriolic amplification' of his case at a public meeting. Yet the book was reviewed seriously, and at length, in the *BMJ*. No one tried to defend in public the practices he had dragged into the light. Some distinguished professors began to come over to his side; and the public response was very supportive. Even his old enemies, the grandees of the Royal College of Physicians, attempted to write a voluntary code of practice for their members, for which he scored them savagely – 'a whitewashing, worth-less document, purposely vague, and adding nothing to the publicised but often ignored recommendations of the World Health Organisation'.

John Rundle, Pappworth's former student, said thirty years later that what made the book work was its underlying passion and anger on behalf of 'the outpatients sitting on those long wooden benches in hospitals, who were the ones used in these experiments. The attitude was still, somehow, that they were lucky to be seen by a doctor, and therefore they were fair game. Pappworth hated the undervaluing of people, and that was only partly because he had been undervalued himself.'

The medical establishment was mobilized by the state during the Second World War, when sensational breakthroughs of immediate military use were made – the control of malaria, the discovery of penicillin – and this attitude was carried over into peacetime. Vast funds flowed into medical research centres for 'wars' on heart disease, cancer and polio. This was especially true in the USA, but the same culture of emergency also touched British medicine.

Pappworth and Beecher were sensitive to the darker side of this cult of medical 'war', and did much to undermine it. They contributed, like the women asking for recognition as intimates of their children's pain, to a change in the way people were addressed at important moments of their lives – in sickness, at the time of their children's births, and even on their own deathbeds. It could be argued that all kinds of people in the 1960s were discovering their rights, and that the work of these two 'whistle-blowers' was merely about 'patients' rights', but that does not quite measure the lessening of avoidable distress that they brought about. Pappworth's ideas about ethics are now accepted, in theory, in every research institution that takes the human body as its object.

The BMA's *Handbook of Medical Ethics*, published in 1993, runs to 325 pages; it includes 35 pages alone on the issue of consent. The revelation of doctors' involvement in torture in the 1970s made explicit the link that Bamber began to suspect, and forced doctors to consider the roots of medical abuse in their own clinical attitudes. Bamber would later, through her work with Amnesty, play a part in changing the stance of the British medical profession towards issues of human rights. Jim Welsh, the medical co-ordinator of the International Secretariat of Amnesty International and the author of *Medicine Betrayed*, the BMA's major statement on medical complicity in torture, locates 'the foothills of some human rights violations in the way that doctors *see* patients; if you see them coldly and indifferently that is also the way you will see prisoners when you are called to examine them, and eventually torture victims too.' Pappworth was far-sighted enough to understand that no society can afford to tolerate a corps of desensitized physicians.

The lesson that Helen Bamber drew from her association with this extraordinary man was that the individual had to be protected from the ethics of emergency. This was an obvious link with Amnesty International, which tried to stop the rot of politics by the state of war – writers in the East jailed because 'objectively' they aided the imperialist enemy, land reformers in the West murdered because they resembled communists. 'In each case, power was being used to inflict great short-term hurt in the name of long-term good. I began to see that medicine and human rights are linked quite profoundly.'

As the decade ended, it would be harder for her to keep apart the twin concerns that were beginning to rule her life. After her marriage failed she became more involved in Amnesty. 'It was for my own sake. I needed something to build on.'

Maurice Pappworth helped his friend and former assistant as practically as he knew how, just as she was beginning her association with Amnesty. Rudi Bamber had not collapsed into depression after the divorce, as some of his friends thought he might; he had remarried, and happily, in a relationship that has endured longer than his first marriage. In the early 1970s he contracted viral pneumonia and his lungs were dangerously close to failure; he was attacked by waves of hallucinations, 'talking to people who weren't there,' he remembered, as he drifted in and out of consciousness; he seemed to be dying. Gill, his second wife, grew much closer to Helen than had been possible before; and Helen suggested that they bring Pappworth in to take a second look at Rudi. The man who revered diagnosis was as good as his theory said he should be. According to Helen, the younger doctors gathered around Rudi Bamber's bed to watch the legendary outsider examine the patient. Pappworth altered the course of treatment. In Rudi Bamber's view, 'He was instrumental in saving my life.'

*   *   *

In Europe the middle of the Cold War still meant an absence of war. The West basked in full employment, its consensus hated by young radicals, but threatened by peaceful revolution from the right, not the left.

The dull but total control that Brezhnev reimposed on the Soviet empire after 1964 was mean even in its use of violence, but the police states of 'actually existing socialism' had few crevices in which organized pressure from below could build up. The leaders also realized that terror would always rebound on themselves. It was only possible in these countries to be a 'dissident', to refuse the party's right to rule on behalf of the people. Torture of the Algerian type was hardly needed: medical and pharmacological torture would do – dosing with sedatives and hallucinogens, incarceration in dreary 'hospitals' which were little more than psychiatric jails.

Outside Europe, the 'great contest' brought the furies of war. Wherever power was fragmented, or difficult to impose on nations still struggling to form themselves, violence could be almost measureless. South-East Asia, Vietnam above all, suffered havoc, the worst combination of undeclared world war and internal civil conflict.

In Latin America, Castro's seizure of power with a small band of guerrillas let loose utopian hope and conservative fear, in dangerously equal measure, throughout the subcontinent. The obvious injustices – of a land system resembling feudalism, of squalid shanty towns, of discrimination against the descendants of the pre-conquest inhabitants – suddenly began to look vulnerable to elementary and radical gestures.

In the context of the Cold War, every local argument was translated into apocalyptic, global terms. Language was charged and romanticized; words that in more settled societies would have remained empty now conjured real violence.

What the rival systems shared, whenever they were challenged, was a view of opposition as a form of illness. Peasants demanding land reform, strikers, writers true to their gift rather than the state, and religious believers were seen as germs, or tumours. Cancer was the disease of the age, and it crossed into politics. The atmosphere of the time was hectic: every questioning of legitimacy was a threat, a potential invasion. The enemy within was a mutating cell; if it was not stopped it would spread and destroy the body. War came home, in too many societies. Colonel Trinquier saw disease in Algeria; Generals Pinochet and Menendez would see it in the turmoil of Chile and Argentina. It had to be cut out, and to find it probing and interrogation would be necessary.

* * *

The massacres on the Indonesian islands in 1965, after an army coup and the fall of the radical nationalist Sukarno, were among the worst anywhere since the Second World War. After all opposition had been crushed, thousands were held on prison islands and forced to labour in harsh conditions, with constant surveillance.

The Hampstead branch of Amnesty adopted Beni Tjung as its prisoner of conscience. All they knew about him was that he was a poet, and that he had been held on Buru Island since 1965. Through him Helen Bamber learned the trade of human rights campaigning. 'This was what you did: you were told that you had been assigned a certain prisoner, in a process known within Amnesty as an "urgent action", and you wrote letters to the head of state (in this case General Suharto) and his ambassador to the UK, you visited the ambassador if he would see you, you collected information and encouraged others to send letters.' It was simple and so novel that it still seemed to have an effect. Amnesty's very interest in someone had a powerful resonance: the name itself had already come to signify a certain moral position that governments were loath to attack.

Unfortunately little of Tjung's work was available, and although he may have been a fine poet, what she read in translation 'rather tested one's Voltairean instincts', as Bamber later remarked. 'The Ballad of Upit' seemed to be an ode to women workers on the tea plantations:

> Upit!
> among the tea shrubs on the slope of the hill
> your fingers dance from twig to twig
> the leaves are gently swaying
> kissed by the mountain breeze.
> Eight hours you have sweated
> on the verdant sunlit hill
> why is it that your heart
> fails to find repose?

British writers – Adrian Mitchell, Stephen Spender – lent their names in support of the prisoner; and International PEN helped. A balloon race was held, leaflets were handed out, and John Conteh, a then-famous boxer, failed to turn up to publicize an event; the chairmen of companies doing business with Indonesia were asked to take a stand. (None did, though Arnold Weinstock of GEC, Britain's biggest industrial company, sent Bamber's group a cheque for £500.)

This was the usual small change of grass-roots Amnesty work, the kind of campaigning it is easy to see as do-gooding, but which has made a contribution to civilizing the world in the late twentieth century – or at least to making power more cautious. Amnesty's rather stiff, formal, polite expressions of concern hooked onto a government and dragged at it, making more difficult the purchase of weapons and the getting of credit. The left in the 1960s rather despised Amnesty's focus on the individual, and the non-violent individual at that: what of collective and justly violent action against oppression? Yet the organization went on insisting that the persecution of those who criticized without violence had to be refused whenever it occurred; beyond that limit lay moral chaos.

Bamber learned that in order to have any effect it was necessary to be absolutely consistent, and always do the next time-consuming boring task – mailing the letters or phoning the friendly vicar; and that the press would take more interest if there was an angle, or a local connection. Amnesty could not free Beni Tjung, or any of the 6000 other prisoners on Buru Island. Suharto knew he had the West's backing; and the British public did not care what happened in Java.

Those who came into contact with Helen Bamber in these years say that she worked for Amnesty with the same uncanny energy she seems to have brought to everything she has done. It was a grim tirelessness: that old insistence on walking around the room, the lesson the German–Jewish refugee taught her in her father's house. She read all the circulars from the Amnesty International Secretariat, volunteered for everything, and typed letters and statements onto flimsy stencils that wrapped around an inked drum and were turned to print onto cheap paper. 'So many leaflets', she remembered; 'I had moments when I saw them stuck to wet pavements in Camden Town when I wondered if any leaflet shoved into someone's hand has ever touched anyone's mind.'

*   *   *

In the Chilean port of Valparaíso an enormous monument stands in the square outside the naval headquarters, facing the docks and the Pacific Ocean. On the central pedestal the national hero Arturo Prat flourishes a sword. Around him at the four compass points are his three officers from the warship *El Huascar*, and the figure of a single seaman, all standing on ships' prows. In 1879, during the War of the Pacific against Peru, the young captain's gunboat ran into a massive Peruvian ironclad. In a gesture from the age of Trafalgar, Prat grappled his little vessel with the enemy. He jumped across the gap between the ships, sabre in hand, calling his men to follow, but the *Huascar* was rolled back by the swell and he found himself alone, with a hostile ship's company surrounding him. The Peruvian crew, not used to repelling boarders and dirty work with cutlasses, could not stop him making his way to the bridge, cutting at anyone who came near him. He was only three steps away from the enemy commander when the ship's cook, who happened to be on the gangway leading to the bridge, shot him in the head from behind.

The liberal, rational Chilean film-maker who related this story in 1997, acting out the young hero's last moments, insisted that Prat was a few seconds away from seizing the enemy ship. If only he had made it through the door onto the bridge!

The point of the young captain's legend was brought home by the wife of the man who told it with such gusto. She said that Chileans were obsessed with perfecting their modernity: the perfect capitalist economy, or the perfect revolution, and with addressing it in sonorous self-dramatizing periods, as though a Nerudan ode could solve a historical problem. Like Arturo Prat, leaping the gap and hoping to win the prize by sheer will. This shrewd woman seemed to be saying that in Chile words had the power not just to do harm, as they always do, but to kill, the distinction between language and reality blurring disastrously. The coup against the government of Salvador Allende that made General Augusto Pinochet a dictator for seventeen years started in front of the Prat memorial on 11 September 1973.

Salvador Allende was elected in 1970 on a programme of import substitution, nationalization and land reform – a radical redistribution of wealth. Allende had the backing of roughly half the population. The other half hated him. He was a Marxist, a Freemason, a haut-bourgeois – a mass of contradictions, hoping to bring about the transformation of his society by exhortation rather than force. He was not a Leninist; he had no instinct for violence or civil war. But the left was drunk on verbal Bolshevism; and Allende was surrounded by people who talked a good revolution. The Secretary of the Socialist Party, Carlos Altamirano, gave fiery speeches as though he had divisions of armed workers at his back, and he had none. The far-left MIR (Movement of the Revolutionary Left), which believed in guerrilla war, did have a small military capacity, but it consisted mainly of students. Chile is too long and thin and urbanized for guerrillas to hide in, unlike Cuba, where Fidel Castro and Che Guevara sheltered in the mountains of the Sierra Maestra from an inefficient dictator.

Allende's declarations of friendship with Cuba and the USSR helped create in Chile the spectre of communism, in which Allende insisted, truthfully, that he did not believe. (Nor, ironically, did the Chilean Communist Party, which was more temperate than the left of Allende's own party.) But the left had no strategy, and as the economy went out of control – prices shooting up, productivity going down, investment stagnating and employers of all sizes in revolt, along with sections of organized labour – Allende played for time. Some of his ministers demanded implementation of the full programme, while the communists – more lucidly aware of hemispheric realities – were prepared to compromise with the opposition Christian Democrats. As the conflict worsened, a failed coup by an army unit led to a new round of factory seizures by workers, which in turn exacerbated the resentment of the right. Allende, meanwhile, put his faith in the constitutional tradition of the national army.

These events were taking place in the third decade of the Cold War, a time of heightened tension between the superpowers; and the Chilean state in its present form was less than a century old, a form created by the army, the disciplined, German-trained force that had wrenched a tract of mineral-rich territory from the Peruvians and Bolivians in the war that made a hero of Arturo Prat. The military chose to assume that the left was serious about strategy; Richard Nixon and Henry Kissinger, unyielding believers in the dogma of global strategic struggle, were happy to encourage them; and words called up deeds. In 1973 the generals turned out to have a mind of their own, shaped by geopolitical doctrines, by paranoid theories of national security and subversive warfare, and crude social Darwinism. Allende's failed revolution would be followed by a war against civil society, a remaking of Chile in deadly earnest.

All the 'germs' (the word was General Pinochet's) would have to be cleaned out. At first the army shot people in droves, or condoned orgies of personal revenge. They used the word 'war' to describe a coup, which had no precedent in Chilean history for its violence, against a helpless enemy. There were stolen guns in the hands of the left, hidden in factories around Santiago, but the workers had no capacity to use them. The young conscripts who rode into Santiago hyped up for battle with terrorists found themselves guarding disorganized crowds, herded into football stadiums and temporary camps.

Pinochet needed an enemy. The mainstream parties were broken quickly. There was massive quiet resistance, from churches and unions and decent individuals, but in the first year his only armed opponent was the MIR, which had 'military' and 'intelligence' sections and tried to fight back. They had dreamed of turning the Andes into one giant Sierra Maestra; and they were tragically influenced by the gloss on Che's life tossed off by Regis Debray, the French publicist who believed that the *foco*, the liberated area, would become the nucleus of a chain reaction, outflanking the armies and cities of Latin America and touching off a continental revolution. This was Theory. In the introduction to his patronizing book-length interview with Allende in 1971, a tragically absurd document, Debray showed his grasp of Chilean history by declaring that if there were a coup, 'the revolutionary river would leave its bed and burst the banks in which it is confined today.'

The river was a trickle. Among the young MIRistas hiding out in Santiago was Luis Muñoz, a member of the group's intelligence service; the Enriquez brothers, the group's founders and leaders, issuing bulletins of 'mass resistance' to fascism; and Andres Pascal Allende, the dead president's nephew, with his lover Mary Ann Beausire, a dancer from a conservative Anglo-Chilean family. They ran between safe houses, hounded by army intelligence services, secret police agents and informers; curfews and roadblocks were everywhere. Soldiers in high Prussian boots stood guard, cocks of the walk in a nation that had once seemed to itself so English and tranquil. Miguel Enriquez was shot resisting arrest; his brother died soon after. It was a one-sided little war: at most four or five soldiers and police agents died that year. The MIR lost hundreds, among the thousands who were executed; the country was held in a state of siege. The rumours from the football stadium and the camps in the south were terrifying; even worse stories were told of houses in the suburbs.

* * *

For part of a generation, 11 September 1973 became a myth like the fall of the Spanish Republic thirty-five years before. The first democratically elected Marxist in history had died by his own hand rather than surrender; the idea of peaceful revolution was buried with him. The role of the CIA was clear enough – they encouraged those who wished to bring Allende down – but for many outside Chile, the internal divisions, and the sheer utopianism that wrecked Allende's government were harder to grasp. Helen Bamber was deeply affected by it. More than any other event since the end of the war, it sealed her determination to help draw a line against cruelty.

She said that it was the much-vaunted Englishness of Chile – that image of 'tea-drinking, constitutional, orderly progress' – that made the coup obscene for her, and revived memories of the 1930s, of fascism, and childhood fears of gleaming boots on the garden path. These fears were echoed throughout Europe in a time of industrial militancy, student revolts, neo-nationalist terrorism and shadow armies of the right. 'What was unbearable was the sense of a light going out; the failure of an entire vision of reform, which was being crushed along with the nonsense. And the violence of the coup was so grossly excessive: it was not about stopping revolution. The worst violence was done to an utterly helpless and defeated enemy. It felt very close to home.'

In the course of Amnesty's work for those who had died and disappeared in Chile, Helen met two men who would become close collaborators and inflect the course of her life. Gordon Wills, a City accountant in a pinstriped suit, seemed an unlikely ally. Outwardly prim, careful and restrained, he combined total reliability with spiritual hunger and a commitment to justice. He had grown up in Newcastle, a working-class boy with a gift for figures, but money and numbers were never enough. In Nigeria in the late 1960s, he had seen evidence of the state's capacity for extreme violence during the war against the Biafran separatists. To his own surprise, he had accepted that this was not a fact of nature, or of African barbarism, and that it was necessary to stand against it.

The second man, Dick Barbor-Might, was a character more familiar to Helen Bamber. He had worked in the Ministry of Supply after leaving school – the government department that bought arms for the services. A liberal Catholic, he was revolted by the Vietnam War; he couldn't face spending any more days working out the cost-effectiveness of, as he later put it, 'the best way to roast people alive in tanks'. At Leicester University as a mature student he soaked up anti-imperialist theory, the neo-Marxisms of Gunder Frank and Wallerstein and the older writings of J. A. Hobson. After graduation he became a lecturer at a London polytechnic. He went to Chile in August 1973 as Popular Unity was falling apart, and he was briefly locked up, more frightened than he could ever have imagined, in the changing rooms of the National Stadium hearing the screams and gunfire from under the bleachers. After his release the studied neutrality of the British Ambassador, Sir Reginald Seconde, infuriated him. Back in England, he entered the solidarity movement as though he had found God for the second time.

He had a rapid, urgent fluency, an ability to weave tight connections between the smallest local events and large global patterns. He would often invite his hearers to see one pattern in a dense net of inferences as the only possible explanation of a certain action by the state; he could see it in a silence. He was an Amnesty activist because he was a sincere anti-totalitarian, steeped in Orwell and Koestler, and yet he also desired a total refusal of any compromise with the interests, as he saw them, of world capitalism. He wanted Amnesty to be more than it could ever be: a movement for moral and social change. He could never be satisfied with a received story, or a mere prisoner of conscience. Like Sartre he was fascinated by the invincibility and seamlessness of power, the Sartre who once wrote: 'We must achieve revolutionary socialism all together everywhere.' That is, it can never happen, and yet it must.

Events in Barbor-Might's world could not escape the control of the system; there was little space for the contingent. Power concealed itself, and infiltrated even the organizations that resisted it. Only those who were radically outside the system could form a nucleus for change.

This was very close to conspiracy theory. His views are summed up here from the recollections of people who knew him in the 1970s, and from later conversations with him. Some found him impossible; all thought him difficult. The ex-civil servant revealed himself in the driving prose of his long, single-spaced letters, divided into points, qualifications and summaries. He drowned his case in words. Many who worked with him were aware of his over-investment – of himself, and of inflated, intricate hypotheses – in the cases he adopted. In a group like Amnesty, inherently pragmatic, anxious to criticize only provable violations of human rights, Barbor-Might would always be a volatile element. By the end he was so tangled in a web of speculation and fact that no one could tell them apart.

Helen Bamber, even after the final débâcle, speaks warmly of him. He could be deeply persuasive. She pays tribute to his energy, and she was fascinated by his almost effortless ability to explain, intervene and theorize. To her, who had never been to university, he must have had the seductive attraction of the men who dominated small magazines of the time with their eloquent *tours d'horizons* of east and west; the kind of man who seemed to take the pulse of the world every morning. 'He could bring a sense of global politics to bear on what had been, quite often, a rather sentimental Amnesty picture of the world. He could at least offer some political explanation of why repression was taking place. There was nothing churchy about Dick; in British Amnesty he was a ball of fire. All that was positive. But he was also obsessional.' How could she resist him? And of course she and Gordon Wills shared much of Barbor-Might's impatience with Amnesty, its reluctance to see beyond the prisoner to those who had built the cell and armed the guards. She believed that she could handle Dick, but in the end no one could save him.

They all became obsessional; Dick gave up his lectureship and became an unpaid full-time volunteer; by the end he was working as a night-porter in a hotel. Gordon Wills, an extremely sober fellow, says that he was then almost as zealous as Barbor-Might. He was, as he recalls with a wistful air, 'supposed to be married at the time'. Helen describes them all as 'living on the edge'. An Amnesty official who knew them well said later that 'work was an inconvenience for them'. Dick would sleep on her sofa, or Gordon's; and they would call each other in the early hours of the morning, or drive late at night from her place to Gordon's house in Blackheath, ten miles across London, to pick up a vital piece of information. Once they all slept on mailbags on the floor of the British Amnesty office.

In Bamber's case, her need to draw a line was beginning to centre on the most intimate form of repression: torture, which aroused all her old fear of being singled out, had become the response in too many countries to any offence against the state. 'It was to do with total power, exercised over the human body, and it was the singling out of people for a particular type of obscenity that I couldn't bear. I had a horror of it and I tried to retreat from thinking about it too much; but of all forms of repression it seemed the most immoral.'

Amnesty International agreed, and published an important *Report on*

Torture in 1974. Torture is now 'an instrument of government', a 'method of political control', the authors wrote; and they argued that while the propensity to torture may lurk in most human beings, it takes a state decision to use this potential to make torture significant.

In the beginning, however, Bamber was very much the activist. She became chair of the Hampstead group and was later elected with Gordon Wills to the Executive Council of the British Section of Amnesty, as a representative of the London region, which she, Wills and Barbor-Might tried to turn into a pool of energy on which Amnesty could draw for sustained campaigning.

Amnesty already had, by 1974, some 2600 members in Britain, and the numbers grew fast, reaching 17,000 by the early eighties. By then the Director of the British Section was Cosmas Desmond, a former priest jailed in South Africa for his stand against apartheid. The office was small; the section relied on volunteers who were willing to take responsibility for campaigns, like Bamber and her friends. One of them, Antonia Hunt, said later, bluntly, that they were 'the cuckoos in the nest'. Their graft was vital, but it could escape the control and reproach the sluggish routines of the paid office. Apart from a certain animosity between campaigners and traditionalists, the British Section was troubled by its closeness to the International Secretariat of Amnesty, which has always been based in London, and which produces the careful documentation and research that is the heart of the organization's work. This could seem a painful contrast to the efforts of the local body; and the temptation to influence international policy, and to believe that events in London are occurring at the centre of the world, could cause a rush of blood to the heads of the excitable. But for the moment, these were latent problems.

Gordon Wills said later: 'I didn't really notice her at the beginning. I thought she was the usual plummy Hampstead lady. What I first noticed was her *extraordinary* energy.' He still has a note of disbelief in his voice, after knowing her for twenty-five years. 'An incredible determination and tenacity. If we had to meet about something late at night there were no limits on how long she would continue.' He tells a story of Helen working all night for several days running in the crypt of the Church of Christ the King in Gordon Square, lent them by a supportive priest. They were preparing a dossier of case studies for a London region conference, and wished to show how investigation, propaganda and campaigning could be connected with interests in the UK – companies trading with repressive states, trade unions benefiting from the companies' prosperity – and how famous well-wishers could be brought to bear on a case. It was an expression of their desire to change the direction of Amnesty, to make it more of a campaigning movement for human rights, less exclusively focused on the fate of individual prisoners, no matter how symbolic.

A benefactor had given them some yellow paper. As the dossier grew, they ran out of paper and Wills drove around in rush hour traffic, an earnest man red-eyed with exhaustion, looking for the right horrible shade of stock. The Gestetner machine cranked away in the church crypt while Helen edited the document and worked steadily on an old manual typewriter. Forty volunteers collated it standing in line, piecing together thousands of loose badly-inked pages.

This is one of the Bamber myths: a judicious person like Gordon Wills believes that he did not see her sleep for nine days. She may, he concedes, have nodded off now and then, but he is sure she worked all night and then left each morning for her paid job in Harley Street: a burst of insomniac, exalted dedication. Her form of courteous energy often evokes this mixture of admiration and fantasy, and perhaps also guilt and fear. Stamina is an attribute of those who hold real power – like the famous light sleepers who have run great states in time of war. Bamber is willing to live at a pitch of intensity in the act of challenging power. There is of course a different kind of power in such activity, which can be hard to accept. It may already have begun to affect her relationship with her sons.

It is so easy not to know; never to ask the question that opens onto a past, and easier still to keep that question at bay. Bamber had lived a silence with her husband, and they had, without intending to, imposed their silence on their children. Anything to do with the Holocaust remained unspeakable, despite its centrality to everything that they were.

They were hardly alone in this. It was in the late 1970s that Helen Bamber worked for Andrew Matthews, who was then a successful gynaecologist. Her son Jonathan wrote his very first letter to Matthews' daughter, who was dying of cystic fibrosis. Bamber was close to the father in his grief. Yet neither of them mentioned their experiences in

Belsen, which had changed both their lives. It was only after his death, when his other daughter brought his scrapbook of atrocities to the Medical Foundation, that Bamber realized he had been there at all.

The tacit agreement not to speak of certain things inside her family was now, perhaps, too long-standing to change. The boys had their independence, and were already resourceful and self-sufficient. But what can start as anxious tact can become habit, and become so hardened that it seems like a secret. David Bamber remembered that, even when his parents were together, 'You could sense that there was a complete unspokenness about something, which as a small child you could not put your finger on; it was like a ghost that was too terrible to talk about.' His self-reliance and ability to do things for himself he traces to the origins of that silence. 'I think I was brought up by my mother to be a *survivor*. I was a frightened child, in many ways, and was afraid sometimes even to leave the house — I had a fantasy that I would be killed. She tried to manage that fear by sending me to judo classes to make me stronger. She felt personally responsible for any weakness, and wanted to put it right; she put immense emphasis on tutors outside school to help me with my dyslexia, for example.'

He believes that both he and his brother have pushed themselves nearly to destruction by setting themselves extreme challenges. He took up white-water canoeing. ('You can't afford to make a mistake on big water, and the pleasure of weaving a way through using your skill gave me real satisfaction.') Jonathan became a talented, almost addicted mountaineer. 'That we both do things like this says, I think, something about testing ourselves, about surviving.' David thinks of one incident from his childhood that for him sums up his mother's reticent anxiety about the world. 'She gave me a gold watch that had belonged to her father and said, "Hang on to this, you may need it; gold is valuable and it is a good thing to keep." Years later, I realized that Jews exchanged gold objects for water on the trains, when they were being transported to death.'

Helen remembers coming in late at night with Dick and Gordon, like guilty teenagers, to find the boys standing at the head of the stairs, her worried parents. It was in the late 1970s; David must have been almost twenty. She recalls this with affectionate laughter — delighting in the absurdity of the situation — because she believes that the boys were doing well, and that they liked her collaborators. It seems that they did; and the combination of discipline and freedom they were given sounds enviable. But perhaps one of her sons was not really joking: the world could seem more important to her than him. David Bamber says he began to wish he had a more normal childhood: 'Nowadays I keep meeting people who say she's a hero, but I see her from a different side. She always had a mission. And I think she viewed my brother and me as a mission too, as though she could only see the world in terms of victims and victimizers, and victim helpers. It was as though my needs were met as a victim, to help me survive.'

*   *   *

Dick Barbor-Might did not have cases, in the normal Amnesty sense; prisoners for him were keys to unlock the secret relations between dictatorships and the forces in the West that propped them up. When he met Helen Bamber he had found such a key: a young Anglo-Chilean businessman called Guillermo (William) Beausire Alonso. His family called him Bill.

Beausire was, officially, last seen boarding a flight in Santiago on his way to France in November 1974. It was known that he had landed at Buenos Aires, and then he vanished. The Chileans denied all knowledge of him; so did the Argentineans. But a picture of the absent man began slowly to form, as more and more refugees escaped from Chile.

His mother Inès and sister Diana arrived in Britain, both distraught, in June 1975. Helen speaks of Doña Inès as a handsome dignified woman, and of Diana as a gentle person shattered by what the DINA, Pinochet's new secret police, had done to her. They told Amnesty about Mary Ann, the fugitive sister, and about her MIR boyfriend, and about their own persecution. They spoke of hearing Bill's name called in a secret prison, the look of his shoes seen from under a blindfold, the sound of his voice.

A woman called Adriana Borquez was allowed into Britain in February 1976. She had been tortured, she believed, in Colonia Dignidad, a cult based in the south of Chile and led by Paul Schäffer, a paedophile fraudster on the run from West Germany, who had placed his remote settlement at the disposal of the army. The cult was notorious long before the coup for its abuse of its own members, its rackets, its consumption of tranquillizers – swallowing more in a year than the population of the province in which it was located. Adriana Borquez had seen Beausire in a DINA house as recently as July 1975. After that, the trail dried up. But they all believed against themselves that he was alive, his mother, sister, Helen, Dick; and perhaps Adriana most of all, because although she had more reason to fear the worst she had in a way loved him in the course of a brief life together that none of the others could share.

Helen believed she could manage Dick's enthusiasms, but he truly infected her, in ways he could not have intended, with this enigmatic young Chilean. For both of them, Beausire was a case that dramatized the nature of the regime, and because he held a British passport (thanks to his English father) he provided leverage on the British government, to keep it at arm's length from the Chilean junta. This larger issue mattered to the campaigners; but a subtle distinction began to develop between them. Barbor-Might, in a knowing echo of Cold War spy stories, speaks of 'running' William Beausire. He was a thread: if you pulled on it, you might be able to unravel the whole web of deceit. Helen Bamber, however, began to be affected more personally. Beausire haunted her: he was an emblem of the victim, but also of the normal man singled out for special treatment by a vindictive state. There was something uncanny about the thought of this decent, spoiled, conventionally right-wing young gentleman suffering extreme agony for views he did not even hold.

The standard left cult of the working-class hero slightly irritated her, she now says; that image of the stoic victim loyal to his party. Far too many who were suffering had no party. 'There are different kinds of heroism, and it seemed to me – it was my fantasy of him – that Beausire had to live with himself. He had nothing he could play games with. He was everything the left would have sneered at, and yet he came so well out of the other survivors' accounts. He had a quality of resistance of his own, different from the others. He was incorruptible, and that may have killed him.'

The British Labour government had stopped selling arms (new ones, at least) to Chile in 1974; and after the British doctor Sheila Cassidy was tortured by the DINA in 1975 they broke off diplomatic relations as well. British arms companies were anxious to restore a more value-free foreign policy, and Amnesty International and the Chilean solidarity campaigns were aware that if a Conservative government succeeded the weak Labour administration, General Pinochet would have no further problems with the supply of frigates.

This is – to anticipate a little – exactly what happened after Mrs Thatcher's victory in 1979. Diplomatic ties were resumed in February 1980. Nicholas Ridley at the Foreign Office made no secret of his wish also to resume arms sales. On 15 July that year, the 21-year-old British student Claire Frances Wilson was arrested with her Chilean boyfriend and tortured, following the shooting of the chief of Army Intelligence in Santiago. Dick Barbor-Might picked up her case when news of it first came to the British Amnesty office, and made it front page news. He was able to establish that Nicholas Ridley had deliberately delayed acknowledging the fact of her torture, which he must have been told about by the Embassy in Santiago, in order not to interfere with his announcement on the 21st ending the ban on arms sales. Together with the lawyer Geoffrey Bindman, Dick Barbor-Might and Helen Bamber called the young woman in Chile over a special link, the stunned telephone engineers listening to her cry as she described her torture. Amnesty publicized her testimony very effectively. The case showed how high the stakes could rise, and how serious a game Bamber and her friends were playing. It also exposed, of course, the weakness of human rights demands on a strong and hostile government.

Bamber was given an insight into how little she mattered when she and Dick Barbor-Might, accompanied by Cosmas Desmond, called on Nicholas Ridley at the Foreign Office that July. They pointed out that the information about Claire Wilson must have been known to the government, and asked how they could restore arms sales, knowing what the regime was still capable of doing. She said of the encounter: 'There were polite words, and officials looking at their watches, and total confidence in what they were doing and saying; they assumed that they held knowledge that we did not. It was a dialogue of the deaf. Ridley didn't say much; he was indifferent to the case, and he looked utterly contemptuous of us. The officials had made up their minds, and patronized us.' Bamber distinctly remembered that Ridley's hands were shaking, his cigarette trembling in his fingers, as he sat in his palatial room lined with crimson studded-leather sofas, behind a great leather-topped desk surmounted by green shaded lamps. Behind him, ten-foot-long mirrors reflecting heavy chandeliers and roof beams were set between high windows looking out onto Whitehall.

As they walked out into the summer evening the TV cameras caught them, and, exposed garishly by the lights, they gave an interview to Independent Television News, expressing their hope that the British government would now put pressure on the Chilean authorities, and so on – the usual guarded phrases after a hopeless encounter with a government.

In the mid-1970s, however, the thread still clung to Bill Beausire (they had all started calling him by his first name, as though he were their brother). As long as he could be made to live, he was a scandal, a pebble in the shoe of the junta. Dick Barbor-Might and Helen Bamber built up the layers of a convincing narrative from rumours and witness statements. In December 1976 another refugee came, the young MIRista Luis Muñoz Gonzalez. His own sufferings had been prolonged. He spoke of seeing Beausire, in January of the previous year, shaking and emaciated, in a place called the Villa Grimaldi.

Luis Muñoz had left school at fourteen and joined an organization that seemed to be part of a movement setting fire to a continent. He became a leading member of the MIR's 'intelligence section'. He was a Guevarist, but he had worked in factories and had a clearer grasp of the situation than the upper-class MIR leaders who had decreed after the coup that there would be an upsurge of the masses, and that the group must give it a lead. Luis Muñoz thought they should save themselves, and keep their powder dry; but he stayed, and for a year he evaded capture. On the morning of 18 November 1974 he parted from his second wife (his first wife, who was not in the MIR was, he thought, already safe, and living with their daughter) and when she failed to keep the evening rendezvous he knew she had been taken. He stayed free for another three weeks.

In the Villa Grimaldi, a converted farmhouse–restaurant on the eastern edge of Santiago, he was beaten, racked and electrocuted. On the second day his blindfold was removed. The army captain in his immaculate fatigues asked, 'Don't you remember me?' Luis had been at school with him; he did then recall the boy showing off his splendid blue cadet's uniform when he was accepted by the military academy. His name was Miguel Krasnoff Marchenko, the only son of a White Russian officer, whose wife had emigrated to Chile. A strange dialogue began, which Luis Muñoz believes may have saved him: very few militants with his record ever came back alive. He seemed to fascinate Krasnoff Marchenko: 'He wanted to know how I had ended up like this; he also had the chance to show off his power to someone from his childhood; he was full of mad energy. I was insolent to him, called him *tu* instead of *Jefe* as we were supposed to do, told him he was a fascist killer.'

The torture resumed, guided by his old schoolmate. Luis Muñoz was laconic about it, twenty-four years later, but his voice sank to a whisper as he elucidated what Krasnoff had supervised. 'There was hanging by the arms, they used a hammer, I remember suffocation with a plastic bag; the hanging is very painful, your wrists are twisted; with the electricity you feel your brain is going to explode, they put things in your anus; on your ears it is very bad, and on your penis. That night they tied me up to a bed in a big room with other people, I was shaking with the convulsions of electricity, you see lightning, and your mouth feels as though it is going to crack. I could hear voices whispering, "Be strong."'

He told Bamber that some of the torturers wore his own clothes. Krasnoff sat by the side of the man working the generator. 'Give him more,' he would say. 'God, you jump,' said Luis Muñoz. Krasnoff told him that he had shot Luis's wife.

In January 1975, during the fourth week, Krasnoff Marchenko would come every day to talk to him. They had put him in a closet handcuffed and chained. It was 'about the size of that', he said, and he pointed over to a wooden cupboard, about four feet high, that stood in the corner of the room in which he was speaking. There was a hole in the closet door to let in – just enough – air, and they kept a radio on all night so that he couldn't sleep. He could hear a man, in another box nearby, crying, begging for his life.

Luis knew he smelled terrible by then. Krasnoff would come and open the door and look at him, smoking a cigarette (Luis remembers that it was a Marlboro), careful to breathe only tobacco-scented air. He would offer cigarettes to Luis, who never accepted one.

Krasnoff came once to the box and said, 'We're going to bring your daughter.' 'Bring her,' said Luis. 'I don't care.' He believes that his in-difference, which was by then real to him, may have stopped Krasnoff from doing it.

After his release from the box Luis met William Beausire. 'He was very depressed, ill and anaemic; but he had great intelligence and strength.' He said that Beausire helped other prisoners, and he told Dick Barbor-Might about how Bill had once cradled a prisoner's head for hours after a torture session. Luis surprised himself, he said, by admiring this 'Englishman'; he had always hated the Anglophile Chilean upper class.

They transferred Luis to a prison camp. One day Krasnoff Marchenko came to visit. 'I hope you're not sad any more,' Luis recalled his torturer saying to him. They seem to have let him go eventually on a promise of good conduct; the MIR was by then extirpated. He flew to Britain, which gave him asylum and where he had nothing. 'You come out a different person. I was afraid of myself. You're meeting somebody inside yourself that you don't know; you are totally disconnected. When I first met Helen I wanted to kill myself. I would go to the psychology department in Foyle's and sit on a chair and read, use it like a library.' He was fascinated by *The Feeling Child* by Arthur Janov: the idea of a primal scream, a violent purging. 'I needed to recover my body.'

Bamber first met him at a hunger strike by Chilean refugees in a church on the Euston Road. (Billie Whitelaw, the actor, interpreter and friend of Beckett, came to show her support; she and Bamber became friends, and Whitelaw does public readings for the Medical Foundation.) But Luis Muñoz struck deep into Helen Bamber. 'I felt the first kind of recognition that there was work of a different kind, that couldn't be avoided, that actually needed to be done. He was more severely depressed than any survivor I have ever met; and there was nothing for him, no concept anywhere that he might need help. After the hunger strike I met him in his home in North London, sometimes riding along on top of the 134 bus which goes down past Muswell Hill and Highgate. I remember sitting up there with him describing to me how helpless and hopeless he felt, and how he was without any feeling of wanting to go on living, and I remember thinking how I was gliding through pleasant residential Muswell Hill and those beautiful trees in Highgate Wood sitting beside a man who was telling me of the most appalling obscenities.'

She was struck by how they took his clothes and wore them when they were torturing him. 'It's as though they want you to feel you are torturing yourself; something that you've honoured and bought and worn, your leather jacket, your jeans, your shirt; they are suggesting to you that they have completely removed your personality, and it reverses everything, takes a personality and destroys everything a person loves, like playing music while torturing.

'We went on meeting and talking, and tried to find ways of looking at a life in which he had lost so much. I could do so little; but I think that in talking and facing a lot of difficult things together we did some useful work. I always think about him. He is writing now, and once we talked about others who had written, like Primo Levi; and he said to me, I do not wish to commit suicide when I finish my book. That journey between a hopeful life and the past: survivors move constantly between one and the other.

'It was also necessary to think about Luis's physical disability; from the time he was hung from a beam and they applied electricity he felt something go in his lower abdominal area, and it returned to him, awful pain. We talked about whether it was a "real" pain, or a pain of memory, a pain that he could let go. Pain *becomes* memory, for some torture victims.

'I began then to think what one might be able to do for survivors of torture. Luis showed me the possibility of this. I actually wanted to escape it, because it's much easier to be the agitator, the active campaigner; to run around, to make statements, get on the phone, and feel you are doing something; that can be very comfortable, you are keeping your own demons away. But when you look into someone's experience; when you share that with them, it is different. Once you've done it, and once you've understood that there is this other dimension, it is difficult – or it was difficult for me – to go back to the ordinary way of working.'

In the activist world that still held her, Dick Barbor-Might suspected that there was collusion high in the British establishment to suppress the Beausire case; 'The enemy was here,' as he said later: the Foreign Office could have saved Beausire, and did nothing. Barbor-Might spoke of 'the dog that didn't bark'. He had also begun to suspect that the British secret service was attempting to destabilize Amnesty. The blockage of arms sales to a robustly anti-communist regime would not have endeared the organization to MI6, but proof was a series of 'threads leading into nothingness', in his own striking phrase.

For now, at least, Dick Barbor-Might could focus on his one great case. He and Helen Bamber produced an Amnesty booklet about Beausire, which was mainly Dick's work, and it was very competent. They reported what they had discovered from talking to the exiles, and called on the British government to demand Bill's release, or at least to find out where he was being held. Bamber remembered 'one of the most appalling evenings of that whole period when I worked on the Beausire document with Veronica Aurens, a friend from the orthopaedic hospital. She drew pictures based on Luis Muñoz's account of the Villa Grimaldi, simple sketches of the *parrilla*, of electrocution, of a man hung from a frame. You had to place yourself there, and we were both shattered by it.'

The pamphlet was description; but it was also a way of paying heed to memory. Bamber understood from talking to Luis Muñoz and Adriana Borquez that they felt forgotten, that they needed to connect their stories with the ordinary world of those who had not been tortured. The Beausire dossier would ensure that there was at least one more brief, carefully sifted account of an individual's fate, told in the many voices of those who saw him after he 'disappeared'.

But Helen and the others were campaigning without hope. Bill Beausire was dead before she ever heard of him; it was a question, now – although they did not know it – of how forgotten he would be.

7

POOR GHOST

It is easier to die than to remember.

Basil Bunting, *Briggflatts*

He who listens sins.

Paul Schäffer, cult leader of Colonia Dignidad

On a warm night in a Santiago garden, the leader of the Chilean mountaineers who climbed K2 in the Himalayas spoke about the bodies they found in a glacier. He and his friends stood and looked in silence at a headless torso, and a frozen body with its arms torn off, its bearded head smiling widely, projecting from the ice. They had died on the worst mountain in the world, a remote, vertical Arctic, where the solidarity among climbers is so great because of the extreme risks, and the Chileans did not even know their names. This apparition of the disappeared unsettled them. They went on with the climb, but they noted the place and came back to bury the bodies. They were interred in a deep crevasse, and as a grave marker some words were scratched on a titanium plate. Further down the mountain the Chileans put up a cairn of stones on a level space commanding the field of rock and ice thrusting up out of Asia: a monument to all the men and women who had died there, ten days from the nearest village. Some of the names were scratched out with crampons or nails, but each now had a piece of writing to commemorate them. All the climbers felt that some memorial was necessary; it was fitting.

*   *   *

In the General Cemetery in Santiago there is a wall of names:

Bastias Sandoval, Luis A.   28–9–1973   28
Beausire Alonso, Guillermo R.   2–11–1974   24
Becarra Avello, Manuel M.   13–9–1973   18

And so on, 3200 of them incised in black on white stone; it recalls the inscriptions cut into the sides of mountains in the northern Chilean deserts, which can be seen for miles. Archaeologists call them 'geoglyphs': carvings on the earth. 'Salvador Allende Gossens/Presidente de la Republica' is written in larger letters at the centre of two intricate wings of script spread out on either side. The 'Disappeared/Detained' to the left; 'Political Murders' on the right. Beausire is among the disappeared, high up among the Bs, too awkward to photograph. The base of the wall is sunk below the level of the cemetery path and rises out of a fall of rock, like a cliff, seeming to balance itself on the rubble. There is a tiny water-font under the rocks, the words *Para que Nunca Más* inscribed on its edge, and a bunch of white, red and purple carnations strewn over it. The containment of the names here, the waste of it, is overwhelming.

An unruly democracy, with its capacity for extravagant gestures, was beheaded and terrorized. This high wall, a simple list of known facts, also represents a boundary in this 'muffled society'. The past is on the other side of what is still the only public memorial to the victims of the military dictatorship. In Constitution Square, behind the presidential palace known as La Moneda, dead leaders stare gravely from their plinths, but there is no record of the Allende period or the dictatorship. It was a time out of joint, best forgotten, like a bitter civil war. The General Cemetery is at the far end of the long Avenida Recoleta, miles from any site of official state memory. And being so far from the centre, the wall doesn't disturb the booming economy of the city, its endless present.

The memorial is surrounded by the strongbox mausolea of the Chilean upper class, set amid pine and yew and cypress – little temples to sound money, large estates in the south, German and English antecedents and carefully cultivated privacy.

On each corner of the viewing platform in front of the wall are four large human heads, smiling at a secret happiness, half-stuck in the rough grey matrix from which they were sculpted. This further echo of pre-conquest Chilean culture must be deliberate. The Nasca people of the northern desert had a cult of the severed head: they made pots and cups in the form of rounded, beatific faces, serene and peaceful, symbols of fertility and well-being in an ecology that was harsh and getting worse. These great fallen heads seem also to remember an unattainable future.

*   *   *

Bungalows painted in lurid shades — blue, pink, green — line the streets in the Santiago suburb of Macul, off the long straight avenues that run out from the centre of the city towards the south. Many of the houses are built of pre-cast concrete, the lawns weedy and rough; the heat and dust feel oppressive: a long way from the clean sidewalks and brick-and-hardwood villas — masked by bay trees and pristine hedges — of Las Condes and Providencia, where Beausire grew up and where gardens are gently sprinkled even in the drought. But even in Macul the larger gardens have pomegranate and pear trees, and vines. The light, the easy fertility, the vivid colours are numbing.

The house, no. 3037 on Calle Iran, is situated at the corner of Iran and Los Plátanos. On that side there is a park, a dry square of earth without a patch of grass, on which two lines of trees cut across the grey surface diagonally, like the flagpoles on Constitution Square. It was probably never the sort of place where people walked much, except to relieve their dogs. Perhaps the house was chosen because although it is on an ordinary street and is overlooked by other ordinary houses, it also faces this silent empty field of dirt.

No. 3037 had its curtains drawn. A short man, very darkly tanned, wearing black sunglasses, opened the gate as the car stopped. He was dressed in a white shirt, with his jacket over his right shoulder. In his hand he carried a red plastic folder. He stood and stared, very confident of his ground. He did not move for several seconds, and then walked carefully across the street, marking his time, his attention, and then along the edge of the empty park, looking back once.

The house is painted in light green and terracotta, and all the ironwork — railings, gutters, gates — is the same bright rusty colour. It is as garish as a Road-Runner cartoon. The building is larger than it first appears, shaped like an L; the upper storey juts out over a patio, and the garden is bigger than on any of the adjoining properties. A short path leads from a locked gate up to the patio and main door. The place is half concealed by a wall; and the garden is fronted by a six-foot iron fence backed by wire mesh. It is not a daunting fence, easy for a fit person to climb. A stringy black German Shepherd lifted itself from the shade of the patio to the gate, its ears back, snarling, muzzling through the bars.

The house is not even set very far back – about ten paces, less, but it is striking how much of it remains invisible from the street. The shrubbery breaks up the line of sight, even of the ground floor; tall palm trees hide the windows on the upper storey, and balconies deepen their concealment. It would be difficult to get a glimpse inside even without the drawn curtains.

It was more or less the same twenty-two years ago. The security must have been so casual, though they had a dog then too. It was ideal, really, central enough to be an office for the processing of subjects, easy to get to from the government ministries and army headquarters, and just isolated enough to diminish attention and muffle sounds. And it was after all a halfway house, a rehabilitation centre. It was meant to reassure the inmates, to show them that there was hope: they were living in a normal house, just like ordinary people. It would have the look of a colourful doctor's clinic, were it not for the dead air, the shut-in garden, the drawn curtains and the attack dog. But people were changed here; were never the same again afterwards. The state cured them of subversion, and then tried to cure them of the cure, a double therapy.

The street is quiet. Didn't anyone ever hear a particularly sustained cry, or wonder at the constant loud music? There must have been a subtle repulsion, stopping the neighbours looking, and if they had wanted to know it would have meant standing in the street and gazing with the kind of confidence that only the very courageous might have had in Santiago in 1975. Yet the condition of the tall young man working in the garden in May of that year, his clothes draped on him, must have given some neighbour a disturbed few minutes on her way to work.

Does the man in the white shirt know that this was a house in which people were tied to metal bedframes and hurt with electricity? To cover the sounds of human pain, the boogie shuffle of early 1970s dance tunes was heard so often and so loudly that the house became known as 'La Discoteca'. Torturers are jokers: they have such unpleasant stuff to displace. Does the man know that the house he lives in was also called 'La Venda Sexy', the Sexy Blindfold, because women with scarves tied around their eyes were raped here by army officers and their accomplices, men like Osvaldo Romo?

Adriana Borquez could draw the man a sketch to lay over his own private map of the place where no doubt he feels safest, where he feels at home. The bathroom on the ground floor is where the guards came to her in the shower several nights running; here, perhaps where he sleeps, is where they kept Bill tied to an iron frame on the floor for a month; this room in which his children may sleep they used for putting crocodile-clip electrodes on men's and women's most sensitive flesh; Bill regularly watered and pruned that pomegranate tree; and back there is the water tank where she and Bill talked about jumping over the wall and wondered how far they would get on those straight suburban avenues that go on for miles, with her hardly able to walk and Bill shaking and shambling along.

She did come back to the house once, accidentally, when a taxi driver taking her to meet one of her daughters in Santiago took a short cut through Macul. 'I asked him to stop. I was looking at the house and I couldn't believe it; I tried to imagine myself behind that window, behind the curtains, trying to see a bit of the outside world and I suddenly had this image again, from the inside to the outside, the room to the garden. And from where I was sitting in the taxi I could see the lemon tree, it had grown bigger; and then I saw this child's tricycle, and I couldn't stop crying, I couldn't, it was terrible. I said to the driver, please go. I looked at the balcony there, below the balcony is a porch, and inside the porch is a window, and that was my room, *our* room – with Bill. It was not good to go back there.'

In the utter silence and the heat, the absorption of the house in itself is repellent – an undischarged bankruptcy of imagination in the total lack of acknowledgement of what was done here. Dante in the 'Inferno' has a line that evokes despair, facing the wolf that symbolizes malice, in a place 'where the sun falls silent'. Light is silent here. Photos of the house come out as dead and distant as crime-scene pictures: the flat refusal of the unkempt garden, the brown gates, the dog. But of course none of this is evidence of anything; it happened a long time ago, life has come back to normal and there are no skeletons under the patio. After all, it's only a house.

*   *   *

On Saturday, 2 November 1974, Guillermo Beausire Alonso drove to the airport from his mother's house in Calle Alferez Real, in the wealthy suburb of Providencia. He was going to live in Paris, where he hoped to work in finance. His intention was to stop over for the weekend in Buenos Aires, in order to buy clothes, so that he would look the part when he arrived in Europe. His mother Inès went with him to say goodbye. She had married an Englishman, Wilfred Beausire, in 1943, and though he had died in 1958 his children had dual nationality. There were four of them, three girls and the boy.

Bill still lived at home at the age of twenty-five; he was close to his mother and sisters and enjoyed the life of his class, its servants and summer homes. He sailed in the Pacific off Valparaíso, ate in fashionable restaurants on the coast or in the foothills of the Andes, hung out on the gilded strip at Viña del Mar. He had gone to business school in Valparaíso and worked on the Santiago Stock Exchange; his passions were yachting and girls. His mother later told Helen Bamber that he had voted for the Conservative candidate, not Allende, in the 1970 election.

People like Beausire had every reason to feel safe in their world, even under a dictatorship. But his youngest sister Mary Ann was the lover of Andres Pascal Allende. That November she had been underground for over a year. Andres Pascal's mother was Laura Allende, Salvador's sister, who was herself on the left of the Socialist Party. These were dangerous family connections, but Andres Pascal was far worse. He was now the senior surviving leader of the MIR, which was – at least in the person of the young militants who were still alive, like Luis Muñoz – engaged in a pathetic 'armed struggle' against the regime. In that first year, at least 2000 people died at the hands of the army; it lost four men.

Mary Ann dragged the whole family down. A month before Bill left the country, the founder and secretary-general of the MIR, Miguel Enriquez, died shooting it out with soldiers. The DINA, the new secret police, became more aware of the Beausires. The atmosphere around the family grew heavy and unpleasant. Juana, Bill's eldest sister, took the infant child of the fugitive couple into asylum with her at the Italian Embassy.

Family is not lightly abandoned in Chile. Bill seems to have had at least one meeting with Mary Ann, which was observed by others, as all his movements may have been for who knows how long. They may have let him run because they were hoping to net Andres Pascal. His grief-stricken mother and sister Diana insisted to Helen Bamber, seven months later, that he was innocent, an apolitical young businessman, and this was true; but it was their truth, not the regime's. In those meetings with his desperate younger sister, to whom he was very close, he may, according to the last person known to have seen him alive (and who is the last to wish to muddy his innocence), have crossed the shifting line that separated the enemy from the merely indifferent.

Inès watched Bill cross the runway and stayed on the viewing jetty until the plane took off. That was the last she saw of him, striding along with his briefcase, waving to her, a tall, dark-haired, overweight but good-looking young man, and then he was gone up the aircraft steps. But although she was certain that she never saw him again, she was equally sure that she heard his voice once more, not long afterwards.

She was arrested less than an hour after she got back from the airport. Her daughter Diana had just come by. Men walked into the kitchen hung with machine pistols, demanding to know where her son was, and where Mary Ann was hiding. Inès told them that Bill had left the country. But in her bag they found a notebook with the aircraft time and flight number – she had made a note of it, just in case. How she must have felt about her fussy competence, in the years that were left to her; and how much time her daughters must have spent convincing her that the secret policemen already knew.

Two of the DINA agents hurried out of the room with Inès's note. The others ripped Scotch tape over the women's eyes, put sunglasses over the tape and took them out to a Chevrolet van. All the women connected with the Beausire family who were picked up that day (including Laura Allende) were taken first to a DINA detention centre known as Cuatro Alamos.

They took Inès from there to a house in the suburb of Nunoa, on Calle José Domingo Canas, and read to her a statement by Bill. She was not harmed, but was made to sit, blindfolded, and listen to the sounds from other rooms.

Four days later, on the 6th, they took her back to that house from Cuatro Alamos. Her interrogator was Osvaldo Romo, who is a famous man in Chile. He asked Inès again about her missing children. He shouted at and insulted her, but did not strike her. Under the Allende government he had been an organizer in a *población*, a working-class shanty town. He was a tinpot caudillo, a bit of an ultra-left thug: El Presidente is not moving fast enough, the people are tired of waiting – the fog of cheap maximalism in which the government had to work. But the day after the coup he turned up in his shanty town dressed in fatigues, accompanying a squad of soldiers, and began pointing out his fellow-activists. It is not clear that he had changed his mind very much: a certain kind of nihilistic resentment can simply reverse its direction. The new regime would have a use for violent losers.

When he spoke to Inès, Romo had probably come from torturing her son. Bill mentioned the man's name to at least two surviving witnesses. Inès told Helen later that Romo revelled in frightening and humiliating her, that he was full of leering respect for Doña Inès.

It was later on that day, the 6th, that Inès heard Bill's voice, speaking to one of the guards, and the next day she heard him again, asking a guard where to put the wet mop and dirty water from the toilet he had just cleaned. That afternoon they took a roll-call, and read her son's name from a list. She heard her daughter Diana say that Guillermo Beausire was her brother, and a guard say that he was in the cell next to hers.

Diana Beausire was also kept in a cell in Cuatro Alamos, and transferred to the house on José Domingo Canas, blindfolded; her mother was in the same van. They were made to lie on the floor in a room with other female prisoners. The guards kept them awake all night with curses and threats. In the morning Diana was taken to another room, with a scarf over her eyes. She could hear laughter, typewriters clattering, talking. They asked her questions about Andres Pascal and her sister. The pretence at conversation turned to screaming rage, punching, kicking, blows on the ear. 'I cannot remember how long this took.' Back in her cell, she heard all night 'the screams of prisoners being tortured'.

The beating and abuse lasted for two hours on 6 November, and afterwards she heard her brother addressed by name when they moved him from his cell. She spoke up and was heard by her mother. She heard them tell him that they had found Andres Pascal Allende, and Bill saying that he did not believe them.

Another week passed in Cuatro Alamos, to which they had returned her, without much violence, and after that Diana was sent to a different house – she was not sure where – and they worked on her for seven hours a day for three days, with electrocution, more blows, and always the screaming, demanding threats. Her testimony notes that when she was not being tortured she was forced to sit silent and unmoving on a chair, and forbidden to use the toilet. Helen Bamber remembered that detail, many years later, and commented that it is one of the least costly forms of torture: the victim's body is allowed to humiliate itself.

On 5 December Diana was taken to the Villa Grimaldi. In the heat of the Chilean summer she was left blindfolded in the open courtyard for hours. A guard asked a prisoner how he was feeling. She heard Bill's voice. Under her blindfold she could see his shoes and trousers. 'I could not afford to look at him more closely.'

Inès was taken back to Cuatro Alamos and released after ten weeks. Her daughter was freed a little later.

*   *   *

He had escaped. It is easy to imagine his light heart when he walked onto the concourse of Ezeiza airport in Buenos Aires, for the first stopover of his long flight. He was looking forward to some serious shopping. He heard his name over the PA, calling him to the International Police Control. Felipe Dumonceau, a school friend he met on the flight, who was then a young Chilean diplomat on his way to Ankara, saw Bill walk casually away from his future towards a desk against the wall of the airport. A few minutes later Bill disappeared from public view and official existence.

When Dumonceau enquired, as the plane was about to fly on to Paris, what had happened to his travelling companion, he was told that there was a problem with Beausire's immigration documents. The young diplomat did that much: he was working for people who took kindly to discretion; but he made a statement later about the message over the loudspeaker and Bill's short walk across the terminal.

Helen Bamber and Dick Barbor-Might thought they knew enough, from those who had heard Bill tell the story, to state that he was shown into the office behind the desk. DINA agents were waiting there. The agents punched and kicked him, in order to stun and frighten him. Then they gave him chocolate to eat – a little energy for the shock. For a while he was kept in a toilet closet at the rear of the office. It is not clear how long he was held back there as tourists walked through the scenery of shops and bars feeling important and a little fearful, as intercontinental travellers always do, while yards away behind a wall he sat terrified and disoriented on a toilet pedestal.

Later, probably in the early part of Sunday, they handcuffed him and led him through the service areas and onto a Chilean Air Force plane. He told Luis Muñoz and Adriana Borquez later that they beat him during the two-hour flight, and the plane landed at Cerrillos, a military airport near Santiago. Some ex-prisoners who met him say that he was actually kidnapped by SIFA, the air force's own secret service, and that they held him for a few days before handing him over to their DINA rivals.

However he got there, by 6 November Bill was in the house on Calle José Domingo Canas. The beatings and the rest probably started in earnest there, but perhaps not yet with full intensity; it is impossible to say. Those who know are serving out their commissions in the Chilean Army.

From then on we get only glimpses, fragments, images of a pale, physical wreck, a man fainting with pain and nausea, losing weight, becoming kilos thinner, his clothes hanging off him, stooped and shuffling because of the injuries to his spine; a human being systematically shocked, dislocated and bruised. There are contradictions in the stories, almost all told by people who were tortured themselves and more than lucky to have escaped with their lives from the places in which they met Bill. He seems to have repeated his story again and again, as though he knew he would never be able to tell it in his own voice, adding some new detail each time he was moved around the branches of this peculiar institution.

After Calle José Domingo Canas they took him to the Villa Grimaldi. Before the coup it was one of those roughly elegant, out-of-town restaurants of the kind that Beausire seems to have liked. It was surrounded by a high wall, it had gardens and terraces with views of the cordillera, and a swimming pool, which was kept fresh by a pumping mechanism housed in a small tower at the north-east corner of the property.

In the main wing, along one wall, the prisoners and their guards were housed, and rooms were set aside for goods stolen by the DINA, whilst in another building the secret policemen kept offices, a dining room and a billiard table.

In the grounds, they had built a minute free-standing 'room' in which they would place prisoners for days at a time, huddled up in darkness in a space a metre square. It would have been possible, if Bill was not blindfolded, for him to have looked up as they put him into the hutch and seen the enormous formations of the Andes to the east. They had similar boxes indoors, we know that, which they called 'wardrobes'. The effects on the spine were predictable. Luis Muñoz was kept in one of these boxes, and Krasnoff Marchenko would visit him, smoking his Marlboro to mask the smell from his schoolmate's body.

At the Villa they also had the submarine; the *parilla*, which means barbecue; and the strappado, or *pau de arrau* – the literal meaning is parrot's perch. None of these require much ingenuity: a bath full of cold water, often dirty; a metal bedframe hooked up to a generator; and a couple of hooks and pieces of rope. Torture is an improviser's art.

Those who shared in his abjection say that Bill was subjected to electric shock in every part of his body, stretched out on the bare springs of a bed and wetted to make his body more receptive to the current of electricity, while sticks were thrust up his rectum, and he was suspended for long periods in the *pau de arrau* so that the joints of his shoulders and arms were dislocated. The men who tortured him almost certainly included Captain Krasnoff Marchenko and Osvaldo Romo. And he could presumably tell them nothing, nothing at all about where Allende's nephew was hiding.

Every simple thing that we associate with safety or convenience – the bath of water that cradles the body and cleanses it of sweat and dirt, the energy that gives light and heat, the safe enclosure of the room, the bed, the very idea of a house – were parodied and inverted here. Wardrobes turned into crippling, suffocating doll's houses. Elaine Scarry, in her great meditation on torture, calls this process 'the unmaking of the made'; the room itself, 'the simplest form of shelter' and the basic unit of civilization, is in torture 'converted into a weapon'. 'Made to participate in the annihilation of the prisoners, made to demonstrate that everything is a weapon, the objects themselves, and with them the fact of civilization, are annihilated.' At the Villa Grimaldi the world of the victim like Bill Beausire contracted into an intense space of pain and fear; and in the literal contraction of the body in a box, the prisoner was made to understand that his or her expansive world had come to nothing. The prisoners were told: this is all the room you have. If they survived, every room, for some of them, would have the capacity to close in and crush instead of protecting their bodies. Scarry rightly calls the ending of Poe's 'The Pit and the Pendulum', in which the walls of the chamber begin to draw in on the victim, 'the single distilled form of torture that in many ways represents all torture'.

A crude pen and ink sketch, drawn by Helen Bamber's friend Veronica Aurens for the Amnesty pamphlet about Beausire, shows a naked male tied to a rough frame. The body is splayed out, like a carcass: an utter abandonment of its sovereignty. The event the drawing describes is taking place in a vault-shaped room, meant to be the tower of the Villa Grimaldi. The man's head is covered by a dark hood; thin wires pass under the hood, and from his penis and his leg, to a generator, a little machine on a table operated by a man who stands by it looking quiet and efficient. At another table, a man writes with a pen, and off to the right a fourth man holds a sheaf of documents and seems to address the blinded person. The torturers are relaxed and untheatrical; they are doing unhurried work, as the executioner and the torturer are so often represented, with great acuity, in Western art – like the muscular bowmen redrawing their crossbows in the Pollaiuolo version of the killing of St Sebastian, which hangs in the National Gallery in London. In Veronica Aurens' drawing, the man in charge of the generator might be an anaesthetist during an operation, vigilant, sober, competent; and perhaps in his own mind he had become a kind of physician.

This simple sketch, based on the testimony of people who had been at the centre of scenes like this, tells us a little about Beausire's pain, more than many of us feel comfortable with knowing. It is probably an accurate image of what was done to him in the Villa Grimaldi. But in its echo of the idea of martyrdom, of suffering as an emblematic event, it can't show that the word 'disappearance' has a narrative within it. Beausire still had a long way to go.

Luis Muñoz remembers that Bill was profoundly depressed when he met him, but he also remembers a person who encouraged his fellow-prisoners, even the Guevarists of the MIR, to hold out when Krasnoff Marchenko was deriding them with the appearance on TV of four of their leaders who had capitulated. Perhaps it was wishful thinking to believe that Bill was on their side against the fascists; but there is no doubt that he had become an enemy of the state – the position was assigned to him. (Young soldiers returning from Vietnam in the late 1960s reported a joke that had become standard after the torture of civilians: if he wasn't a Viet Cong before, he sure as hell is one now.)

The DINA tried to bait a trap. Three times, over a period of ten days in December, Bill rang the Italian Embassy and spoke to his sister Juana. She later testified that he said he had come back from Europe and needed to reach Mary Ann and Andres Pascal, that he had urgent information to give to them; but she also said, according to Helen, who was told this story by the mother, that 'Bill did not sound like Bill'.

A young woman who had been to business school with Guillermo Beausire was taken from Cuatro Alamos to the Villa Grimaldi in late December 1974. One day she was washing dishes, blindfolded, and heard his voice. She peeked from under the binding and saw a thin man who had once been fat. He told her he had lost ten kilos, and that he was fainting all the time. He said, 'They have tortured me very badly.' He told her that he had been in the houses on Calle José Domingo Canas and Calle Iran.

After two months, which remain unimaginable no matter how much we think we know, Bill was taken away from the Villa Grimaldi. Luis Muñoz may have witnessed his departure: he heard the guards tell Bill that he must change his clothes, that he was being sent back to Argentina to continue his journey to Europe. In fact he was transferred to no. 3037 Calle Iran, where he may already have been tortured.

Bill later told Adriana Borquez that he had been kept for a long time tied to an iron frame on the floor at La Discoteca, as the guards called the house, and that he had been untied only to make further calls to his sister in the Italian Embassy. Once, he said, he managed to get free and make his way upstairs to the phone, and got through to a friend, but was discovered by a guard and had to cut the line.

It is unclear how much he was tortured during his second stay in Calle Iran. A woman lawyer held there for a single night in early May 1975 remembers him telling her that he had by then lost twenty kilos, nearly a quarter of his body weight. She was struck by how loosely his clothes hung from him. He described the 'house of torture' at the Villa Grimaldi, and she recalled him saying that he had caught a brief glimpse of his sister there. He was, this woman testified later in Caracas, wearing the same clothes in which he had been arrested, along with an old sweater they had given him. He seemed to be free to move about the house and garden, watched by the guards. 'He requested me to inform his mother of his existence in that place.' And, he told her, he had been subjected to some form of 'psychoanalysis-type treatment' by a man who was known as 'The Doctor'.

*   *   *

Adriana Borquez lives in a *mediagua*, a half-water house. Proper houses have two 'falls of water', two slopes to drain water from their roofs. Hers is a lean-to shanty made of cladded brick with a kitchen extension built of cheap, thin wood. It is like standing inside a packing case, especially in her tiny kitchen – two layers of plasterboard pinned to supporting struts. A raw brick wall supports the end of the kitchen. The shower stall in the toilet is of plain concrete, with seashells pressed into the cement for decoration. She has a smaller shed at the far end of the yard at the back, which she rents to those even poorer than herself.

The house is neat and tidy. It contains almost no possessions – no television, few books, no comfortable furniture. She does, however, have souvenirs: an Irish linen tea towel printed with the words of 'Galway Bay' and 'Molly Malone'; another towel with the image of the Radcliffe Camera in Oxford; a set of postcards of Scottish islands; a Guinness sign from a pub; a tiny cup from County Kerry. She has never been to Ireland, but she did have Irish friends, and she has lived in Oxford. The careful kitsch of the returned exile, these objects are not sentimental, but mnemonics for more serious issues – friendship, loyalty and solidarity. They suggest that anything more durable would make their owner vulnerable, would hurt her if it was destroyed; it would cost too much. Here she has nothing to lose.

Her yard was very hot in the afternoon. It is a ledge of dry earth falling away to the river bed, choked with brush except at the narrow central stream, which was down to a trickle because of the drought. She said that in the winter there were herons along the river, perching on the willows, and that the men round here shoot them for food. The cordillera loomed up across the river, as it seems to do everywhere in central Chile, grand and dwarfing, great barren slopes and hard little trees.

Adriana is a small woman of sixty, who smiles a lot, the way very angry people often do. She has a mop of short brown hair, and strong wide eyes behind heavy glasses. Her body twists from the waist on two walking sticks. This was a good day: most of the time, she needs the wheelchair in the corner near her desk, which was littered with documents and press cuttings relating to Colonia Dignidad, a book in German on the cult, and a Bible, which was surprising. Pain is familiar to her: after three hours talking on a rough two-by-four wooden bench in the yard, she could hardly move. Yet her voice is warm, almost caressing; she has a watchful, slightly mocking kindliness towards those who wish her well. She is very alert and passionate, and lives in a past from which there is little prospect of escape.

She has been waiting for years for a hospital to see to her hips. The operation would cost the equivalent of $6000 if it was carried out privately. This was a matter her friends abroad had wished to explore, but she politely and fiercely cut through expressions of interest in the Chilean medical system by saying pointedly that in case her English friends were wondering, 'This is between me and the Chilean state. They *owe* me.'

Her hips were bad long before she was tortured: much of her childhood was spent in bed, her legs weighted to correct an asymmetry in their length, and the treatment weakened her hips. The torturers discovered this, and beat and stretched her so that her spine was damaged and her hips ruined. Hence her constant pain.

So she swings herself along, feisty and damaged, telling the Chilean government what it can do with their boom, their compromises and their bland 'renewal'. 'Every time anyone wants to tell the truth about what happened under Pinochet there is the phantom of a coup; they dress up in fatigues and bring their tanks into the street, but this time who will they kill? There is no one to kill any more.' The myth of Chilean civility enrages her. 'No, we were so proud that we were not *tropical*, like Brazil. Well, now we have become so *bloody* tropical. That was the worst crime, to have triggered the transformation of Chilean society, which used to be so clear, so naive, there was such a solidarity, such kindness, and now you have people living on islands, one island beside the other. There is no togetherness any more.'

She won't be assuaged, and of course the democrats who took over in

1990 have been able to do almost nothing to assuage her. The officers remain untouchable, the army a closed and dangerous because un-defeated institution. The army's victims, like Adriana, mimic it, defiant, fixated and rigid.

Adriana Borquez was born into a prosperous family of German origin. She married a solicitor, when she was very young, and had two children. Then one day – she tells it as an epiphany – she visited a *población*, a very poor one, and saw a different Chile. Soon afterwards, she joined the Communist Party, broke with her family – her father with his large ranch in the south, her whole well-ordered German–Chilean world – and left her husband. She went to live in a *población* in the rural town of Talca, and returned there after her exile in Britain. One of her English friends summed up her conversion like this: 'You make up your mind and you start fighting for it and you don't look at the flaws because to do that would reveal all the domestic and other impossibilities.'

Supporting herself by teaching French in a local school, she had three more children before 1973, with two different men. She was one of the rank and file, selling party newspapers in the *población*, organizing women, agitating in the teachers' union – an obvious target. Yet she was allowed to go on teaching for the first year of the dictatorship.

She continued to distribute papers, and to act as a courier. Notes would be pushed under her kitchen door asking her to go to such and such an address and to see what she could do. She was given money to distribute to the families of people on the run. 'It was so dangerous but I was very lucky. Anyway, you always think it can happen to other people, not to you.' Adriana may have benefited in that first year from the army's determination to wipe out the MIR and the left wing of the Socialist Party, and she was a very small fish.

The violence of the repression surprised her, as it did everybody, even those Marxists who saw the iron heel in every capitalist state. She may deride the myth of Chilean constitutionalism now but it was seductive enough for her to be lulled by it in the early 1970s, and to have been shocked by what followed.

She should have been scared off when they first came for her, on 11 September 1974. She had refused to celebrate the first anniversary of the coup with her pupils at the local stadium. When she got home from the barracks the house had been ransacked and her kids had disappeared.

Then a neighbour opened her door and called out that Adriana's close friend, the local priest, had taken them, and that they were safe.

All the soldiers did then was warn her, and make her come back every week to the local military base to sign a form of parole, and every week her friend the priest stood in the street with his bicycle until she came out again. She must have felt a little blessed, for two weeks later she decided to provoke the army.

'Every Monday after the coup, teachers had to present a "civic act" in the school assembly, and for a whole year I avoided doing it. There would be a homily about order and discipline and then a remembrance of the heroes of the homeland, Arturo Prat and so on, and students had to write poems about them. But on Monday, 24 September it was inescapably my turn, and I thought my God, I have to speak about a soldier, I can't stomach this. So as it was the spring I chose as my character the season itself. I talked about the spring coming out in the sky, which meant freedom, chained birds, free birds and all those silly metaphors, and suddenly the electric address system went off. I climbed on a chair and started shouting to the students. I had written down my speech, and I distributed it afterwards, and some students copied it and passed it around.'

Her frightened headmistress called her in and, surrounded by education officials, asked her to sign a letter of resignation. Adriana refused and was told to leave the building. She walked back to her classroom. The room was empty; nor were there any students in the yard. She went to collect her things from the teachers' room, which was also deserted. 'They must have ordered everybody to stay with their students in their classrooms.'

Though it was the end of the month, she was not paid off. She could not find work of any kind — not much demand for a communist ex-schoolteacher under a right-wing dictatorship, with unemployment at 20 per cent. 'I didn't manage very well; I didn't manage at all. I had to give up my children, except my eldest daughter, to people who could look after them. But even she had breakfast in one house, and lunch in another. I was not eating very much; down here by the river, all this used to be a wood, and I collected herbs and roots, and some fruit, and lived on food like that, and bread, for months.'

She travelled to Santiago to confront the Education Ministry, and seems to have shamed the regional director of education into offering her one more chance, asking him why she was supposed to be so dangerous. 'They sent me to a boys' *liceo*. I managed to teach for ten days but after that I fainted in the classroom because I had not eaten properly for so long. So I was taken home, and someone came to see me, and then the Party realized that I was in a bad way, so someone came with a parcel of food, and a doctor came and gave me injections. But as soon as I recovered somebody also came with a big packet of bulletins for me to distribute.

'On Monday, 22 April [1975] I went back to school. I distributed the newspapers on my way home; it was raining, it was late and I went to bed. At three o'clock in the morning on the 23rd they came, smashing the door down. There was a display of weapons, many men surrounding the house, gunmen in the yard, shouting. I tried to be calm. "Sir, identify yourself." "Bitch." '

She was driven out of town in a bus full of people blindfolded and hooded. The bus drove south, and then after a few hours she thought she could identify the town of Linares, and after that they turned to the left, towards the mountains. In darkness, and still blindfolded, they were pushed into a building.

'I had a bad time. Gosh, I had a very bad time. I was so scared at the beginning. I was more scared before it happened than after it had begun. At first I could hear the shouting and crying and the noises of blows; but I could see nothing, every moment you expected to be beaten. I was trying to keep in one piece, because I had been taken with some young girls, who came back to our room in a very bad state. Nobody dared to speak about what had happened, but you could guess because of the bleeding, and I was the last to be taken for a "talk". Then it started; it went on for twenty days, I think. It was terrible; terrible. I don't count the last day, when they gave me a shower. Beatings, electric shocks everywhere. On and on. They used dogs, for sexual assault.'

While speaking about what they had done to her, she laughed. This laughter was warm, knowing, desolate; and her voice would trail off, at moments, in wonder at other human beings.

The disproportion between what they did to her and what she was and what she knew seems enormous. Rationalist views of torture, like that of Major Trinquier, theorist of special methods in Algeria, can never give a reason for the excess, the need to reach in and destroy the core of the person long after they have talked. Cesare Beccaria, whose essay *On Crime and Punishment*, published in 1764, was the first modern denunciation of torture, wished to substitute a geometrical calculation of penalties for the old torments; yet this very rational Enlightenment economist suspected that torture had something utterly destructive in it, not simply compelling the prisoner to confess but 'purging him in some metaphysical and incomprehensible way of infamy'. Adriana was a paper-seller; her party wasn't even in armed rebellion against the illegal regime. Yet to her torturers she was infamous. 'It was inconceivable. It was like a revelation of how deep human beings can go. After the coup I did not grasp the full dimensions of the thing. I was naive. They said they were looking for information about the organization, contacts, things like that. But it went on and on. They tortured the young people even more badly, they were hurt very, very much.'

She suspected that she was in Colonia Dignidad when she heard people conversing in German near the guards' room. 'By then I could not stand up, I was bleeding, I was soiled with my own excrement, covered in vomit. I was in the dirt.' One day, towards the end, one of the team who had violated and crippled her brought her some sandwiches. She had grown up eating German food, and recognized the meat in those sandwiches as German *Wurst*. 'Another day he brought a piece of *Kuchen* and some stewed fruit. It was such a luxury after the horrible things they made us eat, the soapwater that passed for soup, and to have a plate, so I brought it up to my blindfold, which had loosened a little. It was half-dark in the room but I could see that the plate had a golden rim. It felt silky, like a plate in my omamma's [grandmother's] house, and I turned it and it was stamped "Dorf Bayern". Then I took the spoon and started caressing the spoon, and I brought it up close too and I could just read "Weihnachten" and a date, and years later I talked with Lotte Pachmore [a cult member who escaped from Colonia Dignidad] and she spoke of the silver brought from Germany and inscribed "Weihnachten 1958". I thought it was 1953 – I couldn't see the other side of the figure eight in the dark.'

Adriana said, 'They had taken away all our human qualities. I remember being taken back to my cell – the smell of shit, urine, vomit and sweat in my cell nauseated me. I realized this terrible smell in my cell is me. For many years after I wanted to wash myself, all the time.

Now I can control it, but every time something really upsets me I go to the shower. My friends say I'm always apologizing for being smelly. Chilean people embrace each other a lot, and my women friends are very warm and when they want to kiss me sometimes I say no, I'm dirty, but I can't go on explaining that I have a "trauma".

'Death? I don't fear death. I longed for death so many times when I was in Colonia Dignidad. And torture?' Here she paused for a long time, and breathed deeply, so that her voice came back up as a whisper. 'Oh, gosh, I would choose death.'

After these defilements, and when she could barely stand up, they put some women in with her and told her to get them to talk. Adriana realized that this was perhaps the most dangerous moment she had faced. In her abject state she had to summon up sufficient strength to placate and delude these men who had already erased her from civil existence. She and the other women – all equally small fry – whispered together and worked out some harmless declarations which would not worsen their situation. 'We had to give the appearance of talking, of telling things. I knew that if I was to survive I had to make the DINA think I could be useful to them.' Who can tell, or who dare judge, what she promised them? She smiled at them when she could, and acted harmless, and they seem to have begun to think that she was 'curable'. The DINA put some effort that year into turning women and using them as agents, and succeeded with a few.

'One night they said you are so smelly, you must shower, and I showered for the first time. Then they said we are taking you to a special place, a nice place for people like you. But I didn't want to feel special. I felt very safe with the other women, they were company after so many days on my own. And they did not bring the bloody dogs any more.'

They drove her north through Linares to Talca. She was taken back to her house, which was torn apart and empty, but her Bible was on her night table, and they allowed her to take it with her. (It was the only book she referred to with respect in many hours of conversation; her anchorite socialism owes more to a renunciation of the world than to Marxist theory.) She changed out of her filthy trousers into a pair belonging to her daughter, and Adriana hoped her dirty clothes would tell someone she had been there. She also took a knitted jacket made a long time ago by her estranged sister.

The 'special place' they took her to was the house on Calle Iran. She remembers the date precisely: 17 May 1975. 'It was the morning. I was taken out of the van into a house and into a room with a bunk bed and a wooden partition that went all the way up to the ceiling, and through a slit in the partition I could see another bunk bed with a young man lying on it. I thought he was a guard. When I was nervous I had to urinate all the time. So I told this man, who said he would call the guard, and asked me who I was. I said I was Adriana, a prisoner from Colonia Dignidad. He said shut up, don't say anything, and he called the guard. He said let her go to the toilet, she smells so bad she will be worse than ever if you don't. Take her, go on. He seemed to know how to get them to do things.

'What I saw when he stood up was a very big man; *weak*, physically, floppy, a large man who had lost so much weight, but handsome and very sad. His eyes were exhausted.'

Once she began to talk about Bill, Adriana's voice became meditative and slow, as though she was remembering happiness. 'We started our friendship very slowly. He said look, don't worry, you won't be tortured systematically here; they do something else to you. They will try to brainwash you. He said don't worry, I'll help you. I didn't know yet who he was, which side he was on; and there were only two possible sides at that time.'

She found that Calle Iran was an office. The agents would arrive during the morning, complaining about the public transport, the traffic, the cold, or the weather, and go to work, either in the house itself or out in the city. It was like a branch of some social service. The agents wore cheap suits, or blue jeans; like ordinary working people, and with the same frustrations. Some would go for the day to the Villa Grimaldi.

At night there were at least five guards in the house; some of them used it as a dormitory. A big yellow dog called Volodia was released after dark. It is said to have been used in the past to assault women, and was probably named after Volodia Teitelbaum, a leading Chilean communist. Another torturer's joke: the dog was a son of a bitch. During the day, if they were working in the house, Adriana and Bill, the only other occupants, were confined to their room and had to ask permission to go to the toilet, which was just across the hall. But when they were alone with their guards, they were free to move around the ground floor.

Adriana was the given the job of washing and cleaning; Bill was ordered to look after the garden.

Adriana had to wash clothes all the time, as neither of them had much to wear. She was still wearing the clothes she had when she was picked up, with her daughter's trousers, some underwear, and her sister's knitted jacket.

Bill was given clothes that had belonged to other prisoners, but he kept his good brown shoes. They were worn now, misshapen because his leg had been injured and he limped, but also because of his odd way of walking. (Inés Beausire was shaken by this detail when Adriana mentioned it in London: it proved that she had known Bill.)

To keep the place warm, as the weather changed, the guards burned confiscated belongings that none of the agents wanted, the books and furniture of the disappeared going up in smoke in the cold Chilean autumn.

Neither Bill nor Adriana were ever called by their real names: she was La Chica, The Girl, and he was El Gordo, Fatty. Torturers destroy not only the emotional and physical integrity of their victims, their sense of their own bodies and their trust in the world, but even their identity, renaming them as derisively as possible. Perhaps it helps to distance them. They made Adriana loathe her own body, carrying her own stink around with her, and then called her what a desirable girl would be called; and having wasted Bill's imposing solidity, they reminded him of the comfort he had lost.

Poor Gordo, he's had a bad time, some of the guards would say.

During the day Bill and Adriana whispered through the partition. He spoke about his family, about Diana and her daughter Carolina, Mary Ann and her baby, and about his mother. He would talk about that world in which he was so settled, which she had run away from. 'We tried not to talk about the terrible things that had happened to us; didn't linger, once we had established what had happened. We had nothing but each other in that house. I was a communist teacher and he considered himself a cut above me, and let me know it. He couldn't believe I had chosen to live in a shanty town. But I didn't mind. There were things we could give each other. Bill had had a good education at St George's, an English school, and could recite Shakespeare, and I would recite Racine, Molière and Lamartine – we filled our talks with what we could remember. We both had a good memory for poetry. In Colonia Dignidad I think I had kept sane partly through reciting poetry to myself – some Neruda, like the *Twenty Poems of Love*, but also Baudelaire – especially "L'Albatros". But I have not read any of them ever again. When I was in Oxford I bought some editions of their work, but I couldn't read them.'

Adriana's way of sharing intimate terror and solidarity, as she remembers her time in that house, is a constant nervous laughter. 'Bill was *very* neurotic. Some days I would say to him in the morning, "Bill, good morning" and he would snap, "Don't talk to me today. I want to have silence." I couldn't speak, sing, do anything! But by then we had these routines. He would try to get me to exercise my legs, which were in a lot of pain; and he would say "Aaah, you are an *ugly* woman! Such a *skinny, yellow* woman!" So I felt absolutely safe.'

He was actually very gentle with her. Her back teeth were smashed, coming through the gums and infected, and although this prevented her from eating solid food the guards would not bring her a dentist. So Bill, she says, chewed food for her: meat, which he insisted she must eat, and hard fruit like apples.

He also prepared her for their 'doctor'. Bill had attended some fashionable relaxation class and he knew a little about meditation and control of breathing, and he taught her as much as he could.

Someone in the Chilean high command must have given permission for Osvaldo Pinchetti to practise his version of 'medicine' at La Discoteca. It is one of the strangest examples of the torturer's gift for parodying the civilized world in which knowledge is obtained by disciplining the mind with learning and argument. Adriana believes that they hoped to turn the house into a kind of 'clinic' for the psychological treatment of potential collaborators and informers. Perhaps the army merely saw it as a slightly exotic way of collecting information. Whatever their intention, she found herself under the care of Pinchetti, whom the guards called El Doc, or El Brujo, The Wizard. His technique was hypnosis. And he did, in a way, represent a kind of magic – the infantile magical thinking that believes a person can be cut up and reassembled like a paper doll.

She describes El Brujo as a tall man with olive skin and an aquiline nose, bold, stocky and unclean. 'The smell was terrible. I would guess he was near because of his smell. He had yellow-stained fingers – he chain-smoked cigarettes.' Bill told her that other prisoners had said that when El Brujo was torturing them he smoked all the time; and that his fantasy of medicine was such that he wore a white coat even in Villa Grimaldi. In La Discoteca he pretended to her that he had actually had medical training.

He would come, needles in hand, and speak to her in a low, soothing voice, acting out his idea of bedside medicine. She tried to intimidate him as subtly as she could. 'He would say, "We need to do this treatment. I will count up to ten, and you will sleep". He tested whether you were hypnotized or not by inserting a needle into your arm, and I learned not to move a muscle. I had to listen to all his rubbish, but he never really managed to hypnotize me. Perhaps I was no longer very suggestible. He would tell me I was a poor woman, so stupid, with no house, no profession – "and look what has happened to your children," and I would nod along, but I was so scared. He would make propositions to me when he thought I was in a trance, asking me what certain names meant to me and offering me a way out if I helped them. And I was supposed to sleep after the "doctor" went away.'

An officer once came, to see how she was responding to her 'treatment'. He asked whether she missed her children, and she surely did not have to falsify her distress and anxiety when she answered that she did. 'They were trying to implant the idea of the failure of my whole life, with no man, no job. They were preparing me for something, for a proposal: "You have a hope with us, if, when you collaborate." I took a day to say yes, yes to everything. I would have said yes to anything in order to get out of that place.'

Adriana emphasizes how polite she was with the guards, how correct, saying 'thank you' and 'please': that smiling tense civility, her rage held down – her description could have been of herself as she is today. In order to survive she had to act as though she had power – to soothe the guards, to put the torturers at their ease – and conceal the fact that she was living in pain and fear. So Adriana jollied them along, making them lunch, playing billiards with them, responding to their menacing friendliness with laughs and ready grins.

Other officers in plain clothes came to talk with Bill about what he could do for them, but they also talked – he was after all a *caballero*, a Chilean gentleman – of sailing, clubs and fast cars. But Bill could not wear the mask, and would rage at them, calling them fascists and killers. When they had gone he would kick things around the room. The communist militant behaving like an obedient housewife; the gilded youth like a hothead. Nor could he help treating the guards as social inferiors, letting them know they could not dent his pride. But they never beat him while Adriana was there, either because they were under orders or because, as one of them said, '*Gordo esta loco.*' He's mad already.

Adriana was still vulnerable, despite her careful role-playing. The house had two names among the guards, and although it was no longer a place where they needed to play loud music to cover other sounds, it was also La Venda Sexy.

'Already I had developed this mania for washing, and although it was winter at the foot of the cordillera, I insisted on showering early in the morning in the freezing cold. I think one of the morning guards told one of the night guards this, so they would come in the middle of the night and say, "Come, Chica, have a shower," and I would say I didn't want one, but they would order me. So I would shower, but the shower came with other things too. It was a very narrow bathroom under the stairs, and there was a step down, then the washing basin, the loo and beyond that the shower. A very small space.

'The third time it happened I was there in the shower, under freezing water, being touched and so on by two men, and suddenly I had this vision of this enormous gorilla in the door, occupying the whole space and startling the guards away from me, and shouting like mad, "Leave her alone!" The guards were so surprised that they backed out of the room and I was left with him, and he said wait a minute, and he took something from his room – it was an old home-made shawl – and wrapped this around me and took me back to the room and started drying me and said, "Why didn't you tell me?" And then he took my clothes – he was big, you know, I was hanging from him – and told me to dress. He was very angry with me. And I said, "But Bill, it was *me* who was being attacked," and he said, "Yes, but you didn't tell me!"

'The next time they came he was awake and he told them no, you will never touch her again, you won't do it again. And there were five men with machine guns in that house. It was his honour, I think, his manhood, everything in him was revolted by it. It could have been any woman, but he couldn't allow that. He was so crazy by that time that he could defy them. For someone he didn't really know.'

Soon after this he gave her a present. One of the guards asked him to mend an old-fashioned fuse with copper wire, and he kept some of the wire and twisted a copper flower out of it. He bowed low and called her 'Madame', a piece of tender mockery because she had told him her students had to call her that, even though she was a communist.

It wasn't a love affair, but it is taken for granted that she loved him and remains obsessed with him — a spoiled young brat she would have despised had she met him in the world outside, the world before torture. Dick Barbor-Might once asked her whether there had been a sexual relationship. There was none, but she was so offended that she asked him to apologize, and yet what they had was at least as intimate as sex.

She and Bill never talked about politics. It was important never to tell anyone your whole story. 'It's something you never lose, you never trust anybody absolutely afterwards.' She said that she could never speak to Dick about certain things, that he had needed to know so much, in order to fit it into a pattern, that it seemed he could never know enough. 'I think that was part of Dick's problem, he demanded to be trusted, to be told *every*thing, when I wasn't prepared yet. He was so kind, so caring, but he wanted to *know*. You can't force something like that.'

While there was the remotest hope that Bill might be alive, she could not speak about one thing that he had not so much told her as hinted at. She believes that he may, at Mary Ann's request, have bought cars needed by fugitive members of the MIR. Perhaps it was simply one car, for his much-loved younger sister. She was, after all, under effective sentence of death. But for the watching men, who must have been following him for a long time, he was no longer innocent, and therefore less than human. 'If you have gangrene in an arm, you have to cut it off, right?' Pinochet said to an interviewer in 1986.

Disease, cure, putrefaction, surgery: at the end of all the metaphors was the house on Calle Iran. 'We were in an ordinary suburban house surrounded by *other ordinary suburban houses*.' Her voice was low, as she said this, baffled by what the world can come to. 'On Sundays I was allowed to walk in the garden. There is a car entrance there and behind the garage is the neighbouring bungalow. And one day I was hanging my washing there, and I saw on top of a ladder a man trimming the creepers off the next door house. I thought, my God what if I call him, if I tell him, and I could do nothing. Though I never did it in front of the guards, I was crying to myself all the time, and I cried now, I took my pants from the line and suffocated my sobbing. I wondered whether the neighbours were part of it, or if they realized what was happening.

'I broke once more in La Discoteca, again when I was hanging out my clothes, and I heard this crying of a child, I thought it was a little girl, and the voice of a mother scolding the child because she wouldn't walk fast enough; she was really abusing the girl. I thought, my God she doesn't know what she has got.

'I didn't allow myself to think of good things. I had this image of my daughters, I refused to accept that image, to linger on thinking of them, because I knew it was my weakness. They could catch me out and do something bad to them, perhaps. I didn't even allow myself to think of my friend the priest. I *erased* as much as I could. And I'm not sure that I have managed to remake the past from memory because I have forgotten many, many things. In there, it had to be a denial of the past the whole day long.'

If memories of her children had to be refused, one way of doing it was to focus on certain pictures, and to try to remember every detail of them. She mentioned a nineteenth-century painting, *El Perla del Mercador*, which is in the Palacio de Bellas Artes in Santiago. Whenever she went there as a young woman, she said, she would gaze at the picture; and in La Discoteca she dwelt on it again.

Seen in the gallery, it seems a piece of orientalist kitsch, reminiscent of Bouguereau or Alma-Tadema, a strange painting to have stayed in the mind of a woman like Adriana Borquez. A beautiful, naked European woman is displayed on a rug in a bazaar, guarded by a tall Arab. The woman is languid, revelling in her own sexual power, tantalizing the viewer, confident of her ability to dominate even the Arab looking solemnly down on her blonde nudity. The hint of erotic rebellion in the painting may have attracted Adriana when she was young; but perhaps the reason she remembered it so well in that ugly house is simpler: the image represented a vision of the perfect body, a captured body unmarked, as yet, by violence or pain.

After seeing this picture it was easier to understand why Adriana repeated Baudelaire's 'L'Albatros' to herself while she was under torture. A metaphor for the poet bogged down in everyday existence, the poem is also a description of physical beauty degraded and humiliated, and of human cruelty to another animal. Bored sailors catch albatrosses, which glide so gracefully 'over the bitter waves'. Ciarán Carson's version catches the violence of the game:

> But they slap him, Emperor of Blue, down on the salty planks.
>   They taunt him.
> Spat at, tripped up, his wings creak helplessly like oars, and
>   haunt him.
>
> This wingèd voyager, now bedraggled, ugly, awkward, how
>   pathetic!
> Someone pokes a pipe into his mouth, and someone else who
>   mimics him is paralytic.

'There is an English phrase: living on the razor's edge. I lived like that, felt it physically. It was only three months, the whole thing, but it cut so deep, my life was broken in two, before and after. And there is no way to compare life before and after. It is like a brand inside, you will never be like other people. You can be worse or better but never the same. Sometimes I think I am privileged; I have been able to see a side of life that nobody else knows. Well, I survived, and that's it.'

But the survival she describes, speaking very slowly and carefully, is a half-life. 'The worst thing is the marginalization. We don't want a *medal*. But where your voice is not heard, you become a person without voice. Your thoughts are nothing; you have no means of communicating. Then you go backwards and backwards, with resentment, life becomes so *mean* ... it's a harsh struggle to keep alive, in that way.'

Adriana lives in a shack because she is poor, and she came back to Chile partly because she wanted to be near her daughters. Yet she could have stayed in England, and had a better standard of living and medical care. The house she lives in is so fragile that it is as though she is relearning the most basic forms of safety, unwilling to trust the world further than she can throw it. Binswanger, the existential psychologist, speaks of a narrowing of the space of life in certain conditions – the occupation of all the mind's exits 'as though by armed guards'. This is all the room Adriana has; torture has boxed her in.

On another summer night in Santiago, two British expatriates, with long records of opposition to the dictatorship, were talking about the unreconcilables. One of them grew almost exasperated. 'The Adrianas are a sect; they possess the truth society does not have. Nothing can help them,' he said. The other man replied: 'But the problem is that they are right. And because the question of truth or justice is unresolvable in Chile, they live in agony.'

* * *

How much can a society forget? Can bodies remain unburied, without poisoning the state?

At the core of Helen Bamber's work with the Medical Foundation for the Care of Victims of Torture is the belief that testimony, the open and public recognition of the truth of what was done to people, is part of any achievable measure of healing, small though that may be. Bamber drew this familiar idea from her own experience with survivors of the Holocaust, and saw it embodied in Maurice Pappworth's fight to name cruelty for what it was, even when it was carried out by well-meaning professionals. She realized in her work with Luis Muñoz that good history is also crucial in speaking about torture; and that denial of the truth, and lack of proper acknowledgement of the victims, can be damaging in itself. Impunity for torturers is also a denial of reparation for their victims.

Bamber, one of many who support this argument, is not putting the case for revenge justice. Justice may demand that those who torture and kill should be brought to trial, but this is not always possible; and the first step in that process may be the only one that can realistically be taken: acknowledgement of the truth, and the naming of the perpetrators.

This is not mere Freudian politics, as though to say repression hurts and speaking helps. The demand for a proper memorial involves needs much older than depth psychology: Antigone is walled up in a tomb for giving her brother his funeral rites; and it is also Hamlet's demand. The Danish court is corrupted by the effects of unrecognized violence; power and action are baffled by the denial of truth. The ghost demands revenge, but also a memento, and will not rest in his son's conscience until he has that recognition. The revenge tragedy, bloody and cruel, enacts the cure of the diseased civil body; but moral recognition of wrongful violence is at the heart of the play. Hamlet, at the end, suffers a last panic that Horatio's 'Roman' gesture of drinking from the poisoned cup will succeed, depriving Hamlet in turn of honour and understanding.

> O good Horatio, what a wounded name,
> Things standing thus unknown, shall I leave behind me.
> If thou didst ever hold me in thy heart,
> Absent thee from felicity awhile,
> And in this harsh world draw thy breath in pain,
> To tell my story.

In Chile, the dictatorship was not defeated in war, as the Nazis were; nor humiliated by a stronger power, like the Argentinean generals in the Falklands. Pinochet retired as head of state in 1990, after losing a plebiscite designed to keep him in power for another eight years. He conceded power to a coalition of moderate democrats, but stayed on as commander in chief of the army. His regime was played out, and its corruption and violence had alienated the middle class. The economy was thriving, but Pinochet had overseen two deep recessions and was no longer trusted. Yet he could still get over 40 per cent of the vote, and many of those who voted for him remain defiantly unrepentant about what he did. There is no nostalgia for Popular Unity: the left is relentlessly self-critical, seeing the Allende government as a utopian episode that got out of hand, exacerbated by the Cold War. But on the right it is easy to find Chileans who praise their army's restraint, by comparison with other Latin American forces: look at the massacres in El Salvador and Guatemala, the wild and uncontrollable death squads in Argentina! The killings in Chile were precise, targeted, limited. Torture? There was very little, and the reds exaggerated what little there was.

Pinochet's 1980 constitution had put in place a Senate weighted to the far right and a Supreme Court unsympathetic to raking over spent coals. His army's budget was guaranteed; no politician can, or dare, interfere with the generals. An amnesty blocked any prosecution of the culprits in the disappearances and the torture. The only perpetrators caught outside this zone of silence have been low-level thugs like Osvaldo Romo, and

General Contreras himself, the former head of DINA – but only because his hand in the murder of Allende's former ambassador Orlando Letelier was so visible. A car-bomb near the White House was an act of terrorism that the US could not ignore; justice had to be seen to be done, especially after a campaign by human rights activists based in the USA made some gesture expedient. But the army officers like Miguel Krasnoff Marchenko who planned and administered the Villa Grimaldi, Calle Iran, and all the other houses, continue to prosper.

A commission to establish the truth was set up by Patricio Aylwin, the first democratic President of Chile for seventeen years. A former judge, Raul Rettig, chaired the commission; his secretary, and the commission's driving intellectual force, was José Zalaquett, a Christian Democrat human rights lawyer imprisoned under the dictatorship and, in his exile, a prominent figure in Amnesty International. He is an articulate defender of the necessary impurity of compromise in the situation faced by Chilean democrats.

The Rettig report scrupulously records the names, and the probable fates, of all the victims it was able to trace. Its careful research makes its silence on the identity of the torturers and killers all the more striking. 'We were not a court of law,' Zalaquett emphasized in conversation in 1997; 'we could not attribute guilt to individuals, but simply impute moral guilt – guilt of an impersonal kind – to the state. A person could have been stigmatized by us without due process. We dared not fall into the temptation of weakening the rule of law by assigning guilt without any defence; we *had* to err on the side of defending the principles of the rule of law.'

Zalaquett claimed that Aylwin wanted to name the perpetrators, but that he was persuaded not to, since it would have reintroduced into Chilean society the principle of the kangaroo court. So even though most of them were well known, they remain legally and morally unconnected with their cruelty. Although many historians and journalists know the truth and can name the names, so that it would be wrong to speak of complete silence, in Chile itself the torturers have been granted a kind of absolution.

Is not this a hyper-delicacy of legal scruple, in the case of men known to have tortured thousands of people? For Zalaquett this question embraces 'the foremost question of political ethics of our time', the question that must be answered in different ways in Sri Lanka, South Africa, Bosnia and Ulster. 'The precedent of Nuremberg rested on the material condition that the evil had been defeated. There was no messy tie in 1945; but all other situations have been messier. Without a decisive military defeat you have to ask how you can accomplish what you want: how you can get both truth *and* justice. It is a question of optimizing your principles. You can't prosecute a million Afrikaners. And in Chile it was even harder: the army never lost real power, and certainly not cohesion. The democrats played by the rules of their game and won; so it was impossible then to change the rules. Perhaps the people should have ousted Pinochet – but they did not.'

The past is dangerous in Chile: any attempt to reopen the question of the amnesty causes unexplained army manoeuvres, with tank battalions in combat fatigues posing around central Santiago, even though the army can no longer be a pretender to rule: there is no internal enemy against which it can rally any significant fraction of Chilean society, as Pinochet undoubtedly could in the 1970s. It may be an imperfect democracy, a *protected* democracy, in Pinochet's sinister phrase, yet the transition was handled with dignity and skill by Aylwin and his political allies, who faced down Pinochet over Rettig's enquiries and restored genuine civil liberties. This may be the most that anyone can get: a grudging acceptance of former enemies, truth without recompense, peace without reconciliation. (It took more than two generations for the Irish Civil War to begin to lift from people's minds – and that was a war in which *both* sides were armed, and inflicted serious casualties on each other.)

What is disturbing in Chile is a complacency towards the past, and the absence of imaginative forms of remembering. There is a lack of concern at the pain that impunity causes, except among the embittered and isolated former victims themselves. Instead there is a willed political amnesia: the price of democracy is a belief that onward movement in a sound economy is the cure for bad dreams. Something is missing in the state, even if the democratic wish of the majority is to forget.

Here are two visitors' anecdotes. The Rettig report, so beautifully put together by Zalaquett and his colleagues, was supposed to be made available to as many people as possible so that a civic and moral lesson might be learned; but in the summer of 1997 it was impossible to buy the report in any Santiago bookshop. It was not even on the stock computer of the best of them. The report has become a rare book.

The second anecdote is well known to visitors to Santiago. No. 38 Calle Londres was a Socialist Party headquarters just off the main avenue of Santiago, the Alameda, and five minutes' walk from the presidential palace. It was taken over by the DINA and they tortured people there. Now the pale sandstone building, restored and blasted clean, houses the Bernardo O'Higgins Institute of Chile. The plate on the wall carries the number 40. The buildings on either side of it are now 36 and 42. No. 38 Calle Londres is transcended, changed in number and name.

Zalaquett, a deeply impressive and humane man, was sensitive to the dangers of the compromise, saying that 'You never give up on your dead.' We must, he admitted, 'acknowledge' the truth, as well as 'having knowledge' of it; and someone, eventually, has to say in the name of the army that what it did was wrong. If this does not happen, he said, the belief that in extreme circumstances you can murder those in your custody is passed on inside the military.

He would be right to point out that Hamlet's search for absolute truth and justice ended in massacre and the ruin of the state. That dramatic resolution could not, and should not, be scripted by democrats; nor is it usually available to anyone in real life. The Chileans have had to accept a society in which the survivors live with torturers revelling in immunity and sometimes in wealth; one in which violence of the most extreme kind lurks as a remedy, whenever the tension and argument of democracy become difficult.

* * *

In no. 3037 Calle Iran, the guards were sure that their prisoners would not run away. A gas tank stood propped against the wall of the garden, which was not very high. Bill and Adriana could easily have stepped from the tank onto the wall. But Adriana could hardly walk; and the guards knew what terror makes of somebody. 'We looked at the wall and we said, too high. Then we said, no, it's not that high. And days after that I said, you try. He had been very disagreeable with me all that day. He said, "Are you crazy, they would kill you if I ran." He was a gentleman: it would not have occurred to him to get away on his own. He was a naughty gentleman.'

He had a very old threadbare sweater. It was cold that year by late June. She talked one of the guards into giving her some odd wool, another old jumper and a pair of knitting needles. Out of these materials she made Bill a new sweater. She had only enough wool to make it short, but she made it with a big turtle neck. He was very particular, she says, asking for certain stitches, and they had to be well done. When it was finished he moved around the garden more comfortably, stooping like a ghost of himself in this patched-up garment.

From the little we know of Bill Beausire in his last weeks it is fairly clear that he knew he would die without ever leaving this lawless zone of parody and violence, like an animated cartoon of the world he thought he knew. Every auspicious thing had deserted him. He became morose and withdrawn, and increasingly hostile to the guards. Adriana remembers him saying: 'How could they present me again to the world, I know so many things about them; they can't risk it.'

Yet they were willing to risk it with her. Helen Bamber has a theory that they decided not to let him go in the end because he could not *pretend* to submit, and that he had such confident upper-class contempt for them that he gave them a reason to kill him. This was part of her own romantic idealization of Bill, the good man fallen into hell, but it is probably not far from the truth. Bamber also speculated that the very common ground that the officers shared with Bill was slippery: his Britishness, the yacht club, the good school, the friends in the diplomatic service would give his evidence a lot of weight.

Adriana, on the other hand, they found in a *población*, and they thought they had crushed and turned her. 'With me they had nothing in common. And what I showed to the outside was very different from what I was feeling.' Helen Bamber recalled Adriana telling her that she tried to get Bill to play along, to wear the mask, but that he was no good at it.

Bill said to Adriana one day in late June 1975 that he couldn't go on any more. It was eight months since he had 'disappeared'. He wrote a letter addressed to the DINA chiefs and took it to the guards on the first floor, and came back looking very thoughtful. Adriana does not know what he said in that letter. Then he wrote another letter to his mother and asked Adriana to keep it safe. 'For many years I remembered every line of the letter. He closed with the phrase *Garde ta foi*. I did not understand the meaning it held for him, until I repeated it to Señora Inès in London and she said that it was their motto, from the Beausire family crest.'

In mid-June, two air force intelligence men in plain clothes came to see Inès Beausire. They walked into her house and into her bedroom. One of them sat on the end of her bed. He told her that they now wanted Mary Ann and her lover dead; but he promised her that Bill would survive if she would tell them where her daughter was hiding. They must have known that she did not know, but they tried anyway, just in case, forcing her to imagine that she might have to make a choice between her children.

A few days later, she was advised by the British Embassy to leave Chile. She and Diana flew to Britain, arriving on 21 June. She was soon in touch with the Chile Committee for Human Rights and Amnesty International, which wrote to MPs of the governing Labour Party, asking them to publicize her son's case. Everything that Inès now did would cost her energy she did not have, and have effects she could not control, although nothing she did could have saved her son. It may even be that these first steps of a campaign to save him were the last straw for those holding him.

On 2 July 1975 Adriana was washing clothes, as usual. 'I had washed and mended his shirts that morning. Some men came in at a very unusual time; not at lunch or the end of the day, but in the afternoon, suddenly. I was washing up after lunch in the kitchen when he came out of his half of the room into the kitchen. I dried my hands on a towel.'

Bill stood in front of her in his loose ill-fitting shirt, looking like a gentle scarecrow, and said, 'Shit. It's over. They are taking me.' In her testimony in London six months later she would provide an inventory of Bill Beausire's worldly goods, which she put into a large paper bag: 'Two shirts, one sweater and his underwear. We looked for his jacket, navy blue with golden buttons, the same one he was detained in at Ezeiza and which was too big on him. Bill had a pair of Terylene trousers, brown shoes slightly deformed from his peculiar way of walking, a black turtle-neck sweater, that I had knitted for him from the wool of an old one the guards had given him; a royal blue sweater that I had also fixed for him, turning it inside out as it was old and faded. He had one white poplin shirt and a white nylon one. All this he took with him and two or three very old and faded hand towels.'

She seems to have insisted with her careful absurd gestures that he was going somewhere from which he would return. They embraced, he reaching down to hug her crippled body. He put on his jacket and shambled awkwardly, a big man still not used to his own fragile lightness, out along the passageway and through the front door. He passed under the overhang of the first floor and down the path to the gate, the three DINA men walking in front and behind him, as casual as old friends. Just before they reached the front gate – there would have been a car, maybe two, out on Calle Iran – the door of the house was pushed to by one of the guards and the tall figure was shut out.

*   *   *

Afterwards she kept asking the guards as they came in where they had taken him, and one of them said, 'Well, he was left in Ezeiza to continue his trip'; another said, 'He's in Argentina'; and then one said, 'He's gone to Puerto Montt,' a port city in the far south of Chile. Adriana said, 'It seemed that some disappeared people were used to build the southern highway, and I thought that was what the guard meant. But a DINA agent later made a statement about the code they used, La Moneda for one set of prisoners, Puerto Montt for the other. One for the ones to be buried on land, the others to be thrown in the sea.'

Francisco Scilingo, a former Lieutenant Commander at the Naval School of Mechanics in Argentina, described how they did it in his country, cruising over the vast estuary of the Rio Plata in a boxy transport plane and dropping the bodies of often still-living people out the back, watching them falling one by one into the water.

In Chile the air force sometimes used helicopters; but the navy is also said to have helped, heading out to sea with the dead or comatose bodies of those who were about to disappear for good, a sea-burial without honour or memorial. What did the captain call it in his log? Did he use the word 'jettison', the act of lightening a ship in distress? Did one of the officers who came to the house and talked sailing with Bill ever think of him as he beat into the wind on a Sunday cruise, the tiller shaking in his hand like a living thing?

Whatever happened, nothing will ever be done about it now. The event has parted company with history. Bill went to sea for the last time, perhaps from Valparaíso, sailing from under the hill covered with brightly-coloured corrugated-iron clad houses, past the grey warships at their long dock, and out into the limitless Pacific.

*   *   *

There was, after all, an element of whimsy in their decisions over life and death. In some of them it is difficult not to see a lazy contempt for the survivor, as though to say we don't care what you tell the world, whether you live or die. Adriana discovered that she didn't matter very much on 23 July, three weeks to the day after Bill left.

'They made me write a letter to my sister, and I said I had none, that I had parted from my family long ago. "No, start again," they said, "we have located your sister." So I wrote a letter saying that I had some needs but that I was well. I sent her the cardigan, the one I had taken from my house, and she knew it was hers, so she sent me something I had given her. She went to the Archbishop's human rights group, and they said that they did not know what state I would be in when I was released. So they prepared everything.

'A guard who said he was a hairdresser came one day and cut and shampooed my hair. Then they told me I was being taken away. I used to carry Bill's letter along with anything useful in my underpants, so I went to the loo. I was so scared that I tore the letter in little pieces and flushed it away. When they put me out of the car in front of her house and I took the blindfold off, I stood there thinking, when will they shoot? A woman started coming towards me and I realized it was my sister, whom I had not seen for years and years. She looked at me and from the look on her face I saw how I must look.'

*   *   *

From the Villa Grimaldi, the foothills of the Andes filled the line of sight, a red mass blocking the low sun. The long roads back towards the centre of Santiago were lined with tiny brick houses with tarred plastic roofs. Scrubby allotments, oil and bits of cars, shanties in small orchards choking in dust: the city map didn't go this far east.

The place was overlooked by new houses. Presumably it would not have been like this in 1974; then there was probably a shack in the field opposite, a few lemon trees, some vines.

The original side walls and the gateposts of the Villa – hexagonal blocks of weathered brick – were still standing. They must have been part of the walls of the country farmhouse. A high-tension chain fence had replaced the front wall, so the whole property was visible from the road. The tower and the buildings along the western wall were all gone.

The Villa was levelled years ago after General Salas Wenzel, a former DINA officer, bought the property (using his wife and daughter as a front) as a site for luxury apartments: an entrepreneurial way of uprooting the past. Human rights groups raised enough Cain to stop the development.

A builder's sign announced that this was the *Parque por la Paz ex-Villa Grimaldi* under the direction of the *Ministerio de Vivienda y Urbanismo*. Two old sunburned workers were eating bread on the step of a Portakabin near the far wall. Someone had written along the wall behind them, '*No a la impunidad!*' No to impunity. When José Zalaquett defended the compromise that allowed the democrats a kind of power, he had asked, unanswerably, 'Which is better? The mantle of righteousness, and bloody clandestinity, or the rule of the majority, peace and free speech?' But when he was asked why there was so little imaginative recognition of the victims, apart from the memorial wall in the cemetery, he was briefly at a loss for words. Schoolchildren, he remembered, had been asked to design a poster for the campaign for the peace park at Villa Grimaldi; and as for the park itself, 'Somehow that project seems not to have gone apace.'

A sprinkler whipped water back and forth over young trees in plastic tubes, and over new grass at the back of the compound. A mosaic sculpture like an upturned starfish was laid out in a scoop of ground inside the gate. It would no doubt have water in it eventually, and copper coins and bits of bright plastic would be thrown into it. The park would be a small, remote and dreary municipal garden. The poverty of imagination and effort: a gesture made with half a heart. A black tree stump, just higher than the railing, had been left standing a few inches outside it. The tree could be aligned with the place where the tower once stood in the far corner of the site, where Bill Beausire had been tortured. This column of dark ugly wood was one of the few things on the site original to it; the only true memorial there.

A memorial is often the substitution of an attribute for the whole: cannon on a victory monument, a strand of barbed wire on a sculpture for ex-prisoners of war. In rhetoric this is the figure of metonymy, but there were so few attributes of the Villa left that the park was empty of meaning. The Greek word for metonymy means, literally, 'change of name', and that was more like what was happening, an embarrassed changing of the subject, a silence.

8

LEARNED ON THE BODY

But it seems that the Government had a true Account of it, and several Counsels were held about Ways to prevent its coming over; but all was kept very private. Hence it was, that this Rumour died off again, and People began to forget it, as a thing we were very little concern'd in, and that we hoped was not true ...

Daniel Defoe, *A Journal of the Plague Year*

El Brujo, the 'doctor' from Santiago, may have been a sad thug, mimicking what he could not have; yet if he was a fantasist, he was accurate in his mimicry in at least one respect: certain doctors in Chile, and in many other countries, had become servants of the torturer. For some, their involvement was limited to the reluctant examination of a prisoner, under threat of violence to themselves, to determine if the victim could sustain more abuse. Others willingly passed men and women as fit for torture, and revived them when they lost consciousness. And a few devised systems of pain and demoralization, and helped to implement them: they became torturers themselves.

Helen Bamber had heard of doctors passing through the Villa Grimaldi, doing their rounds as though it were a hospital, and affably conversing with the guards. In the Beausire pamphlet she and Barbor-Might reproduced the clinical notes of a doctor who had examined his colleague, Dr Batista Van Schowen Vasey, grossly tortured and near death in the Navy Hospital at Valparaíso. The notes were bland, neutral: a doctor registering symptoms without the smallest concern for their context. Dr Van Schowen never reappeared. That medicine could be tricked by power and turned on itself had been demonstrated too often, earlier in the century; and yet it still seemed incredible.

Many of the Chilean doctors who collaborated with the DINA were employed by the army, and subject to military discipline and intimidation. The same bad excuse could not be found for Dr Dolcey Brito, head of the Department of Psychology at the Catholic Institute of Philosophy, Science and Letters in Montevideo. Uruguay, once the most stable and prosperous of Latin American countries, had slipped into military dictatorship under the impact of economic crisis and an urban guerrilla campaign by the Tupamaros, an elitist organization given to spectacular and noisy gestures – kidnappings for ransom, assassinations of high-ranking army officers. The character of the dictatorship that followed, perhaps owing to the small size and relatively sophisticated infrastructure of the country, was highly organized and totalitarian. The purest expression of the regime was Libertad Prison, a model institution for the breaking of prisoners, after they had been tortured and interrogated. Its routines were, according to former inmates, devised and administered by Dr Brito.

Absolute silence was the rule, especially on the second floor of the jail, filled with prisoners who were particularly stubborn; each prisoner had to walk with his or her eyes gazing ahead – looking at another prisoner was an offence; the warders were rotated to avoid the smallest build-up of sympathy with inmates, and had to signal their orders with a bell or whistle, to preserve an environment without voice. The rules were also infinitely variable: meaningless, repetitive activities would suddenly be replaced by more lenient measures; a gesture of the head could be interpreted as a rebellious act, and result in solitary confinement in a special cell called 'the island', dark, wet and cold. Cell-mates were switched without warning; tasks were assigned and taken away without warning. The only rule was that there were no predictable, and potentially calming, rules. In Bamber's words, 'Their lives were governed by uncertainty, the most terrifying component of torture; unsure whether you are going to live, whether you will be allowed to urinate, defecate, whether they will bring your wife, what they will do next, will you break, will you die.' Drugs were used as punishment: strong sedatives or tranquillizers alternated with more direct physical abuse. The inevitable breakdowns led to self-accusations and new charges against other prisoners, methodically encouraged by Dr Brito, often with the aid of further doses of drugs. Libertad ('Freedom') was a machine, carefully designed to stamp out personality and mental integrity.

Brito was said by witnesses to have a text displayed on the wall above his desk: 'I will pluck out your eyes and put them in me, and you will pluck out mine, and put them in you, so that you will see me through my eyes, and I through yours.' This enigmatic sentence was written by Ludwig Binswanger, existentialist psychologist and advocate of humane treatment of the insane, whose work inspired Michel Foucault's critique of the modern idea of madness. Brito's adoption of it as the legend for an institution more regimented and intrusive than the worst nineteenth-century penitentiary must have been a conscious joke, perhaps inspired by some academic vendetta. Where Binswanger intended to signify greater mutual understanding, Brito meant the opposite, a remoulding: a political cure of mistaken ideas.

The existence of such physicians was an open secret by the mid-1970s. Dr Brito was, for Helen Bamber, a symbol of all that Maurice Pappworth had railed against. It is not surprising that in 1975, in the midst of her hectic activism with Dick Barbor-Might and Gordon Wills, yet still almost as a sideline, a distraction, she agreed at their urging to help establish a medical group of Amnesty in Britain.

The year before, the Danish section of Amnesty had set up such a group under the single-minded leadership of the neurologist Inge Kemp-Genefke, to call attention to medical abuses of human rights, and to campaign on behalf of doctors and nurses who were victims themselves. The common factor in both cases was torture. In Britain, one of the first doctors to respond to this initiative was Elizabeth Gordon, a surgeon who launched the group with Neil Evans, a hospital administrator.

Betty Gordon was already a Fellow of the Royal College of Surgeons: she had risen high in a male-dominated craft. When she qualified, she was one of the very few women surgeons in Britain. She speculated that this may have alerted her to issues of justice, and interested her in human rights; too many men had asked her what she was going to do after she qualified – the idea that she might wish to practise her art was too exotic. She also spoke about one of her patients in a civilian hospital in Vietnam, where she did a tour during the war with an Australian medical team. The man was taken away by the South Vietnamese police, despite her attempts to protect him. She knew, she said, what would happen to him.

Gordon and Evans held their talks and slide shows in various London hospitals, speaking to half-empty rooms, puzzled medical students. It did not seem an issue that could ever touch the British profession very closely. But Gordon, a quiet, undemonstrative doer, kept the group in being, posting events and sending out leaflets. Bamber was struck when she met her by her careful economy with words, as though she would only say what she could prove. This quality of precision, of exacting standards of examination and diagnosis, would be useful later.

Bamber's arrival put a charge into the small group. The two women became friends, respecting each other's ethical commitment and differing gifts. Jan Pollert and Peter Kandela, doctors and members of Amnesty, were encouraged to write articles for the specialist press, describing abuses of medicine in Latin America and the USSR. Kay Daly, an Irish volunteer in the British Section, would later edit a small magazine, *Medicine and Human Rights*, reporting and interviewing doctors and survivors. Helen Bamber became a regular speaker at events in hospitals and medical schools, and according to her colleagues often had a mesmerizing effect on audiences. Her depth of experience was obvious, but her projection of herself and her mellifluous voice – a slightly old-fashioned, actorly self-awareness – also worked extremely well. The medical group became a force inside British Amnesty, one of its most active and creative sections.

The case of a young Uruguayan woman held in Punta Rieles Prison was typical of their very small victories. She was suffering from a chronic circulatory disease and in great pain from that and her ordeal at the hands of the army. The group organized a large number of doctors to write to the prison authorities and the government requesting her release. All they achieved was the woman's transfer to a less harsh jail; but the case showed that the Uruguayans were sensitive to pressure, and that attention from well-connected doctors could embarrass governments. The idea that physicians should care for their patients has the force of a categorical imperative, in most cultures, and the shame of torture can taint the good name of a country's medical profession.

The most notorious case of corrupted medicine was the use of psychiatry as an instrument of state repression in the Soviet Union. Under

Brezhnev, political murder was considered unseemly: the party bureaucracy had learned from Stalin that unrestrained violence would recoil on themselves. Instead, opposition was redefined as pathological, as a form of mental illness. (Dissenters were still, of course, often sent to labour camps.) Novel psychiatric conditions were diagnosed: 'nervous exhaustion brought on by a search for justice'; 'mania for reconstructing society'; 'psychopathic paranoia with overvalued ideas and tendencies to litigation'. (The satellite countries shared in the discovery of new diseases: a Czech couple who had converted to Seventh-Day Adventism were found to be suffering from 'Paranoia Religiosa Adventistica'.) The 'patients' were then sent to one of the 'Special Psychiatric Hospitals' controlled by doctors from the Serbsky Institute in Moscow, and by the KGB.

Their treatment in these places was a pharmacological version of torture. Sane individuals were given heavy doses of strong tranquillizers, the neuroleptic drugs that reduce the intensity of nerve function – chlorpromazine (better known as Largactil), tizertsine and haloperidol. Designed for patients suffering manic delirium or paranoiac hallucination, their impact was described by Helen Bamber in notes for a talk that she gave to an audience in the late 1970s: 'They produce frightening side-effects, skin and blood disorders, extreme sensitivity of the eyes to light, weight gain or loss, intense pain – some victims writhe in agony; worst of all, many victims suffer "Parkinsonism", their muscles become rigid, they move slowly and sluggishly, their bodies feel restless and experience a constant desire to change position.' One of the commonest drugs used in Russian hospitals was sulfazine, a solution of sulphur in peach oil that induces high temperatures and fever and which was once fashionable in treating 'general paralysis of the insane', but which had not been used in the West since the Second World War. It was described in the *Lancet* as long ago as 1930 as 'painful and useless'. This was, as Alexander Podrabinek described it in a samizdat, a system of 'punitive medicine', tightly integrated with the legal apparatus of the USSR.

The medical group lobbied and published on behalf of those condemned to prison hospitals, who included the founders of an independent trade union, religious believers, and doctors who had refused to mislabel the sane. It focused on the cases of imprisoned psychiatrists like Semyon Gluzman or Anatoly Koryagin, with some effect among British doctors, but it was far from the most important organization working to expose medical cruelty in the Soviet bloc. The Campaign Against Psychiatric Abuse, associated with Vladimir Bukovsky, Viktor Feinberg and Peter Reddaway was so effective that by the early 1980s Soviet psychiatry had pariah status. Its national organization resigned from the World Psychiatric Association in February 1983 rather than be expelled. The poet and translator Richard McKane, whose work on the dark late poems of Osip Mandelstam – those written after his torture and in his last exile at Voronezh – would draw him to Helen Bamber, recalls that CAPA was using the word 'glasnost' to mean 'publicity' as early as 1977. 'We must give him *glasnost!*' they would say of some imprisoned Russian democrat. (Thus words become irritants in the mind of a ruling class.)

The medical group's work helped Bamber to persuade more and more doctors to take a stand in defence of humane medicine. Her network steadily widened: neurologists, paediatricians, psychotherapists, general practitioners, and forensic pathologists were drawn in. The moral and intellectual climate of British medicine seemed to Bamber to be changing. To some extent, this was a response to her old friend's work: Pappworth's demand for committees to oversee research on human beings was no longer scandalous, and even the Royal College of Physicians finally agreed in the mid-1970s that research should be regulated. The government issued an order to health authorities to set up ethics committees, and the BMA committed itself to the principle of 'sound ethical controls on medical research'.

The BMA had already taken a stand on unusual punishment close to home. In August 1971, after internment was introduced in Northern Ireland, the British Army subjected a group of detainees to a radical combination of sensory deprivation and physical stress. Standing against a wall balanced on their fingertips, hooded, struck at random by unseen guards and surrounded by loud, unbearable and toneless noise, the men were severely disoriented and shocked. It had the character of an experiment, testing the quality of information produced. But most of the real IRA men the interrogators were seeking had escaped the net; and the victims of the experiment took Britain to the European Court of Human Rights. Two government committees (chaired by Sir Edward Compton and Lord Parker) attempted to defend the practice of 'interrogation in depth', with qualifications, using the now canonical justification of the ticking bomb. Compton wrote that in dealing with terrorists, 'time is of the essence; information must be sought while it is still fresh so that it may be used as quickly as possible to effect the capture of persons, arms and explosives and thereby save ... lives.' Lord Parker defined brutality as 'an inhuman or savage form of cruelty' and cruelty as 'a disposition to inflict suffering coupled with an indifference to, or pleasure in, the victim's pain'. As long as the interrogator didn't enjoy his work, what he did could not be brutal or cruel. Parker suggested that a medical practitioner be on hand for such interrogations. Here was a moral crossroads, both for the British government and the country's medical profession: whether to euphemize torture, permit it and assist in it, or to refuse it outright.

Lord Gardiner, the third member of the Parker Committee, wrote a powerful dissent from his colleagues' interpretation of the evidence. 'If it is to be made legal to employ methods not now legal against a man whom the police believe to have, but who may not have, information which the police desire to obtain, I, like many of our witnesses, have searched for, but been unable to find, either in logic or in morals, any limit to the degree of ill-treatment to be legalised. The only logical limit ... would appear to be whatever degree of ill-treatment proves to be necessary to get the information out of him, which would include, if necessary, extreme torture.' This is an excellent definition of the gradient that indulgence in torture sets up, and the temptation to slide down it was very great, amid chaotic sectarian violence in Ireland and terrorist bombing of civilians in Britain.

To his enduring credit, Edward Heath, the Prime Minister, rejected the majority report and listened to Gardiner. Although there were serious beatings of suspects by police in Castlereagh Interrogation Centre during the mid-1970s under a Labour government, the British state refused to institutionalize torture in Northern Ireland.

The doctors supported Gardiner, and the BMA did not forget the issue of torture. Its document for the 1975 meeting of the World Medical Association, heavily influenced by Amnesty, contributed to the Tokyo Declaration, which explicitly ruled out any medical participation in torture 'or other forms of cruel, inhuman or degrading procedures'. This declaration remains a touchstone in any discussion of medical ethics, and is at least theoretically accepted by all members of the WMA.

Amnesty exploited this cultural shift to develop closer links with the leaders of British medicine. The death of Steve Biko in South Africa in 1977 sparked a massive campaign, but Bamber and her friends focused on the role of the three doctors who had examined him and announced that the brain-damaged man with a lumbar puncture showed 'no evidence of any abnormality'. They then allowed the police to transport him over 600 miles on the floor of a Land Rover to Pretoria, where he died. Doctors, nurses and medical students in Britain were encouraged by the medical group to write to the Medical Association of South Africa; and the group drafted a letter which was signed by a large number of physicians. The South Africans refused to find anything unethical in the behaviour of the three doctors – a stance that led to the expulsion of MASA for three years from the WMA.

One of the most valuable results of this work among doctors was Bamber's relationship with Dr John Dawson, the young head of the BMA's ethics committee. Bamber went to see him with examples of their material on the USSR, Chile and South Africa, and appealed to him, in effect, to form an alliance with Amnesty. Dawson enchanted her: he was alert and responsive, and passionate about human rights, and saw a way of developing these concerns in his work for the BMA. He looked to the medical group for support, and they derived considerable strength from him. The medical group gave him a brief on 'Doctors and Torture' before the annual meeting of the BMA in 1981, which helped to ensure the unanimous passage of a motion condemning 'the usage of medical personnel in enforcement of inhuman laws and degrading measures', and committing the organization to work for freedom from torture, and not simply to assert a duty of doctors to refrain from it. This was a signal event, in the history of an association of notably conservative hue in the past. Its international prestige could be brought to bear on other national medical associations, encouraging them in their resistance to government pressure.

The medical group was not Bamber's only commitment in the late 1970s: the work on Chile continued, she was also chair of the Amnesty Hampstead group, and had become interested in the origins of the equipment she was hearing about – the shock batons (essentially, cattle prods for humans) widely used in Latin America and elsewhere, and the leg-irons and handcuffs that featured in so many reports of torture. It was not then Amnesty's policy to call for trade sanctions against governments, or to target particular exports. Bamber and her friends began to argue for the banning of military or security transfers of any kind, to any organization implicated in torture. Barbor-Might became a very energetic 'repressive technology co-ordinator', occupying a desk for four months in the British Amnesty office; relations between officials and volunteers were not improved. Since almost anything – from a chair to a generator – can be turned into an implement of pain, it might be difficult to set limits to such a ban. But their intention was to focus not on the technology, but the agency – not on what was being exported, but to whom. They lost this argument inside Amnesty at the time, but they had started an important debate.

Bamber had now gathered an extraordinary range of medical sympathizers around herself. She could go on campaigning and lobbying; or she could go further into that more demanding terrain that Luis Muñoz had first opened up to her. Helen Bamber seems slowly to have realized, as she grew more involved with the medical group, that for her the central issue was the perversion of medicine in the service of injustice, and the healing potential of medicine for its victims. The intimacy of the linkage between torture and cure had never seemed so obvious. The group also offered an even more sharply focused and irritating challenge to power than most Amnesty work: it was no longer simply about writing letters and demanding the end of individual imprisonment, but about ending a whole set of practices and habits.

Three strands were now weaving together in her life: the urge to campaign for human rights, and to publicize violations of human dignity; the belief that medical ethics were poorly understood and vulnerable to abuse; and, inexorable in its pull on her, the need to pay attention to the victims.

*   *   *

Before any such clarification could be made, her friend Dick Barbor-Might was consumed by the stories he told to make sense of an evil world. Helen Bamber once described him affectionately as a star that shone too brightly for its own good; what happened in the late winter of 1981 was a spectacular gravitational collapse, with so much information trapped inside him that no one could read it coherently.

He had resigned his academic job years before, and worked as a night porter, spending his days working for Amnesty – a relentless life. He became so messianic and over-eager that even Helen Bamber was tested to her limit. 'You had to be very strong to work with him and stand up to him, but he was also intensely vulnerable, and that, coupled with his theoretical assurance, had always formed part of his attraction for me. He often brought understanding, but he also drove people to one side.'

It began as a row inside the British Section of Amnesty. The volunteers, like Helen Bamber, were now acutely frustrated by what they saw as a sluggish office staff, headed by the affable and well-meaning figure of Cosmas Desmond, the former priest from South Africa. Their impatience with bureaucracy led Helen Bamber, Gordon Wills and Dick Barbor-Might to resign from the Council of Amnesty in 1980; their stature (the chairman's report for that year singled them out as 'indefatigably gifted campaigners') made this a serious gesture.

Gordon Wills, the quiet anchor of the group, now decided that he had had enough. His reasons for withdrawal were complex. The difference he wanted to make, he had come to feel, could not be made through Amnesty; and he was tired, he said later, of the 'sentimentality' of writing letters and feeling good about oneself; tired above all of 'working at a distance'. Exhaustion had set in – his marriage had broken up, he had sacrificed a great deal, and he did not have Helen's iron will to 'pace the room'. He also wished to explore the spiritual impulse which had always been important to him, and his searching led him to an undogmatic Buddhism. His departure from Amnesty removed a firebreak.

Barbor-Might later acknowledged that the dispute was 'nasty, complex and internecine'. Helen Bamber, her friend Antonia Hunt (who worked on human rights in Uganda) and others supported Barbor-Might. The dispute worsened with the charge that Dick's aim was to oust Cosmas Desmond and replace him. It is difficult to reconstruct the events in detail, but no one seems to dispute that a strike by the majority of the office staff in support of Desmond led to a situation in which volunteers, among them Bamber and Barbor-Might, found themselves in occupation of the office. An investigation by Peter Archer, former Solicitor-General in the Labour government, concluded that Barbor-Might may have been 'over-demanding' and 'abrasive' but that he was not guilty of organizing an internal coup. The enquiry paid tribute to his ability, energy and dedication; Archer wrote that Dick and his collaborators 'worked almost incessantly, sometimes throughout the night'. This now reads like a warning of a fever about to break, but meanwhile Cosmas Desmond lost a vote of confidence and resigned, amid great bitterness.

The end-game began with the entry of the stooped figure of Jeremy Thorpe, former leader of the Liberal Party and a disgraced showman of British politics. The weak Labour government between 1974 and 1979 had for a time depended on his small party's support; the charisma of power softened his long face. He had always been a split man, contending with himself: a power-loving disciple of J. S. Mill, an impeccably married cottager, a believer in human rights and democracy and a manipulator of secret party funds; the instinct of a caudillo within the gentry politician in his bespoke suit and trilby hat.

Thorpe used a crew of tax exiles, party grandees, a crooked MP and a shady ex-pilot to frighten an unstable ex-lover, a former model and stable lad called Norman Scott. Scott had broken the unwritten code that then governed same-sex relationships between the lower orders and the establishment: Take the money and walk, and never complain. He hung around, embarrassing and annoying. The pilot, recruited as a hit-man, shot Scott's dog in an encounter on Dartmoor. In 1979 Thorpe went on trial for conspiracy to murder. The old loyalties still had enough inert power in them to let the judge direct the jury to acquit, in a summing up so biased that only parody could do it justice. (Peter Cook's savage and still soberly hilarious caricature of the judge's speech, 'Entirely A Matter For You', was performed on stage at a benefit for Amnesty later that year.)

An Ealing comedy death-squad, the episode carried faint echoes of more violent cultures, of informal executions in quiet places, and it was an event of its time – of strikes led by Marxist trade union leaders, proposals for secret armies of the right, and black propaganda and bag-jobs by British secret policemen on politicians they considered disloyal. At the trial only the accomplices, the small fry, were defamed, and Thorpe walked free. But no one believed him, or in him; he was a moral ghost.

On 8 February 1982 the British members of Amnesty International discovered that this ruined man was the successor to the unfortunate Cosmas Desmond. The traditional channel back to respectability had been oiled and opened, the sinner seen to be doing charity work, or taking up the directorship of some worthy cause. Out of no less than forty-two candidates, Thorpe had been chosen by Amnesty's selection committee as the best person for the job. His application was kept secret from the wider membership, for reasons that were never properly explained. He did a brilliant interview, according to someone who was there; charming the pants off a group unused to effortless confidence and authority (and vacuity, a dangerously soothing property). He was now the public face of the founding section of the world's most important human rights organization.

Thorpe did not waste time, somehow taking public credit for a forth-coming event that linked the repression in El Salvador with the banning of *Solidarność* in Poland, and moved smoothly around the Amnesty office with the press in tow, charming the staff and rigging photo-opportunities with practised ease.

The members of Amnesty, however, felt stung. It was as if the people who had made the decision had been sleepwalking. James Nichol, who had been on the selection committee, left the executive, and in his resignation letter he wrote: 'Central as my own position may have been, I do not now understand all that has happened or that has failed to happen.'

His bewilderment at what he had done was widely shared. Thorpe's supporters could never make a positive argument for him, and blustered, saying that now the decision had been taken they had to stick to it, otherwise Amnesty would look foolish and inconsistent. Another council member wrote that she and her colleagues had 'believed that Amnesty's reputation was such that Mr Thorpe's past would not tarnish our organization'. Bamber denounced the appointment as soon it was made public. Looking back on it, she said that 'the trouble is that British Amnesty was made up of good people who didn't want to be nasty, who wanted to be diplomatic and enlist powerful friends.' She spoke of Max Frisch's anti-fascist parable *The Fire Raisers*, in which a nice middle-class family are invaded by lodgers who gradually bring in wood and fuel in order to burn the house down. The family cannot believe what is happening to them, and devise rational explanations for the behaviour of their aberrant guests. 'A lot of people in Amnesty were hypnotized by Thorpe.'

The event flipped Dick Barbor-Might into uncontrollable conspiracy-hunting. He did not react for a few days, and seemed at first, according to Bamber, nearly indifferent to what was happening. Then it occurred to him that because Amnesty (often at his urging) had been pushing against arms sales, and was taking up the issue of repressive technology, and had offended Nicholas Ridley at the Foreign Office, then surely the only people who could benefit from Thorpe's appointment were the men at the dark heai t of the British state.

Barbor-Might knows he went over the edge: he spoke later of a 'light bulb' coming on in his head, a moment of epiphany, of utter certainty: they were all in it, the British spooks, BOSS (the South African intelligence network), Thorpe – and certain Amnesty leaders, who had deliberately fostered divisions. 'Something had to explain why they had denied any solution to the terrible organizational problems of Amnesty.' Amnesty, and the group around him in particular, were targeted by MI6, the British counter-intelligence service: this was his 'dark thesis' about Amnesty, in which silent forces had created a zone of collusion and manipulation where doubt and self-destruction would flourish. He also, and fatally, identified his *bête noire* inside Amnesty, his master of puppets – the man who had engineered the conflict. This man was, Barbor-Might believed with unshakeable conviction, an agent of the state and of political evil.

Bamber remembered him making 'this huge jigsaw puzzle, and I wasn't sure it was the right version. What Dick did was to produce a *thesis*. That was what worried me about Dick. There could be other constructions on what was happening, though there was certainly something very odd going on. What you get in any human rights organization is either crass institutional behaviour, or occasionally something much more sinister. In this case, it could not be brought into the light: the important thing was stopping Thorpe.'

The *Observer* told Barbor-Might that his detective work was too thin to print, and so did the *Sunday Times*. He saw his nemesis as devious, genially cynical, a watcher – the perfect intelligencer. Dick Barbor-Might had become like Godwin's Caleb Williams, hounded by a corrupt genius of power.

On a beautiful summer day in 1982, he committed public political suicide. At the AGM of the British Section he demanded to be heard; voices had already been raised calling for his expulsion. He said that he had acted in good faith, but that he was formally withdrawing from Amnesty International, to which he had devoted so many years of his life. Helen Bamber remained silent; he felt that she denied him completely. The wife of the headmaster of a public school stood up and said that they should all remember Dick's good work, that he had had a brainstorm. And damned with that kindly, well-meaning verdict, he walked out into the sunshine and the wreckage of his life.

He admitted later that what happened was inevitable, that he had become impossible, and that he could not blame Helen or the others. He is generous, touchingly self-incriminating; yet he carries the burden of believing in the unfalsifiable. 'I was right, I think, but not in detail,' he said later. He is still convinced that there was an intelligence operation inside Amnesty; and his tragedy is that he may well have been right. Why might not MI6 have dabbled in the affairs of an organization that was threatening arms sales, which so many politicians like Ridley, Jonathan Aitken, and Margaret Thatcher saw it as their mission to promote, no matter how dreadful the 'end-use'? The spies may have engineered Thorpe's nomination in order to discredit Amnesty, and to put in place a weak man whom they could control – but this could never be proved.

In the end, the revulsion against the appointment was too strong, and the *Observer*, and its owner David Astor, who was a founder of Amnesty, pronounced magisterially against Thorpe. He resigned, 'astonished', he said, that 'people who claim to believe in human rights and civil liberties should display such pettiness and prejudice'.

Amnesty International set up an inquiry into the bizarre affairs of its British group. Dick Barbor-Might sat all day in the City Business Library preparing his evidence, surrounded by files of press cuttings about South African banks and their operations, their links with BOSS and MI6, desperately seeking the key – there had to be a chain of transmission of power, nods and winks, and quiet understandings. But he could not make the connections; the task was beyond his strength, the links in the chain impossibly heavy to lift.

He did write an enormous letter, fifty-seven pages long and still unfinished, in a burst of his effortless fluency, a memo that lacks a single thread of hard evidence but is full of intimations against the man he suspected of being a mole. They were drawn from what he called 'the institutional setting', and the inference it compelled him to make that only penetration could explain his suspect's behaviour. The letter was interminable, in every sense, and was never mailed. He placed it in a brown folder, and said later that he had never been able to reread it.

He still worked nights in a hostel in Charterhouse Square among the

Filipinos and Africans who cleaned the bedrooms of the West End hotels. His isolation was complete. At first light he would go out and sit in the square; he said he found he liked looking at the trees as the dawn came up. This is more or less what he did for the next six years. He allowed the scar to grow around the angry welt of dangerous certainty in his mind.

He went to Birmingham, and worked among the lowest-paid public-service workers, the very definition of the failed and the unwanted in Thatcher's Britain. There he found a second life as a union activist, defending the National Health Service against market reforms driving the middle class into private medicine. Pinochet's Chile remained, for him, the laboratory of Thatcherism, the place where the radical right had been able to test out their ideas. But this was restful stuff, after the emotional scorching of the Amnesty years.

Dick Barbor-Might has collected himself; his judgement lacks bitterness. 'Helen dropped me. She is a wonderful person, and I was very hurt. People may have felt that there was something in what I was arguing, but they may also have felt that Amnesty International itself would have been damaged by what I was doing. There's a lesson in humility here for me as I enter my sixties; and Helen and the others moved on so powerfully and have done such good work. With hindsight there is a grace in it, to use Christian language. There has to be compassion and humility and kindness as well as anger; perhaps in the end the logic can't be extended too far. The logics break down.'

The break marked, for Helen Bamber, the final rejection of a certain kind of politics, in which the empire always has terrible power and victims can only gesticulate against it. One of her later colleagues said of her that she has persevered because something in her is suspicious of the 'big idea', the fashionable obsession of the moment; and in the early 1980s she could see that a choice had to be made. There was always a tension within Amnesty between its ethical commitment to defend the most basic human rights, and the desire of some members to attack the sources of oppression. Barbor-Might wanted a movement for change, which Amnesty could never become; and if Helen Bamber to some extent shared this desire, she was now convinced that any attempt to attack structural causes alone would take her too far from a problem that tugged at her, like a person standing next to her quietly reminding her that she had something important to do. But she had also now lost Dick and Gordon, who were friends as well as colleagues; and at times she felt old and alone.

*   *   *

The medical group had taken on a life of its own. Word spread that there were doctors in London who were willing to examine torture victims, and to testify on their behalf if they could discover evidence on the body. Lawyers sent refugees to Helen Bamber, who would send them to Betty Gordon or another specialist. Their medical reports could help an application for asylum. The claim that Britain has always been a sanctuary for refugees escaping persecution may, as the Jews discovered in the 1930s, have been a self-congratulatory myth; but it still had truth in it in the 1970s. Convincing medical evidence was usually accepted by the state. This was about to change.

If the person were seriously injured, one of the doctors would treat them in their consulting rooms or after-hours in a hospital. It was an ad hoc, frantic operation, much of it clandestine: whether the administrators knew that their hospitals were being used to treat the injuries of dictatorship is a question that cannot now be answered.

Helen Bamber survived by doing secretarial work for two doctors, and editing papers for a group of psychoanalysts. One of her employers was an orthopaedic surgeon in Harley Street, Peter French, 'a lovely man' who knew that his distinguished secretary was not spending all her time on his business, and seemed to have strange visitors in his surgery. She has no clear idea how many hours she was working, and there was no one to stop her: David had graduated by now, and Jonathan was at Bristol University. On most evenings she would pass through the Amnesty building, and maintain her web of contacts. The office of the international organization moved from the Strand to Farringdon, to an ugly building occupying most of a city block. It looks like a vast mail-order depot, a place where high volumes of letters count.

In the basement parking garage there was an old custodian's hut, and the medical group was given it to use as an office. With Amnesty workers' cars going in and out, with carbon monoxide and the fumes of petrol hanging in the air, Bamber began to see more survivors and to talk to them. Almost without meaning to, she found herself entering into a new relationship. That it should be developing in a crude prefabricated hut, and with such improvised resources, seems strangely appropriate. Torture takes place in borrowed houses, half-finished buildings, in places where people once enjoyed food and wine. It reverses civilization. Bamber was starting to enter a darker and more intimate place, in which the work of the torturer might itself be undone. She was mimicking the relationship of cruelty in order to subvert it; and imitating its expediency, using whatever came to hand.

The lighting in the hut was a harsh fluorescent tube; for heat there was a three-bar electric fire. They had a typewriter donated by students at Bristol, where Jonathan was studying physics. Bamber remembers seeing a man in the hut, an Ethiopian asylum-seeker with a dead arm, the result of an encounter with soldiers during the Red Terror that followed the revolution against Haile Selassie. The limb waved loosely, in a distressing way; Betty Gordon came to see him with 'an orthopaedic chap' and soon Bamber was taking him to a hospital outside London where a sympathetic surgeon fixed the arm in a more comfortable position.

She also persuaded a neurologist at London Hospital to give free nerve conduction tests. Betty Gordon and the forensic pathologist Sir Bernard Knight began to describe, with their pedantic passion for minute accuracy, the exact shape and probable cause of abrasions, contusions, burns and wounds. As a demonstration of the way in which the body can be read closely for evidence of torture, Betty Gordon published her medical examination of a teacher from El Salvador in the *Lancet* in January 1984. The man was badly scarred on his trunk, arms, buttocks and thighs. The analysis is dispassionate, and unanswerably compelling. She showed that he had been bound at the wrists, and that acid had been poured over him while he was lying down. She showed how it had flowed and pooled. This was forensic pathology with an urgent political purpose. In the years to come, she and other doctors would find that a text can be read in many different ways, and they would find themselves defending their interpretations of injury against critics working for a hostile state.

During this period, Helen Bamber was a borrower of things and people, often in the privileged enclave of Harley Street. She moved between posh consulting rooms after hours, and dank bedsits in Whitechapel and Brixton, responding to appeals for help.

Brian Fisher, a doctor with a practice in South London, had established a relationship of trust with a community of Chilean refugees by learning Spanish and taking an interest in their culture. He had become convinced by what Helen Bamber had begun to suspect in her talks with survivors – that those who had been tortured were often mute about their real suffering. They found it difficult to speak to their partners; they had nightmares and were continually depressed; they had 'imaginary' illnesses. In an interview with *Medicine and Human Rights*, the bulletin of the medical group, he said that because these former victims' 'minds and bodies have been so incredibly abused they do produce a lot of psychosomatic complaints. They are preoccupied with illness and describe pains which are almost certainly not caused by any physical disease... These people have been subjected to a systematic process which totally distorts the way mind and body work. As a result of this they produce a set of very "odd" symptoms which, without some kind of background knowledge, it is impossible for a doctor to treat.' And he added: 'We need people who have some kind of empathy, some real understanding of the overwhelming confusion, guilt, alienation and psychological bruising refugees sustain.'

But it was the case of Ahmed Hashimi that seems to have turned her, practically, towards meeting the need described by Dr Fisher; and in a way this young Iranian turned all their heads. Helen Bamber was introduced to him by a doctor called Wasyl Nimenko. Hashimi had been in one of those gigantic demonstrations against the Shah in late 1978. He ran away when the police came, and they shot him in the back. He was partially paralysed from the bullet lodged in his spine, and they dragged him off to prison where the imperial secret police, SAVAK – high on the scale of cruelty among modern torturers – got to work on him. They gave him only the most minimal medical treatment. The permanent agony of his condition made it easy to inflict further pain, and they degraded him badly. They kept him manacled for months, his wounds untreated. He told Bamber later that the manacles were stamped 'made in Britain'. Khomeini's revolution opened the prison doors, briefly, in January 1979.

His brother came with him to London when the new regime showed its despotic hand. Ahmed was being treated at a hospital in Hackney where the doctors regarded him with suspicion: they could not understand what was wrong with him. They knew he was lying when he said he had been in a car accident, and this antagonized them; he felt that he repelled them. They simply could not imagine where he had been. It is hard to blame them for not considering what had been done to him; in a refrain that recurs in the stories of torture victims, 'He wouldn't tell them.' He and his brother lived in a squat; he was incontinent, and didn't have long to live.

Something about him moved Helen deeply. She still talks about him. He was beautiful, in that dark and patrician way of many young Persian men, and seems to have been intelligent and sweet-tempered. Helen once remarked that he had been shot at exactly the same age her husband was when he had seen his father die. Who knows what connections she made, which led her to organize support for this half-dead young man? 'It was not enough to publicize his case. It was necessary to help him.'

She explained to the hospital what had really happened; and with Nimenko, who was a passionate defender of human rights, raised money for a vehicle, for a ripple bed to prevent sores, and helped secure a flat for Ahmed and his brother through the local council. He read politics and economics at London University while undergoing repeated, painful operations. Above all, she 'entered into a difficult negotiation with him concerning his impending death, because it was obvious he was not going to live for a long time. We talked about how he was going to live his life; I said that some of us lived until we were old, and some of us a short time, and that it was what we did with the time that mattered. If we waste our time wondering about it, it is no good. I know this is trite, but it seemed to help, and he wanted to achieve something before he died.' She encouraged him to read and study, and he enjoyed the work; he was a very good student, determined to finish his degree, working towards it as if it contained a future, though he knew that ahead lay an area of darkness.

Ahmed Hashimi thought he wouldn't make it even as far as his qualification, but he had done the work, and when he slipped into a coma in Hackney Hospital he had, after all, achieved more than his torturers had wished. The university awarded him a degree. Helen Bamber was with him at the end, and had helped to turn the nurses' dislike of this mutilated stranger into something more than respect.

*   *   *

The Danish medical group formed the International Rehabilitation and Research Centre for Torture Victims (known as the IRCT) in 1980, when it was given permission to admit and treat torture victims at Copenhagen University Hospital, with funds granted by the Danish state. The IRCT is now also one of the world's leading research groups on its subject matter. Bamber's own formal split from Amnesty International would not come until 1985, though her new group had been operating inside the host organization for two years prior to that. The Danish group set a powerful example, although there was no prospect of the British government allocating funds for a similar service.

Bamber said of this transition period: 'Amnesty was working with paper and urgent actions; they could not treat people, and we wanted to. What they were doing remained crucially important, but our work began to be uncontainable inside Amnesty.' One more step had to be taken, however, before something new could precipitate out from the stream of campaigning events. Betty Gordon and Bernard Knight were the catalysts. In January 1985, they went on a semi-clandestine mission to examine refugees from Uganda in what they had to refer to as 'a neighbouring African country'. Killings and disappearances under the direction of Milton Obote, once considered the decent alternative to Idi Amin, were laying waste parts of Uganda. Obote was still supported by the British government. Six years after Amin's overthrow, an Amnesty report, in typically restrained and measured language, concluded that 'all but a few of those detained in military custody are tortured.' Gordon and Knight were to gather as much physical evidence as they could from survivors.

They flew on 'holiday' to Nairobi, the Kenyan capital, checked into a hotel, and rented a room nearby where they could examine Ugandan refugees. The two doctors examined each person who came to them and tried to match their verbal narrative with the story told by their wounds. Gordon's instruments consisted of a pen and paper, a tape measure and a magnifying glass; and a camera loaded with black and white film, which gives better detail of physical injuries than colour stock. She was learning to be very careful to distinguish old childhood scars and sports injuries from those inflicted by the state; it helped if each person would give her a history of their own body's mishaps. Gordon said that although she was doing a technical job, she had to try to get a feel for what it might have been like in the person's particular situation, in order to understand how their injuries were sustained. She knew how to distance herself from trauma as a surgeon, but here she found her defences threatened.

The flat and careful technical language of the doctors' case histories of sixteen people is a merciful screen between them and the reader. Unlike sensory deprivation and electrocution, which leave few visible physical marks, the methods of threatened African dictators were gross and reckless, as if they lacked the slightest concern for the scandal that the bodies of their subjects would advertise. The Ugandan material is of baroque nastiness. It did have an impact on government policy in the UK, which was no longer able to deny Obote's savagery. And one unforeseen result of the mission was Helen Bamber's meeting with James Mubiru, one of the people examined by Betty Gordon. He would become the first person cared for by a range of specialists as a victim of torture, by doctors, physiotherapists and psychotherapists – and set the pattern for the rest of Bamber's life.

The most obvious thing about James Mubiru is the tranquil beauty of his face, and his immaculate dress. In that instant of recognition the eye also registers the dark scarf at his throat, and the fact that it is not a scarf. It is a muff of skin, rearing up around his face, as though supporting it. The technical term is 'keloid scarring', which happens when some skins are cut or burned: they do not heal in neat, tear-shaped or flat patches but create bunched, florid scars. His body's protest against atrocity has taken this extraordinary form, grafting a part of itself as though it were a foreign thing that could be cut away, like thick ivy from a tree. It cannot: thirty-nine operations have failed. The keloids always return.

He is courteous, articulate and confident; he smiles warmly, and seems genuinely happy, refusing to behave like a troubled survivor. His life is full – he makes deals, interrupts conversations politely to charm a caller on his mobile phone, and he has a young son. Yet when Helen Bamber met him he had just been excoriated.

His father, a Christian of the Bugandan tribe, was a banker who, after Obote returned to power, became dangerously useful to the president: he could lobby on the government's behalf among international bankers and aid donors. This also meant that he could do Obote harm. In 1981 James was asleep in one of the smaller chalets behind his family's main house; he described the dense starlight and humidity of the equatorial night, as well he might remember his last painless evening. Soldiers surrounded the big house and fired bazookas into it. His immediate family was wiped out, and he was pulled from his hiding place under a bed. 'Our family had seemed invincible, a centre of protection and stability. In those explosions it all went. I was taken in a Land Rover – I've always had a horror of them since, like a rich man looking at you with hooded eyes – with the soldiers treading on my body as I lay on the floor.'

The state – presumably Obote himself – seems to have decided that James's father had an agenda, and that he might have shared it with his fifteen-year-old son, so they began to ask him questions. Perhaps they regretted not taking his father alive. He was kept underground, at first: 'Sunlight was treated as a gift.' Officers came to see him – high-ranking men, some of whom he knew; he felt he was in limbo, but he was, he said, not sure if he was forgiven or was going to hell. When he was transferred to a crowded cell of political prisoners, he thought he had escaped, that he was no longer important. Summoned from there into a garage-like space, with rough surfaces studded with power-points, he was made to stand in front of a man who was, James said, 'eerily quiet and calm, and asked me if my father had any partners, if he ever sent anyone abroad, if he had any girlfriends'. He never raised his voice: 'He was like a man standing in a laboratory, observing me through a micro-scope, gently talking to me.'

All that should be said about what happened next is that the implement the man ordered to be used was a hot-plate, and that they tied rags soaked in paraffin and strips of polythene around James's neck and torso, and set them alight. The statement these words form is not part of civilized discourse; it is, in an overused term, unspeakable. Like many of the propositions about the world in this and previous chapters, it sets a trap: to even acknowledge it is to become complicit with what it describes; and yet not to write it is to refuse part of the truth. 'In Africa,' James said, 'we have to be aware of snakes and other predators. But man, man can be very ... creative. The pain was *very* deep.'

When some of the perpetrators came to him begging forgiveness and offering to smuggle messages for him, it gave him a certain power, added to his – as he put it – 'stupid belief in justice and my own innocence'.

Eventually they decided his body, damaged as it was, was worth more to them alive than dead, so they demanded a ransom from his uncle and handed James over to his surviving family. He was still not safe: a rival faction in Obote's security apparatus, his family heard, was determined to kidnap James to cut themselves a piece of the action; and so he left for Kenya, where he was examined by the two English doctors. Bernard Knight swore continually and violently, James recalled, as he explored the evidence of his body. 'This was my first introduction to English profanity, and I was shocked. For the first time, however, I could see a third party describing what had happened to me without me having to say it. He could see how sustained it had been.'

Because Ugandan agents were operating in Nairobi, it was far from a secure haven for the injured boy, and so Amnesty and his family conspired to get him to London. Malcolm Rifkind, the Foreign Secretary at the time, had been denying that torture was widespread in Uganda. The Amnesty Report based on Gordon's and Knight's work, containing their forensic–medical notes, and the visible testimony of James's body, made the government position untenable.

From the beginning, all attempts to excise the keloids failed, the skin coiling and lumping again as soon as it was cut. Helen Bamber involved herself when money for the operations ran out. She organized for him, much more directly than she had ever done before, a combination of medical and psychic rehabilitation.

At first it was a matter of persuading doctors to accept the challenge of James's injuries: laser surgery, skin grafting, chemical treatments. She was sixty years old when she met James, but the relationship with the teenager worked, and has endured. His first impression of her remains bright: 'She had that curious, quizzical smile on her face; a completely open body language, with a huge heavy bag weighing down her small body. Her demeanour was very welcoming. I remember it was late afternoon, hot, in the Amnesty building: that quizzical expression, giving you enough rope. I felt she had strength and wisdom.' He cares for her, and is one of the people who can rib her about the holidays she never takes and her obsessional work habits – her 'drive and energy verging on zealousness'. He was struck, nonetheless, by how much time she had for him, despite her job in Harley Street, and by the number of people with whom she seemed to have formed relationships – a system he compared to an African network of family and friends, and which he had not expected to find in Europe.

He liked Helen Bamber's unpatronizing empathy, and her work – and it was careful work – helped, but she knew he needed more than she could offer. In many hours of discussion with him she learned a great deal about his courage, and his anger; and about the struggle he faced in the recovery of his body, in making it acceptable to himself again. James can be serene now about what he calls 'the natural affinity for beauty, and the natural reticence towards disfigurement, especially in the West where the media are so driven by images of human beauty'. For someone as young as he then was, and in his condition, alone in a new place, serenity cannot have been easy to achieve.

Bamber met a psychotherapist at around the same time as her encounter with James Mubiru, and in bringing the two of them together, the jigsaw that she had been trying to piece together for so long began to take recognizable shape. The therapist was John Schlapobersky, the grandson of Lithuanian Jews who had emigrated to South Africa at the turn of the century. He and Helen Bamber saw something in each other: a shared understanding of history, and of what is important in thinking about atrocity. His grandfather's brothers stayed in Lithuania, and perished with their families in the Kovno massacres, in the late summer of 1941. In South Africa, his family was no respecter of apartheid, and while a student at Johannesburg University he had spoken and written against the system. Called out from a lecture one day, he found himself in the main Pretoria interrogation centre, beaten under a harsh light and then put standing 'on the bricks' – a pedestal on which prisoners were made to balance for days at a time, deprived of sleep while they were abused and questioned. He had three days of this, but luckily the police discovered that he had a British passport, and the beating stopped. The sleep deprivation did not. He was, he said, 'hallucinating' by the end of the week.

When he was released three months later, he was deported, and came to Britain, where he studied psychology. He was inspired, intellectually and emotionally, by the attempt to link social relations with individual psychology pioneered by the Frankfurt School in pre-war Germany; and in particular by the line of writers and therapists descending from Siegmund Fuchs, who left Germany in 1933 and changed his name to

S. H. Foulkes. He introduced the idea of group therapy to Britain, working with traumatized combat soldiers at Northfields Hospital near Birmingham, and showed that the interactions of a group of similarly distressed people, led by a sensitive participant, can be immensely creative. Social experience – in the symbolic form of the small group – can encourage regeneration in the individual. The technique recognizes that the origins of many difficulties are inextricably personal and social. In Britain, Foulkes's legacy includes institutions – such as the Cassel Hospital, which was the first therapeutic community for non-war-related neuroses – and practitioners like Tom Maine and Robin Skynner, Schlapobersky's own teacher. Schlapobersky is not a dogmatic group analyst – he also sees individual patients – but it was his interest in group work that made him so alert to Bamber's concerns. Together they would begin to define a political, therapeutic community for people who had been grossly abused by state power.

When he met Bamber, he said later, he had no idea that he was 'opening a door', that within a few months he would find himself sitting opposite a man like James Mubiru and listening to him relate his experience of physical horror. 'Outside the birds were singing, the red bus was going by, children were playing; a benign, ordered world, and into it came this irruption of chaos and violence.' He began to see James, as an individual patient and in a group, and their work together helped to reconnect James to a future. And while he was doing so, Schlapobersky was exploring the connection between therapy and human rights with Helen Bamber, their discussion enriched and complicated by the knowledge of torture that he brought to it.

They were still groping towards a method, but Schlapobersky said later that he learned from her 'the principle of positive intervention' – which he is convinced that she learned in Belsen. He meant that you can do something for the survivor with the creative resources that you have as a person, which can in turn evoke what is creative in them. It means not deferring and simply medicalizing the problem, so that if a torture victim complains of a bad back one does not necessarily rush them to an osteopath (though that may be helpful too), but explores the way in which his or her body is experiencing pain – 'somatizing', in the medical jargon, translating hurt into a new physical language. Perhaps it simply means listening, but carefully.

In a brilliant paper delivered at the ICA in 1993, Schlapobersky set down five principles for the 'political application of psychotherapy'. They codify his understanding of the experience that he and Helen Bamber draw on in their work, and can be read as a kind of theoretical charter for it. The first is that torture is not in any significant way a problem of individual sadism, though it may draw on sources of aggression deep in the human psyche: it is organized violence, usually as an element in a conscious political strategy, and often associated with other catastrophes such as war, social conflict and dispossession. The treatment of survivors therefore demands a commitment to human rights, in the largest sense.

The second principle is that of 'positive intervention through medical attention and through sustained ... emotional support in all those cases where people express a need that allows us to engage with them in constructive terms'. Medical examination is so important because 'the separation of body from mind is nowhere less appropriate than in the treatment of torture, where the body has been abused to gain access to the mind.' It helps restore 'the privacy and integrity of their own bodily processes'. Intervention will not often 'cure'; the purpose is to *free* victims, rather than heal them from the lasting effects of the torturer's own intervention.

The creation of a containing environment is the third principle, a community with which survivors can form a relationship; and this community in turn allows those who care for survivors to feel supported, an important consideration for men and women exposed to such appalling knowledge, day after day.

People have had particular experiences, and have developed ways of adjusting to the world before they undergo massive trauma. Schlapobersky's fourth principle is that it is possible to reawaken these inner strengths – to help people renew themselves and 'reacquire a sense of agency and creative endeavour in their lives'. Sometimes, ordinary social relationships can release these energies: 'the needs of others' awaken them in even the most affected victims. 'Victimhood' is a category few people wish to adopt, and the best thing a therapist can do is to help the survivor transcend it.

Finally, the testimony of survivors reduces their isolation, in a place where it is accepted that their memories are important and that the disaster they have been through is worth acknowledging. Stories matter.

Bamber had for a long time been working with four of these principles almost instinctively. (John Schlapobersky compared her to S. H. Foulkes, who had left little that was worth reading, in his view; and yet she, like Foulkes, had an 'extraordinary capacity to make *everything* she did somehow therapeutic, when she was relating to survivors, inspiring those around her with the value of the work'.) She was aware of the systematic nature of torture, when it is used by modern states in the defence of power structures; she had seen the intricate connection between body and mind in the Holocaust survivors, in the Chilean refugees and in too many others; she understood something of the way in which people can be encouraged to reconnect with the world through emotional support; and her sense of the fragility of memory came from deep in her own Jewish heritage. What she did not have was a 'containing environment' – a safe house for speaking and hearing about the unbearable. She needed to find a place where terror could be at home.

*   *   *

The parting with Amnesty was civilized and friendly. In 1985, while she was working with James Mubiru, Helen Bamber asked the hierarchy of Amnesty for money to pay Kay Daly as a part-time administrator for the medical group. Betty Gordon appeared at a council meeting to argue the case, and the money was granted. There followed an outcry from the office staff, who felt that their own needs had been ignored: the old tension between upstart volunteers and full-time officials. These were territorial skirmishes; the real dilemma was that Bamber and her doctors could not go on seeing people in their spare time. Their raids on surgeries did not offer a stable basis for the treatment of survivors; and Bamber had spent too many evenings in the cold hut in the basement garage. She needed funds to go on with the work, and Amnesty could not provide them. In long talks with the chair of the British Section, the lawyer Peter Duffy, Bamber discussed the possibility of leaving to form a new organization. She and her group were valuable for Amnesty: they had won the support of the British Medical Association for an important campaign against torture; but Amnesty could not suddenly grow an arm for the treatment of hurt refugees.

Helen began to cut her moorings. First she gave up her job with Peter French. When Rex Bloomstein approached the medical group asking for help in making a film about human rights, Bamber found him unctuous, a creature from showbusiness. She changed her mind: the media camouflage hid sincerity and astute judgement, and by the end of 1985 he was helping her with the practical business of starting a charity. They met in the office of Bloomstein's production company on the corner of Warren Street. They had to elect trustees, which was not difficult: Bloomstein, suave and cautious, agreed to be the chair; Betty Gordon was the vice-chair; Dr John Dawson of the BMA offered to be a trustee, in an important gesture of support, and so did Sidney Bloch, a psychiatrist who had written about the special hospitals in the USSR. Gordon Wills returned, as though out of the blue, clearer and sharper for his spiritual retreat, drawn to something that would not be action at a distance, but a fusion of human rights work with treatment. 'It was about actual people; it was too compelling and vital to resist.' The heads of the three Royal Colleges, of Surgeons, Physicians and Psychiatrists, agreed to sponsor the organization: the medical profession had come a long way since the 1950s. The first meeting of the board of trustees took place at the BMA, in a grand portrait-lined committee room. At the meeting Helen Bamber was appointed director of the organization they had decided to call the Medical Foundation for the Care of Victims of Torture.

9

REMAKING THE WORLD

Maybe it takes longer to pay for being good than for being bad.

William Faulkner

They were given two rooms in the National Temperance Hospital, connected by wide corridors and leading out onto a covered pavilion. The abandoned hospital, once an infirmary for total abstainers, is set back from the Hampstead Road, a busy artery to North-West London. It is a handsome grey Victorian brick building obscured by the prefabricated extensions and black fire-escapes clamped onto it. Doctors in Bamber's network had persuaded the local health authority to give her the rooms while the building lay empty for renovation. The rent was £16 a week, though no one can remember ever paying it. Bamber had a part-time assistant and a typewriter, a desk and filing cabinet; some chairs and a sofa came later, no one knows how, from the offices of Thames TV. John Schlapobersky brought a plant for her on the day her phone was connected.

Bamber was sixty-one years old when she moved in. The hospital was on the edge of the district where she had earned her living for decades. She now began to pull a lifetime's relationships and obsessions into a final order. After the frantic activity of the early 1980s, it would be a different kind of work. The centre of it would be a room, in which a person's world might be remade – not a new world, because torture can enter too far into the future for that, but at least the existing world made bearable. The room is a holding space, the professionals say, where anger and pain can be acknowledged. Two or more people working intimately in such a room would try to re-enact and reverse what torture does. Above all, the survivors would be allowed to help themselves.

Those who worked there say the hospital was a good building; they could circulate, the clients could walk and smoke on the veranda, and the corridors were wide. It felt both spacious and private. Erol Yesilyurt, who started working there as a translator and became a case-worker and psychologist, made the seemingly obvious point that it was 'neither hospital nor clinic': a place that allowed people to come through the door without feeling that they were declaring themselves sick or mad.

It would have to be a place where time slowed down, if any good was to come of it; 'My body had time to think about pain,' said an Iranian treated early in the Foundation's history. No matter how frantic the work, or how many distractions in the paper on the desk, the listener would have to act as though nothing else mattered but the story she was hearing. Yesilyurt offered what seemed to be his personal charter: 'Every time you listen to somebody *you have to listen to that story as though it was for the first time.* I think this is one of the things I learned from Helen. Every time she sees a new client, she listens to almost similar stories from the same area, but every time she did not betray that. There is no essential set of symptoms: everyone has to be treated as a person.' Sherman Carroll, who knew her in the seventies when he was an Amnesty official, had seen her ability to be 'unhurried' when she spoke to people during the rush of urgent actions; Alison Wood had noticed it in the clamour of Belsen.

The people she began to recruit were, most of them, difficult and maverick. It isn't clear how conscious Bamber was about her criteria, but she knew she would need men and women who shared her own strangeness, and shared her naive refusal of the world as it is. Straight professionals would not do. But at first the most important thing was that they had a place. Helen Bamber could focus her entire, uncanny energy on it. A few years later, they moved a mile north to a back-street of Kentish Town and took over a pair of late-Victorian terraced houses joined by a shop front, with a warren of small rooms behind it. A railway bridge crosses the road a few yards away. When it rains heavily, the Fleet River – turned into an underground sewer by modern London – seeps up into the basement, leaving a damp stain on papers filed there. By the time they moved to Kentish Town, they were seeing 600 people a year.

In 1995 it was over a thousand; by 1997, twice that number. They are crowded, spartan quarters, with no space to walk and think. They missed the long arcades of the hospital, but the fact that the new building was so ordinary, a converted domestic interior, helped make it a very safe house, despite being crammed so tight. One of the therapists who worked there said after she left: 'People get unbelievably attached to the building. It is the brick mother.' For Helen Bamber it could be said that it was the place she had always wanted. It was not the big contented house that she could never find, with her family at ease with themselves around a kitchen table. But the world inside the Foundation was built around a different idea of trust. Bamber would feel at home there, and be there, working seven days a week, well into her eighth decade.

*　　*　　*

She had to learn how to manage, to cope with the needs and anxieties of people working for her. The group around her was marked by exile and violence: John Schlapobersky, with his experience of South Africa; Antonia Hunt, who learned to treat the world with a certain reserve when she was a young refugee from Austria and who had worked with Bamber on Uganda and repressive technology; Tom Landau, a retired doctor and refugee from Hitler's Berlin; Erol Yesilyurt, jailed and tortured after the 1980 coup in Turkey; and Perico Rodriguez, a former prisoner of the Argentinean dictatorship, with all that that implies, who was released after an Amnesty campaign organized from Britain. Gill Hinshelwood, a doctor and psychoanalyst from a working-class Lancashire family, was an early recruit; and Gordon Wills helped shape it all into a coherent bundle of energy.

Wills has worked with Helen Bamber for much of the past quarter-century, and knows her defects better than anyone. He appraises her almost coldly, despite himself, in the way that an adviser thinking about the succession has to do. Like others who have worked with her, he thinks that her charisma and ability to attract good people was at first often overwhelmed by her tendency to try to do it all, to take on too much, and to revel in crisis. Living in a state of emergency had become almost a habit to her. Others say that she can be hard and intolerant of others' weakness, failing to understand that the untiring drive she shares with her father and her sons can't be sustained by less persistent, less haunted people. Many of her present colleagues spoke of how dis-approving she seemed of them at first, until some test of their character that only she understood had been passed. Yet she also, paradoxically, hates confrontation, so that passengers can ride a long way before they are asked to get off. Erol Yesilyurt said that her instinct is to protect, even with the incompetent, and that despite her power in the organization she cannot punish easily. This, he said, 'causes further troubles'. Wills saw this as her 'Achilles heel', and that his task was to bind it up. He wanted to free her to lead an extraordinary group of carers using diverse and imaginative methods.

Criticism of her within the organization can be sharp. Gill Hinshelwood said, only half-jokingly, that she thought they tolerated the relentless awfulness of the material they deal with 'by making the organization itself awful'. She fantasized about writing a paper on 'The Diagnosis of Torture in an Organization for the Care of Torture Victims', but she also said: 'The Foundation is actually very good: a huge amount of work gets done. But we treat each other terribly; we dash around in chaos; and Helen in her way is a complete dictator. But we support her and we moan. It is a very primitive organization trying to do very sophisticated things. We chew over our anger about policy at night, and perhaps that is how we cope. Or make it worse. I think we must reflect patients' experiences all the time. When the Home Office says to some unfortunate refugee, "Why didn't you leave then, immediately after they had tortured you, why did you wait for six months?" I can understand that person from the way we behave ourselves.'

Hinshelwood spoke of 'the constant sense of emergency' fed by the Immigration and Asylum Act of 1993, which withdrew state benefit from many categories of refugee while they applied for asylum. It was an attempt by the then Conservative government to squeeze as many applicants as possible off the island – a quick and safe piece of legislative xenophobia. Some of the Foundation's clients were left with no means of support. Bamber and Gordon Wills responded by organizing emergency handouts of essential rations to clients in extreme need, but some of her colleagues, including Hinshelwood, felt that this was a diversion. Speaking in the winter of 1996, she said, 'We were racked with guilt and felt we should be giving them baked beans and sanitary towels. I thought we should not take this up. We should have been developing an international voice, and our therapeutic work, and we can't do that if we become an emergency service, a charity in the conventional sense.'

Hinshelwood found Helen Bamber 'syrupy'when she met her, and did not take to her at first. 'But the saving grace is that Helen is not lazy. She works damned hard; and I have enormous admiration for her; she has always been on the side of right. And she manages to gather the right sort of people around her: she has a knack for picking winners. Whether she also picks *victims* and knows how hard victims work, I don't know. But if she had an outside enemy I would fight the enemy. But within... She is charismatic, and very knowledgeable, but she can't let go of the day-to-day running. She goes to every meeting, which can be inhibiting. She loves crises, and people who do that need more crises.'

This straight talk raises a question: why does Bamber, or anyone else, do this kind of work – choose to live close to so much trauma? What do they get out of it? In the climate of suspicion which is our inheritance from Freud and Darwin, everything has its price, including altruism: we calculate motives, and value distrust. Every ideal has its genealogy. Nietzsche despised the utilitarian concept of goodness as useful, and found the origins of benevolence in the unapologetic exercise of power; good was merely what the powerful and noble chose to do. He admired the fact that aristocratic Greeks of the classical age could define themselves as 'truthful' simply by virtue of who they were: their word was good. The common man – dark, deceitful and cowardly – was inherently untrustworthy. Only torture could get the truth out of a slave, in a Greek court of law, but Nietzsche disdains to tell us this.

Nietzsche may have hated the social Darwinists, whose descendants have rooted altruism in the blind urge to defend those who share our genes. But the postmodernists – Nietzsche's own heirs – and the modern Darwinians share the view that action on behalf of others must be treated ironically: treated as an almost aesthetic decision, on the one hand, or reduced to a form of moderate self-interest, on the other.

S. H. Foulkes, whose ideas about therapy have influenced the way that Bamber and her collaborators now work, had reason to think carefully about people who carry out the 'thankless tasks' associated with compassion. He wrote that the carer's interest 'must not be overweighted with motives such as "helping other people" because this is too often based on... unresolved conflicts... His interest should be of a more detached, sublimated kind, similar to that of a scientist or artist.' She must resist the temptation to play God; in dealing with people who open themselves up to her, she gains a form of power, and that is always dangerous.

The caricature of the needy carer is a familiar one: bustling in and lavishing sympathy on the wretched survivor; full of the haggard self-pity that comes from doing too much; the lady bountiful, the angel princess: the smug flesh on charity's bones. Foulkes's student Robin Skynner recognized frankly that people who become 'helpers' do so because 'they are also getting something from the process psychologically.'

It is a small step from this to the assertion that all of them, social workers, psychologists, therapists – not to mention those caring for torture victims – are maintaining a system that services their own voracious needs. Is human rights therapy the attempt of professionals to capture and medicalize a political problem, so that they can get funds and resources? Yet to make this claim is to confuse motive with effect, as though medicine itself could be discredited by the buzz of power a doctor feels. Skynner himself drew a more interesting conclusion. If the need of the carer is not recognized, a cycle of deprivation is set up, in which the emptiness and despair of the would-be helper feed on the pain of the victim. The former does more and more, to less and less effect, and collapses in exhaustion. Skynner recommended 'feeding the goose that lays the golden eggs' by acknowledging the carer's own problems, and finding ways of honestly enjoying the work, so that both sides to the encounter gain from it; like a mother, who feeds her child, but not selflessly, for she gets immense satisfaction from the baby's pleasure.

Skynner was shrewd about the families that people like him re-create in their working lives: 'We automatically seek an environment, including a work situation, which is an improvement on the family of origin, but nevertheless similar enough for the psychological attitudes and social skills we learned in that original family to be good enough to cope with it – or perhaps even to be specially valued and therefore an advantage rather than a handicap. In other words, as in marriage and friendship we seek out something better and different but not *too* different.' This statement could be an abstract definition of the complex goodness and sadness of Helen Bamber's life, but like any theoretical summary of a complicated action, it explains everything and nothing.

Her need even now, in her seventies, can still be too acute, too great for practical fulfilment. She is so sensitive to emergency that she can be tossed around by it like a cork; organizing food parcels for asylum-seekers may have been a hopeless task, for which she and her Foundation were not equipped – but she could not face seeing Kurdish and Algerian refugees, who she believed had been tortured, begging on the streets. She has been very good at helping those survivors of disaster that she can reach, and turning her work with them into a sustained protest against cruelty. She has it under control, most of the time; the necessary selfishness keeps her in check, and with old age she is calmly aware of the demands she makes on the world, insisting that she doesn't work 'just for love of humanity; a lot of it is about myself. My need to do it is very strong indeed. And it is not a heroic, or even a worthy need.' She has also, with what seems to an outsider considerable dignity, learned to imagine her own passing, and no longer goes to every meeting. Too many founders with her kind of allure wreck what they create; she has avoided the temptation. But there are still moments when the boundaries are blown down, and she is reaching out as if in the dark responding to cries for help, saving the world in a flurry of desperate gestures.

* * *

This is the side of his mother David Bamber saw, as he neared the age of forty. He believed that she would almost find it a relief to hear that he was not all right, when she asked how he was in her weekly phone-call, for there to be an emergency so that she could swing into action on his behalf. He was harsh about his relations with her; he wore the independence he achieved so early like a thin, hard armour. His memory of childhood was bleak: he spoke of it as though he had been deserted by one parent, and treated and hardened as a survivor by the other. He resented the covert domination of his early life by a Holocaust that was almost a secret, and though he is no more religious than his parents he felt that he had had to discover for himself what it meant to be Jewish. He could see only the compulsive side of his mother's work, as though it were a mere symptom. Yet the neglect he implied when he said that she was never a normal mother is angrily anachronistic: Helen Bamber's late burst of activism only started after the coup in Chile, when David was sixteen. He acknowledged that there must be something unusual about her, but he denied that it touched him. Yet she invested him so powerfully that he was frank about the inadequacy he felt in relation to her energy, her ability to build and endure: 'Everything, in a way, is a reaction against her, to maintain some kind of independence, to find my own voice.'

To help him find that voice, he began attending an art class about ten years ago. 'I think in pictures,' he said, so he thought at first of painting, but when he saw sculptors working he was moved by 'something about the relationship between them and the physicality of their material'. He began to work with clay, guided by a teacher interested in the human figure, who asked him to model a head, and gave him a skull to help him understand the structure. David spent a long time working on this first piece, and 'it was almost as if I wasn't present while I was making it'. The clay head was covered with plaster, and then a form was cast from the mould. 'It made this thing.' The head was a tormented howl of anguish. It is crude, ghoulish, derivative of famous screams, and disturbing in its own right. David described his own reaction to it, when he finally saw the cast: 'I opened it up and revealed the form, and I thought, there is nothing in my personal experience that equates to that scream; there is nothing that horrible in anything I have witnessed. And I felt that it was a scream from the gas chambers. In some way my parents' horror was passing through me in this strange kind of silence.'

For ten years, as he completed an art degree, he worked and learned about form, while holding down a stressful day-job as a management consultant. As time went on he engaged more and more directly with the theme of the Holocaust. In 1994, he began a series of pieces in which a man-made regular metal form pins down, butts up against or tears out of wood; a struggle between organic and inorganic, living and dead. His pieces are massive, often using the root systems of trees that he has found and shaped with a chainsaw. None of the pieces is named. Some of them link four rusty girders arranged as a long open cube with a massive structure of four hewn blocks of timber, two uprights with two cross-blocks notched into them – rather like a country stile; but much more like a heavy wooden buffer, and the girders evoke railway tracks. In one striking piece they begin to converge in perspective, narrowing as they run into a wall, hinting at their eventual fusion into a sharp point, the end of the line. He said that too much of Holocaust art 'doesn't convey anything because it tells you too much.'

One giant sculpture, made for his final year show, resembles the incomplete frame of a wooden hut. Two pairs of uprights, four cross-bars suggesting end walls, and two timbers as a base, are slotted into each other in simple joints; each eight-foot high cube is cut from a tree, apparently roughly, with the chainsaw, though the lines through the centre of each are at exactly ninety degrees. The structure is open on top, a sketch of a room, of basic shelter, as though it could go either way: become a house or a prison.

By the summer of 1996, he felt he was 'getting somewhere', and was ready to intervene in his own family's history, from which he had felt so excluded. He set out with his chainsaw for the Polish National Centre for Sculpture at Orońsko, forty kilometres south of Warsaw. It is close to the concentration camp at Majdanek, where his father's mother and grandmother were killed. He made one piece while he was there, but only after walking around the site at Majdanek 'to see it in its full physicality'. He was allowed to leave the work in the sculpture park, grounding it with foundations as deep as he could drive into Polish soil. It stands under trees by the side of a lake, a place he chose deliberately because it was dark and mosquito-ridden. The sculpture evokes the form of a trough, or of a bier; it is closed at the back, but in front it presents a kind of shelf, and on it are placed three roughly cut pieces of wood in the shape of human heads. The metal pieces under the bisected column that forms the bier are the blades of an old harrow.

In David Bamber's work the conflict between organic and inorganic form is rendered in stark terms. In a local gallery, he collaborated with another artist on an installation in which a tree-trunk, a dark irregular column of wood, was placed at the end of a long alcove, surrounded by a ton of neatly-raked gravel. A metal fence under high tension anchored to the side walls of the gallery sliced through the centre of the trunk, as though the dead tissue of the wood had divided and grown around the net of metal links, whose extreme stress increased the violence of the arrangement. In the gallery's comments book, the viewers recorded their disquiet, evoking images of rape, of killing; one person wrote: 'You have tortured the wood.' David said: 'People project feeling onto it. They look on the tree as a person.' In these massive forms, he has found a voice; he insists that it is a universal voice, speaking of history and identity, but it is also, perhaps, a way of capturing his mother's and his father's voices, and it is at least as eloquent and compulsive as hers. She brought him up, and it may be that because she hid as well as revealed so much he needed a charge of anger against her to reach a vantage-point from which he could claim, if never make sense of, the history that formed them both.

'The cobbler's children go barefoot,' or can think they do. Both David and Jonathan are small, tough and resolute; so at least they might seem to those who do not know them, or have listened only to their more unguarded comments about themselves and their family, and are therefore at risk of seeing them, in David's terms, as isolated survivors. Beneath their reserved, yet almost ruthless frankness about their upbringing, the listener senses complicated patterns of love and rage determined by events that nearly destroyed their father, and which leave little room for conventional sentimentality. They are active and high-achieving men, yet they have paid a price, and David, especially, speaks as though he can feel history chafing his skin. He once said that the burden of the second generation is also a gift; he suffers under it as he seeks to interpret it. So it can appear to the outsider, who is aware of intruding a structure onto lives marked by a violence he can barely imagine.

Jonathan, a physicist who specialized in glaciology – he studies the movement of the polar icecaps – said he believed that his family is 'self-contained, independent, and [that] we don't need or seek much contact with each other.' He admitted to being struck occasionally by the way that families other than the one he grew up in live their more collective lives, but he only knows one family and one self, and he has adjusted to them. In the life he has made for himself he has a loving and stable relationship, and is a father to two step-children. Yet like his mother and older brother, he has inherited motivation, 'the Bamber trait very clear in the whole line'. He sees David as 'very directed, very goal-oriented, with non-stop activity; and we all try to cram twenty-eight hours into twenty-four.'

Until five years ago, he was a passionately keen climber; the mountains were 'the love of his life'. Coming to university at Bristol was 'like being reborn', and the mountains seem to have been one of the most important discoveries of his new life. In his first summer at college he went to the Alps, whilst at weekends he scaled the sheer walls of the Avon Gorge. 'But the mountains were the real thing for me. That's what kept me going.' He spoke of his attraction to high places in terms of loneliness and perfection: 'the isolation, the beauty, the remoteness, the pristine virginal appearance of white snow mountains; they are very pure. It is the ultimate form of escapism; you are very much preoccupied with your own survival; and nothing focuses the mind more.'

In 1993 he went on an expedition to the Himalayas in Kashmir, with a group of climbers, some of them less familiar with high altitudes than Jonathan and his closest climbing partner. 'It was a funny old trip.' He and his friend, after they had done a warm-up route, set off to conquer an unclimbed mountain known as Tupendo. At 200 metres from the summit they were snowed in, and sat it out for a day in a little bivouac. When the weather improved they did two pitches – about 100 metres – and Jonathan's friend was leading when a rock was dislodged and landed on Jonathan's leg, removing, in his own dispassionate account, 'the front of my leg, and the impact, pushing the front of my leg against the rockface, took off a bit of the back, so that the leg was hanging on by tendons and a bit of skin'. His partner struggled for half a day to lower Jonathan to a two-foot-wide ledge, where he could at least lie flat in the tiny bivouac tent, his leg held in a splint of ice-picks. All he had for relief was a small bottle of paracetamol. He told his mother that he had contemplated rolling to the side and ending the pain and the smell, but he had promised his family he would return. Two days later his friend reached him with another climber, bringing proper analgesics. Carrying him off the mountain took another two days.

They reached the base camp forty-eight hours later. The other climbers were sure that Jonathan would lose his leg: 'I had very bad gangrene and frostbite.' A helicopter took him to Jammu, at the foot of the Himalayas, for an emergency operation, and on to Delhi for a second. Two weeks later he reached the UK, for the first of another seven operations. 'I also had osteomyelitis [infection of the bone], which wouldn't go away, until the last operation finally stopped it.' For three and a half years he was on crutches, but to strengthen his leg and to improve the circulation in it he took to riding a bicycle, and soon he was doing very serious long-distance and hill-cycling. His aim was to get back to the mountains as soon as his fitness would allow: in the early spring of 1998 he intended to climb rock in Majorca as a warm-up exercise for the high peaks.

He said of himself: 'I was a lonely child, in many ways, not fitting in with the main stream of things. That may have made me more distant, a more removed kind of person.' He admires his mother, and has a dignified answer to the assertion that her work only services her own demons. 'People never do something totally selflessly for other people. They do it because it does something for them; because it makes them feel better in some way; but why it makes them feel better, and what need it fulfils, is something that is very personal, and I don't think anyone has a right to make a judgement about that. That's all I can say. People can do a lot of good because it fulfils some need within them.'

On the wall of Jonathan Bamber's office he has hung a large map of Antarctica, the great white shape dominating the room with its emptiness. It is the perfect image of isolation, and might look symbolic of a chilly self-sufficiency; but Jonathan's ideal situation is finding a path on a mountain with people he completely trusts – for their judgement, courage and loyalty, in the knowledge that they will remember and search for each other if anything goes wrong.

*   *   *

Certain kinds of extreme experience are no more curable than the un-happiness of families. Not all torture victims need help: the individual with a well-grounded personality, who has strong support from their community and an ideological framework into which violence can be fitted, often seems to survive better than others. (Helen Bamber herself, it should be said, is sceptical even of this exception.) It is the majority of victims who are left so bewildered – the innocent bystanders, the family members punished for their son's crime, the people at the bus-stop picked up in a random sweep. In exile, political militants begin to lose their protective outer casing – the rituals of the leader-cult, the slogans, the songs for the heroic martyrs sounding forced and empty. For most of the people who come to the crowded building in Kentish Town, it is a matter of learning to live with the consequences of violence; of accepting, as the Auschwitz survivor Jean Amery still believed twenty years after the Gestapo captured him, that 'whoever has succumbed to torture can no longer feel at home in the world.'

In this sense, the Foundation is 'not just a sanctuary, but a place of raw terrible truth', in the words of Susan Levy, a South African therapist who worked there until 1996. She had to say to people, in effect, 'This is never going to be all right – you are never going to be as you once were.' Gill Hinshelwood said of a woman client: 'There's no way you can take the story away from her: people think that if you tell the story once, you can take it and throw it away. But it does not work like that. It's your story, your history, and it will never become drawing-room conversation because it isn't; but you're going to have to be able to tell it to yourself, and perhaps your nearest and dearest, without breaking down.' She compared these memories to a plant that can be pulled up, but never thrown away: 'It remains living material.'

It lives, often, through anger and wounding language. The Foundation is not an easy place to work precisely because torture generates a direly untranslatable verbal structure in its victims. 'The *how* of pain defies communication through language,' Jean Amery wrote in his meditation on his own torture in the Belgian fort of Breendonk in July 1943. The impassivity, the unyielding and unself-pitying eyes of the victim can be difficult to meet.

Helping such a person confront reality and hold onto good is an even more daunting task. Susan Levy described an encounter with a woman from an Arab country who had been badly tortured. She had two children, by a man who had himself died under torture, and had been in therapy for two years. It was Christmas. The woman spoke of how much she liked that season in London, with the pine trees, the festive atmosphere, the giving of gifts, how she felt at one with all people – *even the Jews*. Even the Jews, whom she hated with all her heart. She knew she was speaking into the face of a young South African Jew. Then she said she wanted to smoke, though Susan hated people smoking in her cupboard-sized office. She drew her chair close to Susan, who was sitting near the open window and thought her patient intended to let the draught take the smoke out of the room, came closer still and exhaled into Susan's face. This was a patient she had nurtured for two years. It was a perfect reproduction of the torturing relationship; the woman mimicking the controlled insult to her own integrity. (She later broke down and apologized, begging forgiveness: it was not *she* who had been abusive.)

Violence also puts down roots in the minds of children, and can be passed from generation to generation. Sheila Melzak works in a room scattered with crayons and toys, garish drawings and posters – a play-room where nothing is innocent. Here young children who have witnessed what Helen Bamber calls 'grotesque death', who have seen their parents tortured and their houses destroyed, learn about politics.

But politics as Sheila Melzak defines it is not school civics: it is about learning to live in a society that for these children now includes extreme violence – an elemental politics of negotiation, in order to humanize relations with other people and to lessen the potential for violence in themselves. It is necessary, Melzak argues, to think about the inner world of these children in relation to their outer world, and to understand the burden of secrecy that they are forced to carry. They have lost one or both parents, they have lived under a regime in which they learned that speech was dangerous, and as refugees, they have lost the culture of their birth. She thinks that the secrets of these children are often expressed magically: they believe that the losses they have suffered are their fault, caused by their own ambivalent feelings of rage and love towards their parents, and that there is little difference between thinking and doing a thing.

A child like this, who has shat himself in fear at the age of nine, and seen his parents humiliated and even killed, and who is then expected to behave well in an unsuspecting school, can become a hard little knot of aggres-sion. Shall he (or she) identify with the parent or the soldier, the authority of love or of the gun? The feelings of guilt that this oscillation sets up are destructive, and Melzak tries to contain and integrate them. It is slow work. She described her attempts to get a child from Zaire to trust her, a child who has no context for what this Sheila person does, so Melzak encourages him to talk about Zaire, the village he came from, and the violence he saw around him. She gets him to draw, and they discuss his pictures and what they mean. The boy drew an image of a fearsome goon in camouflage battledress with five guns, a big knife, and a classic child's idea of a bomb, a finned turd. He loves to act the tough violent guy, but ten weeks later he drew a red flower, of a type that grows only in Zaire. This was progress, but not an outbreak of peace and love; rather it was the other side of the ambivalence impacted in him. It may be possible to bring both sides into a stable balance, but no one can count on it.

Children punishing themselves for what they haven't done; parents acting out their helpless fear on their children. A survivor of two years' terror in Khomeini's jails has come to terms with his own anger and grief, and has a wife and child, but even when he holds the baby he lets his head hang back, swings him in a way that is not merely affectionate, as though, Helen Bamber said, he were testing the child's physical endurance. She knows a Kurdish father who makes his children stand under the cold shower every morning of their lives. They escape the living room to study the moment he comes home; he is almost incapable of talking to them. As long as they are studying he is proud and happy: he will recite their honours, he loves them and they may come to hate him. 'Not all victims are nice people,' Gill Hinshelwood warned; 'we should not idealize our clients.' Nor can all of them be 'innocent', though it is the basic principle of the Foundation that no one 'deserves' to be tortured; some of their clients are surely former guerrillas, and a few may perhaps be perpetrators themselves.

Michael Korzinski, a therapist and former dancer who tries to work with the bodies as well as the minds of those who cannot distinguish mental from physical pain, explained why he and his colleagues needed to support each other so much, and why each needed a supervisor they could talk to outside the Foundation. 'You don't do this work to be loved by the people you help. Sometimes the healthy thing for them is to attack you; and you have to be ready for that. People who have been tortured really know how to put you through the wringer. This is not a place for do-gooders.'

*   *   *

John Rundle still says that his great teacher Maurice Pappworth showed him what it is to be a good doctor. He is a neurologist, but he finds himself doing work never dreamed of by the Royal College of Physicians.

An Iraqi man in his fifties came to him with pains in his head and back, and perhaps because he was able to trust this older English doctor, he admitted that he had no desire to go on living. He often wished he could kill himself. Tuesdays were particularly unbearable; it was as if he would go on only if he could find a way of abolishing that day of the week. It emerged that his son and brother had been executed on a Tuesday, and in a scene that would be incredible were it not typical of the Iraqi Ba'ath, he had been compelled to watch them die. He was beaten severely when he asked for permission to kiss the body of his son.

Rundle suggested that on Tuesdays the man should go into a room on his own and think about his son. These encounters became an informal ceremony in which the father tried to reconstruct what his son looked like, how he dressed, what they shared; sometimes he tried to bring him to Rundle so that they could imagine him in the room with them. Rundle was attempting to get the man to recognize that his guilt and helplessness were misplaced – that he could have done nothing, and that the boy now deserved a decent burial. That is what they tried to give him.

This act of homage grew out of the careful taking of a patient's history. The Iraqi had refused psychological counselling, and like many torture victims from non-Western cultures he had no framework into which the talk and silences of conventional therapy could be fitted; his pain and despair were accessible by other means. It was not orthodox therapy, but it helped.

For Rundle, his work at the Foundation is an extension of good medicine. He is much older than any of the other doctors who work there; his almost querulous voice, still with the twang of his Palmers Green childhood, seems to declare an irritable old codger, but he is aggravated by barbarism. The tone of his voice recalls Pappworth's prose; his conversation is always jumping up for a fight. 'Clinical medicine is a dying art. You have to *listen* to the patient: there is no substitute for that. Of course you also need a broad and deep knowledge of medicine; you should never stop studying, and the last book you read should be the one they prise out of your hands in the coffin. But the better the therapist the better the result – this is true of all medical disciplines. The quality of the person is what matters.'

Everything at the Foundation starts with the body, and a careful, sympathetic clinical examination. Rundle, like the other physicians, has become expert in the effects of torture: soft tissue damage to muscles and ligaments from beating with sticks and rifle butts, on the trunk, or the soles of the feet (or *falaka*, which is endemic in Turkey and the Middle East); and damage to the lumbar region, which hurts not only the back but also the legs. (One of his many Iraqis, a devout Muslim, has a left thigh so damaged that he cannot kneel to pray, which is a constant torment to him.) Painful shoulder joints because of 'Palestinian hanging', in which the victim is suspended from a rope by their arms tied behind their back; eye injuries, such as degeneration of the optic nerve, so that vision blurs; and many epilepsies, which are caused by blows to the head. He believes that torture often causes hepatitis, when bloody tools are used on prisoner after prisoner.

The examination itself can be therapeutic. Paying careful attention can affect the emotional and cognitive dimensions of pain. The relief of hearing that a condition is treatable is very great. Rundle's ability to offer, in many cases, a very precise diagnosis can be reassuring. His confidence extends to joking with his patients. He thinks it helps to distance the questioner from the memory of bureaucracy and the police that any interrogation arouses. The visitor is often surprised by the amount of laughter in the building: the discovery of pleasure in the horrible, but also a subversion of it.

'These are situations no medical school ever trained you for,' Rundle said. He improvises, as he did with the Iraqi father mourning his unburied son. He described the course of the examination as an identification, an entering-in. 'You have to move into the torture chamber with them; you almost have to be tortured with them. Each question makes the situation less ambiguous and clearer. Were you wearing a blindfold? Was there a light? Were you seated? What did they use to hit you? What shape was it? How were your hands tied?' This meticulous reconstruction, piecing together what their bodies tell him matched with their words, also helps to eliminate the occasional faker.

After the medical examination, other doors open. It isn't all talk. There is no single programme, at the Foundation, for torture victims. Treatment is as flexible and imaginative as the ingenious cruelty that it undermines. Their clients do not come, on the whole, because they feel their souls have been damaged, but for what seem like practical reasons: they have inexplicable back pains, or acute insomnia and nightmares. They may have been referred by some hospital, as when a homeless man picked up off the streets tells a story that horrifies a young doctor in casualty. Or they need asylum, because they are terrified of being sent back to Algeria or Iraq. The darker matter often erupts only in the course of dealing with these immediate problems.

Some go into individual psychotherapy, but the implied contract between counsellor and patient and the unfamiliar demands of the hour-long session make this intimidating for many of the people who reach the

Foundation. More sociable kinds of therapy seem to work better, so that people can form connections with each other, and not just on the basis of their shared injuries. These groups are influenced by the conviction that, to paraphrase John Schlapobersky, they hold within them the resources that any society contains for good relationships. The victim learns to rewrite the story that jagged on torture.

They have a women's psychotherapy group, for those who have been tortured and suffered bereavement. These are strong, articulate women, helping each other to master harrowing experience. A craft group teaches skills like pottery, embroidery, painting on glass, sewing. Little is spoken, but the work often leads to extraordinary discussions, as though the neat work of making an object with the hands had some purgative effect. Another group farms two allotments, using natural growth as a metaphor for ordering and encouraging rehabilitation. A physiotherapist touches cramped and aching bodies that can never find a relaxing posture. All of them have to be ready to face the atrocious when they least expect it. Gill Hinshelwood said: 'You have to cope with yourself in every session: face the unknown, and allow yourself to be shocked, and surprised, to feel disbelief, and go through all that again and again. That's what I think is a therapeutic interview.'

*   *   *

They also have to work with silence. Sheila Melzak has written about the layering of secrecy she finds in her adolescent patients. They have grown up in societies that force on their citizens 'the conscious keeping of secrets, the unconscious internalization of divisiveness and secrecy and limitations on the ability to assess reality'. In exile, these tortured children may be full of anger at their parents, yet also idealize one or both of them; and live a nostalgic fantasy of their homeland, while resenting and fearing Britain, which they may find forbidding and racist. Frequently, they blame themselves for their parents' deaths. They are mourning, they have been subject to 'continuous trauma', and they are at a stage in their lives when even well-loved teenagers in suburban comfort can destroy themselves. Holding back has become second nature to them.

We are used to assuming that there is relief in talking (and among torture victims there often is); but women almost never want to tell, because the torture of women in many countries includes rape. Gill

Hinshelwood works with a lot of abused women. 'You need to know that they feel shame in the telling, shame that they have not been strong enough to lock it away and keep silent. They don't *want* to tell their whole story; at Heathrow airport, they are unlikely to tell an immigration officer they have been raped. And you have to be sensitive to that sense of shame and not exploit it. You have to be terribly conscious of your own power, and sometimes ask for time to think about what to do with what they have told you. What they tell does not go away.' Returning to her image of 'living material', she said that if you pull up a plant, 'it doesn't survive long if you don't look after it.'

These women can almost never tell their relatives or husbands; and this is the torturer's intention, to infect the entire family with shame and anger. It works all too well: sex becomes an ordeal, and the suspicion and frustration of their partners worsen the infection.

Men are raped – by guards, or with the muzzle of a rifle – and it is delicate work making them trust a doctor enough to admit that their sense of themselves has been destroyed. One of the many ironies of torture is that something so crude reproduces itself so effortlessly, even in its cognitive style. Torture almost always denies that it has happened; it is always an official secret; and sometimes the victims themselves collude to ensure that it remains so.

*   *   *

Richard McKane's English versions of the later poems of Mandelstam are beautifully pitched and laconic. *The Moscow Notebooks* and *The Voronezh Notebooks* are a great sequence of meditations on despotism and mental and physical suffering. The poems written after May 1934 are the work of a writer who has been tortured by the NKVD, and who has made two suicide attempts. McKane has a political affinity with these poems, and his imaginative relationship with them is also highly personal. He speaks lucidly of his own depression; and he has resisted political cruelty ever since he became a poet: he was active in the campaign against psychiatric abuse in the Soviet Union, and among his other achievements as a translator are editions of the work of Nazim Hikmet, the Turkish communist poet who spent fifteen years in prison.

At the Foundation, working with therapists and physicians, McKane interprets for Turks and Kurds who have little or no English. His voice is deep, with an actor's resonance and modulation, a voice that has a very British authority of foreign service and scholarship. The intimacy between the subject and the interpreter – their entry into each other – preoccupies him. 'You sit there and hear someone say, "I went to the police station, they beat me on the feet, I could not walk," and then you say, meaning it, "I went to the police station, they beat me on the feet, I could not walk." You cannot help empathizing, almost identifying with them through the language you share, in the act of translation.' Something of them is translated into him. McKane spoke of Daniel Day-Lewis's reputed near-breakdown while playing Hamlet, of how Day-Lewis was taken over by the spirit of his powerful father, to explain how torture gets inside his own psyche. Sometimes it threatens his equilibrium, but McKane loves this work. There is improvisation and creativity: the interpreter has to suggest ways of phrasing experience, and find the right words for pain. He or she even offers suggestions about treatment, if they have understood some subtle hint in the client's language. The restrained silence of orthodox therapy would be callous.

McKane agreed with John Rundle it was important to risk laughter. He spoke with real longing, as all the older workers do, of the late Dr Tom Landau, who was the first real therapist-healer of the Foundation. He could, according to McKane, get into a 'really constructive' relationship with a client before the first hour was up, making them visibly relaxed and trusting – enough to wave his long-handled rubber mallet above his head when he tested their knees and ankles for reaction-times and cry out, 'Now this is *English falaka!*' He could use language to catch and then release the tension, and would judge his moment well, knowing not to say it if it was out of place.

Erol Yesilyurt has a photograph of Landau, who died in 1989, in his office. He was close to him, and said that Landau was a basically pessimistic man, that he seemed to 'know what suffering was about', and that is perhaps why he laughed so much. Landau had come from Germany with his family in 1933 and knew a little about being a refugee; Yesilyurt implied that Landau's jokes were a beautiful kind of gallows humour. Helen Bamber said of her early mentor Oscar Friedmann that he 'could not work with the light as well as the shade'; and it is noticeable that although she is no joker, she too laughs a great deal, a wry and exasperated humour that puts difficult people at their ease. James Mubiru said that Bamber was 'quizzical', and her fun does ask questions. Yesilyurt has reflected on her sceptical but undiscouraged amusement. 'I never thought she treated people like victims, in fact; she has high hopes about clients, and loves to see them doing better if they are given the opportunity, but she does also have this pessimism, thinking that their experience will always be with them, that they will never be free of their experience, and that what they lived through may affect their lives, and their relationships with their children.'

Jokes play on words. Freud noticed that Jewish jokes are usually made by Jews themselves, 'while the anecdotes about them from other sources scarcely ever rise above the level of comic stories or brutal derision.' The language of torturers, though obsessed with jokes and nicknames, is stuck at precisely this level of 'brutal derision': language for them is a weapon. It is often foul and coarse: what used to be called 'bad language', but bad in the sense of a complete breakdown of communicative restraint. Because it contains real power, a phrase like 'fuck your sister' is both curse and threat. Richard McKane said that if he ever did write on torture, it would be a linguistically based study. He has accumulated enough examples of oaths and curses used in torture in Russia and Turkey to think that they can be almost as torturing as blows on the soles of the feet.

In an essay on the effects of torture on women and children, Gill Hinshelwood has unpacked the syntax of the torturer: 'The lesson is always "Our regime is absolutely powerful, and can do anything to anyone. You are absolutely powerless and can do nothing to save yourselves and your family." These are two unreal, mad and primitive statements, and there is no place for them in civilised, adult living. They are, none the less, a description of the prevailing culture in oppressive dictatorial regimes.'

In tolerant democracies, we play more sophisticated language games. Richard McKane spoke at a conference attended by British Home Office officials, and mentioned a Turkish man who had burned himself to death under threat of deportation. McKane thought he was describing a real event, which had affected him enough to write a poem about it. A Home Office civil servant was on his feet immediately to object to the word 'suicide', as 'the matter was sub judice'. Later that day McKane offered the opinion that Kurdish prisoners were 'systematically tortured' in areas of South-East Turkey. A second official intervened asking the chairman of the conference for a comment – as though asking for a ruling, an adjudication that would quash it – on the word 'systematically'.

*   *   *

In everything related to torture, words are an urgent matter. ' "The question is," said Alice, "whether you *can* make words mean so many different things." "The question is," said Humpty Dumpty, "which is to be master – that's all." '

Torture in the ancient world, and again in Europe from the twelfth until the eighteenth century, was 'the queen of proofs' because words were not reliable without pain. Slaves and suspects were 'put to the question'. It was a question of evidence: only true confession could accurately describe certain events. Truth had to be in the first person of the past definite: I saw this; I did that. From the middle of the seventeenth century onwards, however, torture's relationship with truth was itself put to the question. Strong bodies might resist torture; the owners of weak bodies would admit to anything in order to stop it. Hobbes noted curtly that 'Accusations upon Torture are not to be reputed as Testimonies.' New ideas about rights were based on the notion of bodily integrity; new scruples arose about the violation of the body except in extreme circumstances. Notions of truth were more and more based on probability, on reasonable proof and reasonable doubt. This new kind of proof rested on an acceptance that 'disinterested truth' was possible, and on trust among those committed to the same rational standards. Cesare Beccaria, the Enlightenment's most influential thinker on justice, imagined a world in which inquiry and punishment would not 'make pain the crucible of truth.' In such a world – which is still, ideally, our own – torture tears up the compact of trust and replaces it with pure power.

Yet when someone comes to the border of a democratic state and requests asylum, claiming to be grievously hurt, there is now often a regression to pre-modern ideas of justice and proof. All states control immigration, but the notion of asylum as a place of refuge has been more or less honoured throughout the twentieth century in the democratic West. The limitations of asylum were seen when a whole population was threatened in pre-war Central Europe: the doors then opened a mere crack; but after 1945, refugees from oppression in the Soviet bloc, from Arab and African dictatorships, and from military regimes in Latin America, were accepted more or less willingly in countries like Britain, Germany and the USA. Since 1989, especially in Europe, the doors have been closing again. We have elaborate methods for excluding 'bogus refugees', and restricting the rights of applicants. Asylum is no longer a human right, but an immigration problem: the word is shifting its meaning.

Ripples from civil war barely touch wealthy countries like Britain: the vast majority of refugees go to neighbouring countries and return home as soon as they can. The numbers applying for asylum are relatively small (roughly 30,000 a year, or 0.05 per cent of the population, in the case of Britain) and can be mapped exactly onto zones of civil war. Prior to 1988, for example, the former Yugoslavia produced 9 asylum-seekers to the UK; by 1992, over 5000 Bosnians, Croatians and Serbs were applying each year. Algerians, before the cancellation of elections and the declaration of a state of emergency in their country in 1992, showed no desire to invade Britain: twenty applied for asylum in 1990, but nearly 2000 were seeking to escape a ferocious conflict by 1995. The same pattern can be detected for country after country. Asylum-seekers are not, on the whole, economic migrants in disguise.

There is nonetheless a stubbornly inventive 'culture of disbelief' among the state's doormen. Amnesty International called it a 'tendency to summarily dismiss asylum-seekers' claims as "unfounded" or "exaggerated".' The reduction in the number of successful applications that this attitude brought about was, in turn, advanced as 'proof' that most asylum claims are bogus. In Britain, a contentious 'white list' of countries certified free of human rights abuses was drawn up in 1996, while welfare benefits were abolished for anyone not claiming asylum immediately upon arrival at a British port. Those who arrived from a third country – say, via France from Algeria – could be expelled without right of appeal. These regulations breached the UN Convention on Refugees, which is meant to guarantee protection to escapees from disaster and assumes that each country has fair procedures for hearing their claims.

A critical debate has been going on for years now, as the world order changed and language with it, between the Medical Foundation and the

British Home Office. It is civilized and courteous, at times almost academic in tone, though detachment can be sustained only with great self-control on one side of the argument. The texts are the bodies of alleged torture victims. The Foundation writes around 500 medical reports a year for asylum-seekers, and the debate is about norms of evidence and proof.

Scars can be read in different ways. At the Foundation, the medical examination and the background checking of each story are designed to eliminate the liar and the fantasist. If the verbal account is consistent with the marks on the body, or injury deeper in its tissues, then there is a high probability that the person is telling the truth. However, the doctors are always aware that a pattern of wounds confined, say, to the left arm and shoulder could have been inflicted on himself by a right-handed man, and a suspicious pattern of this kind would undermine an account of persecution. Nor can any doctor ever swear that torture is the *only* possible cause of the bodily signs they read. Even James Mubiru's scars might have been caused by a freak domestic accident, and in the mid-1980s the Home Office tried to suggest that they were; but his familiarity with Obote's jails, and Betty Gordon's skilled reconstruction of the way his burns were caused, made any alternative explanation to torture highly improbable. Most forms of knowledge in the modern world are like that: open to challenge, and based on an accumulation of probabilities that make other stories less realistic. The fossil record supports the theory of evolution, though we have never seen trilobites crawl on the sea-floor.

This kind of truth is not enough for the state in a world no longer divided neatly between great power blocs. In December 1995, a man from Northern Cyprus – the Turkish statelet established after the invasion and partition of the island in 1975 – was examined by a doctor at the Foundation. He – let's say his name was Mehmet – was a Turkish political journalist advocating a federal solution to the Cyprus problem, a sharing of power between Turks and Greeks. It is well known that the rulers of Northern Cyprus are determined to hold onto their exclusively Turkish entity. Mehmet had applied for asylum in Britain once before, and had been sent back. We cannot know precisely what happened at Larnaca on his arrival, but the evidence suggests a display of frenzied political rage. When Mehmet removed his shirt, the doctor found more than 170 burn-scars on his back. In the black and white photographs his torso looks like a big spotted cat sitting on a chair. A consultant dermatologist who examined him wrote: 'There was a central, thin, atrophic and puckered centre with a narrow, hyperpigmented zone at the periphery of each scar.' In other words, she thought that he had had a heated metal bar, tapered at the end – something like a red-hot poker – applied to his back over and over again. This was consistent with Mehmet's story. She reported that he described a 'sweet burned smell of "roasting flesh, like a barbecue"'.

In January 1996 the Home Office refused his request for asylum. An official informed him that 'in fact, these wounds were inflicted at your request in an attempt to strengthen your asylum claim... [they are] a cynical attempt to circumvent normal United Kingdom immigration rules.' The doctor who had first examined the man's injuries thought about this construction of the evidence: it wouldn't be the first time someone had themselves hurt to escape a dangerous situation. Soldiers in Vietnam shot high-velocity bullets into their feet. However, on the basis of what he knew about resistance to pain, the doctor concluded that 'though a tough and determined man might agree to having half a dozen [burns], his resolve would disappear soon after and never allow anything like a hundred and seventy to be incurred. It also seems that such a number is quite unnecessary and must be the action of torture by a violent and sadistic operator. Five or more burns would seem ample backing for a claim for admission.' The large bruises on the right side of the man's back further weakened the civil service theory, since they were, in the examiner's eyes, 'consistent with forcible restraint'.

The Home Office still refused to believe Mehmet's story, and turned him down a second time. But now their reading of the evidence shifted to its context. The UN Convention on Refugees is supposed to ensure that no person is sent back to a country in which he or she has a 'well-founded fear' of being persecuted. Here there is ample scope for deconstruction of medical evidence by a hostile critic relying on optimistic assessments of human rights in a given country. In the case of Mehmet, the state insisted that even if he had been tortured, it could not have taken place in Northern Cyprus because 'there is no evidence to suggest that there is any state-sanctioned persecution of individuals there ... Accordingly, we are not satisfied that the authorities in Northern

Cyprus would knowingly tolerate or condone such abuses by the police.'
When does a disfigured body *become* evidence? It can be made to mean so
many different things. It took two years for Britain to relent. In January
1998 the man was allowed to stay 'on humanitarian grounds'. There is,
of course, still 'no torture' in Northern Cyprus.

It would be easy to multiply examples of this kind. An Algerian,
'Peter', working as a merchant sailor, had a dozen scars that matched his
story of torture by the Algerian police during his country's murky,
furious civil war. But one burn-scar, on his arm, *could* have been caused,
according to the officials, by leaning against a hot pipe running from a
boiler on his ship, and this falsified all the other scars. Michael Peel, who
examined him, was able to show that Peter's other wounds, and his
general physical and psychological condition – he also had the familiar
signs of post-traumatic stress, and had been raped – was more consistent
with torture than the hazards of the engine-room. Nonetheless, the state
wanted to throw him out. The immigration officials backed down when
John Sweeney of the *Observer* made 'Peter's' dilemma the centrepiece of
a major article on 25 June 1997; but only so many refugees can be
chosen to embarrass the Home Secretary over his Sunday breakfast.
Eighty-six per cent of all Algerian refugees were refused asylum in 1997.

The state is now demanding of asylum-seekers a level of proof unknown
in other areas of the law, higher than the British courts themselves have set
for asylum cases. It pretends to crave certainty. The formal legal position
is that asylum claims should be supported by evidence that establishes a
'reasonable degree of likelihood' that the person has been mistreated, and
that they would be in further danger if they returned to their own country.
In asylum case law a greater than even chance of the truth of a claim
should clinch it. The Home Office instead demands the kind of proof once
furnished only by torture. A medical report is discarded because it doesn't
provide absolutely irrefutable evidence, which would be available only if
we could witness the infliction of the wounds.

Antonia Hunt was told that as a young child in autumn 1938, in a cold
French village, after her family's flight from Vienna, she said to her
mother, 'Even the dogs don't want us here.' Like Helen Bamber, she now
despairs over the heartless serenity of the democracies; the 1930s are
closer to her than they have been for decades. The whittling away of the
right of asylum threatens the Foundation's work in obvious ways. But it

goes deeper than that, for Bamber and those like her who remember the world before the Cold War. The effective end of asylum would mean a closing of the mind to the fact that the world contains torture: the victory of an indifference that seemed to become morally unacceptable in 1945. So although it is not a refugee organization, the Foundation could not help being drawn into attempts to keep the gates ajar, and has campaigned against the increasingly harsh treatment of asylum seekers, by Conservative and Labour governments alike. John Rundle spelled out what they felt was at stake. 'People who have been tortured often don't have enough to attract them back into life. Their sense of themselves really hits the deck when a hostile democracy also tells them they are lying.'

*   *   *

The Foundation works publicly against the existence of torture. It is a campaigning human rights organization. Any lesser commitment would, in the eyes of its members, turn their efforts into an after-care service for the tortured, a position that they would find morally untenable. Perico Rodriguez, the Argentinean survivor who works at the Foundation, has an acute sense of how certain ideas – like that of the 'national security state' and its variants – invite torture to happen. He insists that torture is not a 'syndrome', but a strategy, and is repelled by the thought that he might be part of 'an industrial system of production in which somebody is torturing at one end, and we are curing at the other end'.

The Foundation produces well-written, well-designed literature that talks about rehabilitation and hope, but it also denounces the export of electric-shock batons, restraints, generators and weapons to governments that torture, and campaigns vigorously for the right of asylum. Far from being fixated on pity and cruelty, Bamber and her colleagues are looking elsewhere, for reasons and solutions. Her own attitude is un-Christian: she is not interested in revering the suffering man, but in who has done what to him and how he got there, and how he can be helped.

Late one night in Berwick, after a day with the ex-fusiliers and after some talk of 'reconciliation' with Japan, she said with considerable measured vehemence, 'I don't know what reconciliation means; forgiveness can only be given if someone actually asks for it. It makes me angry. People talk of "peace and reconciliation" constantly, because it is almost the only way to get money to do work on human rights, but how can you talk of reconciliation in Guatemala, where massacres have been carried out quite consciously by the state for decades? Who can be reconciled to that, even with peace?'

She went on: 'You have to place torture in a proper context. Otherwise, you are not actually honouring the people who have suffered, you are merely looking at a body that has been assaulted or mutilated. If a doctor looks at a disease she wants to look at the causes of the disease. Once you begin to look for them it's not a pretty picture, because it isn't only about sadistic impulses. It's about power, about privilege, about poverty and the distribution of resources; it's about something which is *most preventable*. I get very tired of people looking at it only as some horrible phenomenon, without actually saying this is a preventable thing.

'What I find difficult, and always have done, is how easily we become bystanders. A whole structure of power, even in those states that don't themselves torture, seems to find it necessary to support, or at least not confront, torture states. Rather than put their foot down and say we do not trade, we do not supply, on the contrary, they say we will supply, and then talk about jobs for the boys. I'm putting it in very simplistic terms, but the remedies are available, and they are not used. The legal instruments are there to prevent torture. And states could apply practical pressure, yet nothing is really done by powerful states to stop it.'

The instruments *are* there. The United Nations Convention Against Torture and Other Cruel, Inhuman or Degrading Treatment or Punishment was passed by the General Assembly in 1984. It builds on Article 5 of the Universal Declaration of Human Rights of 1948, which 'declares' against 'torture [and] cruel, inhuman, or degrading treatment or punishment'. It draws on the European Convention on Human Rights of 1950, and other UN resolutions, such as the International Covenant on Civil and Political Rights of 1966, which also ban torture. The 1984 Convention is beautifully detailed and comprehensive. Article 2 states that 'no exceptional circumstances whatsoever, whether a state of war or a threat of war, internal political instability or any other public emergency, may be invoked as a justification of torture.' It denies torturers a safe haven anywhere by placing an obligation on states to arrest them and extradite them, and even to try non-nationals for the offence where extradition is impossible. The UN set up a 'Committee against Torture', which meets in Geneva and reviews evidence of torture, and reports on states violating the Convention. Bamber is a regular attender and adviser to the UN Voluntary Fund for the Victims of Torture, which in turn subsidizes the Medical Foundation. She would appear to be pushing at an open door, yet torture doesn't stop. According to the UN's figures, sixty countries condone or permit torture; a rough calculation suggests that more people live under governments that torture than under regimes that forbid it.

The Foundation may not hold up the suffering body as an icon, but it does use testimony as a form of witness against torture. When it works, the Foundation is a safe place for memories that cannot be recounted elsewhere. One of the therapists at the Foundation uses fables, allegories of power and oppression, to start indirect discussions among a group of survivors. Some clients are encouraged to write their own narratives and discuss them with others. 'It is the only place I have been listened to,' said a Turkish torture survivor, who did not wish to be named. The 'unconditional positive respect' – Erol Yesilyurt's definition of Bamber's attitude – which they try to give everyone they see makes it easier to shape the past. John Schlapobersky believes in 'the redeeming power of narrative itself'. At the Foundation, victims seem to learn two great lessons: that their story matters to someone else, first of all; and also that it is not unusual. Torture has had similar effects on others, and the torturer in their minds is diminished by this knowledge. The standard language would have it that therapy 'empowers' victims, but people who have been tortured seem to know too much about power to use this rhetoric much. They can learn how to live with themselves.

The political effect of their memories is like a signal of alarm. The stories told at the Foundation become a way of re-imagining power. Torture is an attempt to impose silence by forcing speech, and leaves fear embodied in its victims, like frightened animals, easy to startle and hurt. Elaine Scarry writes that in torture 'the prisoner [becomes] a colossal body with no voice and the torturer a colossal voice ... with no body'. Whatever story they had has been degraded: if they had information to give, it becomes a sign of guilt and shame; if they had none, their pain is often incomprehensible to themselves. In a small way, as Scarry points out, the ability to speak reverses the torturer's narrative, which, like pornography, knows only one dull, repetitive kind of ending. By helping the tortured find their voices, Bamber offers the false, necessary promise that their stories will not be meaningless. They are used in the public work of the Foundation; some of these stories have been told in this book. The actress Billie Whitelaw reads the testimonies of survivors at fundraising gatherings, and when she does she remembers Beckett's warning when he directed her: 'Too much colour. Don't act.' She tries, she says, to be 'the mouthpiece: it's the best thing, the only thing I can do.' They hope to challenge the unwritten rules that let us live with torture.

They may seem to be utopian stories, since the response they seek implies the possibility of a world without torture. This has been a persistent dream since the time of the Enlightenment, since Voltaire, Montesquieu and Beccaria, whose writings are often imagined to have led to the abolition of judicial torture in one country after another during the late eighteenth and early nineteenth centuries. Victor Hugo declared in 1874: 'Torture has ceased to exist.' On the eve of the First World War, and the thirty years of dictatorship and genocide of which it was the first episode, the *Encyclopaedia Britannica* could assert sublimely that 'the whole subject [of torture] is now one of only historical interest, as far as Europe is concerned.' Torture returned, with a vengeance. The revulsion against it was real enough, in the late eighteenth century; but historians argue that what stopped it for a time, in Europe at least, was a massive transformation in the organization of the state, and of crime and punishment. In a society founded on markets and rights, jails and police forces were more efficient, and incidentally more humane, ways of keeping order than chastisement of the body.

Moral witness, then, is never enough. Serious enforcement of international law would go a long way to eliminating torture. But relying on legal instruments is itself insufficient. Attention to the results of torture – the effects on other human beings – is a powerful reminder of the cost of regressing to a situation where excuses for torture seem plausible. Edward Peters in his fine book on the subject writes that it is necessary 'to preserve the reason for making [torture] illegal and dangerous – to preserve a notion of human dignity that, although not always meticulously observed, is generally assumed in the public language, if not the unpublic actions, of most modern societies, and assumed, moreover, in a generally universal and democratic sense'. The existence of the

Foundation, like the work of its Danish counterpart and equivalent organizations in other countries, and the larger work of Amnesty International, is a small contribution to that notion of being human.

The vision of a world that does not include torture is essential, and possible; the fantasy of the melancholic healer who imagines that he is saving the world, finding the bomb, curing the plague, is what we have to fear. No one has ever expressed the torturer's vision better than Joseph de Maistre, the lamenter of despotism, in his praise of the hangman, whom he called 'that inexplicable being'. 'All grandeur, all power, all subordination rests on the executioner: he is the horror and the bond of human association. Remove this incomprehensible agent from the world, and at that very moment order gives way to chaos, thrones topple, and society disappears.'

*   *   *

In June 1993, Helen Bamber went to Israel and testified on behalf of a Palestinian prisoner. She said that this was the hardest decision she had ever taken in her life.

Helen Bamber first met Eyad El-Sarraj, a psychiatrist from Gaza, in 1987. He was then studying at Oxford, and came to see her at the Foundation to discuss the kind of work he thought needed to be done in Gaza. Later they went together to a meeting of YAKAR, a congregation of liberal Jews in London, where he had been invited to speak. She remembered him saying, 'I can't help where I was born. I happen to have been born a Palestinian in Gaza.' He described what it felt like to be in that situation, the choices it forced upon him and the limitations it imposed. He talked about a resort town on the Mediterranean which had become a refugee slum, and how lucky he had been that his father – a high official in the judiciary under the British – had a second home in Gaza when he was advised by his colleagues in 1948 to stay away 'for a couple of weeks until the difficulties are over'. That house had been his family's home for forty years, by the time he met Bamber. He spoke about the absence of sanitation, about children dying from gastro-enteritis and viral meningitis, and about the settlers drawing off water from the Gaza River – how there is more and more salt in the water from the wells, and the bad effect this has on people's kidneys. But his main subject was the torture of Palestinian prisoners by the Israeli security forces. The Intifada was in full swing, with riots, strikes and marches, and thousands of prisoners had been taken. He described beatings, hoodings, dunkings, freezings, loud noise and painful postures: the litany had already become routine.

Bamber, with the Foundation barely a year old, was already well enough known to be asked to introduce El-Sarraj at the London meeting. It cost her some effort to stand in front of a Jewish audience and agree that, from all the evidence she had heard, the Jewish state was also now a torturing state, and that they must face that fact and call on the government to find some other way of dealing with the thousands of young stone-throwers on its hands.

Afterwards a man came up to her and asked: 'With friends like you, who needs enemies?' For a woman with her memories, the cliché was wounding enough. She had seen 'displaced persons' escaping to Palestine from Germany, and knew what they were escaping from. The case for Israel had always been irrefutable, for her; partly because she had shared the dream of restoring the past, and partly because the rest of the world had left no room for any other answer.

But hers was a complicated loyalty. She had never, she believed, been able to share fully in the rhetoric of destiny that uncritical solidarity with the new state demanded. It was difficult for her to accept the story of homecoming to a virgin land. The tone of official history had begun to act like an abrasive on her, especially after the 1967 war and the seizure of the West Bank. For her the situation of Israel, made inescapable by the Holocaust, had a tragic quality, in the exact sense of cruelty and injustice unleashing further injustice, a chain of consequences that could never be understood as a simple fulfilment of the nation's inalienable right to a state. When she listened to Israeli spokesmen she said she often thought about 'blindness and danger', and the 'perpetuation of violence by those who have suffered from it'. The iconic image of victory in 1967, when Israel struck pre-emptively at the Egyptians, Syrians and Jordanians and routed them all, was the face of Moshe Dayan, with his black eyepatch, the one-eyed hero gazing into the future.

By the 1980s, with the territories conquered in that famous victory desolate enclaves of conflict, she felt she was becoming a bystander herself while the Israeli state learned what it is to be an occupying power. In the implied historical accounting that equated the displaced

Palestinians with the immemorial enemies of the Jewish people, includ-ing the Nazis, lesser acts of violence could be carried out in good conscience.

Eyad El-Sarraj had remained a friend, and kept in close touch with Bamber. He was already working among the poor in Gaza. At a confer-ence of the International Society for Health and Human Rights in Costa Rica in 1990, he heard her talk about bringing psychological and therapeutic knowledge to bear on a community, of moving in more adept ways than the conventional clinic allows. This was in tune with her insistence that what violence does to people can't be treated simply as an illness, although it can make them sick.

He said later that her influence had been crucial in changing his direction and that his creation, the Gaza Community Mental Health Programme, owed a lot to her and to others at that conference. Until then, he had been planning a purely psychiatric clinic, but since it was hard to find many families in Gaza that had not suffered 'traumatic' incidents (violent death, imprisonment, maiming, torture) he inevitably became involved with rehabilitation.

Bamber's court appearance in 1993 had its origins in an invitation from the Israeli and Palestinian Physicians for Human Rights to speak at a conference on torture, a scandalous event in itself and one for which it had been difficult to find a venue. A lawyer preparing a case in Hebron heard that she was coming, and sent a message asking her to appear as an expert witness for his client.

Bamber started work on the case in the study of Eyad El-Sarraj's house in Gaza city, her feet barely touching the floor as she sat at his large desk. She read the literature on sensory deprivation faxed to her from the Foundation in London, but it became clear that she would also need to read everything the Israeli lawyers had been able to find and it was too difficult to get the papers into Gaza. She was driven up to Tel Aviv and worked for three days in a flat on the northern outskirts, near the Ministry of Defence complex. A giant communications tower, prickly with satellite dishes, towers over the neighbourhood.

She read and took notes, she remembered, in suffocating heat, at a table piled with depositions and copies of witness statements. An old fan barely moved the air, and she was drenched in perspiration. Bamber was rigid with tension and, she says, fear, hoping that she wouldn't be allowed to testify. There was an atmosphere of emergency and menace even among her friends – fraying tempers, loud voices, bad weather.

The accused, Mahmood Adawi, had confessed to driving his taxi for two men who later attacked an Israeli bus. There were no casualties, but the prosecutor was demanding at least seven years for the driver. Among the papers were records of the General Security Service (otherwise known as Shabak or Shin Bet) interrogation of the prisoner, which had been secured by the man's lawyer, Shlomo Lecker. Some 95 per cent of all cases before Israeli military courts during the uprising were resolved by tabling a confession; any legal argument was about the appropriate sentence. Lecker had decided to oppose the admissibility of his client's confession, which the man had retracted, and the nineteen security service documents made interesting reading, for someone who knew how to read their silences. Bamber noticed that there were periods when neither the accused nor his interrogators were recorded as saying anything.

These times were described as 'Waiting'. There was no great mystery about them. During these lengthy periods Adawi would have been hooded in a thick black sack, smelling, in his case, of sweat and puke, with his hands tied behind him while he crouched on a kindergarten chair. He would be left like that, 'waiting' for two days (other periods were described as 'resting'). He would not have been allowed to sleep during that time. His condition in the waiting room was not described in the GSS protocols, but he gave a vivid account to his lawyer; and no one made any attempt to dispute the use of these 'techniques', because they were not illegal. The question Lecker wished to ask was whether the techniques induced people to sign confessions that they knew to be untrue.

While she was in the Tel Aviv flat, Bamber had asked for a hood that resembled those used by the police, and had sat with it over her head for an hour in the hot room, with the fan switched off.

She hoped not have to go to court, but in the end she was called. Shlomo Lecker had persuaded the military judge to agree that on this narrow legal question, her testimony was relevant. With two Israeli companions, Bamber travelled to Hebron, the Arab city with a salient of Orthodox Jewish settlers at its heart, near the burial place of Abraham, which is also revered by Muslims. The city, she said, was 'electric with tension'. The settlers then as now clustered around the centre of town, like militant priests with their skullcaps, machine pistols over their shoulders.

The old British barracks was then still the police headquarters, border patrol post, GSS centre and military court. She heard someone call it Fort Apache. The Israeli journalist Tom Segev, in his report on the case for the daily *Ha-aretz*, described it as 'a sombre concrete building with garbage and rusty scraps strewn around it'. Bamber was disturbed by the casual brutality of gesture and speech among the security men and police. She and her companions had to wait for half a day in the corridors of the dreary block before they were called. Outside the courthouse there was a smell of blocked latrines. When Bamber asked where she could get a drink she was shown a standpipe in the yard.

The court sat in a bare hall, with a table for the judge on one side, and smaller tables set in front of it. Chintzy floral curtains, which Bamber thinks were plastic, set off the brown gloss paint on the walls. The military judge was a young blonde woman, an Israeli Army reserve captain in full uniform, handsome and imposing. Behind her table the national flag and the emblem of the Israeli Defence Forces hung on the wall.

This was not a full trial, but a hearing, a 'mini-trial' to discuss the admissibility of the confessions before the proper trial could begin. According to Tom Segev, this formality was rare: 'Most detainees in the territories do not even get as far as the primitive process called "military trial". Their punishments are determined in plea bargains, based on confessions extracted from them.' The mini-trial was taking place only because Shlomo Lecker had decided to challenge the confession evidence.

When her time came to be heard by the judge, in a side room off the court, Bamber sat at a large table pressed up against the young prosecutor, an officer with a handgun on his belt. The prisoner was standing off to one side shackled by his wrists to his ankles. He seemed to have difficulty standing upright. He had inflicted cuts and bruises on himself, according to the GSS, while he was in detention.

Bamber leaned forward and spoke firmly and calmly, according to a witness who was present. She remembers feeling surrounded by young men and women in uniform, restless, vigorous and loud. She said she thought the prisoner had been tortured; the material she had read made that very probable, and the record of his injuries when he was examined by a doctor was consistent with this judgement. She added that the man's admissions were probably the pleadings of terror and exhaustion. She quoted the European Court of Human Rights ruling against Britain (the one about inhuman and degrading treatment of the 'hooded men' in 1972), the various internationally accepted definitions of torture, and the man's own testimony about the standing, the hooding, the child's chair tipped forward so that the back is forced to arch, the noise, the nights without sleep. From the GSS's own notes it was clear that he denied everything for a long time, and then on day seven confessed to being a member of Hamas and to spraying slogans on walls. And then they went on and on and on. At the end of the sixteenth day he confessed to driving the car for the two terrorists. Bamber asked, she recalled, when would this process stop? She suggested that after a little more pressure Adawi would have confessed to anything.

From the start the young prosecutor attempted to discredit her. Bamber felt she was under attack. He leaned into and over her, and to her he sounded loud and abrasive. You are not a doctor, yet you claim to be the head of this 'medical foundation'. What are your qualifications? He asked how she knew what was torture and what was not. What do you know about terrorist prisoners? 'His voice dinned at me, he was quite relentless; he attacked my status and integrity.'

When Bamber attempted to speak about the man's injuries they told her that she was not qualified to do so: she would only be heard on the validity of the confession evidence. They were leaving her nothing but anger. She told them about herself, about what she had seen before she was old enough to vote and what she had learned from Holocaust survivors, tried to explain why she did this work. It was a halting, inter-rupted speech, but they did hear her out.

The man had been hooded for most of a week, a heavy hood that he said smelled of vomit. Bamber had tried on a clean hood in the flat in Tel Aviv. She told the court it felt like suffocating in pitch dark. She tried to describe the sensation, speaking to the judge – the intense enclosure, the claustrophobia, the gagging, the panic after such a short time. The judge lost a little of her composure. The thought of this elderly woman with a black bag over her head seemed to disturb her and she missed a few beats in her conducting of what was meant to be a run-through of a familiar judicial scenario. But behind her Bamber was aware of soldiers laughing, sneering, of jokes about the old woman soft on Arabs. The sergeant who was in charge of order in the courtroom passed notes to a girl soldier.

Bamber said she finally made what she thought at first was a slip, saying, OK, if I'm not expert enough for you we do have real experts who can say if this man's statement was made under duress. The prosecutor immediately asked, she recalled, for the record to show that she had admitted she wasn't an expert. The story of her life: an ordinary woman without credentials daring to speak about what states do.

The hearing broke up, and most of the soldiers prepared to leave. Bamber was gathering up her papers when the young prosecutor came back and leaned over earnestly to say that he knew what she was trying to do and he understood it, but she should know that he was only doing his job here. Bamber said with great restraint – she was feeling very drained – that that was something she had heard in other places, that this was what was often said and that it was really sad to hear him say that.

The other guards and soldiers drifted out of the room and left Bamber sitting there alone with the judge, and suddenly she too came over, as friendly as though the barbed exchanges had never taken place, and began to tell Bamber about her aunt, who was a survivor of the camps. It was hard, she said, now that she was old, things were worse for her, she was in more pain, there was less to block out the past. Bamber said to the judge–captain that she was not surprised that her aunt was suffering, that brutality inflicted and witnessed had long-term effects. Bamber explained that was why she was there, and she said that what is being done now will have dreadful consequences for all of us. She said she hoped the beatings, the hoodings, the forced standing to attention and sleep deprivation would stop, because it was degrading the perpetrators too. She hoped this. The officer said: 'So do we.'

But in the conversations around the court, talk of international covenants, and of declarations against torture, was met with irritated suspicion – the outside world does not understand, and these people attacking us do not care a damn for human rights or conventions of civility.

Bamber's intervention had made this trial awkward, so the court accepted, in effect, her offer of another expert witness. She wanted Gisli Gudjonsson, the Icelandic ex-policeman who is a Reader in Psychology at London University, and the author of a standard work on the psychology of interrogation and false confessions. They agreed to postpone the hearing until the 'real expert' could come.

It wasn't easy to persuade him to travel a long way for a hopeless case.

Gudjonsson's fare and expenses for his research programme would have to be met, so Bamber raised the money, mainly from among British Jews. She had nothing more to contribute, so she stayed in London.

In court the judge was now much more polite, according to some who were present, almost ingratiating to the former policeman armed with his rigorous methodology of interrogation, his grasp of forensic technique and medical evidence. Gudjonsson testified for over two hours. The prisoner could not have gouged his cheek on a wall while preserving his nose unharmed, especially when he was handcuffed with a sack over his head. Confinement and physical distress – back pain from the child's chair, lack of sleep, exhaustion – had surely overborne his ability to give a voluntary confession. (When Gudjonsson interviewed the prisoner, the man had told him that he felt his brain had 'dried up and that his life was over'.) Based on the GSS's own records, Gudjonsson showed that the man had been kept awake for fifty-five hours, which allowed him to state that the second confession had without doubt been extracted under duress, against his free will, and was worthless. 'As if', Tom Segev remarked in *Ha-aretz*, 'there was anybody there who did not know what had made Adawi sign. It was quite grotesque.'

In the end a bargain was made, in this as in all other such cases; the serious charge was dropped, and seven years' imprisonment became one year, most of it already spent in detention. The prisoner would soon be free. The court made no ruling about the security service's behaviour. This was one of very few successful challenges to confession evidence in the tens of thousands of cases heard during the Intifada.

*   *   *

It was the law that allowed Mahmood Adawi to confess so unwillingly. A democracy can convince itself that it may not live without torture.

On 12 November 1996, the High Court of Israel heard an application from a lawyer acting for Muhammed Hamdan, who was allegedly a member of Islamic Jihad. His intentions may never be known: he may well have been a terrorist, or about to become one. He had been in custody since the middle of October, and his lawyer was asking for an injunction to stop the General Security Service from using force in their interrogation of his client.

The judges summed up their permission to continue with what they called 'the physical means', which they were careful to insist 'do not constitute torture', and which the law allowed under 'the defence of necessity': 'After having studied the classified material presented to us, we are satisfied that the Respondent [the GSS] indeed possesses information which could substantiate a substantiated suspicion that the Appellant possesses extremely vital information, the immediate procurement of which would prevent an awful disaster, would save human lives, and would prevent very serious terrorist attacks.'

The Public Committee Against Torture in Israel gave a useful translation of this sentence. The suspect might have 'some information which will, at some point, lead to revealing some plan to place a bomb at some time and in an unknown place'.

Israelis enjoy the rule of law, unlike all their neighbours. Free speech is uninhibited, allowing for military censorship. The language of the courts is derived from British common law. The citizen is genuinely defended by it from arbitrary state intervention. Judge's Rules govern the conduct of normal interrogations. If prisoners – Palestinian prisoners, and even real terrorists – fall into the hands of secret policemen, their chances of physical survival are far better in Israel than in Syria or Algeria, let alone Iraq. Grotesque and mutilating torture is unknown, and suspects rarely die in custody. Yet Israel is the only state in the world that has an explicit place for 'physical means' in its law code. The High Court hears appeals for restraint of the state's servants, considers submissions, quotes case law and balances the rights of the appellant with the threat to public safety represented by terrorist organizations. It reminds the secret police that it is not above the law. And out of the fog of earnest language emerges the fact of torture.

It is as though there are two legal systems, one for the events of peace (and for Israelis), and another system for the more or less permanent moment of war, in which there is a regression to medieval notions of evidence: only a confession can establish truth, and only torture can extract a true confession.

A retired judge called Moshe Landau wrote a report for the government in the summer of 1987, which authorized 'moderate means of physical pressure' on suspects. Justice Landau saw his task, after two scandals,* as the achievement of 'essential catharsis of the GSS from its failings' – purgation for men doing heroic work. The GSS had, notoriously, been lying in court about the methods it used. 'We hope', Landau wrote, 'that the GSS personnel will have restored to them ... the ability to distinguish between right and wrong, without needing the help of a legal expert at every step and turn.'

Landau insisted on the state's *reputation* for morality. He invoked its 'basic moral principles', those of 'a law-abiding state grounded in fundamental concepts of morality'; dwelt on the immorality of lying; on the 'moral fibre' of the GSS, and the 'moral defensibility' of the methods which it was using; but in the end his learned document is, despite itself, one of the frankest apologies for torture since Major Roger Trinquier's book rationalized the tactics of the paras in Algeria.

Even the structure of the argument, at certain points, echoed that of the French paratroop officer. Landau wrote that terrorist organizations which deprive citizens of the right to life 'have no moral right to demand that the State for its part maintain towards them the usual civil rights'. Suspects – people who *might* be supporters of these organizations – do not have such a moral right either.

Mordechai Kremnitzer, a legal professor at the Hebrew University, wrote a magnificent commentary on Landau's work. Landau, he noticed, believed that whatever human dignity can be accorded to terrorist suspects comes not from their rights as human beings – which is the working assumption of a democracy – but 'from the interest and duty of the State to maintain a certain moral standard'.

Landau drew on the legend of the ticking bomb: there is a bomb in a building, you have caught its maker, you must force him to tell you where it is. Would *you* torture him, to save lives? The scenario is, as always, written in a way that implies only one possible denouement. It is one of the most insidious and durable of post-war fantasies, irrepressible

---

*One of them was the discovery that a serving Israeli officer of Arab origin, Izzat Nafsu, had been tortured and threatened into admitting treason, for which he was serving eighteen years. The other was the Bus 300 affair, the exposure of a concerted attempt to cover up the killing of two Arab terrorists after they had been removed from a bus where they were holding hostages, and the subsequent attempt to frame an officer who threatened to get at the truth of the incident.

despite the almost complete failure of history to furnish a real case that might justify it.* The IRA, for example, put bombs in restaurants, pubs and bus-stations throughout Northern Ireland, killing hundreds of civilians; not once in the thirty years that that campaign lasted was a life saved by use of the third degree. Justice Landau would, presumably, have cited such a case from Israel's long experience of terrorism, had it existed, but he does not do so.

Landau wanted the unexploded bomb to justify the *defence of necessity* in order to give legal immunity to the GSS. In its British version, which he quoted, the defence exists for one 'who performs an act which he believes is immediately necessary, in order to prevent death or serious injury to himself or others, when the danger he believes exists is of such a nature that it would have been impossible to demand of him to act otherwise'. In other words, a person is allowed to break the most serious laws when they are in extreme danger: to hit the knifer with a car-jack; to run down the man pointing the gun.

Landau would have none of this restriction to clear and immediate danger. For him, the harm done by breaking the law during an interrogation 'must be weighed against the harm to the life or person of others which could occur sooner or later'. The idea of the lesser evil could then come into play. Which is it better to do, he asked, slap a suspect's face, or let him get away with not telling us about a cache of explosives meant for future use in mass terror? 'The answer', he wrote, 'is self-evident.'

Torture becomes pre-emptive self-defence. But once a licence is given to torture to stop 'evil which will occur sooner or later', the secret policeman is tempted to write his own moral code and broaden his field of activity. His job, after all, is to protect 'the very existence of society

---

*This writer has come across one notable exception, described by Alistair Horne in *A Savage War of Peace*. Maître Paul Teitgen, Secretary General at the Prefecture of Algiers, was responsible for over-seeing the police. In November 1956, Fernand Yveton, a communist supporter of the FLN, was caught planting a bomb near a gasometer. It seemed that there was a second bomb. If it exploded, it would have ignited the huge container of gas, a major disaster. The police wished to torture Yveton; Teitgen refused. He told Horne later: 'I trembled the whole afternoon. Finally the bomb did not go off. Thank God I was right. Because if you once get into the torture business, you're lost … All our so-called civilisation is covered with a varnish.' It may be relevant to note that Teitgen was tortured by the Gestapo and sent to Dachau for his work with the French Resistance.

and the State against terrorist acts'. Later in his report, as though illustrating a tendency of which he was unconscious, Landau began to enlarge the class of dangers to whose bearers 'physical pressure' might be applied: terrorist activity 'when it exists potentially', and suspected involvement 'in political subversion'. Since membership of or support for the PLO came under that heading, when Landau was writing, the majority of the population in the occupied territories seemed, by definition, to be excluded theoretically from the human right of bodily integrity.

Landau's view of the PLO was that it was a terrorist organization, root and branch. The objective of the PLO was the destruction of the state, which the GSS must thwart at all costs. He quoted from the PLO's covenant and from the political statement of the Palestine National Council in spring 1987, which called for 'armed struggle' above all other means (although the 1987 resolution was already adding 'and political struggle' to the formula). This was one of the traps concealed in Arafat's empty guerrilla rhetoric, and his call for the restoration of the whole of Palestine: that addiction to the maximum demand that ensures changes for the worse.

'A moderate measure of physical pressure'. Landau insisted that 'the pressure must never reach the level of physical torture or maltreatment of the subject or grievous harm to his honour which deprives him of his human dignity'. Mordechai Kremnitzer commented that 'what may be moderate as compared to other methods of torture is not moderate unto itself'. Landau's 'guidelines for GSS interrogators' – his manual of moderate methods – were reserved for the second, secret part of his report, which has never been made public.

One of his recommendations was certainly – given its near-universal use in Israeli jails since the late 1980s – a form of vigorous shaking, known as *tiltul* in Hebrew. Hamdan, the terrorist suspect, was given this treatment. A large, strong man holds the prisoner by the lapels and shakes him like a cushion, as though he were trying to shake the dust out of it. It has innocuous connotations: giving a child 'a good shaking', 'shaking yourself up', 'shaking him out of it'; but it has more in common with domestic child abuse, or 'shaken infant syndrome', a frequent cause of damage to babies' brains. Occasionally a prisoner dies from this treatment. Dr Derrick Pounder of Dundee University examined one such

body in April 1995 and found that death was 'the result of brain damage
due to rotational acceleration of the head', or 'forceful jerking movements of the head'. There is a video of a volunteer being 'shaken', to see
what it feels like, at Amnesty International's London office. The guinea
pig, very distressed, cries out for it to be stopped after a few minutes. It
is so simple and apparently harmless. Dr Pounder thought it an example
of 'regressive creativity'.

Landau had the impossible moral and legal task of reconciling the
violence of an occupying army with the honourable traditions of its courts;
of balancing the threat from suicide terrorists with a belief in human
dignity. His attempt at equilibrium resulted in methods that any reasonable
human being subjected to them would call torture. The intelligence
agents, meanwhile, presented themselves as unsung workers in the dark,
the state's night-soil removers. Landau quoted one of them as saying: 'We
are talking about "the cleaning of the sewers" the existence of which
endangers state security, and this unpleasant mission has been imposed
upon us. One cannot clean sewers without dirtying oneself.' The echoes of
so many earlier workers in political hygiene were lost on the judge, who
seems from the tone of his report a decent, well-meaning man.

In one of Kafka's greatest stories, an officer is weary of having to
explain the harsh realities of his work, the things he has to do so that
others can sleep easy in their beds. The explorer who has come to
inspect the penal colony asks if the prisoner, who is about to be executed
by a machine that will cut the text of the law that he has broken into his
flesh, knows the sentence that has been passed on him.

> 'No,' said the officer again, as if demanding further justification of his
> question from the explorer. 'It would be useless to announce it to him,' he
> said, 'he'll learn it anyway, on his own body.' ... 'Well then,' said the
> explorer, passing his hand over his forehead, 'so this man still does not
> know how his defence was undertaken?' 'He had no opportunity of defend-
> ing himself,' said the officer, and looked to one side, as if he were talking to
> himself and did not want to embarrass the explorer by telling these things
> which seemed to him self-evident....

A CIA interrogation manual from the mid-1960s admitted that
'regression' in the psychic sense is the aim of interrogation; the anony-

mous author wrote that it was necessary to 'obliterate the familiar and replace it with the weird'. He called it 'the Alice in Wonderland or confusion technique', and the object was 'to confound the expectations and conditioned reactions of the interrogatee. He is accustomed to a world that makes some sense, at least to him: a world of continuity and logic, a predictable world.'

Torture under the law is difficult to understand because of the responsibility to Israel felt by every European with a conscience and a sense of history. A language of morality and respect for human dignity empties itself of meaning, when fear and emergency overwhelm it; a judicial logic that permits torture seems both familiar and a stranger to itself, weird and predictable.

Methods of this kind are not unique to Israel; they are mild, as torture goes. Similar techniques were used in Northern Ireland twenty-five years ago. Nor can it be true that in Israel the guilty are never tortured. Perhaps the Israeli state is simply being honest. Yet in the controversy over the legalization of torture, Mordechai Kremnitzer's judgement catches the horror of *modern* law sanctioning physical cruelty: 'The law, which generally grants protection, permits the suspect's injury, obligates him to suffer it (as he may not resist) and thus renders him legally helpless. More significant than the actual physical blow and suffering themselves – which should not be taken lightly – is the knowledge that the "taboo" has been lifted from one's body, that "one has given one's back to the smiters" [Isaiah 50:6], that the legal barrier which protects one's most valuable assets – one's body and one's liberty – has been lifted. The law itself, intended for one's protection, has turned its back and dealt one a blow.'

*　　*　　*

In the summer of 1997, Bamber returned to meet human rights and rehabilitation organizations in Israel and in what had become the territory of the Palestinian Authority. She was concerned about the situation in Gaza and the West Bank, where the abuse of prisoners by Arafat's numerous police forces was already scandalous. Eighteen prisoners had died in custody since Oslo. One of those arrested, beaten and imprisoned was Dr Eyad El-Sarraj.

It was a tense, difficult visit. Travel between Israel and Gaza was not encouraged. After the Hamas suicide bombs in early 1996, the strip was more or less closed to the outside world. In May 1996, after the assassination of Yitzhak Rabin, Binyamin Netanyahu was elected Prime Minister of Israel. By July 1997, the ban on movement and on day-labourers coming in and out to work in Israeli factories and farms was being lifted, slowly. The peace talks were stalled; the Oslo agreement was an empty declaration. Everywhere, but especially in the divided city of Jerusalem, the keen, thin air of menace enfeebled thought, coarsened argument: the politics of the narrow ground. Waiting for the next atrocity, the next step backwards. A secular, liberal Russian-Jewish woman wanted the Palestinians to have their own state so that all contact between Arab and Jew could be brought to an end: 'their civilization is based on an obsession with death,' she said, and a Palestinian in Jerusalem echoed her, talking hysterically about self-sacrifice, 'because we have nothing left, we are not afraid to die'.

Erez checkpoint at the northern edge of the Gaza Strip was a vast empty stretch of tarmac, completely still in the burning sunlight. It had the air of a port abandoned after a disaster, with vacant spaces for cars and lorries, holding-lanes and inspection sheds. Nothing moved. Even the Israeli military post, a jumble of wire and canvas, looked forgotten. It felt less like a border than the edge of a different world.

We walked across the wide, bare lot between the Israeli and Palestinian guard-posts. Helen Bamber walked purposefully on her short fat legs under the overhead glare, carrying two bags. She looked all her seventy-odd years, but was determined to press on after the two-hour wait at the guard-post. She would keep going for days, while encouraging her younger companions to rest.

On the fine sand dunes near the entrance to the strip, there were huts made of corrugated iron, packing cases, plastic sheeting, bin liners, concrete blocks, car tyres. The more stable settlements were rough breeze-block houses, packed together in narrow alleyways. The dirt and the dreariness of endless waiting permeated the atmosphere.

Later that day a woman sat in her worn office at the small hotel where Bamber stays, and wondered whether she would ever be able to leave Gaza and feel normal, be sure of her right to go and come back without indignity. The hotel is her family house.

She was extremely tired, and like everyone else she was depressed. 'At times like this it is best not to read newspapers or watch the television, except to look at the tennis or old movies.' Her cigarette lifted in a tiny gesture. 'Three years ago after Oslo we had such a dream, and now here we are: imprisoned in Gaza.' She spoke as though she were living half a life, the rest of it lost in some other possible existence she had given up hope of ever finding.

Gaza City was in a trance. All over the city were unfinished multi-storey buildings, twisted iron and wire hanging in the open shelves of their floor spaces. Work had stopped at the point where the raw concrete might have been given signs of life – plumbing, wiring, heating, lighting, all the stuff that makes a building human. These were the hotels and office blocks imagined after 'Oslo'. Gaza had been cut off from the world ever since.

Every Palestinian tells you: no one will complete what they have started; the ministers don't work, twenty-six of them struck by the same spell of indecision, few of them working even within the meagre resources they have.

Not everything has come to a halt. South towards Khan Yunis, the second largest town after Gaza City, cars pass five checkpoints in as many miles. The coastal road skirts a mansion on a high dune overlooking the Mediterranean. A private road corkscrews back towards the house, which resembles the villas that Lebanese warlords build for themselves up the coast, but under the overhang of the road a double bank of oil drums is braced against the dune. Their function is to keep the hill from sliding into the ocean, and with it the house of the Gaza commander of Preventative Security, Arafat's secret police.

Sitting on a couch in his father's house in Gaza City, Eyad El-Sarraj said that Arafat refused to forbid torture, because to do so would be to admit that it existed. (Whereas the Israelis admit it exists, but refuse to call it torture. Torture is always somewhere else.) He is a man who relaxes well, perhaps because he is never at rest, his cellular phone ringing twenty times in the course of an evening while he talks about rehabilitation and public health and the disasters of Arafat's government. It was as though he were conserving energy for some really serious crisis; as though nothing in the situation that summer, after Rabin's murder and Netanyahu's election, with Gaza practically shut off, the peace talks suspended, and new Jewish settlements in East Jerusalem, was particularly exciting.

Imaginative applications of medicine had only deepened his interest in human rights. His high public profile as a doctor made him a candidate for the post of Palestinian Independent Citizens' Rights Commissioner in the state that seemed to be coming into being after the agreement between Rabin and Arafat in Oslo. El-Sarraj was elected by the independent Commission that was supposed to safeguard basic liberties in the new state. For Arafat, he was a catch: a famous psychiatrist, internationally respected, and widely admired for his work with prisoners and families during the Intifada; and he had the additional advantage of being from an old Gaza family of notables. He must have seemed very reliable.

'Abu Ammar', as Arafat is called by many Palestinians ('Father of Ammar' – his *nom-de-guerre* from the early days of Fatah), had made yet another misjudgement; El-Sarraj took the job seriously. He attacked the behaviour of the police forces and security branches. He called torture by its proper name. He denounced arbitrary arrests. He spoke to the foreign press. Soon he began to get phone calls from high officials, former liberation fighters who were baffled by his pickiness over a few troublemakers getting roughed up. Their Hamas rivals were, after all, waging a war, and the Israelis were using it as an excuse to stall negotiations and concessions. Eyad El-Sarraj was meant to be part of the new power, not a critic of it. 'Fuck your human rights, I will kill you if you keep this up' was the closing comment of one telephone call from an important minister.

'After the defeat in Lebanon in 1982, we had to do something for ourselves – we knew that no outside force could any longer help us. And there was an ecstatic sense of victory in the first year of the Intifada: people were no longer victims, forcing the Israelis to take them seriously for the first time in their lives. In the end, the rebellion was hijacked by the underground military groups, but the seeds of a real civil society were there. This was a totally different culture to that of Arafat and his people. They were used to the Arab dictatorships, to their exile world in Tunis. They don't understand this society. They were shocked by its outspokenness, its democracy. And they have turned out to be so incompetent, bad at being soldiers, bad at building roads, hopeless at providing hospitals.'

His immediate concern that afternoon was a professor from Al-Azhar

University in Gaza, a stronghold of nationalist politics, who had just been arrested for setting an examination question on corruption in the Palestinian Authority. Denounced by his dean, he had been arrested as an Israeli spy. When El-Sarraj had, privately and tactfully, requested to know what grounds existed for this accusation, he was told that the evidence was overwhelming, but so sensitive that no one could be allowed to see it. The real situation was more likely the exact reverse of this, but 'objectively' the man was working for the Israelis.

El-Sarraj said that his father – who had just become a great-grand-father – never raised his voice; he described him as a profoundly peaceful man. He thought it was his gardening that helped him stay so tranquil. Inside the walls of the house about an acre of ground is densely planted with vines, pomegranates, figs, apples, lemons, as well as flowers – jasmine, bougainvillaea, magnolia, rose. Its precious calm is separated by a wall from a dirty street in the Gaza Strip. El-Sarraj's grandfather, he said, had been a *hakim*, a traditional healer. He was establishing a lineage for himself, but it didn't sound forced: more a doctor's heritage than a politician's. He seemed to lack the obsessive anti-imperialism and relativism of the standard Arab left, and he spoke for a democratic politics that will have to fight its way between Arafat's 'Egyptian' boss-politics and the Hamas fundamentalists. His aim, he said, was 'peace with dignity'.

That night there was a party for the old man's new great-grandson in the garden. The extended family came together, tall young women in tight jeans and summer dresses who had travelled for the occasion from Canada, the Gulf and the USA. The patriarch of ten children and twenty-three grandchildren sat in his white djelabba, surrounded by his family. He raised his hand, saying, 'Welcome, welcome to Gaza.'

In the garden next morning, El-Sarraj described how, when he was pushed towards reconciliation with the President, he was brought to Arafat's villa. In the big reception room Abu Ammar was watching TV. The Israeli election returns were being counted, in the aftermath of Rabin's murder. Aides and guards sat all around the huge room in the house that everyone in Gaza still calls the Palace, from the time when it was the residence of the Egyptian Governor under Nasser. Men with holstered automatics lounged heavily on sofas. Arafat was expansive. 'Ah my friend, this is a great day for us, my friend Peres is going to win, rejoice.'

El-Sarraj was called over to a huge desk, away from the crowd in the room, so that there were only two close advisers within earshot, and sat shoulder to shoulder with the President like a passenger in a car. He was asked, come on, what do you really want, do something serious, give up this 'human rights' nonsense. Become a minister. He had replied that he did not like being a failure, and he knew he would be no good as a politician. 'I said I did not want to be exposed as incompetent, and said I really did believe in human rights for our people, for everybody. I said I had a passion for it. I wanted to go on doing this work.' Arafat put all joking aside, and said something like, 'OK, no more of your foreign friends – no more. You stop, you are attacking our leadership, our nation, you are attacking *me*.'

A few weeks later El-Sarraj was picked up for the first time. Like many before him, he was invited to come to the police station for a cup of coffee to 'discuss some problems'. That first time they were very polite, very correct. The second time they came at midnight to invite him for a coffee and this time he said, 'This isn't such a good time for coffee, I don't want to come. If you are arresting me show me the warrant.'

At the police barracks a son of one of his father's close friends greeted him, very embarrassed, saying he was sure that this was some mistake. But a stranger walked into the room, a heavy man in plain clothes. He took the prisoner by the arm and drew him down the stairs, along a corridor and out into an enclosed moonlit yard deserted except for one soldier holding a Kalashnikov. As they crossed the yard the man stopped, pulled El-Sarraj around and smashed him in the face. El-Sarraj went down and the man started to kick him with his heavy boots. The pain and shock were dreadful, he said, a game had suddenly turned vicious, although the warnings had been clear enough. The kicks and punches – the man was leaning down, chopping at him – stopped, and in the silence the Citizens' Rights Commissioner heard the metallic tick-tock of the weapon being armed. He thought he was going to die, 'shot like an animal on the ground with no witnesses while "trying to escape"'.

After a fortnight, during which there was an international outcry, El-Sarraj was released. Since then he has been at the centre of an informal, democratic and secular opposition to Arafat's sad government.

He had spent the first week suffocating in a tiny cell. He had had no contact with the outside, no idea how long he would be held, so he had asked one of the guards to get a message to a relative of his who was close

343

to Arafat. This relative went to see Arafat who had said that Eyad was important to him, that he loved him. 'Eyad is my *son*. But he needs discipline.' Abu Ammar, the wise leader, punishing for love. The 'Ammar' whose name he so piously adopted all those years ago was a martyr of early Islam, tortured and killed by his enemies.

*   *   *

Bamber spent that July visit with her counterparts at the Public Committee Against Torture in Israel, a small organization founded by a nurse, Hannah Friedmann, whose family had suffered under the Nazis in Holland. She also saw Physicians for Human Rights in Tel Aviv, and talked for hours with the doctors in Gaza and in Ramallah, on the West Bank. They showed her around their occupational therapy projects, their medical clinics and physiotherapy units. It was all rather formal, but with much animated and intelligent discussion.

She was trying to respond to their situation, and was alert and interested; they respected her and looked to her for advice. Techniques that work in predictable routines further west have to function on the West Bank in conditions of near-chaos. Their medical problems were familiar: head injuries, back pain, many epilepsies. But much of the discussion was about language, about finding the right words for the effects of organized violence and social breakdown. They were all concerned, Bamber included, that the power and usefulness of conventional ideas about trauma could also be restricting. All of them spoke about the dangers of labelling, of not grasping the complexity of each individual.

The chief medical officer of the Gaza programme said, 'We don't actually *see* something called "Post Traumatic Stress Disorder" *as such* — we see social problems, we see injuries, we see wrecked families. By restricting ourselves to "PTSD" we miss a great deal of continuing trauma.' Bamber agreed: if it is used carelessly it can be a *diminishing* label, a language that bogs you down. She said that it is a 'minimalist' definition, and to diagnose someone who has been tortured as suffering from post-traumatic stress is to avoid the use of the word 'torture' with all its political and other difficult connotations.

The Gazan doctor hoped to design a more sensitive questionnaire. After all, he said, traumatic stress is big business; you see someone for eight or twelve sessions and you can report a cure. 'It is degrading for the profession,' this quiet bearded doctor said, in his precise thoughtful English. Stress is of course caused by trauma, but has the real problem disappeared? And in the obsession with post-traumatic stress disorder doctors sometimes forget that medication can be useful, and that the patient's immediate suffering should be seen as suffering, not as a disease.

Of course, he acknowledged, you can't develop a private language of suffering, because no one will recognize it. But something better than the formalities of the standard discourse must be possible. The problems of suffering had to be put into a language that can supplement those definitions of trauma. They needed to be able to describe the reality of what they are seeing 'in the room'. But most clinicians do not have this language, yet.

The doctor spoke about women as 'the last recipient' of all the stresses. 'These are not depressive "episodes" that can be solved by cognitive therapy. The real work is done with the family, with the husband who is having problems. Often the woman comes and complains of something that does not quite click and then she breaks down and says it is not me, it's him but he won't come. They then have to get him to come by saying it will help his wife.'

The Gaza programme had started a group, run by El-Sarraj's sister Shadia, that challenges publicly the hidden tradition of murdering girls who 'dishonour' the family. The previous week a *shaykh* at a leading mosque had denounced them for 'encouraging prostitution'.

What we need, the Chief Medical Officer said, are professionals who know how not to be professionals.

But the language of cure stretches and breaks down in certain situations, the chain of violence and victimization allowing no respite for men or women. We were in Jabaliya refugee camp. Shit smelled in the heat. The camp was the usual sprawl of grey block-houses, unpaved roads and potholes. Dust hung in the air. Cars smashed down into and sprang up out of pits in the road. Brown water flowed down the street. A startling magnolia tree erupted in full flower out of a gap between two hovels; orange bougainvillaea smothered a porch made of scaffolding iron.

They took Bamber to visit a 'rehabilitated' client, a former Al Fatah guerrilla. At the centre of his house, which we entered through a living room, lay a tiled courtyard. A blue plastic sheet and dirty netting were drawn over the yard to give it some shade. A large woman, her age hard to tell, was sitting on a rug to the side of this space, her face contorted in pain. Her foot, stretched out in front of her, was grossly swollen. We were introduced only to the thin dark unshaven man with vacant intense eyes, who was her husband. He invited us into a room off to the side of the little yard.

Bamber could not manage the lotus position assumed by everyone else, so she reclined on a cushion. Ibrahim of the mental health programme translated the thin man's story. A tale of physical, political and military 'struggle' out of a tract. First he distributed leaflets; then he threw stones; then he attacked an Israeli post with petrol bombs, and finally he was entrusted with attacks on 'collaborators' – twelve in all, he related, his eyes never leaving the rug in front of him as he spoke, only lifting his face to look at Ibrahim sideways as he translated. It was not clear how many he actually killed.

Then the Israeli raid, soldiers on the roof over the room we were sitting in, arrest, weeks of torture. After he confessed there was another month of interrogation to tie down all his connections. He was sentenced to twenty years in prison. There he had a psychotic breakdown, became paranoid, imagining men in his cell, and had prolonged depressions so extreme that the Israelis released him after seven years.

He rocked and swayed as he spoke, the hero of his own story, a harsh repetitive prayer to his sacrifice. The doctors at the Gaza programme had warned us that some of the former activists could only survive by this kind of self-exaltation. The man bobbed like an abandoned child. Not all victims are innocent. Bamber said during one of the discussions that 'idealizing torture and the torture victim is a corruption for us. We must guard against the tendency to produce heroes.' They wanted her to see this man as an example of the wreckage that the situation in Gaza produced, over and over again.

The people at the Mental Health Programme are my friends, he said, they have helped me, I feel better and can work. He now had a permit to leave the strip, when it was open, this former Al Fatah Hawk labouring quietly on an Israeli building site. He was on strong medication, and in his case there was little else the doctors could offer.

On the way out Bamber went over to the woman sitting nursing her grotesquely inflamed foot. She was now crying, her face puckered in fear and self-loathing. She seemed to be completely ignored; it was as though we had stepped around a giant insect. Her body was enormous from childbirth and bad food – the thin man told us as part of his glorious narrative that he had fathered four children since his release and wanted more. Bamber tried to communicate with the woman and said something to the people from the programme. She suspected that the woman had a serious vascular condition, which might become gangrenous.

The 'cured' hero; his wife neglected with her poisoned foot. In the shocking heat and smell of the refugee camp, it seemed absurd to think of Philoctetes, the Greek archer betrayed by Odysseus, isolated on a desert island because of his wound, which stinks so much that it disgusts and repels all human company. Yet he stands for people no one will cure or rescue. In Heaney's version the archer says:

Nothing there except
The beat of the waves and the beat of my raw wound ...
I managed to come through
But I never healed.
My whole life has been
Just one long cruel parody.

*   *   *

As we were driving away from Jerusalem on the last day, Helen Bamber started speaking slowly, but with great vehemence, her sentences broken and agitated with the force of what she was trying to say. 'The world has paid a terrible price for the Holocaust. I cannot cut off the terrible historical sequence, and unless we understand that, we understand nothing. There is no clearer message for me than the sequence of perpetration. The manipulation of it. I am still angry with the Germans and the British as well as the Israelis. What interests me is what we can learn, what the second generation can learn. The sequence has to be broken. What we pass on to the next generation is crucial. The Holocaust is not in the past, it is now. It has infiltrated people, the fear of annihilation, creating aggression and paranoia.'

Bamber had been saying to her friends that she would come back more often, and hoped to be there for a conference in October. But later, in Jerusalem, she had said that this might be her last visit to Israel. On the road high above the plain of the Jordan River, the friend who was driving now stopped the car to pick up a small stone for her. She had given her last piece of Jerusalem stone to a client in London, as a gift that implied remembrance. Her friend clambered over a barrier and came back after a couple of minutes with a few small pieces of pale red limestone, pitted like soft wood.

She fingered one little piece of rock as we drove on through the Latrun Pass, the rusty old Israeli armoured cars, memorials from the battle for Jerusalem in 1948, pointing up the valley toward the city. She was at home in the memory of catastrophe, the hard material of history; she works with it, but it offers little comfort. It is not the past: time is open like a wound.

*   *   *

'If you were able to look into the spinal cord from the back you would see a representation of the whole body,' write Melzack and Wall, the great theorists of pain. The butterfly-shaped horns of the spine each contain 'a map of the body surface'. Severe injury distorts the map: amputation may leave cells in the spine 'remembering' the ghost nerves of an absent leg, and terrible pain may be felt in a part of the body that is no longer there. And the body can feel mysterious pain, which has no apparent physical cause. A region of the body becomes *terra incognita*; the map that doctors think they have no longer corresponds to the evidence of the patient's senses.

Nearly all victims of torture suffer back pain. One writer thinks that 'this could be due to repeated direct trauma to the spine, to desperate attempts at avoidance during torture, or adverse prison conditions in a cramped, damp cell'. But often there is nothing that an X-ray can see, and still those who have been tortured complain of debilitating agony. Melzack and Wall are frank about medicine's helpless ignorance, faced with such crippling, yet invisible distress. They say that even minor damage to vertebrae and tissues around the nerves of the spine may be cumulative, pain producing spasm and still more pain.

The pain that follows torture may be no more mysterious than 'ordinary' pain, but it has its own quality. It is now suspected that the whole of a person's history influences the way he or she experiences pain; their state of mind and their relationship with their body affect their perception of physical insult. 'Seeing the source of injury, hearing the sounds of a rifle shot or a falling beam, and thinking about the consequences of an injury all contribute to pain.' Substitute what a torture victim sees and hears for these accidents and it is not surprising that if pain is associated with the most meaningless humiliation, it may be difficult to forget.

Back pain is one of the most central, total pains; it can change a person from an athletic free adult into a reclining invalid. The back makes us what we are in our relations with power, standing straight and confident, or hunched and terrified. Having backbone is a condition of respect: you stand up for your rights. It is just as important to be able to bend it, in prayer or sex. The instinct of the torturer demonstrates, typically, a crude instinctual wisdom about the body: to leave someone stiff, unable to run or handle themselves, is to lodge impotence in them. This kind of pain is inescapable, and justifies Jean Amery's insight that 'only in torture does the transformation of the person into flesh become complete'.

In a room at the Foundation, Michael Korzinski works with people whose pain has baffled the physicians, but who can't be said to be simply neurotic, to want or need their pain. The torturer has, after all, reached into their minds through their bodies. 'The body can heal well; what is far more fragile is the person's sense of their body, the way their self-worth is bound up with it.' Korzinski tries to 'restore their body' to them, through infinite variations of touch and movement. It may be no more than relaxation, dance and exercise; but in combination with orthodox medicine, it lessens pain. Korzinski described a man who felt he had difficulty breathing, who sat folded up and who, when he could breathe freely, felt afraid. When he was tortured, he used to try to hold himself together to prevent the torturers from 'pulling him apart': safety in suffocation. He had to learn to want to stand up and breathe.

Perhaps all the Foundation does, apart from speaking as clearly as it can against torture, is to help its clients rediscover the ordinary terrors of having a body, of arousal and old age, without feeling corrupted by fear. A doctor noticed that 'when many Kurds come here first they stand like that' – he got up and hunched his shoulders submissively – 'and later they stand like this, straight, they really change themselves, though it is a painfully slow process'.

One of Helen Bamber's first clients was an Iranian man tortured by Khomeini's Revolutionary Guards. In the prison where he was held, he was first examined by a doctor, who encouraged him to be frank about his medical problems, saying it would help him in what he had to face; so the prisoner told the doctor about his bad back. When the guards tied him to a bedframe later, they concentrated on his back, stretching, beating, pulling. Afterwards, he was held with sixteen other men in a cell which had space enough for four of them to stretch out; they had to adopt contorted postures even to sit down. Ever since, he has suffered chronic pain. It defined him for a long time: 'The pain pushed out, all along the spine; it took me over.'

His pain is much less extreme now. The different 'cures' seem to have helped him – the attention of good doctors, the talking, movement and physiotherapy. He was so desperate with the pain that he once lost control in Bamber's office, and began to bang his head on her table. Other people who were in the building that day remember the hard knock as bone met wood: they could hear it all the way down the corridor. Earlier Bamber had talked quietly to him about her experience, and listened to him; and because 'she seemed to understand the pain', he felt free to talk; she assured him, somehow, that 'it was not going to hurt her'. Now, however, she put her hands between his head and the table, and before he could stop himself his forehead hit her hands. She told him, almost vehemently, that he'd stood up to Khomeini, and that he shouldn't be defeated by him now. It was the first time that she had touched him with her hands. He said: 'These were not the hands of a torturer.'

REFERENCES

Certain books have influenced the text so deeply that they must be acknowledged separately. Anyone who writes on this subject must be in their debt. Jean Amery's neglected classic, *At the Mind's Limits*, is a series of reflections on the Holocaust. His essay on his own experience of torture is a concentrated meditation on cruelty's effects on the mind and body. Zygmunt Bauman's *Modernity and the Holocaust* is a passionate critique of bureaucratic rationalization and its numbing moral results. Elaine Scarry's great book, *The Body in Pain*, particularly the first chapter on 'The Structure of Torture', was a revelation. *Torture*, by Edward Peters, is an indispensable historical and legal survey, written with controlled passion. I am also greatly indebted to Lawrence Langer's *Holocaust Testimonies* for its insistent questioning of the rhetoric of 'transcendence'.

I also want to acknowledge the longer-term influence of Lawrence Weschler's excellent *A Miracle, A Universe* (New York 1990), a scrupulous picture of Brazilian and Uruguayan attempts to settle accounts with torturers: the *New Yorker* tradition at its best. Kanan Makiya's *Republic of Fear* (London 1990) and *Cruelty and Silence* (London 1993) prepared me to see the wider implications of Bamber's life, and Makiya pointed me towards Judith Shklar's essay, 'Putting Cruelty First', in her *Ordinary Vices* (Cambridge, Mass. 1984).

Chapter One: The Liberties of Berwick, pp. 1–21

Interviews with Bamber, Henry McCreath, Archie Veitch, Bill Brown, Jackie Pyle, Joe Cumming, Bill Gibson, Arch Hattie. Transcript of Bamber conversation with Jimmy Virtue.

Siegfried Sassoon, *The War Poems*, London 1983.

'A defence against the sea rather than a pier for shipping': pamphlet published by Berwick Historical Society.

'the clean sequestered town': Iris Wedgwood, *Northumberland and Durham*, London 1932.

'A peculiar jurisdiction....': *Mackenzie's Comprehensive Gazetteer of England and Wales*, 1895.

'The iniquity of oblivion' is from Thomas Browne's *Urne Buriall*: 'But the iniquity of oblivion blindely scattereth her poppy, and deals with the memory of men without distinction to perpetuity': Cambridge 1958, p. 46.
The dream of 'the unlistened-to story' is from Primo Levi, *If This is a Man*, London, 1996, p. 66.

Chapter Two: The Jigsaw, pp. 22–70

Interviews with Bamber, Rudi Bamber.

Epigraph from Walter Benjamin, 'The Storyteller' in *Illuminations*, London 1970, p. 84.

'terrible poisoning of the health of the national body': Adolf Hitler, *Mein Kampf*, London 1992, p. 224.

'blood, sin and desecration of the race': ibid, p. 226.

'the constructive work of the unknown masses': Peter Kropotkin, *Memoirs of a Revolutionist*, London 1988, p. 147. For London anarchism, see Bill Fishman, *East End Jewish Radicals*, London 1978. Kropotkin's letter to V. I. Lenin is quoted in the 'Epilogue' by James Allen Rogers to the *Memoirs* and is drawn from David Shub, 'Kropotkin and Lenin', *Russian Review*, XII, 1953, pp. 227–34.

'drag the nation into the abyss': Hitler, op.cit., p. 343.

'the sentence that threatened them': Golo Mann, *The History of Germany since 1789*, Hammondsworth, 1987, p. 765.

'the Jewish community itself could not imagine ...': Alfred J. Sherman in 'The British Government, the Jewish Community and the Refugee Agencies', *Journal of Holocaust Education*, vol. 4, no. 1, p. 19.

'Hurrah for the Blackshirts!' and other material on the Rothermere press in the 1930s: Stephen Koss, *The Rise and Fall of the Political Press in Britain*, London 1994, p. 985.

For the Bader brothers, apart from Bamber's memories, see Menachem's obituary in *Jewish Chronicle*, 15 February 1985, and the entry in *Palestine Personalia*, ed. Peretz, Jerusalem 1947. Menachem's wartime smuggling of aid and money to Jews in Nazi Europe is praised in Heini Bornstein, *Switzerland, An Island*, published in Hebrew, Tel Aviv 1996. His own brief memoir, *Sad Missions*, first published in 1954, was republished by Tel Aviv in 1995 on the centenary of his birth. I am indebted to Daphna Vardi for her translation of the relevant passages of this book.

On the negotiations between the Nazis and the Yishuv, see Yehuda Bauer, *Jews for Sale*, New Haven 1996. For the dispute over Reszo Kastner and the Hungarian Jewish leadership's relations with the Yishuv, Tom Segev, *The Seventh Million*, New York 1993, pp. 255–310; Justice Heshin's remarks on Kastner and his citation of Ben-Zakkai are quoted on p. 307.

'the best biological material': Eichmann's phrase is quoted in Hannah Arendt, *Eichmann in Jerusalem*, London 1963, p. 38.

On immigration and asylum for Jewish refugees before the war, and the attitude of bodies like the BMA, see Sherman, op.cit.

'the cautious insensibility of the free world': Norman Bentwich, *They Found Refuge*, London 1956, p. 47.

Osip Mandelstam, 'Poem to the Unknown Soldier', *The Voronezh Notebooks*, translated by Richard and Elizabeth McKane, Newcastle 1996.

'... the aliens within our gates': *Daily Mail*, editorial of 1 March 1940, quoted in Arnold Stent, *A Bespattered Page?*, London 1980, p. 46.

On the Café de Paris bombing, see Charles Graves, *Champagne and Chandeliers*, London 1958, and Philip Ziegler, *London at War*, London 1995, pp. 147–8, who quotes Charles Graves.

'Our dream of a feudal city ...': Cecil Headlam, *The Story of Nuremberg*, London 1899.

Thomas Mann, *Doctor Faustus*: new translation by John Woods, New York 1997, p. 39.

'An Alice in Wonderland situation...' and for the account of the *Dunera* voyage, Stent, op.cit., p. 52 and pp. 114–33.

On the liberation of Belsen and its aftermath, I have relied on Eberhard Kolb, *Bergen-Belsen 1943–45*, published by the Central Office for Political Education of the State of Lower Saxony, 1985; Joanne Reilly, *Belsen*, PhD thesis, typescript, published as *Belsen*, London 1998; *The Times*, 19 April 1945; *Daily Mirror*, 19 April 1945; *Illustrated London News*, 28 April 1945; *Sunday Times*, 22 April 1945, article by R. W. Thompson; Robert Collis, *Straight On*,

London 1947; *The Trial of Josef Kramer and Forty-Four Others: The Belsen Trial*, London 1948; Paul Kemp, 'The Liberation of Bergen-Belsen Concentration Camp in April 1945', *Imperial War Museum Review*, no. 5; Hagit Lavsky, 'The Day After', *German History*, vol. 11, no. 1, 1993; Hagit Lavsky, 'The Work of the Jewish Relief Unit', *Journal of Holocaust Education*, vol. 4, no. 1, 1995; 'Belsen in History and Memory', *Journal of Holocaust Education*, vol. 5, nos 2–3, Autumn/Winter 1996; *Bergen Belsen*, introduced and edited by Josef Rosensaft, World Federation of Bergen Belsen Associations, 1965; and *Belsen*, Irgun Sheerit Hapleita Me'haezor Habriti, 1957, which includes essays by Josef Rosensaft, Nahum Goldmann and Norbert Wollheim.

'We go beyond neighbourly love...'; Counselor of Reich Ministry of the Interior on the Eugenic Sterilization Law, August 1933, quoted in Daniel Kevles, *In the Name of Eugenics*, New York 1985, p. 117.

'the last great typhus epidemic in history...': Kemp, op.cit.

'The condition of the prisoners was so bad...': Irma Grese's examination at the Belsen trial. *The Trial of Josef Kramer and Forty-Four Others: The Belsen Trial*, p. 250.

Chapter Three: Grit in the Wheel, pp. 71–114

Interviews with Bamber, Alison Wood, Henry Lunzer.

Epigraph: 'Surely this war ...' Martha Gellhorn, in *Reporting World War Two*, Volume Two, New York 1997, p. 730.

'A small bare window...': Hannah Levy-Hass, *Inside Belsen: A Belsen Diary*, Brighton 1982, p. 27.

For the numbers of Jews at Belsen after the repatriation of the non-Jewish prisoners, see Reilly PhD thesis op.cit.

'... did not represent a recognised category': Norbert Wollheim, 'Belsen's Place in the Process of "Death and Rebirth" of the Jewish People', in *Belsen*, Irgun Sheerit Hapleita Me'haezor Habriti, 1957, p. 55.

'In theory ...': Reilly, op.cit.

'The problem of accommodation is very acute ...': Judith Lunzer, Welfare Report on Glyn Hughes Hospital, *Jewish Relief Newsletter*, no. 20, January 1947 (Wiener Library, Jewish Relief Unit Archive).

'Better to put an end to it all ...': Levy-Hass, op.cit., p. 68.

'It was the most moving and heart-rending sight ...': H. L. Glyn Hughes in *Belsen*, Irgun Sheerit Hapleita Me'haezor Habriti, 1957, pp. 94–6.

'... row upon row of wooden green huts ...': Derrick Sington, *Belsen Uncovered*, quoted in *Belsen*, Irgun Sherit Hapleita Me'haezor Habriti, 1957, p. 72.

'The hut door hung open ...': Andrew Matthews, *Belsen 1945*, unpublished typescript.

'unburdened herself ...': Eva Kahn-Minden, quoted in Reilly, op.cit.

'Our first move was to make contact ...': Senta Ruth Hirtz, notes written July 1945, MS in Jewish Relief Unit Archive, Wiener Library.

'It was made out of cellophane ...': Irma Grese's evidence at Belsen trial, op.cit., p. 256.

'torture camps ...': *Illustrated London News*, 28 April 1945.

'irredeemably beyond the pale of humanity ...': Malise Ruthven, *Torture: the Grand Conspiracy*, London 1978, p. 288.

'the control, disciplining, invasion ...': Richard Evans, *Rituals of Retribution, Capital Punishment in Germany 1600–1987*, Oxford 1996, p. 899.

H. G. Wells, *The Rights of Man*, Penguin Special, 1940.

'In that brief and hopeful interlude ...': Edward Peters, *Torture*, expanded edition, Philadelphia 1996, p. 141.

'After a while everything will become clear ...': Levy-Hass, op.cit., p. 45.

'What happened ...': Fritz Klein's examination at Belsen trial, op.cit., p. 184.

'Of course I am a doctor ...': Klein quoted by Dr Ella Lingens-Reiner in Robert Jay Lifton, *The Nazi Doctors*, New York 1986, p. 16. Lifton also discusses the case of the orderly Karl Rothe.

'rounding off neatly ...': Tony Kushner, 'The Memory of Belsen' in *Belsen in History and Memory, Journal of Holocaust Education*, op.cit., p. 191.

'250 a day were arriving ...': Reilly, op.cit., p. 170.

'at first they were held ...': Bentwich, op.cit., p. 147. Cf. Reilly, p. 174.

Account of the orderly breakout from Belsen/Höhne is in Henry Lunzer, report to JCRA, 2 June 1946, in 'Belsen Reports' file, Lady Rose Henriques papers, Wiener Library.

'brutal apathy': Paul Kemp, op.cit.

The account of the trial is drawn from *The Trial of Josef Kramer and Forty-Four Others*, op.cit., especially Major Winwood's presentation for the defence, pp. 149–54.

'Nobody was going to deny that there were beatings ...': ibid, p. 518.

'while waves of circumstance beat around him': ibid, p. 156.

'... any place was good enough for a latrine': ibid, p. 249.

'one of those great decisions ...': ibid, p. 509.

'stormy and fantastic': Bentwich, op.cit., p. 162.

'grey ghosts at the doorway of the world': JCRA leaflet, in Jewish Relief Unit Archive, Wiener Library.

Isaac Levy, *Witness to Evil*, London 1995, p. 67.

'Those who were persecuted...': ibid, p. 118.

'Tunefully and passionately ...': Abel J. Herzberg, *Between Two Streams: A Diary from Bergen-Belsen*, London 1997, p. 144.

The contrasting US and British policies on Palestine are discussed in Reilly, op.cit., p. 160.

'intense energy ...': Bentwich, op.cit., p. 143.

'the best in the whole British Zone': Levy, op.cit., p. 89.

'If I think back ...': Eva Kahn-Minden, *The Road Back*, 1996.

A. C. Jacobs and Leonard Cohen, letters to Henry Lunzer, in Jewish Relief Unit Archive, Wiener Library. Reilly describes the reluctance of the JCRA to grapple with the political situation of the displaced persons – their growing Zionism, their feeling of entrapment in Germany – as 'fainthearted and rather naive' (PhD typescript, pp. 253–4).

'the important qualification ...': Bentwich, op.cit., p. 151.

Chapter Four: The Discipline of Love, pp. 115–153

The major work on the young survivors and their first years in Britian is Martin Gilbert's *The Boys*. This chapter, which offers a necessarily more partial and personal view of that time, based on Helen Bamber's memories, also draws on interviews with Rudi Bamber, Roman Halter and Ben Helfgott.

'the largest absolute pacifist organization ...': James Hinton, *Protests and Visisons*, London 1989, p. 103.

'Soon he was lost ...' and other quotations from Stuart Smith, *Derrick Preest*, London 1941.

'England has the most gentle society I know of ...': Stuart Smith, 'How it Seemed Then and How it Seems Now,' in *The Objectors*, ed. Clifford Simmons (n.d. but from internal evidence published 1965).

'Italian critic': Franco Moretti, 'The Conspiracy of the Innocents', in *The Way of the World*, London 1987, p. 213.

'a permanent addition ... openings in commerce': quoted in Martin Gilbert, *The Boys*, London 1997, p. 324.

'It is owing to me': Kahn-Minden, op.cit.

'the pretence that from the wreckage ...': Lawrence Langer, *Holocaust Testimonies: The Ruins of Memory*, New Haven 1991, p. 165.

'I cannot claim ...': Speer, quoted in Dobroszycki (ed.), *Chronicle of the Łodz Ghetto*, New Haven 1984, p. IX.

'those who did this work ...': Gilbert, op.cit., p. 208.

'barely escaping murder': Gilbert, op.cit., p. 267.

'discipline of love': 'Thus day by day,/Subjected to the discipline of love,/His organs and recipient faculties/Are quickened, are more vigorous, his mind spreads,/Tenacious of the forms which it receives.' Wordsworth, *The Prelude*, Book II. See also Rosemary Dinnage, 'A Bit of Light', in Grolnick (ed.), *Between Reality and Fantasy*, London 1998, p. 370: 'The key to the making of things, then, is concurrence: when what the child expects and what the world offers intersect, the object is both found and created at the same moment.'

Chapter Five: A Storm from Paradise, pp. 154–184

'The dreams ...': Joseph Conrad, 'Autocracy and War', 1905, in *Notes on Life and Letters*, London 1949, p. 106.

'To introduce ...': Carl von Clausewitz, *On War*, quoted by Roger Trinquier in *Modern Warfare*, New York 1961.

'under active consideration': quoted by James Patterson, *Grand Expectations: The United States, 1945–74*, New York 1996, p. 224.

Iain Sinclair, *Lud Heat*, London 1998.

'This made the people ...': Daniel Defoe, *A Journal of the Plague Year*, Oxford 1990 edition, pp. 113–14.

'a pestilential nuisance': Christopher Booth, *British Medical Journal*, 10 December 1994.

'Beware the crime ...': Maurice Pappworth, *A Primer of Medicine*, London 1960, p. 6.

'Gods in white coats ...': Michael Burleigh, *Death and Deliverance*, Cambridge 1994, p. 157. The phrase 'life unworthy of life', as Burleigh explains, is from the title of a blueprint for medical killing called *Permission for the Destruction of Life Unworthy of Life*, published in 1920 and immediately influential on German eugenicists and, later, the Nazis. It was written by Karl Binding, a lawyer, and Alfred Hoche, a psychiatrist whose speciality was the conduction of electricity by the spinal cords of decapitated people.

Splints for polio victims: Obituary of Sir Herbert Seddon, *BMJ*, vol. 1, no. 309, 1978, p. 41.

'A ten-inch stiletto' and other information about the Pulfer murder: *Hendon and Finchley Times*, 29 March and 5 April 1957; Georgiou's murder-charge hearing and trial, 19 April and 10 May 1957. See also *Edgware Post*, 4 April 1957.

'one thing seemed impossible ...': Jean-Paul Sartre, 'Preface' to Henri Alleg, *The Question*, London 1958, p. 11.

'slow torturous burnings': George C. Wright, 'By the Book', in W. F. Brundage (ed.), *Under Sentence of Death*, 1997, p. 252.

'not much better ...': Friedrich Nietzsche, *On the Genealogy of Morality*, Cambridge 1994, p. 25.

'The torture went on ...': Alleg, op.cit., pp. 60, 68.

'The executioner had his own cup ...': see Richard Evans, *Rituals of Retribution* op.cit., pp. 60–1.

'from which the victim is excluded ...': Stanley Milgram, quoted in Zygmunt Bauman, *Modernity and the Holocaust*, Cambridge, 1991, p. 156.

'writing on the body': Pierre Clastres, *Society Against the State*, New York 1987, pp. 177–88.

'translation of pain ...': Elaine Scarry, *The Body in Pain*, New York 1985, p. 45.

'like demigods': Alastair Horne, *A Savage War of Peace*, London 1977, p. 167.

'a Cartesian rationale ...': the phrase is Bernard Fall's, in his introduction to the American edition of 1964, written with a sharp eye on the escalating US involvement in Vietnam.

'Warfare is now an interlocking system ...' and the quotations that follow are from Roger Trinquier, *Modern Warfare*, New York 1964.

'Ja—, smiling all the time ...': Alleg, op.cit., pp. 44–5.

'the venomous argots ...': Benedict Anderson, *Imagined Communities,* London 1983, p. 135.

'One night ...': Alleg, op.cit., p. 91.

'The nineteenth century was far from pure ...': Pierre Henri-Simon, quoted in Edward Peters, *Torture,* Philadelphia 1996, p. 101.

Peter Benenson, introduction and account of British abuses of human rights in Kenya, from *Gangrene,* London 1959.

'a depoliticized human ground ...': Arthur Miller, *Timebends,* New York 1987, p. 566.

'I am up against a cliff wall ...': Samuel Beckett, quoted by Charles Juliet, *Conversations with Samuel Beckett,* Leiden 1995, p. 141.

Beckett's record in the French Resistance and his later defence of Jerome Lindon are documented in James Knowlson's superb *Damned to Fame: The Life of Samuel Beckett,* 1996, pp. 297–319 and 492–95.

'Europe is at death's door ... violence': Jean-Paul Sartre, 'Preface' to *The Wretched of the Earth,* Harmondsworth 1967, pp. 12, 18.

'the torture of someone ...': Stuart Smith, 'How it Seemed Then', op.cit.

'I have attempted to follow ...': Maurice Pappworth, *A Primer of Medicine,* London 1960, especially the introduction and the second chapter. His definition of 'the good listener' occurs on page 9.

Chapter Six: Taking Histories, pp. 185–228

Interviews with Rudi Bamber, Peg Belson, Rosita Green, Stuart Smith, Norman Franklin, David Bamber, Jonathan Bamber.

Churchill and Gilbert and Sullivan: see Martin Gilbert, *Churchill,* vol. VIII, London 1988, p. 1356.

'The most rapid way ...': Peter Benenson, *Observer,* 28 May 1961.

'Human Guinea Pigs: a Warning': Maurice Pappworth in *Twentieth Century,* Autumn 1962, special issue on 'Doctors in the Sixties'.

'even in skilled hands ...': David Verel and Ronald Grainger, *Cardiac Catheterization,* London 1978.

'the principle of medical morality ...': Claude Bernard, *Introduction to the Study of Experimental Medicine,* quoted in David Rothman, *Strangers at the Bedside,* New York 1991.

'seem to have had little restraining effect ...': *BMJ*, 27 October 1962.

German research reports: see Rothman, op.cit.

'any classification ...' and other quotes from Henry K. Beecher, 'Experimentation in Man', *JAMA*, vol. 159, no. 5, 1959, pp. 461–78.

'the common ingredient ...': Ronald Melzack and Patrick Wall, *The Challenge of Pain*, London 1996, p. 197.

'not only ...': Brian Inglis, 'The Guinea Pig Revolution in Medical Morality', *Twentieth Century*, Winter 1963.

'the worst honest error ...': D. W. Winnicott, *BMJ*, 28 January 1956.

'a very great fear ...': H. E. W. Hardenberg, letter to *BMJ*, 2 February 1956.

Hardenberg, 'Torture and the Subconscious', unpublished MS, summer 1963.

'The man does not die ...': Chris Marker, *La Jetée*, film, 1963.

'she is seen walking apart from her mother': James Robertson, *A Two-Year-Old Goes to Hospital*: A Scientific Film Record by James Robertson, Tavistock Institute for Human Relations, 1953. This was Robertson's explanatory booklet written to accompany his film.

'being alone in the presence of someone': D. W. Winnicott, 'The Capacity to be Alone', in *The Maturational Processes*, London 1958, pp. 29–36.

Only one hospital in twelve: see *Newsletter*, National Association for the Welfare of Children in Hospital, July 1966. Mothers standing outside: a similar scene to the one Bamber recalls is described in the NAWCH 'Group News' as late as May 1972, outside the isolation unit of a hospital in Hull.

'passed over like a parcel ...': Peg Belson, 'Children in Hospital', *Children and Society*, vol. 7, no. 2, 1993, p. 196.

John Bowlby on hospitals in the Third World: see Bowlby, *Child Care and the Growth of Love*, London 1953.

Sir Herbert Seddon, letter to Bamber from Beit Mery, Lebanon, 9 September 1969.

The publishing history of *Human Guinea Pigs* is gleaned from interviews with Stuart Smith, Norman Franklin and Helen Bamber.

Henry K. Beecher, 'Ethics and Clinical Research', *NEJM*, vol. 274, no. 24, June 1966.

'irresponsible exaggerator': Rothman, *Strangers*, pp. 71–9.

'vulgarly abused ...': Maurice Pappworth, letter to *BMJ*, 24 June 1967.

'have never developed the art ...': Maurice Pappworth, *Human Guinea Pigs*, London 1967, p. 10.

'required some restraint': ibid, p. 38.

'It is difficult ...': ibid, p. 184.

Liver patients: ibid, p. 136.

Chief medical officer of Distillers and 'The Nazi doctors ...': ibid, pp. 64–78.

On Western doctors' attitudes to pure science: David Rothman, *Strangers*, op.cit., p. 63.

'Let us have no more of this ...': Charles Fletcher, letter to *BMJ*, 16 September 1967.

'vitriolic amplifcation': *Lancet*, 11 May 1968.

'a whitewashing ...': Maurice Pappworth, letter to *BMJ*, 2 September 1967.

On medical 'war', see Rothman, op.cit.

British Medical Association, *Handbook of Medical Ethics*, London 1993.

'Ballad of Upit': quoted in *Report on Case Work*, Amnesty International London Region, March 1979.

For Chile, see Leslie Bethell (ed.), *Chile Since Independence*, Cambridge 1996;

'germs': President Pinochet quoted in Pamela Constable and Arturo Valenzuela, *A Nation of Enemies*, New York 1991, p. 319.

'the revolutionary river': Regis Debray, *Conversations with Allende*, London 1971, p. 53. On the theory of the *foco*, see Debray, *Revolutionary Strategy in Latin America*.

'We must achieve revolutionary socialism ...': Jean-Paul Sartre, 'Preface' to *The Wretched of the Earth*, op.cit., p. 10.

The pamphlet: Amnesty International, *Where is William Beausire?*, first edition 1978; second edition 1981.

Chapter Seven: Poor Ghost, pp. 229–266

The account of Bill Beausire's last months is drawn from the Amnesty pamphlet,

and from interviews with Luis Muñoz, Adriana Borquez, and Diana Beausire. The chapter is also based on interviews with Alex Wilde, José Zalaquett, Malcolm Coad, Luis Valenzuela, Hugh O'Shaughnessy, Jorge Lopez Sotomayor, Diana Tickell, Monica Gonzalez, Dick Barbor-Might and Helen Bamber.

'muffled society': the phrase is Alex Wilde's (personal communication).

'the unmaking of the made ... Made to participate ...': Scarry, op.cit., p. 41; 'the single distilled ...': ibid, p. 45.

'He requested me to inform ...': *Where is William Beausire?*

'purging him in some metaphysical ...': Cesare Beccaria, *An Essay on Crimes and Punishment*, quoted in Isaac Kramnick, *The Enlightenment Reader*, New York 1995, p. 530.

'If you have gangrene ...': Augusto Pinochet, quoted in Constable and Valanzuela, op.cit., p. 78.

'The Albatross', Ciarán Carson after Baudelaire, in *First Language*, Oldcastle 1993, p. 70.

'as though by armed guards': Ludwig Binswanger, 'The Case of Lola Voss', in *Selected Papers*, London 1978, p. 296.

'O good, Horatio ...': William Shakespeare, *Hamlet*, Act V, scene ii.

Chapter Eight: Learned on the Body, pp. 267–294

The role of Dolcey Brito: 'Participación de medicos, psicólogos y personal paramédico en las torturas', in Uruguay, *Nunca Mas: Informe Sobre la Violación a los Derechos Humanos*, Montevideo 1989, pp. 301–28. Lawrence Weschler's account of the Libertad regime is excellent. *A Miracle, A Universe*, pp. 131–8. He quotes a psychology student who describes the prison's system as the academic behaviourists' revenge on the Freudians, most of whom were fired from their jobs after the coup in Uruguay.

'Nervous exhaustion ...': the case of Nadezhda Gaidar; 'Mania for reconstructing ...': Mikhail Kukobaka, detained for passing out copies of the Universal Declaration of Human Rights. These and other cases were described in Alexander Podrabinek's *Punitive Medicine*. See Peter Reddaway, *Punitive Medicine: A summary*, Amnesty International, August 1977. The case of the Czech Adventists is drawn from International association on the Political Use of Psychiatry, *Information Bulletin 10*, November 1984, p. 5.

'painful and useless': quoted in A. Voloshanovich, in *Medicine and Human Rights*, Amnesty International Medical Group, no. 2, 1982.

'punitive medicine': Alexander Podrabinek, quoted in *Soviet Opponents of Political Psychiatry in the USSR*, Working Group on the Internment of Dissenters in Mental Hospitals, 1980. See also Punitive Medicine, op.cit.

'sound ethical controls ...': see John S. Horner, 'Medical Ethics and the Regulation of Medical Practice', Manchester University PhD, 1995, p. 138.

'If it is to be made legal ...': *The Torture Report*, British Medical Association, 1986, p. 25, see also the important *Medicine Betrayed*, BMA, London 1992.

Steve Biko: see *Medicine Betrayed*, op.cit., pp. 139, 173–4.

'over-demanding ...': Report by Peter Archer, Amnesty International, n.d., p. 3.

The Thorpe episode: see *Guardian*, 8–9 and 17 February 1982; statement by David Astor, *Guardian*, 27 February 1982. Thorpe statement, 5 March 1982. On his career, see Simon Freeman and Barrie Penrose, *Rinkagate: The Rise and Fall of Jeremy Thorpe*, London 1997.

'examination of a teacher ...': Elizabeth Gordon, *Lancet*, January 1984.

'Dr Brian Fisher talks to Amnesty ...': *Medicine and Human Rights*, no. 5, May 1983.

'the flat and careful technical language ...': *Uganda: Evidence of Torture*, Amnesty International, June 1985. Appendix: 'Medical Examination of 16 Alleged Ugandan Torture Victims', Case No. 12, Conclusion: 'This boy, allegedly arrested at the age of 15, reported that he was severely burned. He now suffers gross facial, neck and arm disfigurement by keloid scars, which are consistent with his account of having been burned with an electric hotplate and ignited rags.'

'the political application of psychotherapy': John Schlapobersky, 'The Reclamation of Space and Time', paper given at 'The Political Psyche', ICA, 27 November 1993.

Chapter Nine: Remaking the World, pp. 295–350

'Nietzsche ...': Friedrich Nietzsche, *On the Genealogy of Morality*, Cambridge 1994, pp. 11–12, 15.

'S. H. Foulkes ...': S. H. Foulkes, from *Group-Analytic Psychotherapy*, p. 157, quoted in John Schlapobersky, Editor's Introduction to Robyn Skinner, *Institutes and How to Survive Them*, London 1988, p. xix.

'Skynner himself ...': Robin Skynner, 'The Goose That Lays the Golden Eggs: A Discussion on the Myth of Altruism', in Skinner, op.cit., pp. 157–69.

'the *how* of pain ...': Jean Améry, *At the Mind's Limits*, Bloomington, Indiana 1980, p. 33.

'Paying careful attention ...': see Ronald Melzack and Patrick D. Wall, *The Challenge of Pain*, pp. 197, 249.

'Mandelstam ...': Richard McKane and Elizabeth McKane, *The Voronezh Notebooks*, Newcastle 1996; *The Moscow Notebooks*, Newcastle 1991.

'while the anecdotes ...': Sigmund Freud, *Jokes and Their Relation to the Unconscious*, Harmondsworth 1976, p. 194.

'the lesson is always ...': Gill Hinshelwood in Duncan Forrest, ed., *A Glimpse of Hell*, London 1996, p. 191.

'the question is ...': Lewis Carroll, *Through the Looking-Glass*, Oxford 1973, p. 190.

'Accusations upon Torture ...': Thomas Hobbes, *Leviathan*, Harmondsworth 1986, p. 199.

'make pain the crucible of truth ...': Cesare Beccaria, in Isaac Kramnick, op.cit., p. 530.

'tendency to summarily dismiss ...': Amnesty International, *Slamming the Door: the Demolition of the Right to Asylum in the UK*, London 1996, p. 3.

'in fact these wounds were inflicted ...': letter from Immigration and Nationality Department, Home Office, 17 January 1996.

'though a tough and determined man ...': Medical Foundation Medical Report, 5 March 1996. See also the Medical Foundation's excellent *Annual Review 1997*, pp. 12–15.

'there is no evidence to suggest ...': letter from IND, 13 January 1998.

'the prisoner a colossal body ...': Elaine Scarry, *The Body in Pain*, op.cit., p. 57.

'Victor Hugo declared ...': quoted in Edward Peters, *Torture*, op.cit., p. 5.

'the whole subject ...': *Encyclopaedia Britannica*, Eleventh Edition, 1910–11. The entry on torture was written by James Williams, Reader in Roman Law at Oxford.

'to preserve the reason ...': Edward Peters, op.cit., p. 186.

De Maistre on the executioner: *The Works of Joseph de Maistre*, ed. Jack Lively, London 1965, pp. 191–2.

'the Israeli journalist ...': Tom Segev, ' "Mini" in Hebron', 24 September 1993.

'When Gudjonsson interviewed ...': Gisli H. Gudjonsson, 'Alleged False Confession, Voluntariness and "Free Will": testifying against the Israeli General Security Service', in *Criminal Behaviour and Mental Health*, 5, 95–105, 1995.

'application from a lawyer ...': 'The Hamdan Case', in B'Tselem, *Legitimizing Torture: The Israeli High Court of Justice Rulings in the Bilbeisi, Hamdan and Mubarak Cases*, Jerusalem, January 1997, pp. 14–19.

'After having studied ...': the High Court of Justice ruling quoted in ibid., p. 16.

'a useful translation': 'Answer to the Judge', statement by the Public Committee Against Torture in Israel, Jerusalem, n.d.

'A retired judge …': 'Commission of Inquiry into the Methods of Investigation of the General Security Service Regarding Hostile Terrorist Activity', *Israel Law Review* nos 2–3, 1989.

'essential catharsis …': ibid., p. 149.

'We hope …': ibid.

'a law-abiding state …': ibid., p. 184.

'have no moral right …': ibid. p. 184.

'a magnificent commentary …': Mordechai Kremnitzer, 'The Landau Commission Report', *Israel Law Review*, op.cit.

'defence of necessity …': 'Commission of Inquiry', op.cit., pp. 167–74.

'must be weighted …': ibid., p. 171.

'Teitgen …': Alistair Horne, *A Savage War of Peace*, London 1977, pp. 180–1,202.

'when it exists potentially …': 'Commission of Inquiry', op.cit., p. 186.

'Landau's view of the PLO …': ibid., p. 154.

'what may be moderate …': Kremnitzer, op.cit., p. 252.

'the result of brain damage …': Derrick J. Pounder, 'Shaken Adult Syndrome', *The American Journal of Forensic Medicine and Pathology*, 18(4), 1997, pp. 321–4.

'the cleaning of the sewers …': 'Commission of Inquiry', op.cit., p. 162.

'"No" said the officer again …': Franz Kafka, 'In the Penal Colony', *Complete Stories*, New York 1971, p. 145.

'A CIA interrogation manual …': Kubark Counterintelligence Interrogation (Kubark was the CIA's codename for itself), July 1963. See also Lisa Haugaard, 'Textbook Repression: US Training Manuals Declassified', *CovertAction Quarterly*, no. 57, Summer 1996.

'the law, which generally grants protection …': Kremnitzer, op.cit., p. 251.

'Nothing there except …': Seamus Heaney, *The Cure at Troy*, New York 1991, p. 18.

'If you were able …': Melzack and Wall, op.cit., p. 115.

'this could be due …': Duncan Forrest FRCS, 'The Physical After-effects of Torture', in *Guidelines for the Examination of Survivors of Torture*, London 1995, p. 9.

'seeing the source of injury …': Melzack and Wall, op.cit., p. 132.

'only in torture …': Jean Améry, op.cit., p. 33.

PERMISSIONS

INDEX